SHARON BATT

KU-611-041

Patient No More

The Politics of Breast Cancer

Scarlet Press

Published by Scarlet Press
5 Montague Rd, London E8 2HN

First published by gynergy books
P.O. Box 2023, Charlottetown, PEI, Canada C1A 7N7

British Library Cataloguing-in-Publication Data
A catalogue record of this book is available from the British Library

ISBN 1 85727 067 3 pb
     1 85727 072 X hb

Printed in Canada by Best Gagné Book Manufacturers

"Anyone who wants to understand why Canadian and American women are now daring to raise their voices in the professionally expropriated and closely guarded arena of human health will find [*Patient No More*] engaging and provoking."
— Judy Brady, editor *1 in 3: Women with Cancer Confront an Epidemic*

"... provides the historical framework for the groundswell of activism that has emerged in the last few years ... It is the most comprehensive work I have ever read on the politics of breast cancer."
— Maryann Napoli, *Center for Medical Consumers*

"Feminist journalism at its best — this book presents an extraordinary amount of medical, historical, and personal material in a style as gripping as a novel ... a brilliant analysis."
— Adriane Fugh-Berman, M.D., *National Women's Health Network*

"Batt tells the politics of cancer in more human terms than they have ever been told ... She combines her personal experience of having breast cancer with her professional abilities as a journalist to uncover some uncomfortable truths ... Careful research is rarely combined so well with personal insight and vivid storytelling."
— Arthur Frank, *At the Will of the Body: Reflections on Illness*

"This book inspires action ... it will arm you with facts ... that may save your life. — A truly excellent, much needed book."
— Charlene Day, *Immune System Handbook: Your Owner's Manual*

"While I was researching breast cancer, at least once an hour I had to get up and go somewhere to scream: scream out my rage, my frustration, and my fear for myself, my daughter, my granddaughter. If you don't know what I was screaming about, you owe it to yourself to buy this book and pay attention to it."
— Susun Weed, *Breast Cancer, Breast Health* and *Menopausal Years — The Wise Woman Way*

"Thoughtful ... potent ... compelling ... It is impossible to read this engaged activist without a deepening understanding of the politics of women's health."

— Sandra Butler, *Cancer in Two Voices*

Acknowledgements

I would not have begun this book without the encouragement of friends in the writing community who believed I could carry it off, especially Mary Meigs, Audrey Thomas, Eleanor Wachtel and Jan Walter. Lise Noël provided a title satisfying to all concerned, in the nick of time. I am grateful to three other friends who met my special and peculiar needs: Jeannie Kamins drew me into the wild fabric of her family life; Abby Lippman supplied a never-ending flow of kibbitzing and clippings; and Jan Richman made up the other half of the mountain workout duo, writers-on-the-run. My mother, sisters, brother and nieces admirably absorbed the shocks of my diagnosis and supported my subsequent decision to speak publicly about them.

Through much of the writing of *Patient No More* I have split time and psychic resources between the solitude of my study and the intense arena of breast cancer politics. Carolyn Badger, Vanessa Kramer, Carole Jones and Ginny Soffa are just four of the many activists who helped me sustain this dual existence and to emerge from it more whole than before.

Of the many written resources about cancer that enlarged my understanding, several stand out. Rose Kushner's *Alternatives,* Audre Lorde's *The Cancer Journals* and Ken and Treya Wilber's book *Grace and Grit* were invaluable for their personal courage and insights. *Dr. Susan Love's Breast Book* is the frank and friendly guide to medical practice that I longed for when I was diagnosed; and James Patterson's *The Dread Disease* is an absorbing cultural history of cancer in America.

People who read and critiqued parts of this manuscript are Rosalie Bertell, Dr. Adriane Fugh-Berman, Irwin Bross, Dr. Thomas Dao, Dr. Sally Dorfman, Nancy Evans, Dr. Richard Evans, Heather Goodare, Dr. Ann Johnson and Mary Meigs. Their comments helped me move from the trees to the forest without getting lost in the wilderness. Whatever confusion remains is entirely my responsibility. Lynn Henry, my editor at gynergy books, was a special gift, by turns challenging and supportive, daring and — in the best sense of the word — patient.

Financial support, no small detail in these days of slash-and-burn budget remedies, came from the Canada Council's Non-Fiction Writing Program and the Ontario Arts Council's Writers' Reserve Program.

To the memory of three who showed the way:
Rose Kushner, Audre Lorde and Elenore Pred.

And to the brave women everywhere
who are struggling to confront this disease
on their own terms.

"I am sorry it happened to you," wrote Luria, "but if such a thing happens it can only be understood, and used. Perhaps it was your destiny to have the experience; certainly it is your duty now to understand and explore ..."

— Oliver Sacks, *A Leg to Stand On*

Contents

Introduction

The origins of this book go back five years. I had just undergone surgery, chemotherapy and radiation, all of which came with ominous warnings and no guarantees. I wanted to understand why breast cancer was widely regarded as a medical success story when thousands of women die every year, despite these same treatments. As a feminist, I longed to hear the stories of other women, past and present.

I also wondered why women with breast cancer had not come together as a political force. I imagined an activist movement, like the one men with AIDS had created. I was not too far into the book when such a movement sprang into being. Notebook in hand, I became a participant in the story I was writing. The final sections of *Patient No More* document the rapid evolution of women with breast cancer — from passive optimists to impatient activists.

As a patient with no medical training, I was initially intimidated by disagreements among medical camps. How could I possibly have an opinion when experts disagreed? When I looked at breast cancer treatments in a historical and social context, however, I found recurring themes which reflected values, vested interests and world views. Lay observers can readily understand these debates. In fact, I believe women with breast cancer must take part in such discussions, or risk being pawns in political power struggles. Our central task is precisely to develop and advance a coherent perspective of our own. Our voice must be a counterweight to the medical point of view that dominates discussions of the disease.

With the advent of activism, this involvement has begun. Advocating for ourselves means seeing our own interests clearly — no easy task when others have spoken for so long on our behalf. Initially the public, and many professionals, assumed advocates would simply lobby to increase funding for breast cancer research. Instead, women with breast cancer began by asking why accurate information about the disease was so difficult to come by, and moved on to examine how decisions are made and money is spent. Many now question the premises of past policies, such as the emphasis on treatment rather than prevention and the strictly biomedical model of cancer.

When activists bring ideas like these to the table, tensions are inevitable. I don't know how they will be resolved, but I have concluded the book on an optimistic note. At a conference in Brugge, Belgium, breast cancer specialists from around the world voiced doubts about the paradigm that has guided their research and practice for 30 years. A new order is forming and activists are part of it. In this, I believe, lies hope for change.

— Sharon Batt, August 1994.

Thrown

Down, down, down. Would the
fall never come to an end!
— Lewis Carroll, *Alice in Wonderland*

Thrown

*"What a queer planet!" he thought. "It is altogether
dry, and altogether pointed, and altogether
harsh and forbidding."*

— Antoine de Saint-Exupéry, *The Little Prince*

Until I got breast cancer, I had thought about it on only three occasions.

When I was a university student in Vancouver in the '60s, my mother wrote to tell me that her sister had breast cancer and was moving from Detroit to live with my family in Ottawa. Mom was upset because Helen had known of the diagnosis for some years but had refused breast surgery. Helen was stubborn so her decision would have seemed merely in character — except that she was a nurse. "Maybe she knows something we don't," I said to my mother. My mother had a different interpretation — that Helen wanted to die.

In fact, my aunt did die a few years later. Around that time I went to a clinic for a routine checkup and an intern examined my breasts.

His eyebrows shot up in alarm. "Very lumpy!" he said.

He told me to go for another opinion which, after two sleepless nights, I did. The doctor was a tall woman with greying hair. After she examined me, she asked, "How old was the doctor who sent you here?"

"Maybe 25."

"I don't think he's felt many breasts in his life," she said dryly. "This is perfectly normal tissue. He's given you a needless scare."

After that, I had a marked bias towards women physicians. I didn't think about breast cancer again for 20 years.

By then I was living in Montreal. I attended an international feminist book fair, and a highlight on the program was an address by the black American poet Audre Lorde. She gave an uncompromising talk which set off a turmoil of debates about race. Afterwards, I headed for the bookstalls. All her books were sold out except for a slim volume called *The Cancer Journals*, based on Lorde's experience with breast cancer. I didn't want to read about cancer. But I wanted to read Audre Lorde. Reluctantly, I bought the book.

Four months later I, too, was diagnosed with breast cancer.

ii

It happened this way. In September I took a cycling vacation in France. Late one afternoon, while showering off the day's hard-won sweat, I ran a soapy hand over my left breast and froze. There, in the lower crescent of flesh, I felt a small, hard lump. I continued to shower, focussing on the evening ahead, the delectable dinner I knew awaited me; but some magnetic force kept drawing my hand to the spot. Sometimes the lump was gone. Then it wasn't. Over the next few days, the reluctant search became a nightly ritual.

By day, I didn't think about it. I felt well, ergo I was well. This straightforward philosophy of health had served me well until now. Indeed, at 43, I felt superb. The lump was an incongruous presence in my vibrant body.

Back in Montreal, I confronted the mammogram machine. The technician scrunched my breast between two horizontal plates then tightened the clamp. "Don't breathe," she said, and vanished.

"OK, breathe," she said, coming out, and squashed my breast vertically.

Downstairs at the breast clinic I gave the X-rays to the surgeon on duty, a taciturn man who seemed to know what he was about. He snapped the X-rays onto a lighted surface, he palpated my breast, he pulled out a long needle. "Mosquito bite," he said. The needle pierced the lump and he twisted it around. I winced.

"Sorry," he said. Then, "Ninety-nine percent sure it's nothing."

I believed him. Despite my unease about the lump, despite my aunt and *The Cancer Journals*, breast cancer seemed a distant menace. I held onto the reassuring slogans I'd heard for years: get a mammogram, see your doctor, breast cancer can be cured. As for those 99 percent odds — most breast lumps are benign.

When I came back for the results of the needle biopsy, things turned ominous. Some cells were irregular.

"I can take another needle sample, or remove the whole lump. I'd prefer to take it out. Then we can be sure."

I must have looked doubtful. The surgeon flipped the report around so I could see it. "Ambiguous cells, insufficient sample."

"What does that mean?" I demanded, suddenly aggressive. It seemed to me he'd messed up the test. And what about the 99 percent odds? Or the mammogram, which showed nothing unusual? I was sinking in quicksand.

My antagonism was not going over well. In fact, the whole encounter had tilted, had spun us both out of control. Now the surgeon was protesting vehemently, "I do not cut off women's breasts, I do not cut off women's breasts!"

I hadn't even considered that possibility. And why was he so defensive? Terrified, I fled.

That night, my friend Jeannie came over to visit. I could think of nothing but the lump and when I told her about it, she asked to feel it. By now I'd decided to have it out. Jeannie has strong opinions and she thought I was capitulating to the medical system.

"If I had all my lumps out, my breasts would look like a moonscape," she said.

"The cells were irregular. I want it out."

She insisted on a mutual breast feel, the kind of ritual we had in high school.

"It's really hard," she said, surprised. Then, soberly, "I'd get it out."

To get my bearings before the operation, I read about breast cancer. Already, I'd skimmed the section in *The New Our Bodies Ourselves*, trying to absorb medical jargon: *estrogen receptor assays, permanent section, two-step biopsy*. Everything the surgeon had done checked out, which reassured me, but the book began to undermine my comforting assumptions. For example, it said, "breast cancer mortality rates have not declined significantly in the past half-century despite progressively earlier detection and treatment."[1] And, "mammograms use radiation and radiation can cause cancer."[2] The more I read, the more astonished I was. Breast cancer, I learned, kills thousands of North American women every year, second only to heart disease. In women 35 to 55, it's the number one killer. I was 43.

As a feminist and a journalist, I fancied myself well informed, especially about women's issues. Yet I knew next to nothing about breast cancer. Now, it seemed that the little I thought I knew was wrong. I was puzzled and vaguely irritated with myself.

My life split onto two tracks. One was life-as-usual: my work as a magazine editor, evenings with friends, a screenwriting workshop, swimming at the gym. The summer of regular cycling had given me a taste for rigorous training and I felt in peak condition. I wanted to try triathlon competition. A fitness test at the Y confirmed my sense of well-being. "Remarkable!" said the women who tested me. "Only professional athletes score higher than this." I could hardly have cancer and feel this well.

Between routines, my thoughts were scattered. I sent postcards to friends in other cities and slipped in an anxious phrase or two: "by the way … it seems I may have cancer." Mentally, I sketched out a will. I drew back from long-term projects and thought morbidly about winding up unfinished business: my last to-do list and will.

iii

The morning of the biopsy, Jeannie takes me to the day surgery. She will come back and get me, then stay overnight at my place. After a general anaesthetic, you aren't supposed to spend that night alone.

I lie ready in my hospital gown. A nurse slips on a pair of white cotton boots that go over my knees. "It's cold in the operating room," she says. My surgery boots reassure me; I'm no longer naked. The nurse sticks a needle in my behind and the drug rolls through me in waves.

Only moments later, it seems, I'm back in the recovery room. I feel fine. Just a slight ache in my left breast, which is bandaged. The surgeon has kept his promise. So far, so good. I fade back into the anaesthetic.

I'm awake again and the surgeon is standing by the bed, looking serious. He begins pacing up and down.

"I don't like having to tell you this ..." he begins.

Malignant. I can't believe it.

"How big was it?" My last refuge. Small is better.

"A centimetre. Not very big."

Still, he's ordered scans and X-rays. Bone. Liver. Lungs. All the places breast cancer goes, I recall from my crash reading. *Metastasize*, a Greek word, means "to change place." When breast cancer changes place it usually kills you. And he's lined up another operation, to remove lymph nodes. I'm to stay in the hospital.

I don't want these tests, this operation. I haven't told my family yet. I don't know what lymph nodes are but I think maybe I want to keep mine. I drift back into the anaesthetic. When I surface again, he's gone. I ask the nurse about the lymph node operation.

"The doctor should have explained it." She's annoyed.

"I think he did." My memory of the surgeon's visit flickers and fades, a lost dream.

"It's the anaesthetic," she says, concerned. Now she's on the phone to the doctor, cancelling the operation. A reprieve.

Jeannie comes back. "It's cancer," I tell her. The word doesn't seem real. It catches on the way out. She hugs me and I feel tears on my cheeks. I don't know if they're hers or mine.

iv

Well. Sick. Well. Sick. I can't hold the two ideas in my head at the same time. And all week, I don't. I keep switching tracks. At work at my desk, then to the hospital for a test. Finally, the terrible hours at night when I'm in bed but awake, soaked in sweat.

Sometimes I switch from the normal track onto the cancer track, like the morning I stop at a red light on the way to work and notice the woman in the next car staring at me. I am talking feverishly to myself, gesturing wildly at an invisible other who is listening patiently to my discourse about cancer.

I step up my research. For most of my reading I rely on the library at McGill but find only one book in the catalogue under breast cancer: a battered copy more than 10 years old of *Breast Cancer: A Personal History and Investigative Report* by Rose Kushner. I also find a sociology doctoral thesis called *Decision Difficult: Physician Behaviour in the Diagnosis and Treatment of Breast Cancer.*

Kushner's book, I sense, is outdated; otherwise, it's a godsend. A Washington journalist who had a mastectomy in the 1970s,

Kushner was so outraged by physicians she talked to at some of America's leading hospitals that she carried out an intensive investigation to learn the facts for herself. Then she wrote a book to tell other women what she'd learned.

She also began a personal crusade to change breast surgery practices. She argued that surgeons should separate the diagnostic biopsy, which determines whether a breast lump is malignant, from the mastectomy that was standard treatment for breast cancer in the 1970s. No woman, Kushner reasoned, should come out of the anaesthetic to be hit with the double whammy of cancer *and* a lost breast. She also knew, from her experience as a former med student, that the operating-room test for malignancy could be wrong. A quick-frozen section might look malignant, but the more reliable lab test, done later, could show it was not. If the surgeon acted on the first analysis, he would inevitably remove a certain number of healthy breasts.[3]

Kusher tells her own story with disarming wit, and I feel I'm listening to a big sister who's been there. Her investigation reads like a detective novel — mystery: breast cancer. Her questions are so much like my own, I stop feeling foolish for being confused. And her discussion of diagnostic errors gives me hope. Maybe, just maybe, my lump isn't really malignant.

The sociology doctoral dissertation has a different tone — the dispassionate language of social science. The writer, Kathryn Taylor, spent three years following physicians as they treated women in a Montreal breast cancer clinic. She wanted to understand how doctors stayed motivated "in the face of high degrees of uncertainty and failure in their endeavour to cure." Uncertainty ... failure? I'm not sure I'm ready for this. And it gets worse: "... no overall improvement in breast cancer survival since statistics were first collected in the 1930s. Early detection is not leading to improved mortality rates ..." Breast cancer patients underwent "painful, uncertain, and often unsuccessful treatment plans ..."[4]

At some point as I read, the book falls to the floor. I wander in a daze around my apartment. I can't take this in, I don't want to. Until now, breast cancer has meant having an operation, no big deal. I've had the surgery and I don't feel very different. Now I am truly frightened. *Pain. Uncertainty. Death. No progress.*

Monday, a week after my biopsy, I go back to see the surgeon.

When the doctor is impatient he says things twice. "You have an interductal carcinoma," he tells me. "You have an interductal carcinoma." He's telling me the diagnosis was not a mistake. What's worse, the bone scan has a "hot spot." The cancer could be in my bones. He orders an X-ray of my upper spine. He's obviously miffed about the cancelled operation. He wants to get on with it, but I have some questions.

"Is the operation risky?"

He says it could leave my arm paralyzed.

I'm incredulous. "Permanently?"

"Perhaps permanently."

I imagine a gimpy arm, cancer everywhere. Pains shoot through my neck where the bone scan was positive.

"Will I be able to work? Do sports?"

I've said something wrong. The doctor stands up and calls the nurse into the office.

"I need a witness," he declares. "Doctors have rights too."

The room tilts into the vortex again. It's spinning faster than before.

I blurt out questions while he takes notes and answers methodically. "The operation won't affect the cancer," I say accusingly. "It won't stop it." I've read this. A lymph node operation will only show how far the disease has spread.

"No. It doesn't stop the cancer."

"And my arm could be permanently paralyzed?"

"Perhaps. We have to cut nerves."

"I don't see the point."

"To complete the staging!" He's exasperated. "We need the operation to complete the staging!"

I stare, blankly. Staging is something they do in the theatre. I'm sitting in a surgeon's office with a diagnosis of cancer and he's talking props and lighting.

"I need to talk to another doctor," I shout. "I want another opinion."

"I *insist* you have another opinion," he throws back, seizing the upper hand. "There's no point treating a patient who doesn't believe in the doctor!"

I glance sideways at the nurse. What is she thinking? She's watching the doctor. When he signals that the discussion is over, she leaves.

"What about this bandage," I demand. In the turmoil, we've both forgotten that the bandage is to come off my breast today. "Am I supposed to remove it myself?"

"You could." He's staring down at his desk.

"Are there stitches in there for me to take out?" I know this is ludicrous, but I'm so mad I can't stop.

"No stitches," he says with a sigh. He gestures to the open door of the examining room. "Why don't you let me take it off."

I hesitate a minute, than capitulate. After he removes the bandage, he nods to a small mirror on the wall. "You can look at it if you like." He sounds conciliatory. Awkward emotions hang in the air, like the aftermath of a lovers' quarrel.

I can hardly see my reflection through the tears. I blink. My breast looks the same as before except for some swelling and a bright red line, like a deep scratch, that follows the curve underneath. I try to take in this line — so long; this red — so vivid. I can feel the surgeon watching, I sense he wants me to be pleased. I'm not. I'm still livid from our interview. I reach for my clothes.

In the reception room, I hurtle past the nurse towards my coat. She calls me over and gives me the name of another doctor who works in the same office.

"A different type altogether," she says. "You'll see. Try him, and if you want to change, no problem." She continues talking me down. "Dr. T. was tired. I could see that. But even when he's not tired," — a long pause — "you take people as they come. He can be ... difficult." She lowers her voice and leans forward. "But Sharon, he's one *helluva* surgeon."

She arranges an appointment with the other doctor and persuades me to return to Dr. T. one more time, to discuss the X-rays of my neck.

"Now Doctor G.," she confides, "he's a different type. I always say, when you go to see Dr. G., bring a book. A thick one."

vi

Added to the enigma of cancer is the enigma of doctors. Not only have I never been seriously ill, I've had scant contact with people who work in medicine. Jeannie's father was a doctor but mine was a lawyer, my mother a psychologist. It strikes me now that my whole family and virtually all my friends are journalists, lawyers, writers, therapists. They live by words and concepts. Aunt Helen was a nurse, yes, but she lived in Detroit and never visited. Before I talk to another doctor, I want to understand what motivates them. Perhaps Kathryn Taylor's dissertation will throw some light on this question, I think. Taylor analyzes the way doctors go about telling women they have breast cancer. Typically, she says, they use one of two strategies. One type — she calls them "experimenters" — take a scientific approach. They emphasize rational thinking and technical skills. Their colleagues, whom Taylor classes as "therapists," rely on clinical experience more than on science for their expertise, and view clinical skill as an almost mystical talent.[5]

The two types of doctors have very different ways of talking to patients. Experimenters are explicit. They use medical jargon and statistics; they cite published studies to back up their recommendations. One, for example, announced to his patient, "Your lesion is in the inner upper quadrant, so it may have infiltrated the internal mammary chain of the lymph node system making reliance on the results of an axillary dissection only tentative. The protocol for your stage of disease suggests radiating the internal chain, prophylactically of course ..."[6]

These doctors know the patient has no idea what they are saying and wouldn't remember it anyway, but they reason that full disclosure of a breast cancer diagnosis will protect them against malpractice suits. By talking up scientific research, they hope to discourage the patient from seeking alternative treatments they consider quackery. Finally, the experimenters feel it is useless to evade the hard facts about breast cancer because patients will ultimately get them from the media.

The therapists use a different language. They speak in euphemisms and describe cases from their clinical experience to explain the diagnosis. They meet direct questions with evasion. One begins the interview by saying, "There was something we didn't like about your [pathology] report ..." The patient, shaking and crying, sobs that when she was 16, her mother died of cancer. She asks if she too has cancer. "Well, it's sort of a tumour," the doctor responds, "but mind you ... probably not like [your mother] had ... we call it infiltrating ductal carcinoma, just your everyday garden variety type ..." To which the patient replies, "Oh, thank God! ... I thought I had cancer ... thank you doctor ... I'm sorry I got this upset ..."[7]

These physicians invoke tradition to justify their evasiveness: things have always been done this way. They don't believe patients really want to know the diagnosis and assume a frank disclosure will trigger depression and grief. They take it on themselves to shield the women from such traumatic emotions.

Dr. T. is an experimenter type I muse, as I sit with my thick book in Dr. G.'s office. The reason for the book is becoming obvious. I've already waited several hours and notice that women who disappear into Dr. G.'s office seem to be there an awfully long time. When my turn finally comes, everyone, including the nurse, has gone home.

Dr. G. is a tall, thin man with blond hair and an angular face. As he examines my breast, he seems to take an especially long time palpating under my arm, all the while staring thoughtfully at the ceiling.

"What is it?" I ask nervously. "Did you find something?"

"Oh, no no no," he protests, as if I were trying to corner him. "A manual exam is never certain. You need a lab report to be sure."

So why all this *feeling*, I wonder, as I pull on my clothes. I sit down in his office for the interview. In the window behind his head the October sky is black but I hold firm when he ventures that I am probably in a hurry to get home. I haven't waited hours in his office to be rushed out the door. I tell him I'm not sure I want to have my lymph nodes removed, especially if it might leave my arm paralyzed. "If it doesn't stop the cancer, why risk it?" I want to know. And don't the lymph nodes have something to do with the immune system?

"Well, you're quite right, the operation won't change your diagnosis," he agrees. He trips along rapidly, hurling out information as he goes. The nurse is right. He is totally different from Dr. T. — Taciturn vs Garrulous. Whether he's an experimenter or a therapist I'm not sure; maybe he's a mixed type. The odds of a paralyzed arm are very small, he assures me. "I'd say one percent. In all likelihood, you'd be in the 99 percent that has no problem."

I've lost this gamble before, I think. And don't I need my lymph nodes to fight the cancer?

"Now you may just have something there," he begins. "As a matter of fact, we'll be starting a protocol in January to look at that very thing." This digression disorients me and I recall something

Kathryn Taylor says in her dissertation: *The experimenters often volunteered information that their patients had not requested.*[8]

"We'll be looking at whether it's better to go right into radiation and chemotherapy without surgery," he finishes.

I'm stuck on the word protocol. Whatever it is, it sounds hopeful, an escape from the operation. "Then maybe I should wait until January ..." I begin.

"Oh, no no no!" he cries. "I wouldn't advise that!"

"Why not?"

"You might get in the wrong group."

Another stumper. They have wrong groups? I go back to the immune system. I am almost never sick and have no allergies, so I think mine must be working pretty well. I don't feel comfortable about having it tampered with.

"If the lymph nodes are part of the immune system and you take out the lymph nodes ..."

"Look," he says, "you have cancer. Your immune system let you down."

Low blow. He's hit the button that crashes my logical defenses: so what if I feel healthy? I have cancer.

Now on the offensive, Dr. G. launches into his wind-up.

"I recommend that you have this operation. If you want, I can do it for you. I've done lots of breast surgery, though lately I've been moving into neck and throat ..."

Another spanner. What's wrong with breast cancer, I wonder. Aren't there enough of us packing the waiting rooms?

In the end, both doctors are saying the same thing: have the operation. I thank him and leave.

I could go to yet another surgeon, but see little point. I'm veering back towards Dr. T. The incision on my breast scarcely hurts at all and looks like it will heal without a trace. The nurse's words echo, "One helluva surgeon." Dr. G.'s career shift to neck and throat makes me nervous. What still worries me about Dr. T. is that we can't talk to one another.

vii

"No one can talk to surgeons," declares my friend Eleanor, on the phone from Toronto. "They're the engineers of the medical profession."

The postcards worked. My friends are kicking in, in unexpected ways. One night Eleanor phones and announces that she has an in-law who is an oncologist in Montreal. She sounds pleased, as if offering something useful.

"What's an oncologist?" I want to know.

A suppressed giggle, then, "A *cancer* specialist."

After a late-night consultation about my mishaps in doctorland, she called the family oncologist for inside advice. Doctors, he said, could be placed on a continuum of communicative skills, with surgeons weighing in rock bottom. "Medical students who are totally inarticulate go into surgery," was how he put it. "The ones who like to talk become psychiatrists. Everyone else falls in between."

This makes a certain sense and is curiously comforting. The disastrous dramas aren't all my fault. And I can stop looking for a surgeon-confessor because I probably won't find one. The in-law also endorsed the hospital where I was being treated. "It seems you've fallen into a nest of good guys," says Eleanor.

viii

"Have you had an accident lately where you could have hurt your neck?" Dr. T. begins.

"Yes, in September. A bicycle accident."

Three days before I was to leave for my cycling vacation, a parked motorist flung his door open in my path and threw me to the pavement. Tests showed nothing broken and I opted to take my long-awaited trip despite a doctor's sensible counsel that I spend my three-week vacation in bed.

Now the X-rays show a cracked vertebra in my neck. The hot spot on the scan isn't cancer after all.

The terror that has gripped me for a week melts into ecstasy. A cracked vertebra! I had assumed the bone scan, an intimidating affair, was a definitive test. Down in the sub-basement of the hospital, I'd passed through metal doors marked Nuclear Medicine and was injected with something radioactive. Two hours later, I returned and stretched out, fully clothed, under a large metal disk. To the left, a tiny TV screen sent pulsating signals as the disk passed over my body. The machine looked impressive, but evidently it couldn't tell the difference between cancer and a cracked bone on the mend. Someone might have told me, I think. Still, I am elated and agree to the lymph node operation.

It's Dr. T.'s turn to look relieved.

Breaking the news of my diagnosis is a complicated affair. I have hardly told anyone. My mother, for example. She'll worry, and I'll have to deal with that. Besides, I can still hardly say the word cancer to myself, let alone lob it, grenade-like, into a conversation.

At work, my imminent lymph node operation prods me to tell my boss, the magazine's editor-in-chief. I'll be taking a week off and some explanation is called for. I know I can allude to some vague medical problem and he won't probe, but I decide to say I have breast cancer. His concern doesn't surprise me, but I'm not prepared for his stricken look. Only later, when he tells me his girlfriend's mother died of breast cancer, do I understand the intensity of his response.

I've become so self-absorbed, I am blind to the needs of others. A few days before I go into the hospital, my neighbour Stuart invites me out for supper. Stuart and I have lived in the same walk-up apartment block for years. When he is between girlfriends we hang out together, two singles at ease with each other. As the dinner progresses, the time seems right to explain why I'm not my usual self. Stuart's shock seems to evolve naturally into sympathy; as we part in the hallway late that evening, I feel I've added a plank to my expanding scaffold of support. I learn later that his brother has just died of a drug overdose. The added burden of my news sends him into a serious depression.

My mother is a worrier of the first rank and I put off telling her as long as I can. When I do, she is much calmer than I expect her to be and we have one of our best conversations in years.

"I thought you would freak out," I confess.

"At times like this, I think it's more helpful to be supportive," she says quietly. She offers to send some relaxation tapes that helped her sleep after dad died.

Aside from Jeannie and Stuart, my other close friend in Montreal is Mary Meigs, a writer my mother's age. The previous summer, Mary was one of eight women chosen for the cast of *The Company of Strangers*, a film about older women. Mary calls me a few days after I tell her I have cancer.

"The most terrible thing has happened," she says. "Gloria has cancer too."

Gloria is Gloria Demers, a woman of about my own age who wrote the script for the film. She has lung cancer. Soon afterwards Mary introduces us and Gloria becomes my first cancer buddy: we compare notes about about treatments, doctors and our fear of dying.

x

The operation is slated for Tuesday morning, two weeks after the biopsy. On Monday night an intern comes in to have me sign a consent form for the operation. He's towheaded and freckle-faced, a 30-year-old Dennis the Menace.

"Is the operation difficult?" I ask, fishing for reassurance.

"Well, more difficult than an appendectomy," he offers. "But nothing like a heart bypass."

I picture him late at night, hunched over a textbook at a page headed "Axillary Dissection for Breast Cancer." He's going to assist Dr. T.

"Let's just say I'm glad he's doing it and not me," he jokes.

With the operation over, the orderly wheels me back to my room. We pass a group of interns and I spot my towheaded visitor of the night before. He sees me too and peels free of the ambulatory pack.

"An incredibly clean dissection!" he declares, beaming down as I roll by. Before I can say anything, he's reabsorbed by the multilegged clump which glides into a waiting elevator. Lymph nodes, I imagine, are strung together like Christmas-tree lights. I picture mine slipping free of my armpit, unencumbered by nerves and other vital parts. I sink back on the pillow. I won't have a gimpy arm after all.

I share my hospital room with a woman I'll call Mrs. Salisbury. She's in her 70s and has a colostomy bag strapped around her waist. She used to be a nurse, has raised two children and had a difficult marriage. Most of the day she sits unsmiling in a chair against the wall, reading, her white hair pulled back in a pony tail. Her reading alternates between the *Consumers Distributing* catalogue and the *National Enquirer*. She will probably outlive me, I think.

"You got flowers," she says, glumly, as the orderly helps me into my bed. "And phone calls."

The flowers are from Stuart. One night he comes to visit me, another night Jeannie, then Mary arrives with Gloria. With the operation over, the week goes by quickly. Friday I'll be discharged.

But first there's a tumour conference, a sort of show-and-tell with me, Exhibit A, lying on a bed. My friend Louise Dulude and my sister Sylvia have driven down from Ottawa and are sitting in the shadows, against one wall. A dozen or so doctors circle the bed as the surgeon presents my case.

"A tumour of one centimetre was removed from the six-o'clock position of the left breast," he announces, lifting off my gown. A dozen pairs of eyes close in on the red slit at the bottom of my breast. I shut my eyes. When I open them, the doctors are filing out of the room.

Later the surgeon comes upstairs to tell me the results of the dissection and explain the treatment. The news isn't good. One of the lymph nodes had cancer cells in it, meaning that the cancer has spread beyond the breast area and is circulating through my system. Millions of maurauding cells are busy dividing, looking for a place to settle. The team recommends six months of chemotherapy, then six weeks of radiotherapy to the spot where the tumour was removed, then a drug called tamoxifen for the rest of my life. Sylvia and Louise hold me up.

xi

Chemotherapy terrifies me. Poisons sent into the bloodstream are supposed to kill the cancer cells when they're dividing. They also kill healthy cells that are dividing. Cancer patients often lose their hair during chemotherapy because cells in the hair follicles divide rapidly, like cancer cells.

The surgeon had said the group recommended CMF, a relatively mild drug mix that usually doesn't cause hair loss. Now the oncologist is suggesting I take part in a trial, a study designed to test three levels of a different combination, CAF, with no tamoxifen. The A stands for Adriamycin, one of the most toxic chemotherapy drugs known. I had thought it was used only for advanced cases.

"What about the tumour conference?" I ask, stunned. "Were you there?"

"If it was Friday, I must have been there," he says enigmatically.

I'm back in the baffling world of medi-speak, complicated this time by the issue of research trials. In her thesis, Taylor says that patients in these studies are followed more closely than those who don't take part. They may benefit from a newer treatment. She also points out that experimenter-physicians face a conflict of interest when it comes time to recruit a patient. The physician is obliged to help the patient make a fully informed choice; the researcher wants to place eligible patients in the trial.

In the larger picture, knowledge about which treatments work best won't advance if women don't take part in studies. Sylvia, Louise and I had discussed this after the tumour conference. Louise was especially sold on the concept of collective responsibility. In theory, I agree. Now, faced with donating my body to this particular experiment, I'm not so sure.

The consent form makes the decision exquisitely concrete. Before I take Adriamycin, I have to sign a paper. It's the kind of release form you sign if you decide to go rafting on the Nahanni. If you crack your head open on a rock, you can't sue the rafting company, because you chose to spend your vacation shooting the rapids. The Adriamycin form releases the drug company from liability if my heart suffers permanent damage — one of the risks of a trip with Adriamycin.

I feel I'm not understanding something.

"Heart damage is a possibility," says the oncologist. "However, with the dosage we'll be giving you, and the duration, and your age, it's not likely."

We're back to probabilities. I try to weigh the unspecified high probability of dying of breast cancer with this unspecified low probability of a permanently damaged heart. Fine for the oncologist to say heart damage is unlikely; the drug company obviously isn't taking any chances.

The oncologist is a stocky man of about my own age with a beard and limpid brown eyes. "You just have to trust me," he says, his eyes underlining the plea. "I wouldn't recommend it if I didn't think it was the best choice."

Taking a deep breath, I sign.

I need to talk to someone. A friend recommends her GP, a woman. I like her. She laughs a lot and talks with an earthy casualness, much different from the reserve of the male cancer specialists.

"I don't think there's anything you could have done to prevent it," she says, "except to have had a baby at 15. That seems to help." She grins.

I ask her about Adriamycin. This brings a merry cry. "The red killer!" she exclaims. Her mother, still alive in her 70s, had it.

"Mind you, mother's heart is terrible," she adds. She puts the treatments in this perspective. "With chemotherapy and cancer, we're at about the same place we were when we used to treat syphilis with arsenic. If it doesn't kill you, it can help you."

I expected something more precise from medicine, but nothing about cancer seems precise. The bone scan, the survival odds, now the chemo.

Rose Kushner's book explains that cancer's chemotherapy era is a by-product of war weaponry. The discovery during World War II that mustard gas kills by poisoning cells led research chemists to reason that liquified mustards could be used to combat cancer. The catch-22 was that lethal chemicals are indiscriminate; years of tests ensued before relatively safe chemotherapy combinations were developed. In the testing process, many cancer patients were "lost," not to cancer but to toxic chemicals.[9]

Chemotherapy's great successes, with childhood leukemia and early adult Hodgkins disease, came in the '50s. With breast cancer, the results were more modest, explained *Our Bodies, Ourselves*. "Currently, only premenopausal women have shown much improved survival with chemotherapy and the gain is small — about 15 percent."[10]

I face my first chemo session with trepidation. The drugs are administered intravenously at the hospital's oncology ward in a room with several beds and large leather-covered chairs. I sit on one of the beds, waiting for the nurse to hook me up to the IV drip. Wearing protective gloves, she readies the thick plastic bags of fluid to hang from the metal rack next to my bed. The fluids are yellowish or clear except for the bright red one: Adriamycin.

"How do you feel?" asks the nurse.

"Scared." My hands are clammy.

"I'd say that's normal."

She pokes the needle into a large vein in the back of my hand; the fluid starts to flow, and I feel a cold sensation as it begins to course through my veins. One, two three, four, five packs of fluid. Three are chemotherapy drugs, two are to reduce nausea from the drugs. The whole procedure takes about two hours.

Afterwards I'm drowsy. At home I sleep a few hours, passing in and out of a drugged haze. A neighbour, Mimi, knocks on the door and asks if I want to go to out for supper. I hesitate — I'm a little unsteady on my feet; I also think I might throw up in the restaurant. I decide to chance it. I'm fine through the meal, but walking home I feel woozy and sit down on a step with my head between my knees until the feeling passes. Later that night I'm jolted awake by the sudden rush of saliva to my mouth and I hurry to the bathroom. In the morning I'm a bit dazed but otherwise I feel my usual self.

The day of my first chemotherapy treatment I am menstruating. Ten days later, at the office, I realize I've begun bleeding again. In a panic, I call the oncology nurse. "The chemo's affecting your ovaries," she says. That night, Stuart and I go to Jeannie's for dinner but I'm in a terrible mood. I sense that my body will never be the same again.

Just before Christmas my hair starts to come out. For the most part this happens in the shower, when I'm rinsing it. The wet strands cover my hand like seaweed. I pull them from one hand; they stick to the other. In two weeks, except for some fuzz, my hair is all gone.

I've already bought a wig. Cancer Society pamphlets advise buying a wig before hair loss, so I go to a discreet salon. Inside, the owner's assistant has bright pink hair while Pierre himself wears a toupée which he lifts off and wiggles, like a magician doing a trick for a child. I choose a dark, curly wig that costs far more than I planned to spend. Pierre gives me separate bangs which, he explains, I can sew to the inside of a scarf to wear on days when I don't want to wear the wig.

xii

During the next six months, my sense of crisis subsides and I gradually reshape my life. After my week in hospital, my boss asks if I want to take a leave of absence or to work part-time. The thought of either frightens me — stay home all day thinking about cancer? My job is my occupational therapy. Except for doctors' appointments and the two days a month I have chemotherapy, I don't miss a minute at the office.

After a few months I reconsider and decide to work three days a week. For three years I've been in a job that doesn't challenge me. It pays better than any job I've ever had, it's moderately interesting and my co-workers are congenial, but a sense of urgency sets in now that my future looks like a finite set of months or years rather than a hazy forever-and-ever. The part-time arrangement will give me enough to live on and I can initiate freelance projects of my own choosing. Heading into my third chemo session, I work up a proposal for a radio documentary on a question that's plagued me since my diagnosis: cancer and its relationship to thoughts and emotions. To my delight, it's accepted!

After the surgery I force myself to swim regularly. When I try to reach out with my left arm, a sharp pain runs through my armpit, as if a tough thread that's too short is holding me together. My arm splashes awkwardly into the water an inch or two above my head. I gain gradually, by centimetres, until one day the thread snaps. For a terrified moment I think my arm is going to drop to the bottom of the pool but instead it curves gracefully over my head.

In the communal shower, the fading incision in my breast causes me no embarrassment but my baldness does. I keep my bathing cap on. Out on the street, the wig is another story and feels like part of a costume. I continually worry that it's crooked.

"What does it look like?" asks a friend, calling from Alberta.

"I'm not sure," I tell her. "Sometimes I think I look cute, but most of the time I think I look like a middle-aged lady in a wig."

A few people, like Jeannie's adolescent son Frank, demand to see my head. A pregnant pause ensues as Jeannie and her partner Henri wait for my reaction. We've just finished supper and are relaxing around the table. I pull off the wig. Another silent moment. Then Frank cries out, "baby hair!" and we all laugh.

Usually I'm more comfortable in public wearing a colourful scarf wrapped around my head, with the fringe of hair sewn underneath. No one seems to guess this is a ruse; in fact the scarf so often draws compliments from people who don't know I have cancer, I begin to think it may actually look stylish. In private, though, the sight of my baldness in a mirror unsettles me. The reflected image recalls the haunted faces of prisoners in death camps … and photos I've seen of cancer patients.

Strange bodily symptoms also trigger panic. One evening Mary and I go to see *Bagdad Café*. Halfway through the film, my concentration goes. I see the images flickering on the screen but I'm not listening, I'm thinking about the pains shooting up and down my neck. *The cancer is in my bones.* Just then Mary leans over and whispers, "My neck hurts! We're sitting too close." I'm so relieved I almost laugh out loud.

Other symptoms are real. For several days after each chemo treatment, breathing is an effort. My chest feels heavy yet not congested. Before going to sleep, I wonder if I'll be able to keep breathing the whole night. "It could just be stress," suggests the oncologist. Later he retracts this. "It is the treatments," he concedes. In February, I begin having mild hot flashes. Within a week they're intense and frequent. During the day this is merely disconcerting; I halt in mid-sentence to mop my face. At night I snatch what sleep I can between sweats that leave the bedclothes drenched and clammy.

I spend hours in the waiting room at the hospital. Chemotherapy lowers your resistance to infections so that something as minor as a hangnail can have fatal complications. Before the nurses can give a chemo treatment, the oncologist has to check the results of a blood test to make sure I can withstand another onslaught. While I'm waiting, I often talk to other patients. I want to know their stories. One day a pretty blond woman, younger than I am, comes into the waiting room wearing sunglasses. It's not that sunny, I think, as we tentatively exchange bits of our histories. She has breast cancer too. "I was fine for two years," she says. "Now," she pauses and removes the glasses to dab her eyes, puffy from crying, "it's come back."

Another day I'm next to a Japanese woman. Her lovely face is tense with strain. She tells me she's 40, married, with a young child. She had a two-centimetre lump in her breast which the doctor thought was a cyst, but it turned out to be cancer. "All removed," she says, her hand circling where her breast once was. At first her husband refused to believe it. "So few Japanese women get breast cancer. But we've had to accept it, it's true."

By all indications, I'm "tolerating the treatments well," as the medical jargon puts it. My blood count varies within the normal range and, though I get noticeably more tired as the months wear on, I'm able to swim, ski, and keep up a moderately active schedule. I still vomit the night after my monthly dose of CAF, but the next morning I'm back to normal.

Gloria Demers is not so fortunate. Her blood count is so low she has to have blood transfusions. One night we go out with Mary to a Chinese restaurant. I'm ravenous, as I have been ever since the chemo started, but Gloria won't touch even her soup. When she and Mary drop me off, Gloria gets out of the car, hugs me tightly and says, "I know we're both going to make it." I hug her back, but I don't know what to say. I think she may be dying.

I've asked Kersti Biro, a friend and amateur photographer, if she'll take some photos of me before my hair grows in. Much as I hate being bald, my months on chemo mark an important transition in my life. I need to understand it. Kersti sets up her tripod in my apartment while I make lunch and we spend a long afternoon together, talking and laughing. She shoots four rolls.

xiii

"Is there any chance I will be cured," I ask the oncologist, "or are we just trying to postpone the inevitable?"

I'm about to have my last chemotherapy treatment and I still can't figure out whether this regimen of poison was the right choice.

"There is a chance you might be completely cured," he answers. "You may never have cancer again."

"How good a chance?"

"What odds could you live with?"

"Ninety-five percent," I say. If I had 95 percent odds of surviving breast cancer, I would truly feel cured. I could throw off the burden of worry that has weighed on me since the diagnosis.

The big brown eyes turn doleful and he shakes his head sadly.

Six weeks of radiation mark the last stage of treatment. First, I have to be measured. I'm prone once more, breast bared, while two cheerful young men mark me up as if they are surveyors charting a field. Their gung-ho mood upsets me; I feel vulnerable and exposed. As the chief marker blocks out an area around my breast with a grease pencil, I break into a dramatic sweat. This bewilders him and he asks, "Were you *running* or something?" I don't feel like explaining the intricacies of the female body and its response to chemotherapy, so I give a helpless shrug. By the time he reaches the final step, in which he tattoos five pinpricks to permanently delineate the section to be radiated, I am completely undone. Back home, I burst into tears.

The radiation is scheduled every weekday for six weeks. I insist on an early time slot so I won't miss too much of my three days per week at the office. I sense this demand is interpreted as "patient being difficult." When someone calls to say a cancellation has freed up the eight AM slot, I feel I've gained a tiny measure of control. While the sessions themselves only last about 15 minutes, the whole procedure bites several hours out of my day, including travel time to and from the hospital, waiting for treatment, and more waiting to see the doctor, who has to decide each week if I'm strong enough to continue the invisible bombardment.

I find radiation sessions more impersonal than chemotherapy. The technician positions me carefully on a narrow bed between two fat metal wings, with my marked-up breast poking through the white gown. Then she exits and closes the door. The bed and wings begin moving through a series of positions, each stop punctuated by a harsh buzzing. Someone, apparently hoping to make this experience sublime, has pasted California feel-good posters in strategic spots on the ceiling and on the massive arms of the machine. One shows two cuddly raccoons and the caption, "A friend is someone who gives you a nice warm feeling." The message misses the mark. As the bed glides silently backwards, I imagine I'm on a mortuary slab, moving by remote control into a crypt.

Still, I do have a warm feeling because the end of treatments is in sight and the spring weather is glorious. One night I have a vivid dream in which my hair grows back, thick and long. About the same time, a man I met at a fall playwriting workshop phones and we splurge on tickets to an international theatre festival: 10 plays in two weeks. He seems curious about the cancer rather than frightened by it. "What's that red line?" he asks one night, as we lean over coffee discussing the merits of the play we've just seen. I look down to see a boundary mark poking above the neck of my tank-top. Another evening, we have to park blocks from the performance venue; the play is an experimental piece from Spain that I don't want to miss. As we tear across a parking lot, he begins lagging behind. "Are you sure you have *cancer*?" he puffs. "I think they got the diagnosis wrong."

It's clear that my friends are no more savvy about breast cancer than I was before I got it.

"What's chemotherapy?" asks the one from Alberta, calling for a health bulletin and a chat. "Is that where they zap you with a big machine?" Others ask, "Did they get it all out?" Or they nod reassuringly and say, "At least they can cure it."

When I try to convey the uncertainty of my prognosis, they are puzzled or incredulous. Everyone wants closure, but I'm getting stubborn. I'd like closure too, but the doctors won't give it to me. And if I can't have it, I'm not about to let my friends have it either.

I'm most baffled by my own misconceptions about breast

cancer and those of a close circle of women friends. In the '70s we worked together on a feminist magazine in Edmonton, of which I was the editor. At one time or another, Karen, Louise, Linda and Eleanor all wrote for the magazine or edited sections of it. If we don't know anything about breast cancer, who does? I wonder. I want to understand the reasons for our collective ignorance which, I am now convinced, must be a characteristic of our generation — the very women who are now turning 40, when breast cancer begins to strike. We should all have read Rose Kushner and Audre Lorde when their books appeared, but we didn't.

At the end of April, one of the hospitals sponsors a cancer information symposium and Rose Kushner is the invited speaker. My admiration for Kushner has grown in the months since I discovered that worn volume in the library. I sent for an updated version of the book and was delighted when it arrived, complete with an autographed inscription: "For Sharon Batt, Good luck, Rose Kushner, January 1989." That Kushner is alive so many years after her diagnosis gives me courage. I wait expectantly for her to appear before the packed auditorium.

She's in her 50s now, rather heavy-set with a broad, open face. She shows slides and tells wry jokes with the ease of a practised public speaker. But her voice is hoarse and she sounds weary.

"What causes breast cancer?" she asks, rhetorically. "Well, the latest theory is ..."

She dies the following February, 16 years after her diagnosis in 1974.

I hate the mysteriousness of my disease and desperately want to know what causes it. One of the astonishing things I learned from Kushner's book is that breast cancer was known in ancient Egypt, as far back as 3500 B.C. The Greeks knew about it too and it was the crab-like appearance of advanced breast tumours that inspired the Roman physician Galen to give cancer the name it has today ("cancer" is Latin for "crab"). What have researchers been doing all these centuries, I wonder.

Many of the books I've read say that environmental carcinogens don't cause breast cancer, but they never explain what *does* cause it. When the cancer centre at McGill advertises a talk on the environment and cancer, Mary and I attend. The lecturer, an epidemiologist, explains the difficulties of epidemiological research, in which patterns of illness in the population are used to suggest disease causation. "Epidemiologists study useful relationships but we can't say anything definite about them," he quips. "Laboratory scientists establish causal relationships, but they don't study anything useful."

One thing he is willing to say is that the effect of environmental carcinogens in causing cancer is cumulative. He illustrates this point with two slides of a camel. In the first, the camel stands tall, proudly bearing its multilayered pack. In the second, an extra item has been added to the pack and the camel, spindly legs splayed, is about to collapse. People worry that a whiff of exhaust from a passing truck will give them cancer, he says, but apparently it takes many whiffs — an unspecified number. Those elusive cancer probabilities.

He goes on to talk about specific environmental causes of cancer. It turns out that he has just completed a large study that examined every recorded case of cancer in Montreal during a certain period of time. He then traced the employment history of each person in the study. When he finishes analyzing the data, he tells us, he will be able to suggest which occupations pose hazards for specific kinds of cancer. There's only one catch: he excluded women from his study. He mentions this casually, in passing. So much for finding out if breast cancer has occupational causes.

After the lecture, Mary and I exchange impressions. We are both distressed that the epidemiologist omitted women from his study — all the more so because his manner was sympathetic. He simply spoke as though a study without women was perfectly normal. Even worse, neither of us was brave enough to stand up and challenge his assumption.

By June, I'm midway through my radiation treatments. The Montreal papers are filled with news of the Fifth International AIDS conference, which has drawn thousands of medical researchers to the city — and thousands of AIDS activists too. I'm impressed by the AIDS activists, even envious. They seem to know so much about the disease and they have such nerve. They are out on the streets staging angry demonstrations; they are in the meeting rooms, telling the scientists to hurry up with their research; they are in the media, talking about AIDS and wearing buttons that say Silence=Death. The AIDS quilt is on display at the Olympic Stadium and I go to see it. Stretched out the length of a football field are hundreds upon hundreds of squares, lovingly made by friends and relatives in memory of their dead.

After seeing the quilt, I go to Jeannie's to watch a TV program about breast cancer. It's an NBC special called *Destined to Live* and it features about 20 women, some famous, some not, speaking of their experience with the disease. They tell moving anecdotes about their terror upon diagnosis, but the overall tone of the program is upbeat. Everyone feels and looks great. They talk about the wonderful changes that have taken place in their lives since having cancer: a baby, a new job, marriage. "Cancer is the best thing that ever happened to me," beams one woman. Watching this show, you would think no one ever died of breast cancer. The long list of sponsors names every cancer agency and medical organization imaginable.

Something inside me snaps. The documentary captures one side of breast cancer — the need for hope — but so much is missing.

I remember an essay in Audre Lorde's *The Cancer Journals,* called "The Transformation of Silence into Language and Action." In it, she talks about her need to overcome her fear of speaking out. When she learned that she might have cancer, she became aware that her greatest regrets were her silences, those occasions when she lacked the courage to put her beliefs into words. She urges women to confront their fears, especially the fear of being visible. "For those of us who write," she says, "it is necessary to scrutinize not only the truth of what we speak, but the truth of that language by which we speak it."[11]

The feeling I have to put into words is obvious: it's my fear of death from breast cancer. I sit down and write an article in which I reject the chipper, optimistic attitude that seems so prevalent. We have much to learn from AIDS activists, I argue. We must educate ourselves about the disease, about the amount of money that is spent on it, and about the policies that govern where that money goes. We must ask why the cause of breast cancer is still not known after all these years. We must also voice our anger about the thousands of women who die each year of breast cancer.

I send the article to the local newspaper and enclose one of Kersti's photos showing my bare, bald head. When the article appears, the photo enlarged to twice the original size, the effect is shocking, even to me. I am more than out of the closet, I have thrown myself into a public arena where the rules are as mysterious as the disease itself. One thing I do understand: there's no going back.

Notes

1. Boston Women's Health Collective, *The New Our Bodies Ourselves*, (New York: Simon and Schuster, 1984), p. 531.

2. Boston Women's Health Collective, p. 495.

3. Rose Kushner's successful fight to have the two-step surgical procedure made routine is described in Rose Kushner, *Alternatives: New Developments in the War on Breast Cancer*, [a revised version of her original book], (N.Y.: Warner, 1986), pp. 181-197.

4. Kathryn Taylor, "Decision Difficult: Physician Behaviour in the Diagnosis and Treatment of Breast Cancer," McGill University Doctoral Dissertation [Sociology], (Montreal, 1984), p. 2.

5. Taylor, pp. 33-34. The chapter on how physicians tell women they have breast cancer has been published as "Physicians and the Disclosure of Undesirable Information," in *Biomedicine Examined*, Margaret Lock and Deborah Gordon (eds), (Dordrecht, The Netherlands: Kluwer Academic Publications, 1988), pp. 441-464.

6. Taylor, p. 37.

7. Taylor, p. 43.

8. Taylor, p. 38.

9. Kushner, p. 63.

10. Kushner, p. 535.

11. Audre Lorde, *The Cancer Journals*, (San Francisco: Spinsters Ink, 1980), p. 22.

TWO

Mapping the Grey Zones

*After a century of pursuit of medical utopia,
and contrary to current conventional wisdom,
medical services have not been important in producing
the changes in life expectancy that have occurred.
A vast amount of contemporary clinical care
is incidental to the curing of disease, but the damage
done by medicine to the health of individuals
and populations is very significant. These facts are
obvious, well documented, and well repressed.*

— Ivan Illich, *Limits to Medicine*

Early Detection
The Mammography Juggernaut

... Here at least was Q. He dug in his heels at Q. Q he was sure of.
Q he could demonstrate. If Q then is Q — R — ...

A shutter, like the leathern eye of a lizard, flickered over the intensity of
his gaze and obscured the letter R. In that flash of darkness he heard
people saying — he was a failure — that R was beyond him. He would
never reach R. On to R, once more. R —

— Virginia Woolf, *To the Lighthouse*

It's February 1993. I'm sitting in a packed meeting room at the Holiday Inn in Bethesda, Maryland, just outside of Washington. While I wait for the proceedings to begin, I browse through my papers on mammography screening until I come across an article bearing a photograph of a woman. She is middle-aged, with a pleasant face, short straight hair and glasses. Her loosely clasped hands fall against a cotton print skirt and she's smiling — shyly I think. I can't see her feet but I imagine she's wearing sensible shoes. She stands next to a mammogram machine. Her name is Dr. Maureen Roberts and she was clinical director of the Edinburgh Breast Screening Project for 10 years. The cruel twist to her story is that she was herself diagnosed with breast cancer while heading the Scottish mammography program. She died eight years later, at age 53.

If Roberts were alive today, no doubt she would be a featured speaker at this two-day workshop. The speakers are an elite group.

They've been brought here by the National Cancer Institute (NCI) to review the world's clinical trial data on breast screening. Sam Shapiro, now in his 80s, will describe the first scientific study of breast screening ever done, the one he conducted in New York in the 1960s. Anthony Miller is here from Canada, to talk about the results of the National Breast Screening Study (NBSS), published a few months ago. Miller's study has provoked an uproar; this gathering is designed largely to restore order to the world which "the Canadians" (Miller and his colleague Cornelia Baines) threw into chaos. In between God and the Devil are: the Swedes, whose trials set the standard for state-of-the-art mammography; Jocelyn Chamberlain from Britain, who will talk about the trial in England as well as the one Maureen Roberts headed in Scotland; and J. Mark Elwood of New Zealand, who has just completed a meta-analysis to assess the combined results of the studies done by the others.

The mood is electric. This is not your usual boring medical conference. The study from Canada accounts for the expectant buzz in the room. Its finding challenges two assumptions about the value of mammography: it questions whether women in their 40s benefit at all from breast screening; and it suggests mammography may provide no significant benefit to women in their 50s if they are already practising breast self-exams and having regular clinical breast exams.

I'm here as press, seated in an area on the right. My assignment is to prepare a short documentary for the Canadian Broadcasting Corporation (CBC) radio back home in Canada. Miller's prominence at the meeting makes this a story with a strong Canadian angle — CBC television news has sent a whole crew. The Americans are interested for other reasons. Five years ago the NCI joined the American Cancer Society (ACS) in recommending regular mammography screening for all women in their 40s. Millions of American women in their 40s go for regular mammograms. It's both an accepted health practice and a thriving business. If this review of the research calls the practice into question, the story will reverberate through the cancer community at every level. Gina Kolata is here from the *New York Times* and Chris Russell is reporting from the *Washington Post*. Other reporters are from the *Economist* and some specialty medical publications: *Oncology Times Newspaper, American Medical News*, and

Radiology Today. I was told when I registered that the NCI hopes the press will give the workshop's conclusions wide and accurate play.

To say that women are confused about breast screening would be an understatement and coverage of Miller's study hasn't helped matters. When the NBSS appeared in the medical press in November 1992, the first story about it in my local paper was headlined, "Mammography doesn't cut breast cancer deaths." Five days later, another story appeared under the headline, "Study criticizing mammography is flawed, radiologists argue." The NBSS results shocked women, and for good reason. Trust in mammography goes to the core of breast cancer's most sacred truth: early detection is your best protection. This conference will weigh the scientific evidence behind the motto.

Before I found the lump in my breast, I had never had a mammogram. Eight months before, my gynaecologist had suggested I go for a "baseline" mammogram. The very idea made me nervous. At first I thought maybe she had felt something, but she assured me the X-ray was just a preliminary precaution, so she would have a record of what my breast looked like. This sounded vaguely sensible, but I still wasn't particularly eager to get one, and I was relieved that she said I might as well wait a few months, until the spring. When spring came, I decided to wait a few months more and by the time I found the lump, in September, the unused referral form was still sitting on a shelf above my telephone. Better late than never, I figured. The mammogram would tell me if I had cancer.

In fact, the lump didn't show up on the X-ray. The needle biopsy was "suspicious," but the surgical biopsy was the test that finally determined I had a cancerous tumour. I was shocked. How could this be?

Looking back, I can see that I was as muddled as most women about mammography. I didn't know the technique is fallible, particularly in women who have dense breast tissue — which is fairly typical of women who have not gone through menopause. For this very reason, and because the risk of breast cancer increases with age, many professionals reason that mammography makes most sense for women who are 50 or over, unless the woman has a suspicious symptom, or a family history of breast cancer. Once I had found a lump, I did have a suspicious symptom, but at that point the mammogram was no longer a screening device — it was a tool for diagnosis. The purpose of screening is to find breast cancers in women who are asymptomatic.

Since that time, I've learned that scientists have been arguing for several decades about the proper place for mammography screening in the fight against breast cancer. Two camps have evolved; I think of them as the minimalists and the go-getters. Those in the first camp say we should use screening mammography only when we know the benefits outweigh the risks. Those trained in preventive medicine are drawn to this camp. The other school of thought takes a more aggressive approach: start routine mammography at the age when breast cancer begins to show up in the statistics: 40 or even younger. Find as many early cancers as you can and root them out. Radiologists, the people who do mammography, rule in this camp.

Members of both sides are well represented in the audience today. The list of participants includes radiologists, nurses, consumer advocates, epidemiologists and administrators of screening programs. Some of the organizations represented are the American Cancer Society, the Food and Drug Administration (FDA), the National Cancer Institute, the Centres for Disease Control and the Eastman Kodak Company. Even Rose Kushner's widower, Harvey Kushner, is listed, from the Rose Kushner Breast Cancer Advisory Center.

Chairing the meeting is Dr. Suzanne Fletcher, president of the American College of Physicians. She's a tall, vibrant woman. As she welcomes us all, her warm exuberance dissipates some of the tension. Perhaps she will be able to reconcile the divisions that are sure to emerge as the discussion gets underway.

Fletcher gives a brief history of scientific investigations of screening. Studies have been going on for 30 years and include eight major randomized controlled trials. These are studies in which women who have no symptoms of breast cancer are assigned at random to one of two different groups — a test group that has some type of regular screening and a control group that does not. Periodically, or at the end of a set period of years, the groups are compared to see whether those who were screened have fared better than those who weren't. An effective screening program would be one in which the screened group showed fewer deaths from breast cancer.

"After the early results of several trials were reported, experts and organizations began making their recommendations on breast screening," says Fletcher. These groups agree that scientific evidence supports breast screening in women aged 50 and over. Screening can mean either mammography or a clinical breast exam by a professional, or both together. However, Fletcher says, getting to the nitty gritty, "recommendations by these groups regarding breast screening for women ages 40 to 49 have varied."

I can't help admiring Fletcher's diplomacy. She accentuates the positive and the field of consensus, and understates the acrimony in the main area of disagreement. She runs through other points of uncertainty: the frequency of screening and the test to be used — that is, mammography, a clinical exam by a professional, breast self-exam (BSE), or machine methods other than mammography. Finally, Dr. Fletcher emphasizes the purpose of this meeting: to interpret the scientific results. The political question — how these results are translated into policy — is not on the agenda.

This point is significant. One reason for the confusion over when to begin mammography — and another reason for the tense atmosphere at this meeting — is what I think of as the War of the Guidelines. When the NCI changed its guidelines in 1988 and began to recommend that women begin routine mammography at age 40, the balance of power shifted from the minimalists to the go-getters. If the outcome of the workshop is that scientific evidence supports beginning mammography at age 50 rather than age 40, all eyes will be on the NCI to see whether they revert to the guidelines they rejected just a few years back.

The three opening speakers don't address the hot issues — whether, and at what age, mammography screening saves lives. They talk about the perceived risk of breast cancer, the impact of false positives and negatives on the woman, and breast self-exam.

Although the risk of breast cancer rises with age, from a low risk at age 30 to 34 of developing breast cancer in the next year (1 chance in 3,731), to a medium risk at age 50 to 54 (one chance in 435), to a relatively high risk at age 70 to 74 (one chance in 222), research has shown that women's perceptions don't jibe with these realities. Sixty-five to 70 percent of women feel age makes no difference to risk. This inaccurate perception of risk may affect women's behaviour, says the first speaker, Dr. Russell Harris from North Carolina. Young women may be seeking mammography because they believe their risk is higher than it is, while older women may not bother to have regular mammograms because they underestimate their risk.

The second speaker, Barbara Rimer, is also from North Carolina. She highlights the psychological effects on women whose screening mammograms give incorrect results. When a woman with a suspicious mammogram learns from follow-up tests that she doesn't have breast cancer, she is likely to feel anxious about having future mammograms and is less likely to perform breast self-exams. These women also bear a financial burden. Of the $216 million a year spent (in the U.S.) on post-mammogram biopsies, $41 million is for false positives, notes Rimer.

The third speaker, Cornelia Baines from Toronto, is Anthony Miller's collaborator in the controversial National Breast Screening Study. She reviews the world literature on breast self-exams. One argument for advocating breast self-exam is the belief that it empowers women and gets them in touch with their own bodies. A second is that the technique is valuable in countries or regions where women have no access to mammography, or for women who refuse mammography. I am surprised to learn that no well-designed study has ever evaluated breast self-exam. Of 13 papers that looked at the effect of BSE on tumour size, says Baines, most found that BSE does enable women to find smaller tumours than they discover by chance. Unpublished results of studies that are still ongoing in the United Kingdom, Finland and Shanghai suggest that a reduction in mortality is likely, but more data is needed before BSE can be advocated as a lifesaving measure with a solid scientific foundation.

I like the fact that all of the introductory presenters illuminate the women's perspective on screening. The talks by Harris and Rimer point out problems in mammography screening that tend to get lost in the heated arguments over mammography as a technology. "A benign biopsy is not a benign situation for the woman undergoing the ordeal," is how Rimer sums up her findings. Baines points out that women describe mammography as "cold and inhuman " What brings them back to the screening centre for rescreening is the clinical examination, because they feel more comfortable.

The second session shifts the tone to science and technology. The featured speaker, Professor Sam Shapiro, is something of an icon at this meeting. One of the other participants says he is humbled to be at the same table with him; another calls him the "grandaddy of mammography."

Breast X-rays, or mammograms, have been around since 1913, but were not put to practical use until 1960 when Houston radiologist Dr. Robert Egan demonstrated that the technique could find early breast cancers. Mammography was quickly accepted as an aid to diagnosing women who had a suspicious lump, but its real promise seemed to lie in screening women who had no symptoms whatsoever. Enter Sam Shapiro and the study he initiated in December 1963. Shapiro and his colleagues began their research in greater New York using women who were enrolled in the Health Insurance Plan (HIP). The researchers randomly assigned 62,000 women between 40 and 64 to either a test group or a control group. They offered those in the first group a free checkup by physical exam and mammography every year for five years; the other women were given no special encouragement to be examined and were left undisturbed. The researchers monitored both groups for breast cancer and breast cancer deaths for an impressive 10 years. Those in the test group, as hoped, suffered fewer deaths from breast cancer. Thirty percent fewer women in the test group died — a statistically significant reduction. The implication seemed clear: detecting early breast cancer saved lives.

In Shapiro's study, which became known as the HIP trial, the women who were screened had a manual exam plus mammography. Therefore, the manual exam could have accounted, at least in part, for the reduction in deaths. And although the study had not set out to compare screening at different ages, analysts noted that the benefits of screening were confined to the women over age 50.[1]

One of the panelists invited to lead today's discussion of the HIP trial is Dr. Charles Smart, a surgeon from Utah. In the course of the discussion, Smart refers several times to something called the National Breast Cancer Detection Demonstration Project (BCDDP). Mention of the BCDDP brings a swift reminder from the moderator that it was not a randomized trial and is therefore not on the agenda. Smart presses his point — that the BCDDP saved lives — but he is overruled. Yet I know from reading Rose Kushner's account of the era that the BCDDP, which followed on the heels of the HIP trial's seven-year results, was a significant chapter in the breast screening story.

In 1973, struck by the promising results of the HIP study, the ACS received funding from the NCI to mount a nationwide screening demonstration program — the BCDDP. The project was vast: 27 screening centres around the country would screen 10,000 women per centre, aged 35 to 74, annually for five years. The screening would be free and thorough. Every volunteer was to have an annual mammogram and two other machine tests, a xerogram (a mammography-like technique which produced Xerox images instead of X-ray pictures) and a thermogram (a type of infrared photography which maps body heat). All would have physical exams and be taught breast self-exam.

The NCI provided $45 million for the project. With neither a control group nor a rigorous plan for data collection, however, the plan was not designed to generate scientific data.[2] The announced purpose was to introduce screening to physicians and women. Critics charged that the HIP study gave no grounds for screening women 35 to 50, with or without mammography.

If the goal was to show that women would attend publicly funded, well-publicized breast screening clinics, the project was a success. When the first centre opened in 1973, women flocked to have their free tests. The next year Betty Ford and Happy Rockefeller had their highly publicized mastectomies; demand skyrocketed. Some centres had waiting lists two months long. By 1976, with 280,281 women signed up, recruiting stopped.

John C. Bailar III, a biostatistician and physician who now heads McGill University's department of biostatistics and epidemiology, was then the NCI's Deputy Associate Director for Cancer Control. He watched the demonstration project with increasing unease. In 1976 he published the first of a series of articles questioning the assumptions behind mammography screening. Regular screening clearly can reduce mortality, he said, but it was not clear how much of the reduction could be attained by clinical screening only — a manual exam plus a medical history. In the HIP trial, he noted, only 15 percent of the diagnoses made by screening in the test group were the result of mammography alone. All the other cases were found by clinical exam, or they turned up between the screens, or after the five-year screening period was over.

Even in cases where mammography had detected the cancer, said Bailar, a variety of statistical biases might account for some, if not all, of the improved survival. And because screening is imprecise, its promotion meant that a great many women would have to undergo investigative surgery, with all the accompanying medical risks, emotional trauma and financial cost.

The part of Bailar's analysis that drew the most fire, however, was his discussion of mammography's radiation hazards. Using the best available data (which he admitted was far from perfect) he estimated the HIP trial would cause between eight and 32 cases of radiation-induced breast cancer. Because the cancers would take 10 to 20 years to develop, they would show up after the study's five-year follow-up period had expired. In his analysis, the number of deaths likely to be caused by radiation was almost identical to the number of lives that would be saved by early detection. The risk was greatest, he said, for women under 50, whose breast tissue was more sensitive to radiation and who had more years ahead of them in which to develop cancer.

The HIP trial did not address the question of radiation. Rose Kushner later commented that she could not understand why, when the HIP trial was planned, no one was concerned about the effects of radiation on the women's healthy breast tissue. "After all," she wrote, "by 1963, data from the atomic-bomb raids over Japan had already proved the harm X-ray could do to people. But somehow, the Japanese data were neglected."[3]

Once Bailar raised the alarm about mammography radiation, government agencies from all levels scurried to test the machines in their jurisdictions. They found BCDDP equipment that emitted amounts of radiation everyone agreed was unsafe. They discovered mammogram machines in other sites that showed leaks, or used industrial X-ray equipment and films never intended for use on breasts. As the popular program evolved into a vote-losing nightmare, politicians jumped to attention.

Media stories and government hearings went on for two years. Rose Kushner herself was in the thick of the controversy as a patient advocate, speaking and writing against the BCDDP, which she described as "a well-intentioned program that was not well planned."[4] She discovered that the NCI had not checked with government radiation experts before launching the program and that the director had even ignored a letter from New York's health department warning of radiation risk. Kushner opposed the government program with some regrets; she saw potential in mammography. "I believe good mammography and good mammographers can save women's breasts by detecting cancer when it is microscopic and needs no mastectomy to be cured," she wrote.

Bailar's concern about excessive surgery was also prophetic. As part of the official inquiry into the BCDDP, a panel of expert pathologists reviewed its 1,810 cases of breast cancer diagnoses and singled out 506 which pathologists had defined as "minimal." The panel concluded that 66 of these cases were benign lesions. Another 22 cases were "uncertain." At least 30 of these 88 women had had complete mastectomies and most operations were the deforming radical, which removes chest muscle as well as breast tissue. The story of the "66 benigns" generated another wave of sensational headlines.[5]

A government-appointed jury, made up of people with no involvement in mammography, developed guidelines for government participation in mammography screening programs. The guidelines recommended that all women over age 50 continue being screened, but that mammography screening in women under 50 be selective. In women aged 40 to 49, mammography screening would be limited to those with a first-degree family history of breast cancer. Only the highest risk women between ages 35 and 39 would have mammography — that is, women who had already had cancer in one breast. By the end of the '70s, the American experience had set mass screening for breast cancer on a cautious course, or so it seemed. The HIP study justified screening in women over 50 to gain a limited but real reduction in deaths, while the BCDDP was a cautionary tale against excessive zeal in mammography.

Over the next decade, however, breast screening in North America underwent a curious evolution. By the early 1990s, many women believed mammography was synonymous with early detection and saved lives. And women under 50 who, according to the research, had the least to gain from the technique and the most to risk, were its most enthusiastic adherents.

The transition began in the early 1980s. Ironically, John Bailar's critique of the BCDDP was the impetus for a new X-ray film that gave sharper pictures with a lower dose of radiation.[6] Mammogram radiation exposure, which is measured in rads (radiation absorbed dose) dropped from eight rads per exposure in the HIP study, to between one and three rads in the BCDDP and was down to 0.6 to 0.2 rads in the Canadian project that began in the early 1980s. Because of Bailar's intervention, said Rose Kushner, "low-dose X-ray film was perfected, more special-purpose mammography equipment using film-screen was acquired by radiologists, and more care is taken by everyone involved."[7] Mammography adherents were quick to point to the improvements in the quality of mammography. They questioned whether the cautious guidelines drawn up by the NCI jury were necessary now. In fact, the argument ran, if the HIP study showed a benefit of 30 percent in the reduction in deaths with the crude equipment available at the time, surely the new equipment would permit an even greater reduction in deaths. As for women under 50, a new analysis of the HIP study — an 18-year follow-up — showed that screened women in this group had six fewer deaths than those in the unscreened group. The difference was not statistically significant — the disparity could have arisen from chance factors; nonetheless the argument was made that if screening with old equipment had saved six lives, new equipment would save even more.

Following this reasoning, a number of organizations began to promote mammography screening as a lifesaving measure for younger women. The American College of Radiologists and the American Cancer Society, in particular, championed routine screening with mammography in women 40 to 50. In 1983, mammography checkups became the centrepiece of the American Cancer Society's campaign against breast cancer. The ACS actively promoted mammography with television advertising, highway billboards and ads in American news magazines. The prescription was: a first (baseline) mammogram between ages 35 and 40, a mammogram every one to two years until age 50 and annual mammograms thereafter.

At the same time as the ACS and the American College of Radiologists promoted screening mammography, other agencies stuck by the moderate policy recommended by the post-BCDDP task force. And so it was that two sets of official guidelines vied for physician and consumer loyalty in the U.S. Their main point of difference was the age at which mammography for asymptomatic women with no history of breast cancer should begin. In the minimalist camp, recommending routine screening mammography only to women over 50 and in special cases of younger women, were the American College of Physicians, the United States Preventive Services Task Force and a screening committee of the International Union Against Cancer. As recently as 1988, the NCI and the American College of Obstetricians and Gynecologists were also aligned with this group. In Canada, Great Britain and Sweden, government guidelines recommended routine mammography screening for women over 50 only.[8]

In 1988, the year of the shift, the NCI left the minimalist camp to side with the go-getters and the American College of Obstetricians and Gynecologists did the same. The Canadian College of Radiologists, which had initially sided with the minimalists, joined its American counterpart. The Canadian Cancer Society, in contrast, is aligned with the camp that would restrict mammography in women under 50 — except in the province of British Columbia, where guidelines encourage women to begin mammography screening in their 40s.

That same year, John Bailar restated his critique. For women under 50, he saw no rationale for screening mammography. Other studies of mammography screening in Europe confirmed the conclusion of the HIP study: screening in this age range did not reduce deaths. As for radiation, he concurred that the risks from regular mammography are much reduced by a combination of best technique and state-of-the-art technology, but the reality was, "not every centre can meet these standards."[9] He reiterated that the costs of mammography — not only monetary, but the emotional toll of false-positive and false-negative diagnoses — had to be weighed in the equation. He also dismissed the concept of a "baseline" mammogram: "On current evidence, they do little more than make the radiologist (and perhaps the surgeon) a bit more comfortable about the same decisions they later would have made anyway."[10]

Maryann Napoli of the Center for Medical Consumers in New York has followed the evolution of mammography guidelines since the 1970s. Her organization advocates screening mammography at age 50 and older. She's here at the conference, so I ask her why she thinks the NCI changed its position on the guidelines, in 1988.

"There was a lot of politics involved," she replies. "The different groups felt they had to come to some agreement and the agreement was that screening should start at a younger age. What was amusing to me," she adds with a laugh, "was that whenever I've asked why they changed to go with the ACS in 1988, they said they didn't want women to be confused."

As for the heavy promotion of mammography, "It's a business in the U.S.," Napoli says. "There is a strong advertising effort to get younger women to be screened in this country because younger women have more money. And they have been very successful efforts. In New York you see subway ads placed by private radiology clinics that suggest women start screening at age 30. A lot of the ads are guilt-provoking. If you're not being screened, you're not taking good care of yourself." And, she continues, "The ads have been effective. Women have bought it."

Certainly the parties behind the ads, companies like Kodak — one of the leading manufacturers of mammographic films — and General Electric — which makes mammography machines — are not wholly disinterested in mammography. Some physicians invest in mammography clinics, then refer patients to the same testing centres. A study in the *New England Journal of Medicine* showed that doctors with a financial stake in imaging equipment (such as that used in mammography) are four-and-a-half times as likely to order those tests than doctors with no vested interest. They also charge more for them. Physicians make up 50 percent of the ACS board and many of these doctors are radiologists. And campaigns to promote mammography can have a "serendipitous fall-out," says medical sociologist Patricia Kaufert, since these campaigns also promote the sponsoring agency and the virtues of giving it money.

Everyone acknowledges that mammography screening is extremely costly. Harvard professor John Cairns estimated in 1985 that it would cost $100 million per year to offer free mammography screening to every American woman over 50 every one to three years.[11] In the U.S., with its private system of medical care, most women either pay for their mammograms out-of-pocket or they have insurance that covers regular screening mammograms.

In countries like Canada, Britain, Sweden and the Netherlands, which have comprehensive state-funded medical coverage, the results of the HIP study suggested a means of controlling breast cancer deaths — and medical costs related to breast cancer treatment — through organized government-run mammography screening programs. In fact, the post-HIP trials were all carried out in countries with both high breast cancer rates and comprehensive national medical plans. To make efficient use of their health care resources, health policy planners in these countries needed to know what the most appropriate interval between screening sessions was, how often it was necessary to screen to effectively prevent deaths, how many years of screening and follow-up are necessary to achieve a reduction in deaths, which age groups could most benefit, and the effectiveness of different screening modalities.

In the mid-1970s, inspired by the HIP study, Sweden's National Board of Health and Welfare began a series of randomized trials of mammography. A large study known as the "two-county trial" — it compared two adjacent counties, one that offered mammography screening and one that did not — began in 1975-76. Another group of randomized studies were begun in Stockholm and Malmö between 1976 and 1982. Early results from the two-county trial were reported in 1985. Two researchers are here at the conference from Sweden, bearing new data from the two-county trial, as well as some early data from later trials. They have put it all together into a combined analysis that will be presented for the first time at this meeting.

I'm curious to hear what the Swedes will say. One prominent Swedish mammographer has apparently taken a vigorous stand against the Canadian study. In an interview on public radio in September 1991, more than a year before the Canadian study was published, Cornelia Baines stated that "certain very prominent people in the screening world have decided that they are sure they're not going to like what the National Breast Screening Study releases as its results." These people had undertaken a systematic program to undermine the results of the study, Baines asserted. She went on to name Laszlo Tabar, the mammographer who headed Sweden's two-county study, as the "leading light" in the campaign. Tabar, she acknowledged, "takes beautiful films. His screening trial in two counties in Sweden has been sort of the gold standard ... But, as I've told Laszlo in personal conversations very often, you can't compare a two-county study — even if it does deal with thousands of women — with a study that has to cross half a continent and involves many autonomous people who are providing what the community can provide locally at its highest level." The underlying issue is a classic one: whether findings from laboratory-perfect conditions can be transferred to the real world.

Laszlo Tabar is not one of today's Swedish guests, however. Lars-Gunnar Larsson, of Umea University Hospital presents the data, aided by Lars Rutqvist and Lennarth Nysbrom. The upshot of the combined analysis of the various studies is that the results are inconclusive. For women under 50, more follow-up is needed (at least three or four more years). In one group of women who began screening when they were in their 40s, five more died in the test group than the unscreened group. Based on the available data, screening for all ages up to 74 has had only a marginal impact on mortality. At one point, someone in the audience mentions Laszlo Tabar. "We don't agree with him," is the abrupt answer.

Like the HIP trial, the European studies show conclusively that mammography screening can detect cancers that are not palpable. They also show that regular mammography screening can reduce (but by no means eliminate), breast cancer deaths in women over 50. And, like the HIP study, they give no basis for using screening mammography in women under 50.

The last person on the program for Day One is Anthony Miller, who will talk about the results of the NBSS for women in their 40s. In the style of the workshop, two panelists will critique his study before questions are taken from the floor. One of the panelists is Daniel Kopans, a Harvard professor and radiologist at Massachusetts General hospital in Boston. Kopans has been vocal throughout the day and clearly takes the view that Miller's mammograms weren't up to snuff. Miller, a small, wiry man with a long face and a British accent, seems unruffled by Kopans and other hostile members of the group. He comments that the Canadian study was almost stopped before it began because of the radiation scare. "In 1980," Miller says, "the concern was with the radiation dose, not with quality of images. This was true in all North America; now we know that image quality is more important."[12]

The 10-year, $18 million Canadian study headed by Miller and Baines set out to answer two questions inspired by the HIP. One was whether combination screening — that is, an annual mammogram, plus manual examination, plus BSE — could be shown to benefit women in their 40s compared to one initial manual examination plus BSE. Although earlier studies showed no such benefit, the Canadian study had a large sample — 50,000 women in their 40s — and used mammography equipment far more sensitive than that in the HIP study. The study was conducted at 15 different centres from Halifax to Vancouver. The women were randomly assigned to one group or the other. The researchers found that mammography increased the detection rate of cancers, as expected. The finding that most disturbed the study's critics, however, was that survival of those in the group that had annual screening, including mammography, was no better than survival in the group that had no screening. In fact 38 women died of breast cancer in the screened group and only 28 died of breast cancer in the group that wasn't screened. The difference was not statistically significant, but gave no support for widespread mammography screening at this age.

Apparently, with two extra years of follow-up, a shift in the figures has narrowed the gap between the two groups. At a medical meeting in England in 1991, Miller caused an uproar when he said that the death rate after five years was "significantly higher" among younger women who were screened. At that time he and Baines refused to release statistical details of the study. The *London Sunday Times*, however, ran a front-page story headlined, "Women who have breast screening are more likely to die of cancer." In the newspaper story, Miller speculated that radiation and surgery after a mammogram might cause secondary cancers to grow faster and hasten deaths. He was roundly criticized for these musings and disputes over the study began to take on a life of their own. In January 1992, Samuel Epstein of the University of Illinois referred to the still-unpublished study in an article he wrote for the *Los Angeles Times*, entitled, "Mammography radiates doubts." The National Cancer Institute and the American College of Radiology responded with press releases defending mammography in women under 50 and attacking Epstein for citing the deaths of women in the NBSS before its results were in print.

The following June, the *Journal of the National Cancer Institute* printed an article quoting radiologists in both Canada and the U.S., all of whom criticized the NBSS. In screening circles, it was no secret that a series of consulting radiologists had quit the study, complaining that the equipment used in the NBSS was outdated and the technologists poorly trained. One radiologist at the Bethesda meeting, Edward Sickles of the University of California in San Francisco, alludes to this high turnover with a quip that he was "the only member of the American College of Radiologists who hasn't resigned from the Canadian study."

Now, with just a trace of feistiness, Miller details the measures taken to ensure quality mammography in the NBSS. Centres that had expertise in mammography were selected, he says. High sensitivity was encouraged, two-view examinations (two X-rays of each breast) were used, the radiological physics were monitored, there were external reviews of the quality of the mammography, and so on.

Joining Daniel Kopans in the discussion of Miller's presentation is Alvin Mushlin, of the Department of Community Medicine in Rochester, New York. Kopans begins, citing a long list of the study's problems, including inappropriate technology, poor training for those involved and flawed randomization. Mushlin, on the other hand, says his overall assessment of the trial is quite favourable. Real things happen to real people, he says. Many of the "faults" cited by the radiologists are indicative of the real-world problems that are inevitable when women have mammography: the equipment will not always be state-of-the-art, some women may not attend all the screening sessions and staff may not be as well trained as one would ideally like.

"Significant decisions are going to be made in this country on the basis of this study," counters Kopans. "It is very imporant for us to know exactly what was done."

Nancy Lee, from the Centre for Disease Control responds, "The Canadian study has probably more rigour than we have in our centres. In that way the Canadian trial is more illustrative than the Swedish study."

A radiologist named Stephen Feig from Philadelphia, who is one of those who resigned from the study, asserts, "I didn't want my presence to be seen as lending credibility to the quality of the mammography. There was resistance to changes, such as grids, that wouldn't have been expensive."

For me, this exchange focusses the dynamics of the day's debates. One group demands maximum control and has a high degree of faith in technology. The other doesn't believe rigorous control is possible, or even that it should be held out as the main object. As well, each camp has a perspective rooted in the daily work of its members. Radiologists see the tiny lesions on a mammogram; public health workers must cope with the panic of the woman who is told that same lesion looks suspicious. In the same way, the dominant American view suits a free-enterprise philosophy of medicine, while countries with comprehensive state medical coverage reflect more closely the ideology of a non-profit system of medicine. A few people, like Edward Sickles, valiantly straddle the divide. "The NBSS has heightened awareness among radiologists in the U.S. for accreditation," he says. "That may be its greatest effect."

Mark Elwood of New Zealand is the highlight on Day Two. In his meta-analysis, he reviews results of all the studies after seven years. The HIP study showed the greatest decrease in mortality, he said, "and is least relevant today." The Swedish studies showed a minimal increase in mortality, the Edinburgh trial showed no difference in mortality between screened and unscreened groups, while the Canadian trials showed a substantial increase in mortality. Overall, he says, there is little difference in mortality between screened and comparison groups, and there is no scientific support for routine mammography screening in women under 50. The Swedish trials, he concludes, because of the high quality of their mammography, give the best estimate of what a mammography screening program could accomplish.

The overview is clearly a blow to mammography enthusiasts. Elwood goes on to suggest why mammography might not benefit younger women. Breast cancer may be a biologically different disease in younger women, or their cancers might grow more rapidly; treatments might be less beneficial to younger women; the greater density of normal breast tissue could decrease effectiveness. Another possibility, he adds, is that mammography screening or therapy may actually pose a hazard to younger women. "Given the small excess of death in several studies on short follow-up," he says, "we have to admit it's a possibility."

This brings an objection from the audience. "The differences are not statistically significant!"

"Well, if we're going to look at trends in one direction, we have to be willing to look at them when they go the other way," responds Elwood. A negative effect, he says, could come from the mammography itself — compressing the breast could stimulate dissemination of the cancer; or the treatment in a younger woman could weaken her system.

"The idea that mammography squeezes cancer cells into the blood stream came from the press!" objects Kopans. "It's irresponsible to suggest mammography does that. Why not say that a clinical exam disseminates cancer cells?"

"Irresponsibility is in the eye of the beholder," retorts Elwood, who seems steeled for the flak. "The onus is on those promoting a service to demonstrate its benefit. There's no empirical evidence to recommend screening for women under 50. The false negative rate is quite high. For high-risk women, more tumours will be found, but not necessarily more benefit. I accept that mammography techniques have improved greatly, but it's only an hypothesis that this reduces mortality. The evidence shows a small non-significant hazard with short follow-up and a small, non-significant benefit with long follow-up. A doctor who wants to recommend mammography to a woman under 50," he says, "should be required to obtain informed consent."

"A very well-done meta-analysis," comments Thomas Chalmers, of the Harvard School of Public Health, who has been asked to critique Elwood's presentation. The scientific evidence does not point to significant benefits in routine mammographic screening in women under 50, he says. He agrees that screening prevents deaths in older women, but says we can't conclude screening by mammography is crucial, even in women over 50. "Perhaps a more important question," he says, "is if mammography lengthens life. None of the studies ask that question."

He adds a plug for the Canadian study. "It's a disgrace that Tony Miller had to scrape together money to do this study when people were getting money to study drugs, the effect of which was to have one more week of misery."

It's time for the wrap-up. Fletcher, still exuding enthusiasm, says she celebrates this opportunity for exchange with the foremost experts on breast screening. She commends them for their contributions to reducing breast cancer mortality, and sets out the conclusions of her summary team. The conclusions are somewhat anti-climactic: for women 40 to 49, no evidence links screening to reduced breast cancer mortality in the first seven years. Too few studies have long-term data to draw conclusions in the longer term. The question may remain unanswered, since large randomized trials are unlikely to be launched elsewhere in the western world for this age group. For women 50 to 59, the data show a reduction in breast cancer mortality due to screening (although not necessarily by mammography). She lists some areas for future research: "We still don't know the optimal interval for mammography or whether a single view mammogram is as effective as a two-view mammogram. We don't know the most effective screening modality." It's a rout for the go-getters.

Kopans objects. "I've been hearing references to the vested interests of radiologists," he says. "I'm on a salary. I teach at Harvard. I can earn a living doing other things, and I'm beginning to think I should." He dictates a statement that he wants added to the summary report: There have been no studies with sufficient numbers of women, design, or follow-up, to demonstrate with statistical power the benefit of screening of women aged 40 to 49. "Should women be denied screening because investigators didn't do proper studies?" he asks.

At the end of the workshop, I ask Maryann Napoli if she thinks that the NCI will change its guidelines to bring them in line with the workshop report. Napoli has her doubts. "They've painted themselves into a corner," she says. "It's very hard to go back and tell the American public that 'we made a mistake. We really didn't have the evidence.' Now they have a problem of dealing with public perception — the perception on women's part in this country about mammography is that this is beneficial, that early detection does equal salvation. And that's because they've given us this one-dimensional view of the technology."

In the months that follow the February meeting, the NCI goes through several drafts of guidelines, all of which get thrown out. In October 1993, the agency calls an all-day meeting to discuss the guidelines issue. As Gina Kolata describes it for the *New York Times,* an 18-member board of Scientific Advisors, and various NCI officials, hear 10 hours of "pleas from groups that wanted it to keep, or change, its current guidelines." At the end of the day, they decide that the agency should just publish information that will allow women to make their own decisions. "We're essentially a research organization," says the director of NCI's division of cancer prevention and control. "We think that's our role." An advisory group member, Dr. David Alberts of the University of Arizona, says he doesn't see any point in telling women to consult their doctors either. "I find it almost a no-brainer to tell them to go to their doctor, who may be less informed than they are."

For me, the missing voice in the debate has been that of Maureen Roberts. If she had been alive to take part in the Bethesda discussion, I think she would support the idea of letting the woman be the judge. Before her death in June 1989, Roberts wrote an article that ran posthumously in the British Medical Journal. The death-bed manifesto belies the mild appearance of the woman in the accompanying photograph. "Breast screening: time for a rethink?" is a hard-hitting critique which questions the whole philosophy of mammography screening — the means of fighting breast cancer to which she devoted much of her professional life.

As a strategy for disease control, she pointed out, screening is always second best: when we don't know how to prevent or treat a disease, we resort to screening to detect it early. Reviewing the various research trials to evaluate breast screening, in which reductions in mortality ranged from 30 percent to no statistically significant impact (her own project), she said, "We cannot ignore [these results], and it is not enough to say that our techniques weren't good enough a few years ago but are adequate now. We all know that mammography is an unsuitable screening test: it is technologically difficult to perform, the pictures are difficult to interpret, it has a high false-positive rate, and we don't know how often to carry it out." However disappointing the admission may be, she concluded, "We can no longer afford to ignore the possibility that screening may not reduce mortality in women of any age."

Even a 30 percent reduction in mortality is a very limited achievement, Roberts contended. "This is not offering any certainty of a cure or normal life to the women who attend [mammogram screening clinics], merely a prolongation of years for a few. Not only that, we cannot predict who will have these extra years."

While they ignore the psychological impact of their interventions, Roberts said those who work in mammography focus on technical questions of quality control. Adopting "an air of evangalism," they urge women to come for screening and approvingly label the comers as "compliant." Screening advocates view a low compliance rate as a problem and worry about how to raise it. "Have we brainwashed ourselves into thinking we are having a dramatic impact on a serious disease, before we brainwash the public?" Roberts asked.

She concluded, "The government is prepared to put a large amount of scarce resources into a national breast screening program, yet is unwilling to take on the tobacco industry at a political level; this despite overwhelming evidence that a truly preventive program would save thousands of lives each year from lung cancer and other diseases. It was clearly a matter of politics, a decision taken in an election year and now out of perspective."[13]

Roberts' plea addresses the power imbalance between professionals who work in the mammography milieu, and the women who use the technology. She wanted to create screening and diagnostic centres that respond to the needs of users. She sought to demystify screening technology, recognizing it as a limited tool to be used when appropriate, not worshipped or imposed.

Her critique suggests to me that the split in values underlying the screening debate falls roughly along lines that are traditionally feminine or masculine. On the feminine side are the concerns with emotional costs and quality of life, the stress on human contact as a component of healing, the holistic, non-linear approach to problem-solving, the concern with conserving resources, and a minimalist approach to medical intervention. On the masculine side are the belief in technology, the bent for grand projects with large financial outlays, and heroic measures to save lives.

Curiously, women of my own generation — baby boomers, who are generally well educated and often financially independent — have thoroughly embraced this second pole, at least where breast cancer is concerned. As Maryann Napoli says, women now in their 40s have bought the idea that if we're not being screened, we're not taking good care of ourselves. Breast cancer advocacy groups in the U.S. have lobbied successfully on a state-by-state basis, to have regular screening mammograms covered by medical insurance, even for women in their 40s. "The NCI and the ACS guidelines have caused these grass-roots activists to lobby for reimbursement, and the politicians supported it because it's Mom and apple pie," says Napoli. "So now what do we do? Undo all these laws and admit the guidelines were misguided?" In Canada, except for British Columbia, the official guidelines have never recommended screening for women in their 40s, but when the Quebec government tried to curtail the massive trend towards screening by women in their 40s by cutting reimbursement for screening mammography in this age group, women's organizations protested the threatened cut.

Our love affair with mammography fits critic Ivan Illich's description of industrial hubris, the dream that we can find technical answers to irrational fantasies. We imagine that we can escape sickness, pain and the threat of death through the medicalization of health. In truth, says Illich, beyond a certain point, the marginal gains cease to be equitably distributed and overall effectiveness begins to decline. We see this clearly in mammography. No society has the trained people and financial resources to devote to the constant operation and upkeep of state-of-the-art mammography equipment for every woman who is susceptible, by virtue of her age, to getting breast cancer. A few women, in privileged pockets of certain countries, will get the best technology mammography has to offer. The majority will be younger women. The rest will be excluded, or will risk the consequences of poor X-rays, interpreted by ill-trained staff.

The way out of the circle, says Illich, is to recover our personal autonomy in health care through an ethical awakening, reinforced by political action. Thus awakened, he argues, "people will limit medical therapies because they want to conserve their opportunity and power to heal.[14]

The concept of an ethical awakening challenges us to view health care spending in a broad societal context. Where breast cancer is concerned, women in their 40s would forego screening mammography, despite the tiny theoretical possibility that a mammogram could be life-saving for them. We would all confront the frustrating fact that we don't know how to limit the ravages of the disease in younger women. Putting mammography in its proper perspective could be the first step in trying to find answers.

Notes

1. John Cairns, "The Treatment of Diseases and the War Against Cancer," *Scientific American*, (Nov. 1985), 253: pp. 51-59, [citation on p. 54]; and Kushner, p. 165.

2. John C. Bailar, "Screening for Early Breast Cancer: Pros and Cons," *Cancer*, (1977), 39:6, pp. 2788-9.

3. John C. Bailar, "Mammography: A Contrary View," *Annals of Internal Medicine*, (1976), 84:77.

4. Kushner, p. 165.

5. Kushner, p. 167.

6. John C. Bailar, "Mammographic Screening: A Reappraisal of Benefits and Risks," *Clinical Obstetrics and Gynecology*, (March 1978), Vol. 21, No. 1, pp. 1-14, [citation p. 10]; Kushner, p. 168.

7. Kushner, p. 167.

8. Kushner, p. 169.

9. David M. Eddy et al, "The Value of Mammography Screening in Women Under 50 Years of Age," *Journal of the American Medical Association*, (1988), pp. 1512-1519.

10. John C. Bailar, "Editorial: Mammography Before Age 50 Years?" *Journal of the American Medical Association*, (Mar. 11, 1988), 259:10, pp. 1548-9.

11. Cairns, pp. 54-55.

12. Anthony B. Miller et al, *Canadian National Breast Screening Study*, 1. "Breast Cancer Detection and Death Rates Among Women Aged 40 to 49 Years,"; 2. "Breast Cancer Detection and Death Rates Among Women Aged 50 to 59 Years," *Canadian Medical Association Journal,"* (Nov. 15, 1992), 147: pp. 1459-1488.

13. Maureen Roberts, "Breast Screening: Time for a Rethink?" *British Medical Journal*, (Nov. 4, 1989), pp. 1153-5.

14. Ivan Illich, *Limits to Medicine*, (London: Penguin, 1990), pp. 264-275.

Cut
Against the Grain

Out, damned spot! Out, I say!
— William Shakespeare, *MacBeth*

When the 19th century British writer Fanny Burney noticed a heavy pain in her breast, "which went on augmenting from week to week," her husband urged her to see a surgeon. The idea revolted Burney; she hoped simple "care and warmth" would take care of the problem. In the ensuing months her spouse enlisted several women friends to bring her round and eventually Burney consented to a physician's visit. After examining her, Dr. Antoine Dubois "uttered so many charges for me to be tranquil, & to suffer no uneasiness that I could not but suspect there was room for terrible inquietude." When she looked to her spouse, "his features, his whole face displayed the bitterest woe." Burney guessed what they could not bear to say — she would need an operation, "to avert evil consequences!"

That was in 1810. Burney and her husband, General D'Arblay, were living in Paris. In a long letter to her sister, Burney described the mastectomy in excruciating detail. Her medical team was the best in France, led by Napoleon's surgeon Dominique-Jean Larrey.

In preparation for the ordeal, Burney made up her will[1] and, on the advice of her surgical team, collaborated in a scheme to have her husband called off on business during the operation. On the appointed day, seven men dressed all in black arrived at her home and readied the salon. "[T]he sight of the immense quantity of bandages, compresses, sponges, lint," she confessed, "made me a little sick." To busy herself, she wrote farewell notes to her husband and son Alex, "in case of a fatal result."

The operation took 20 minutes. During the initial proceedings, Burney remained feisty. One of the men bid her to mount a bed, which they set in the middle of the room and piled with two old mattresses. They covered her face with a handkerchief but the cloth was transparent enough for her to observe the quickening drama. Eight figures circled the bed; polished steel glittered. Dr. Larrey intoned, in a voice of solemn melancholy, "*Qui me tiendra ce sein?*" ("Who will hold the breast for me?")

From his question, and hand signals which described first a cross then a circle, Burney understood they would remove her *entire* breast. Horrified, she started up and threw off her veil. She cried out her reply to Dr. Larrey's question: "*C'est moi, Monsieur!*" Placing her hand under her breast, she demanded to know why they would remove the whole of it. The pain darted through the entire organ, but came from one point.

The men listened attentively but said not a word. Dr. Larrey repositioned Burney on the mattress, spread the veil back over her face, and once more signaled with his hands: the cross — and the circle. Burney sank back in defeat and closed her eyes, "sadly resolute to be wholly resigned."

She did not watch the operation, but monitored every sensation (two chasms in her memory led her to conclude she fainted twice). She writes, "when the dreadful steel was plunged into the breast — cutting through veins — arteries — flesh — nerves — ... I began a scream that lasted unremittingly during the whole time of the incision." At the first cut, air rushed into the wound, "like a mass of minute but sharp & forked poniards." The next cut was circular and went against the grain of her resisting flesh. Midway through, the effort of inscribing the curve so exhausted Dr. Larrey's right hand he was obliged to transfer his knife to his other hand. Just when Burney thought the ordeal over (by now her eyes were "so firmly closed that the Eyelids seemed indented into the Cheeks"), a new procedure ensued: a rackling of knife against breastbone, as the surgeon scraped over and over to eliminate every atom of diseased tissue. At last Dr. Larrey gathered Burney's exhausted body in his arms and carried her to her bed.

Only now did she open her eyes: "& I then saw my good Dr. Larrey, pale nearly as myself, his face streaked with blood, & his expression depicting grief, apprehension & almost horror."

In Burney's day, any operation was a last ditch procedure in which the patient often died of shock, blood loss or infection. Like a war hero, a successful surgeon had to take swift, decisive action. Indeed, the surgical profession has historic links to the military. In the days when the church controlled medicine and forbade the dissection of corpses on religious grounds, working the battlefield was a doctor's best opportunity to find out what was inside the body. Burney's surgeon, Dominique-Jean Larrey, fit the classic mold. Just after he performed Burney's mastectomy he left for the Russian campaign where, at the Battle of Borodino, he amputated 200 limbs in 24 hours.

By the late 19th century, anaesthetics and antisepsis had utterly transformed the trade — but the old attitudes prevailed. All medicine is hierarchical, but as a specialty, surgery is the most hierarchical of all, a physician friend tells me. Surgeons are the prima donnas of the profession. Many surgeons regard their medical school teacher as their master, and to go against his instruction would "besmirch his reputation."

When I first read Burney's account, I gave thanks for my own painless and relatively safe operation. But in the grey zones of medical theory, ethics, values and politics, I also saw parallels to contemporary breast surgery. I wonder, for example, if a surgeon today would have agreed to give Fanny Burney the limited surgery she wanted. I wonder if Dr. Larrey's contemporary would tell Burney of the surgical team's uncertainty about whether an operation would do her any good. Dr. Dubois' first judgement (which was kept from Burney) was that "the evil was too far advanced for any remedy"; surgery would only hasten an inevitable end because, he believed, the cancer had already spread internally. Most of all, I wonder if Fanny Burney had breast cancer.

Today we are told that we have choices in breast cancer surgery; but the evidence is that the surgeon still pilots the patient, gently but firmly, towards the option he or she prefers. This, despite research showing that the extent of surgery doesn't affect survival outcome.

When they operated on Burney, Dr. Larrey and his colleagues followed the wisdom of the time. If the patient with breast cancer was to be subjected to the pain and risk of surgery, the surgeon was obliged "to free the patient of the whole diseased structure" — anything less would "endanger a recurrence of the mischief."[2] At the end of the century, with the advent of anaesthetics and antisepsis, operations became commonplace and a more extreme version of breast surgery gained wide acceptance.

The "super-radical" mastectomy, commonly known as the Halsted, was introduced in the U.S. in the 1880s by William Halsted, a prominent professor of surgery at Johns Hopkins University. Halsted began his incision at the shoulder and removed not just the breast but muscles of the chest wall, lymph glands and all the fat under the skin. The Halsted leaves the woman with a sunken chest, restricted movement on one side of her body and, frequently, a painful chronic condition called "milk arm," caused when lymph fluid fails to circulate properly and accumulates in the arm. Capacity to breastfeed and derive sexual pleasure are, of course, lost from that side of the body. American surgeon George Crile Jr., one of the leaders in the fight to overturn the operation, remarked, "Halsted's radical mastectomy seems to have been designed to inflict the maximal possible deformity, disfiguration, and disability."[3] Yet the Halsted radical soon became the standard operation for breast cancer throughout North America and enjoyed this privileged status until the 1970s.

Halsted's operation arose from both practical realities and from a theory about how cancer spread. Even critics of the operation concede that Halsted had reasons for advancing his technique. The typical breast cancer he treated was an ulcerating malignancy as large as an orange, with extensive spread to the lymph nodes.[4] The theoretical basis for Halsted's operation was much shakier. He believed breast cancer was a local disease which spread from the breast and axilla to the pectoral muscles, before invading the internal organs.[5] A competing view, popular in his day, held that breast cancer was a systemic disease which spread through the blood (before the late 19th century, cancer was thought to be a blood disorder). As well, some of Halsted's contemporaries believed the lymphatic system was the vehicle for distant metastases.[6]

If, as Halsted thought, breast cancer was local, it followed that the operation should be extensive and done as soon as possible.

The goal was to prevent local recurrence. If the patient died of breast cancer after surgery, Halsted assumed the operation had been done too late. If, however, the disease was systemic and not local, catching the cancer early would not save the patient. Some of Halsted's contemporaries questioned his operation on exactly these grounds. In 1894, a perplexed Dr. Gay cited cases of breast cancer which recurred fatally, despite an early operation. "Is there ever a time in the the career of carcinoma of the breast when it is purely a local disease, and hence capable of being permanently cured by an operation?" he asked.[7] Dr. Matas, another American physician who had studied the lymphatic system with anatomists in France, returned to the U.S. to promote the idea that cancer spread via the lymph system.

Halsted's view prevailed, but the evidence today supports Gay and Matas — breast cancer is now considered a systemic disease that spreads through the blood and lymphatic system. This paradigm shift occurred in North American over a period of several decades, beginning in the 1960s. The author of a study published in 1963 calculated the average doubling time of a cancer cell — the time it takes for one cell to become two. Typically, the process is slow: one cell doubles in about 100 days; those two cells take another 100 days to become four, and so on. At this rate, a cancer takes about eight years to grow to one centimetre, the size at which it would be found on a mammogram. By the time a breast tumour can be felt manually, it is about 10 years old.

This finding led Pittsburgh surgeon Bernard Fisher to advance a different theory to the one behind the Halsted. He reasoned that removing the lymph nodes would not have much effect upon survival. Microscopic cells very likely begin circulating in the blood stream and lymphatic system many years before a cancerous lump is detectable. Fisher theorized, therefore, that survival depended on how well the immune system handles whatever cancer cells have already spread from the breast, rather than on the surgeon "catching" the cancer before a specific moment in time.

Although, in North America, this theory was not widely accepted until the 1980s, the Europeans endorsed it long before and quickly passed on its practical benefit to the patient — routine lumpectomies. In the United States and Canada, many surgeons have settled on a half-way solution: "simple" mastectomies (as opposed to the more deforming "radical") for the majority of patients.

Politics played a large role in the acceptance of Halsted's operation, say Theresa Montini and Sheryl Ruzek, two sociologists who examined Halsted's legacy.[8] By introducing an operation that was complicated and difficult to do well, Halsted helped nurture surgery as a specialty. Surgeons, wrote Halsted, "should not cast about for easy operations, that anyone can do at any time and in any place." Many 19th century physicians could perform ordinary breast amputation; it was relatively common and had a low mortality rate. With the Halsted mastectomy, surgeons were able to "differentiate their specialty from the rest of medical practice, but also to gain power and prestige for their specialty."

The Halsted has been called "the greatest standardized surgical error of the 20th century."[9] Its reversal began when a few researchers in the United Kingdom, Canada, and Finland, spurred on by their patients, began to do simple mastectomies or operations that removed only the lump. Sometimes they followed surgery with radiation. One of the renegades was Vera Peters, a young radiologist who took up a post at Toronto General Hospital in 1935. She thought the standard treatment was too severe and began treating those patients who wanted to keep their breasts with a lumpectomy and local radiation. Over the next 25 years, she followed 8,000 women who had either radical mastectomies or a less extensive surgery, recording their progress. Those who had lumpectomies did just as well as those who had mastectomies, she found. Often they survived five, 10, 15 and 20 years or longer. Doctors in Britain and Scandinavia also found that the radical mastectomy gave little or no survival advantage over simple mastectomies, which removed breast tissue only, or lumpectomies with radiation.

Breast specialists in the United States dismissed the studies from Canada, Finland, Scotland and Wales. "Selection bias" could account for the results, they argued; that is, women with small cancers were more likely to be selected for the less radical surgery, and their survival chances were good to begin with. To answer these objections, research of a more rigorous design — the randomized trial — was undertaken in Edinburgh and England. Participants agreed to be randomly assigned to different types of breast surgery: radical mastecomy vs simple mastectomy and radiation, or radical mastectomy vs lumpectomy and radiation.

By 1972, women in the randomized studies had been followed 10 years or more and showed equivalent survival rates regardless of the type of surgery they had undergone. Medical journalist Lynn Payer attended a conference on non-mutilating breast surgery held in Strasbourg, France that year, and observed, "The French were ready to accept the English trial as well as other, uncontrolled, trials as definitive. The English thought there should be more trials and kept trying to point out to the French participants why. And the Americans mostly didn't come."[10]

When American researchers finally decided to study breast cancer surgery, they did it with gusto. In 1971 a team of 200 physicians headed by Pittsburgh surgeon Bernard Fisher launched B-04, a multimillion dollar randomized clinical trial comparing the radical mastectomy with simple breast removal, with or without radiation. The study recruited 1,765 women from 34 medical centres throughout Canada and the U.S. Then, in 1976, Fisher and his team began another trial, B-06, to compare simple mastectomy with lumpectomy, with or without radiation. This study involved 2,500 women. Three years later, the National Cancer Institute (NCI) undertook a clinical trial of its own at the clinical centre in Bethesda, Maryland, in which 300 women were randomly assigned to have either a radical mastectomy, axillary dissection and breast reconstruction, or a lumpectomy plus radiation to the breast and "booster" irradiation at the point of the incision.

All three American studies found what Europeans had accepted to be true years before — that radical surgery offered the women no survival benefit over the simple or "modified" radical or the lumpectomy.[11] Women who had lumpectomies without post-operative radiation were more likely to have local recurrences and had to be treated again, but these recurrences did not affect their ultimate survival.

While this research was in progress, public pressure mounted to provide women with choices in breast surgery. Montini and Ruzek argue that lobbying by women, not new scientific evidence, ultimately cracked the wall of orthodoxy in the United States. In the early 1970s, two prominent American surgeons, Dr. Oliver Cope and Dr. George Crile Jr., began to challenge the Halsted in books and articles aimed at the general public. Medical colleagues opposed them, but their patients took up their views as a political cause. Cope was a retired Harvard professor. At the urging of patients, he wrote a ground-breaking article in *The Radcliffe Quarterly* on the need for non-mutilating treatment. He also appeared in a documentary film produced by the Boston Women's Health Book Collective. Crile, a retired Cleveland surgeon who had lost his wife to breast cancer, reached even more women with a bestselling book called *What Women Should Know About the Breast Cancer Controversy*. With two prominent medical specialists onside, the burgeoning women's health movement singled out the radical mastectomy as "a treatment which could not be justified scientifically and which violated women's body-self callously and cruelly without regard for their fears, feelings, or other psychological needs."

In the decade from 1974 to 1984, the breast surgery controversy and women's right to choice in treatment became stock themes in mass market women's magazines. The number of radical mastectomies in the United States declined dramatically, from 46,000 in 1970 to 5,000 in 1983. Whereas 83 percent of surgeons had favoured Halsted's operation in 1971, by 1982, 89 percent favoured the modified radical. The numerical shift was dramatic, but the change in practice that it represented was less so. The change from radical mastectomy to modified radical sidestepped the key controversy, which centred around radical surgery compared to minimal surgery coupled with radiation and/or chemotherapy. "We believe," said Montini and Ruzek, "that this nominal change in treatment practices reflects surgeons' attempts to appear to be changing their practice (without doing so too drastically) in the face of mounting extra-professional pressure.

"If minimal surgery becomes the treatment of choice," continued Montoni and Ruzek, "surgeons' prestige is likely to diminish because in the medical world at large, technically complex procedures are accorded prestige." Surgeons historically "owned" breast cancer treatment, and ownership rested on the belief that complex, extensive surgery was the crucial factor in survival. Now surgeons had to jockey for place with an ever-crowded field of specialists, including proponents of mass screening programs, chemotherapists and radiotherapists; accepting "small surgery" as the norm would undermine surgeons' already-threatened role in the medical team, said Montini and Ruzek. Studies of attitudes towards breast surgery in Italy, the U.K., the U.S. and Canada show that there are indeed biases within specialties. Surgeons more often favour extensive breast surgery than do medical oncologists and radiotherapists.[12]

Economic incentives are another factor that skew the physician's choice of surgery. Countries with comprehensive medical plans favour cost-saving measures. The American fee-for-service medical system favours more expensive procedures. Montini and Ruzek estimated that a total mastectomy would ring up charges, on average, of $2,843.18 (1981 figures), while a less-than-total mastectomy would cost the patient or her insurer $2,471.12. A total mastectomy is more lucrative to the surgeon and the hospital, because the hospital stay is longer. With a lumpectomy and five weeks of radiation therapy, the radiotherapist pockets the largest share overall.

Research scientists take credit for turning the tide against the radical mastectomy, yet practising physicians in North America were remarkably slow to accept the results of clinical trials. "A trial ignored is almost as bad as a trial not performed and is also a waste of scarce research resources," say the authors of a U.S. government report. "Randomized trials are expensive and often difficult to perform. Why did it take seven separate trials, performed over 15 years, to change expert consensus?"[13] At a public lecture, surgeon Susan Love answered the question with a comparison of data from an American clinical trial with the results of an Italian clinical trial. The two curves were identical. "But the American surgeons said, 'those were *Italian* women,'" she comments dryly. "'They had *Italian* breast cancer. We can't believe that!'"[14] Lynn Payer also suggests American chauvinism was a factor that slowed the acceptance of lumpectomies in the United States. When a vice-president of the American Cancer Society was informed, in the mid-1970s, of a study in the *British Medical Journal* that showed the equivalent effectiveness of lumpectomies and radical mastectomies, he remarked, "We don't read much foreign literature here."[15]

Women's own fears were another barrier to overturning surgical orthodoxy. To the woman reeling from the shock of a cancer diagnosis, the idea that removing the breast will remove the cancer has strong intuitive appeal. Susan Love urges women to fight the initial impulse to just remove the breast as quickly as possible. "There is a feeling that your breast has somehow betrayed you and you should punish it by cutting it off. Somewhere in your brain you think that if you can remove the offending part (and offer it to the gods maybe), you will be able to go back to your life as before." She emphasizes, "Breast cancer is not an emergency. It is very important that you get a second opinion ... [then] make the decision that is right for you."[16] One study of women who were interviewed a year or more after breast surgery found that 56 percent of those who chose mastectomies regretted their choice. All of those who chose lumpectomies said they would do so again. The researcher concluded, "The most important thing that came out of the study is that women should be given a choice." He added, "It's a tactful way of saying maybe they should be told that those who use mastectomy often regret it later."[17]

Within the profession, the efforts of a strong patriarchal figure like Bernard Fisher were probably necessary to bring the surgical troops into line. But political action made a difference too. In some states, American women pushed state legislators to enact breast cancer informed consent laws. The first of these bills passed in Massachusetts in 1979; by 1989, 19 states had the laws in place.[18] The higher rates of breast-conserving surgery are in states that have the laws.[19]

Another question with modern echoes from Burney's case is the diagnosis itself. Did Fanny Burney have cancer? The eminent physicians who attended her certainly believed so or they would never have risked the operation. Physicians who have since read her account aren't so sure. Breast pain, her main symptom, isn't usually a sign of breast cancer. When pain does accompany breast cancer, it usually signifies a type of tumour not curable by surgery. As Burney concluded her account, however, "all ended happily." The wound healed without infection and she survived 29 more years, outliving both her husband and her son.

The number of false or highly questionable breast cancer diagnoses that go to treatment is one of those mysterious grey zones; greyer still is the proportion of those diagnoses that are relayed to women. I was stunned when my mother told me of a friend who learned, after a mastectomy, that she didn't have cancer. Yet a breast cancer diagnosis is not straightforward. A certain number of false positive diagnoses are inevitable.

Medical personnel have ample motivation for concealing diagnostic errors. When Karen Nikkel of Quebec City discovered her mastectomy was based on a faulty diagnosis, she successfully sued the surgeon ($137,000), the pathologist ($166,000) and the hospital (an undisclosed out-of-court settlement). Nikkel found out about the error by accident, six years after the surgery. She was in the doctor's office and the nurse left her file on the table. She looked through it and spotted a letter that said she never had cancer. "I came home and cried for two months, then I decided to do something about it," she said.[20]

For six years, Nikell had lived the life of a cancer patient. She went for check-ups every four months even after the doctors suggested she switch to bi-annual appointments. She was so frightened of a recurrence that she considered a prophylactic mastectomy of her other breast. She had three reconstructive operations and was awaiting a fourth when she discovered the letter in her file. Her husband had had a vasectomy because he couldn't face having more children knowing his wife might die.

Nikkel had what Rose Kushner called one-stage breast surgery. The surgeon biopsied the suspicious lump and gave it to a pathologist in the operating room to analyze. The pathologist examined a sliver of the tissue using a standard procedure called a quick frozen-section. He pronounced the lump cancerous and the surgeon performed the mastectomy. The quick frozen-section is not definitive, however, and Nikkel's pathologist hit the unlucky odds. Immediately after the mastectomy, tissue samples were sent to a nearby hospital for the permanent section, a test in which the tissue is stained and embedded in paraffin. Within 48 hours, the doctors at Nikkel's hospital learned that the samples were non-cancerous.

When Rose Kushner had breast surgery she remembered a joke that had made the rounds among students when she attended Johns Hopkins Medical School 25 years earlier: A young man who arrived at the student health clinic complaining of pain in his penis was sent for a biopsy under general anaesthesia. The surgeon, looking grim, visited him in his room a few days afterward and announced that he had good news and bad news. When the student heard the bad news — "I had to cut your penis off" — he flinched and cried, "My God! What can the good news be?"

Smiling, the surgeon put his hand on the student's shoulder and replied, "It was benign on permanent-section study. The frozen section was a false-positive."[21]

The one-stage procedure for breast cancer was virtually universal in the United States when Kushner found her breast lump in 1974. She resolved she would never go into an operating room unsure if she would wake up with one breast or two. She had to call 19 surgeons before she found one who was willing to do the operation her way, and she felt he did it only to humour her. Afterwards she launched a personal crusade to promote the two-stage procedure. She believed one-step operations, not excessive surgery, were the "real breast-cancer scandal." Her objection to one-step breast surgery went beyond the risk of a frozen-section error. The patient's emotional well-being, she argued, was best served by a two-step procedure. A woman whose biopsy was positive needed a few weeks to adjust to the shock before having cancer surgery.

Various vested interests, including women's groups, insurance companies, and many surgeons, backed Kushner. In 1979 she won a major victory. At conference held to set national guidelines for breast cancer treatment, Kushner was a consumer representative. Her pitch for a two-stage procedure was accepted and became the recommended procedure in breast surgery throughout the United States.[22]

Another diagnostic grey zone is the condition called "in situ" cancer. Mammography finds irregular cells inside the breast lobes and ducts that are tagged *in situ* cancers (meaning "in place"). The term "in situ cancer" is an oxymoron because cancer refers to invading cells. "In situ cancer" literally translates as invading-non-invading cells — a clue to the state of medical thinking on the subject.

When *in situ* cancers appear in the lobules, the portion of the gland where the milk is made, they don't spread, but women who have the condition have an estimated 16 to 27 percent chance of developing cancer *somewhere* in the breast, over 30 years. Most doctors recommend careful monitoring of lobular cancer *in situ*; some, however, recommend bilateral mastectomies. The reasoning behind the drastic operation is that the woman's risk of a future cancer is higher than the population average, but removing a particular local irregularity won't prevent cells elsewhere in the breast from developing into cancer.

In situ cancers in the breast ducts, the tubes which carry the milk to the nipple, are called "ductal carcinoma in situ" (DCIS), and they also signify a higher-than-average risk of breast cancer — an estimated 20 to 25 percent risk over 10 years. This calculation is very much a guesstimate. When DCIS cancers were first found, they were invariably treated by mastectomies so very few untreated cases have been followed explains Susan Love. Extrapolating from those that have, it appears that a local operation for cases that do progress would usually be just as effective as a mastectomy. The rub is that the majority of these lesions simply sit there or even regress, but the life-threatening cases are indistinguishable from the harmless ones. The safest course, in the view of many doctors, is to treat every patient as if she has a lethal cancer.

Consumer advocate Maryann Napoli of the Centre for Medical Consumers in New York calls *in situ* cancers "the downside of mammography screening that women don't hear about." She explains, "We're always told that there are enormous benefits to finding a cancer early, but nobody tells you about the risk of finding something too early. In the last eight years or so, ever since American women accepted mammography screening, we've seen a massive increase — a triple incidence — of the diagnosis of ductal carcinoma *in situ*.

"What's interesting here is that they're going out of their way to find something that they don't have a lot of information on how to treat in the best way. They have been overtreating this non-invasive lesion in the breast by mastectomy up until the last couple of years. Now there's a rethinking, largely because it's being treated more radically than invasive cancer. Because they're not sure how they should be treated, there's a lot of variation depending on what door you walk into. I think it's interesting that after so many years of promoting mammography we still have so much indecision on how to treat this non-palpable lesion which is the *raison d'être* for mammography — to find something so small that it couldn't be found with a manual breast exam."

The shift to small surgery and the accompanying change in the theory of how breast cancer spreads are widely viewed as the greatest advances in breast cancer in this century. The long, drawn-out process of burying the Halsted, however, was less a scientific advance than a roll-back of a procedure that should never have become entrenched. For women, as well as physicians, the Halsted dramatically illustrates the folly of trusting too much in authority. An editorial in the *Lancet* concludes, "The most important lesson we need to learn from that bleak period [of Halsteds] is the extraordinary capacity of the profession for self-delusion."[23] Yet, recently, a new challenge to breast surgeons has met with resistance. Studies in Britain, the U.S. and Canada suggest that a woman's survival odds are almost doubled if she has breast surgery at least two weeks after her last menstrual period, in the luteal (post-ovulaton) phase of the menstrual cycle. So far the results have come from retrospective studies — analyses of past cases from hospital files — and some of the results have been conflicting.

In January 1993, I listened to Ruby T. Senie talk about a retrospective study she did on the timing of breast cancer surgery and the menstrual cycle. Senie, an epidemiologist at the Memorial Sloan-Kettering Cancer Center, spoke at a workshop in Bethesda sponsored by the National Cancer Institute. Like other women in the audience (many of whom had breast cancer), I was fascinated by Senie's presentation. It suggested a surgical practice which could actually improve survival odds — without a drastic intervention that would have lasting effects on the woman, and without adding to the financial cost of the treatment. When I interviewed her afterwards about her work, Senie remarked on how pleasurable it had been to speak to such a receptive audience. When she had addressed a group of surgeons, many argued that, if the theory proved to be true, scheduling their operations to coincide with a particular phase of the patient's menstrual cycle would complicate their lives.[24]

Senie described another telling response from the cancer community to her work. When her analysis was published in the *Annals of Internal Medicine*, in 1991, the publication invited prominent breast cancer specialist William McGuire to write an editorial for the same issue, giving his views on the optimal timing of breast surgery. Using case information on patients from the data bank in San Antonio where he worked, McGuire asked a pair of biostatisticians to perform a statistical experiment. They randomly assigned each of the women a day in the 28-day cycle for when they had had surgery and ran an analysis like the one Senie and her colleagues had run. He concluded that he could produce the same results as Senie with a random procedure, so her results could have happened by chance. The exercise obviously stung Senie: "He basically made a mockery of what I did," she said.

When I read McGuire's article myself, I was struck by its subtle sarcasm. He proclaimed himself sceptical of the view that, "many important biologic phenomena in humans are regulated in no small way by earthly rhythms." He did not reject the optimal timing thesis out of hand; indeed, he concluded, as Senie had, that the findings should be confirmed with a prospective study. He also urged, as she did, research into cyclical changes in immunologic function and other factors associated with women's hormonal cycles. He was emphatic, though, that the current evidence did not warrant a widespread change in current surgical practice. And he completely dismissed the potential of additional retrospective studies.[25]

Despite criticisms, Senie and others have begun to develop a theoretical rationale for the finding. Their thinking builds on the idea that a woman's immune system operates in tandem with her menstrual cycle. At a certain point in the cycle, the immune system peaks, and is better able to fight off tumour cells that are released at the time of surgery. By contrast, before ovulation, the immune system seems to take a bit of a dive, she says. This makes sense, because the woman's body is naturally preparing for pregnancy at this point. With the release of the egg, at ovulation, a reduced immunity creates a receptive environment for the sperm, which is foreign matter.

"Invariably you have to cut across lymphatics that feed into the lymph nodes when you do the surgery," explains Senie, "and of course across blood vessels." In her analysis of files, she found that timing of surgery makes a difference for those patients who are node-positive — the women in whom cells have spread from the breast into the lymph channel. "So to me, it all fits nicely together," says Senie. "Women with positive nodes treated in the luteal stage had survival that was comparable — no significant difference — from the node-negative patients. It was very striking. A recurrence was twice as likely if surgery was in the follicular time [i.e., pre-ovulation], instead of luteal."

That's an enormous potential benefit for women with breast cancer, and one that could be achieved without expensive and debilitating treatments. Yet when I spoke to a Montreal breast surgeon about the menstrual cycle hypothesis, his reaction too was cold. "If the prospective studies show an effect, we'll have to do it," he said grimly. "We'll have no choice." But unless he had unshakable data in hand, he wouldn't entertain any disruption to his operating schedule.

To gather prospective evidence on the menstrual cycle hypothesis will take many years. Who will decide when the evidence is conclusive? Ironically, while this benign innovation has the surgical community grumbling, high-tech interventions proceed apace. In the 1980s, a technique called vascular reconstruction revived the flagging specialty of breast surgery. Halsted's super-radical mastectomy is fading into history, but his admonition that surgeons "not cast about for easy operations" lives on. The new wave of breast reconstruction makes the Halsted look like an apprentice's exercise. The spirit of heroic intervention also animates a new movement towards double prophylactic mastectomies as a means of preventing breast cancer. The preventive value of the operation has never been demonstrated, yet as researchers push into the uncharted regions of breast cancer genetics, the double mastectomy is shaping up as the "treatment of choice" (for want of any viable alternatives) for women who carry the threat of breast cancer in their genes. "Progress" in breast surgery is far from being the end of our struggle for true choice.

Notes

1. Account of Fanny Burney's mastectomy, from her letter to Esther Burney of Sept. 30, 1811, [#595], in *The Journals and Letters of Fanny Burney (Mme D'Arblay)*, *Vol. VI*, edited by Joyce Hemlow et al, (Oxford: Clarendon Press, 1975), pp. 596-616.

2. From *Practical Surgery* by Robert Liston (1837), cited in Hemlow, p. 613.

3. George Crile, Jr., *What Women Should Know About the Breast Cancer Controversy*, (N.Y.: McMillan, 1973), p. 38

4. Crile, pp. 39-40.

5. Theresa Montini and Sheryl Ruzek, "Overturning Orthodoxy: The Emergence of Breast Cancer Treatment Policy," *Research in the Sociology of Health Care*, Vol. 8, (Greenwich: JAI Press, 1989), p. 7.

6. Montini and Ruzek, p. 7.

7. Montini and Ruzek, p. 10.

8. Montini and Ruzek, pp. 3-32.

9. Dr. Ray Lawson, cited in Crile, p. 39.

10. Lynn Payer, "Medicine & Culture: Varieties of Treatment in the United States, England, West Germany and France," (N.Y.: H. Holt, 1988), p. 37.

11. Ralph Moss, *The Cancer Industry*, (N.Y.: Paragon House, 1991), p. 51.

12. Liberati et al, *American Journal of Public Health*, (1991), 81: pp. 38-42, cited in Ganz, p. 1148.

13. Schachter and Neuhauser, "The Implications of Cost Effectiveness Analysis of Medical Technology," [Background Paper #2: *Case Studies of Medical Technologies*, Case Study #17: "Surgery for Breast Cancer"], (Washington, D.C.: U.S. Congress, Office of Technology Assessment, 1981), p. 20, cited in Montini and Ruzek, p. 21.

14. Susan Love, "Breast Cancer in the 1990s," public lecture, Burlington, Vermont, (June 1992).

15. Payer, p. 28.

16. Susan Love in the afterword to Joyce Gadler, *My Breast*, (N.Y.: Addison Wesley, 1992), p. 177.

17. Gerald J. Margolis, cited in newspaper article, "Study Finds Many Women Who Had Mastecomies Regret Making That Choice," *New York Times*, (1988).

18. F. Mullen, Barbara Hoffman et al, *Charting the Journey: An Almanac of Practical Resources for Cancer Survivors*, (N.Y.: Consumers Union, 1990), p. 202

19. Ganz, p. 1147.

20. Geoff Baker, "Breast removal was unnecessary, Quebec woman awarded $303,600," *The Gazette*, Oct. 21, 1992, p. A5.

21. Kushner, p. 183.

22. Kushner, p. 186.

23. Editorial, "Breast Cancer: Have We Lost Our Way?" *Lancet*, (Feb. 6, 1993), 341: p. 344.

24. Interview with Ruby T. Senie, Bethesda Maryland, (Jan. 29, 1993).

25. William L. McGuire, "The Optimal Timing of Mastectomy: Low Tide or High Tide?" *Annals of Internal Medicine*, (Sept. 1, 1991), Vol. 115, No. 5, pp. 401-403.

Radiation
An Amazing Recovery

So hell has regulations to enact?
Good, for with law a man can make a pact,
Then why not with you gentlemen of hell?

— Goethe, *Faust, Part One*

When Vanessa Kramer, a friend of mine in Montreal, learned she had breast cancer, she did not want to undergo radiation. "I just see it as part of the nuclear industry. I thought if I was going to take the treatment I would somehow be sanctioning our use of this whole side of things."

Vanessa's treatment team just assumed she would have radiation after her lumpectomy. "I asked them, 'Why do you want me to do it? If it's a small lump, is it really really necessary, or is it just The Treatment? What's the evidence against it?'" That was in 1990, and Vanessa could find no readily available information against post-lumpectomy radiation.

"When I came to make the decision," she recalls, "the doctor I was dealing with gave me the 39 to 40 percent recurrence figure if I didn't have it. So I had to weigh that. Forty percent is a significant number. Like everyone else, I'm a child of my age and naturally I want to live as long as I can, within reason." Although her tumour had "clean margins" (no sign of cancer in the outer part of the tissue that was removed), her surgeon explained that he saw the radiation as "an insurance clean-up," in case microscopic bits of tumour were missed during the surgery. This argument, and the fact that she saw no political value in a silent and individual act of refusal, swayed her to accept the treatment.

Radiation was presented to me, as it was to Vanessa, as "standard," as insurance, to "sterilize" the breast in case a lethal cancer cell had somehow been left behind. Although I felt anxious about exposing myself to radiation, I wanted to keep my breast. I did not have enough information about possible ill effects on my health to challenge the recommendations of a tumour board.

Radiation after breast-conserving surgery is usually done in a two-stage procedure. First the entire breast is irradiated, a procedure that usually takes five weeks of treatments, five days per week. Immediately following, a procedure called the "boost" irradiates the scar area, and is intended to kill any malignant cells left behind at the site of the operation. The boost itself is administered in one of two methods. In the implant boost, plastic tubes containing radioactive pellets are threaded through the breast and left for about 36 hours. The woman emits radioactivity during the time the implants are in her breast, and so must be kept in isolation. A boost by electron beam is administered by a machine, on an outpatient basis, in the same manner as the treatments to the whole breast. The choice of boost depends on the equipment available to the radiotherapist and, if both options are available, on such factors as the amount of surgery, the size of the tumour and the size of the breast. The implant method penetrates more deeply.[1]

Women are told radiation will be painless (mine was) and that the burns to the skin will pass quickly (mine did), but I found the experience of radiation treatments strangely traumatic. The nuclear medicine wing of the hospital had the impersonal feel of a science-fiction movie. The treatment was individual, in a sealed-off room with outsized machines. After I'd stripped to the waist, a technician (sometimes male, sometimes female) fussed to get my body in the precise position indicated by markings on my chest. Once I was positioned, the technician told me not to move, then disappeared into an anteroom, closed the heavy door, and monitored the proceedings on a screen. I knew correct positioning and stillness were important to minimize damage to my internal organs by the invisible rays. I also knew that if something vital got hit, I wouldn't feel it.

With the advent of lumpectomies, radiation has recovered lost status as a post-surgical treatment. For six decades, radiation therapy was standard practice after a radical mastectomy. The treatment often caused long-term harm, including burns on the skin and hardening of vital organs such as the heart and lungs. Evidence accumulated in the literature showing that radiotherapy after a radical mastectomy did nothing to improve the survival rate; eventually the practice was overturned. When lumpectomies came into favour as an orthodox treatment, acceptance of adjuvant radiation was cautious. Not all women have recurrences after a lumpectomy and breast irradiation does not always prevent a recurrence. Data on long-term effects is still sparse. The risks and benefits of post-lumpectomy irradiation tumbled into a grey zone.

Acceptance of the treatment has grown in the last 10 years, however, to the point where radiation after a lumpectomy is the norm. I was puzzled by this seemingly blanket endorsement of a treatment with limited benefit. As I explored what we know about radiotherapy's benefits and risks, the ideal goal of providing each woman with choices and the best treatment began to retreat like a will-o'-the-wisp.

Members of the cancer community have a longstanding ambivalence to radiation, explains James Patterson in his cultural history of cancer in America. Cautious critics warned that radiation was "at best an inexact science, at worst highly dangerous to patients,"[2] but politicians, always under pressure for quick solutions to the cancer problem, believed radiation might eventually be the breakthrough everyone was waiting for, if only they sank enough money into improved technology. Throughout the 1940s and '50s, says Patterson, "grant-seeking researchers promised that cancer could be defeated with technological 'guns' and omnipotent rays."[3] Leaders at the American Cancer Society (ACS) and the National Cancer Institute (NCI) followed a double policy. They advised radiotherapy mainly as an adjunct treatment, and meanwhile gave generous support to radiotherapy programs and research.

Doubts were expressed quietly; the public heard mainly optimism about radiation. The development of atomic weaponry skewed the information flow even more. With no particular medical advances, articles in the popular press hailed radiation cancer treatments as "one of the most fantastic events in human history"

(*Reader's Digest* in 1944) and "The Sunny Side of the Atom" (a 1947 CBS documentary). The medical magazine *Hygeia,* published by the American Medical Association, asserted in 1947 that "medically applied atomic science has already saved more lives than were lost in the explosions at Hiroshima and Nagasaki." Radiation therapy had found its niche in popular mythology — the silver lining in the mushroom cloud.

About the same time, in 1946, a scientific article was published demonstrating the limitations of radiation after a radical mastectomy. Entitled "The Role of Roentgen Therapy in Carcinoma of the Breast," the study showed that radiating the axilla after a radical mastectomy merely reduced the number of local recurrences. Women who had radiation treatment developed more distant metastases than those who had no underarm radiation. The survival of the two groups of women was the same.

Rose Kushner was shocked when her surgeon, Thomas Dao, showed her this article in 1974. She had expected the usual 20 radiation treatments after her mastectomy, but Dao looked at her "as if I had suggested coffee enemas."[4] He was, she soon learned, a conservative in the use of X-rays for breast cancer treatment. "I do not think irradiating the breast afterward is necessary," he told her. "I am more afraid of the possible dangers of large doses of X-ray than the relatively small risk of having another cancer growing somewhere in the breast. No one knows what can happen," explained Dao. "If it's the left breast, X-rays might burn her heart; on either side, the lungs and esophagus might be injured. Women develop severe lymphedema from irradiation and I am afraid of it."[5]

To back up his position, he showed her studies that had been published between 1946 and 1960 by scientists all over the world. They compared the fate of women who had been treated with radiation to the breast and axilla after a mastectomy, and those who had not. "The general opinion was that the increased incidence of metastases to other organs after axillary irradiation made routine X-ray therapy risky when the nodes had been removed." By the early 1960s, many specialists had concluded that preventing recurrences did not warrant the risk, "because new local tumours could be treated surgically. On the other hand, metastases occurring far from the orginal tumour site might not be found until too late." Yet in 1974, when Kushner had her treatment, most "average doctors in average hospitals" in the U.S. were still giving the order to irradiate axillas.[6]

When breast conserving surgery began its slow ascent as an orthodox treatment, the role of radiation was not clear. One lumpectomy pioneer, radiologist Vera Peters of Toronto, believed the method of treatment had little effect on the patient's survival. She therefore tailored treatment to the emotional needs of the patient and encouraged the woman to take part in treatment decisions. After a lumpectomy, she usually irradiated the breast for a minimum of four weeks. She discontinued irradiation after a mild skin reaction could be observed.[7] Another early advocate of limited surgery, George Crile Jr. of Cleveland, felt the available evidence supported selective use of radiation with a lumpectomy, as with a modified mastectomy.

The same randomized trial that was so influential in making lumpectomies a standard treatment in North America, also compared lumpectomies with and without radiation. When the five-year results were reported in 1985, press attention focussed on the surgical aspect (mastectomies vs lumpectomies). The comparison between the two lumpectomy groups received relatively less play. Both these groups showed better disease-free survival than the mastectomy group, but only 6.7 percent of the women who had radiation after surgery had recurrences; 27.9 percent of those who did not have radiation suffered recurrences.

When the eight-year results of the study were published in 1989, the gap had widened; 10 percent of those who had radiation had recurrences, while 39 percent of those who did not have radiation recurred. Until a recent data-fraud scandal (see Part Four) tainted the reputation of the NSABP and Bernard Fisher, its chief investigator, this study was widely viewed as the Gold Standard in research on breast cancer surgery.

Although the higher recurrence rate for women who had no radiation still showed no effect on survival, the panel of experts who made up the 1991 consensus conference on standard breast cancer treatment concluded that, as an optimal technique, radiation to the whole breast be routinely used. "Although local control can be obtained in some patients with local excision alone," the recommendations continued, "no subgroups have been identified in which radiation therapy can be avoided."

We still don't know the long-term effects of radiation after a lumpectomy. Studies by Fisher's team and others have not continued long enough to reveal whether the long-term morbidity and mortality that halted post-mastectomy radiation will show up 10 years or more after post-lumpectomy radiation. Thomas Dao, Rose Kushner's former physician, remains cautious about breast irradiation. Now semi-retired, Dao says he never used radiation routinely after a lumpectomy and still doesn't advocate its routine use.[8] He still believes radiation should be given in some cases, but most practising surgeons tend to follow the recommended practice, rather than making case-by-case judgements. And the recommendation of the 1991 Consensus Development Conference is that radiation should follow a lumpectomy.

Texas surgeon Richard Evans does not believe the research on recurrences supports routine irradiation after a lumpectomy. Noting that some women undergo a mastectomy either because radiation is not conveniently available or because they do not want to undergo the month or so of radiotherapy, he argues that patients should be informed that lumpectomy without radiation is a reasonable choice for many women.

Evans reviewed the data from seven studies which followed women who did not have radiation treatment after a lumpectomy. Based on this data, from the U.S., Britain, Sweden and Canada, he concluded not only that radiation therapy doesn't improve survival but that local recurrence rates can be as low as 10 to 15 percent in carefully selected patients.[9] Patients with larger tumours and those with positive lymph nodes were more likely to suffer a recurrence. Evans also concluded that meticulous surgical technique could reduce the recurrence rate.

The elimination of routine radiation reduces the small risk of radiation-induced cancer, and (since breast tissue can't be irradiated twice), saves radiation therapy for later use to treat a recurrence, reasons Evans. Women, he says, should be made aware of the good odds that breast-conserving surgery alone can control their disease, and they should be told that a second tumour in the breast is not the ominous sign it was once believed to be.

Evans uses the term "local persistence" to describe most breast cancer relapses, in order to distinguish them from a "local recurrence," which typically signals a symptom of distant metastasis.[10]

He theorizes that a woman who resists the initial tumour will likely be able to do the same with a second tumour, as long as the tumour is detected and removed.

A woman may also want to ask for a lumpectomy that takes a wide margin of tissue, says Evans, a view supported by the Italian method of local surgery, which removes more of the breast. "George Crile always did a partial mastectomy," Evans told me when I phoned to ask him to elaborate on his views. "He had the recurrence rate down to 10 percent or less — that's if you leave out patients who have interductal disease and I wouldn't quarrel with radiation in that case."

Evans doesn't understand why radiation is recommended as the standard practice after a lumpectomy. "Everyone agrees there's no benefit to survival. There's no debate about that. And cosmetically the results of a wider excision are actually better without radiation. I close the skin over a cavity and it fills up with fluid. The cosmetic result is excellent and nearly comparable to a narrow excision." He attended a seminar to observe a demonstration of the technique used in Fisher's lumpectomy research trial. In his view, "the margin of incision was too narrow, a half a centimetre or so."

"I've been fighting this battle now for 15 years," says Evans. "At the beginning we were arguing against mastectomies and it seemed prudent to do radiation — the people who were on my side were radiotherapists. Now they're the ones fighting against me." As for the patients, he says, naturally they want to do anything they can to eradicate the disease.[11]

Rose Kushner also argued that, from the woman's perspective, breast conserving surgery without irradiation could be an important option. She worried about the effects of poorly done breast irradiation and the practical difficulties women in outlying areas face in obtaining radiation. These concerns are still relevant today.

In Canada, which now has about 15,000 women diagnosed each year, the move to lumpectomies, in conjunction with the growth of screening programs, has created a squeeze on publicly funded facilities. Two major centres, Toronto and Vancouver, have been the first to feel the pressure. With a 20-fold increase in the use of breast conservation, Vancouver radiation oncologist Ivo Olivotto told the Parliamentary committee studying breast cancer, "the resources to provide timely radiation therapy do not exist. This is one of the reasons that contribute to the big waiting list for radiation therapy today."[12] Faced with a wait of five to seven weeks for treatments from the time of initial referral, many women opt instead for a mastectomy.

For women in small centres, the dilemma described by Rose Kushner still holds: local facilities don't have radiation equipment or staff for post-surgical follow-up. "In Vancouver we have patients who come down from Whitehorse and stay in the lodge next to the cancer institute for four or five weeks," said Olivotto. "For some women it may not be possible to leave their home communities for that duration of time." Medicare pays accommodation for women who must travel for their treatment, but does not cover child care costs or compensate for lost salaries.[13]

Some of these women no doubt have the increasingly common diagnosis of ductal carcinoma in situ (DCIS). A number of trials are currently in progress, in the United States, Italy and the U.K., to determine whether irradiation is appropriate for these cases. When Hazel Thornton was diagnosed with DCIS, in August 1991, she was asked to consider volunteering for the U.K. trial. She was given a leaflet explaining the need for a DCIS trial to evaluate four widely differing treatment options: no further treatment, a four-to-five week course of X-ray therapy to the breast, one tamoxifen tablet daily for five years, or both radiotherapy and tamoxifen. She subsequently questioned not only the wisdom of giving radiotherapy to women with this condition, but the use of the clinical trial as a tool for investigating the procedure.

As Thornton wrote later in the *Lancet*, she had an "instinctive reaction against radiotherapy for this non-invasive condition." She read two articles on the question, written by experienced doctors and radiotherapists, which reinforced her feelings. One article stated, "To give healthy women who have volunteered for screening a five-week course of radiotherapy, with its associated short-term morbidity and its potentially more serious effects after treatment, seems hard to justify." Because she was unwilling to undergo radiotherapy, she declined to enter the trial. She went on to ask, "Should the radiotherapy arm of the trial be dropped? I am not willing to damage the quality of my life to reinforce a conclusion that has already been drawn by many: that 'radiotherapy does not appear to produce any improvements.'" An analysis of treatments for selected patients would allow a better assessment of post-operative management, she suggested.[14]

An ironic twist in the story of radiation is that ionizing radiation, the type delivered by X-rays and radiotherapy, is one of the few environmental contaminants known unequivocally to cause breast cancer. There is concern that radiation treatments may induce cancers in the healthy breast.[15] A study published in 1991 used files from women treated with mastectomies in Connecticut between 1935 and 1982. Researchers from the NCI compared the rate of subsequent breast cancers in women who had radiation after their operation with those who were not irradiated. Fewer than three percent of the irradiated women had later breast cancers that could be attributed to the radiation, but in women who had their treatment when they were under 45, the risk was significantly greater. "It seems prudent to minimize exposure of the contralateral [other] breast whenever possible, particularly for women under 45 years of age," the authors concluded, although they still recommended that radiation be used.

Nova Scotia physician Ian MacKenzie found the first evidence of this link between breast cancer and ionizing radiation in the early 1960s with a study of women who had been treated for tuberculosis (TB) in the 1940s. In those days, TB was often treated by collapsing the infected lung to "give it a rest."[16] Physicians used a daily X-ray test called fluoroscopy to check on how the infection was doing. MacKenzie compared the medical records of women who had the X-ray tests with others who had TB but didn't have fluoroscopy. Of 271 women who had the test, 13 (4.8 percent) developed breast cancer 20 years later. Of 510 who didn't have fluoroscopy, only one (0.2 percent) developed breast cancer.[17]

Although this treatment is now obsolete, women who were treated for TB decades ago may still turn up in doctors' offices with breast cancer. Susan Love describes such a case from her own practice, a woman who had TB three decades before, when she was in her early 20s. "She lived in France and was treated with intensive radiation in the sanatorium. Her two best friends at the sanatorium, treated with the same radiation therapy she was given, have also developed breast cancer."[18]

The bombing of Nagasaki and Hiroshima was another real-life experiment that demonstrated a link between radiation and various cancers, including breast cancer. Records of female survivors showed the same relationships observed in the TB studies. The cancers do not begin to show up for about 10 years. Women who were exposed to radiation before age 40 are most likely to develop breast cancer, but radiation-induced breast cancer appears at about age 40 and thereafter — the same period in life that breast cancer begins to show up in general population statistics.

The data from atomic bomb survivors is still coming in. The increase in breast cancer is most dramatic for those who were under 20 when they were exposed. This finding was taken for years as an indication that adolescence was the most vulnerable age for a woman to experience radiation to the breast area, but the most recent Japanese data show an even more devastating impact on breast cancer incidence rates for survivors who were 10 or under in 1945. These women, who were aged 46 to 56 in 1991, show a 39 percent increase in breast cancer per unit dose of radiation, compared to a 6.2 percent increase for women who were adolescents in 1945. Women aged 20 to 29 in 1945 showed a 2.3 percent increase and those who were 30 to 39 experienced a 1.1 percent increase. The full impact on the youngest group of women won't be known for several decades.[19]

Physicians are reluctant to face doctor-caused cancer squarely, says biostastician Irwin Bross. In the 1970s, Bross headed a large research project at Roswell Park Memorial Institute in Buffalo, set up to study an increase in leukemia that had been noticed in the 1950s. The Tri-State Leukemia Survey used the tumour registries in New York, Maryland and Minnesota to follow 16 million people from 1959 to 1962. One of Bross' researchers was Rosalie Bertell, a nun whose love of mathematics led her into biomedical research.

We looked at "just about everything you could think of" in the records of people with leukemia, recalls Bertell. That included family background, cause of death for parents and grandparents, the person's own health history, complete occupational history, residential history, whether they'd been exposed to farm animals or not, whether they had pets, and whether those pets had ever been sick.[20] In the early 1970s, after about four years of analysing the data, it became clear that diagnostic medical X-rays were the main cause of the leukemia effect. This was one of the first indications that low levels of medical radiation, as well as high levels, were harmful to health.

"The increase in leukemia that we were seeing was really nothing more than premature aging," says Bertell. "People were getting leukemia that they might not have gotten until they were much older." Through a mathematical analysis, Bertell concluded that the X-rays accelerated the body breakdown we call aging in a very systematic manner. Bertell's analysis also showed that radiation had a more pronounced effect on people who already showed signs of premature aging — "those with heart disease, diabetes, or signs of inability to cope with the environment, such as asthmas and allergies."[21]

Unlike X-rays, therapeutic radiation is delivered at high doses. While a mammogram delivers only 0.2 to 0.5 rads (radiation absorbed dose) of radiation, a six-week course of radiotherapy delivers about 5,000 rads. In a sense, the high levels of radiation are safer, because they kill cells rather than damaging them. "The high levels used in radiotherapy will kill more cells and cells that are dead will not cause a cancer," explains Bertell. The theory is that radiotherapy won't cause cellular mutations. However, the cell deaths cause extensive damage to tissues and organs.

"So why does radiotherapy cause secondary cancers?" I asked Bertell in a telephone interview.

"The cancer danger in radiotherapy is at the edge of the beam, where you can't control it," she explained. "Radiotherapy can damage some cells. They will be abnormal. Whatever these cells were doing, they will do in a mistaken way. If they were producing a hormone, they will do that in a way that's abnormal. This is an acceleration of the aging process and in radiotherapy it happens to the cells on the fringe, where the radiation beam scatters."

Accelerated aging should not be equated with early dying, Bertell continued. "It's something you can live with. It has to do with quality of life. A lot depends on how much bone marrow was exposed and with breast irradiation, you're not hitting as much of the bone marrow."[22]

Bross' interpretation of data linking X-rays with cancer and heart disease was published in 1979, in the *American Journal of Public Health*. In the same issue, the journal ran a disclaimer saying that Bross "stood alone" in defense of his data and interpretations of it. The journal had published the report, the article said, because Bross was a respected investigator and published critiques of his work were rare.[23] Shortly afterwards, the National Cancer

Institute cut his funding for the project. The research team of nine professionals had to disperse and find other jobs. They also lost permission to use the basic data from the tumour registries. "We still can't get access to that data," says Rosalie Bertell, who has since resettled in Toronto.[24]

In a special report on the dangers of low-level radiation published in 1979 after the Three-Mile Island disaster, *Science* magazine discussed the Bross affair in a special dossier which included an article called "Low-Level Radiation: Just How Bad Is It?" The report concluded that the political nature of the radiation issue makes the hazard of irradiation used in X-rays and medical therapies a grey zone. Most research into the health effects of radiation came under the jurisdiction of the Department of Energy, "the domain of the atomic energy establishment," the report noted. The Department of Health, Education and Welfare, which is usually responsible for health research, has a minor role. Yet 90 percent of man-made exposure to radiation comes from medical uses of the technology and only 10 percent from occupational exposure in the nuclear fuel and weapons industry.[25]

Long-term effects of cancer treatments, including therapeutic radiation, are one of the "survivor issues" identified by an American advocacy group called the National Coalition of Cancer Survivorship (NCCS). The NCCS wants the National Cancer Institute to commit a larger proportion of its budget to studying long-term effects of cancer treatments and the psychological, social and economic impact of cancer. The current NCI budget allocation for these issues is currently about one percent.[26]

"We're supposed to be grateful just to be alive," commented Susan Leigh, a founding member of NCCS, during a panel discussion of the long-term effects of cancer treatments. Leigh wonders if her own diagnosis of breast cancer was the result of radiation treatments she had for Hodgkin's disease 20 years back. Physicians say she could just be one of the 'one in nine' American women who gets breast cancer but, she notes, cancer survivors are not followed for the long term unless they are in a clinical trial. Ellen Stovall, who is now the NCCS' executive director, is another force behind the initiative to have attention paid to long-term effects of treatments. Stovall was treated for Hodgkin's disease in 1970 and subsequently experienced chronic pain, including a sensation of shock whenever she bent her head. Her radiation oncologist assured her the pain was not related to the therapy. Her first reaction was guilt for complaining. Stovall later found a neurologist who explained that her symptoms made perfect sense, given the treatments she had had.

Stovall encourages people who have had cancer treatments to acknowledge such symptoms and the anxiety that accompanies them, and to seek out advice on pain management. "Oncologists aren't the ones to help with these long-term problems," she says. "They're there to look for tumours." After much searching, Stovall found a physician who would talk to her about the long-term effects of her radiation and chemotherapy treatments.

Although women have begun to openly explore the deep emotions associated with breast surgery and reconstruction, the effect of radiation treatments on the emotions is largely un-charted. The few published studies on the subject say that patients experience radiation as frightening. They associate the treat-ments with radiation damage and they feel the physician does not give satisfactory information. In one study, many patients ex-pressed concerns about being alone during exposure, about the size of the machines and the noise they make (a periodic harsh beeping when the machine is on). Most received so little informa-tion before treatment began, they had scant idea of the number and length of radiation sessions and they did not know what reactions to expect.[27]

Carole Jones, a friend in Ottawa, told me her biggest dread when she first learned she had breast cancer was chemotherapy. "That just sounds so horrible. Radiation was certainly the better of the two in my mind," she said. After the fact, she feels radiation was much worse. "I *hated* that whole radiation area — I didn't like the staff, I didn't like the atmosphere, I didn't like anything about it. I hated the way the staff talked over you. And stripping off at the door and then walking over to the machines, instead of keeping you covered until they had the machine down and then uncover-ing you — there was no dignity at all."

Her treatment included an implant boost to the scar area, which was very different from my experience of boost by electron beam. For Carole, this was the nadir of a thoroughly awful ex-perience. "They actually thread plastic tubing through from one side of the scar to the other. Some were quite large, like a ball-point pen if you took out the cartridge and some were very tiny. There were seven tubes all together and they were held together with a piece of plastic." Carole was under a general anaesthetic for this portion of the procedure. Back in her room, they put threads of radioactive material into the seven tubes and closed them back up again.

"You are put in an isolated room and because it is a room for radioactive materials, it's got the double walls with the lead lining. The rooms are double-doored, so that people have to go through the second door before they actually get in to see you. And whenever someone comes in and out of the doors an alarm sounds: Beep! Beep! Beep! A red light over your bed goes on and off all the time, to warn anybody that comes into the room. Even at night, you've got this red light going above your head. You could only see a nurse for half an hour per shift. She stood and talked to you from behind a sort of podium, where she was shielded from the radiation."

Carole was shocked when she saw the implant for the first time. "I had no idea it would look so goddam awful. I wish the doctor had shown me a picture first. You look down at these pins sticking out of your breast and it's like something medieval, they were so ugly and huge."

She had understood that she would feel quite well during the boost treatment. She had bought some new tapes and brought in books she wanted to read. "I kind of looked forward to it because I hadn't had a lot of time to myself since I first got breast cancer. And here I would have a room to myself and my own bathroom. But you don't feel well. I think partly because of the general anaesthetic, but maybe it's the radioactive material too. I found I couldn't listen to any of my tapes and I couldn't read."

Because she'd just finished the regular radiation, she had a sore from the burn and it started festering before she went into the hospital. At one point one of the nurses came in and Carole asked her if she could have the wounds covered. "She just took some bandages and threw them on the bed at me and said, 'Do it yourself,' and walked out of the room. I burst into tears."

During the whole time she was in isolation — 48 hours — she didn't receive any meals. "The kitchen staff aren't allowed into the room. They put the tray down in between the two doors and the nurse is supposed to bring it in. But the nurses would forget, and the kitchen staff would just pick them up again. So I didn't get anything to eat the whole time I was there."

The final assault came when she was to have the implants removed. "I understood from my doctor there would be very little discomfort. They would give me a local anaesthetic and it would be much less painful to take them out than it was putting them in. And so the nurse came in at about six in the morning and she said nothing had been ordered for me to get these needles out. And I said, 'Well is it going to hurt?' She said, 'I don't know.' She gave me a Tylenol 3. The resident came at about seven AM and the first thing he did was take off the piece of plastic that was holding these needles together, which meant they splayed apart, which caused incredible pain. When I screamed, he called the nurse back in and the nurse held me down while he took them out. It took about 45 minutes to get them all out and the pain was just indescribable. I screamed and cried the whole time they did it."

Carole's doctor was furious when she described the resident's behaviour and the fact that a nurse had held her down. "But the point is," says Carole, "that's what happened." She also told her doctor, "If you are going to have any other patients do it, for God's sake don't have them call me because I wouldn't recommend it to anybody, I wouldn't do it again. It was the worse thing I have ever been through in my life. It was so horrible."

She had agreed to the boost because the treatment team said it would reduce her risk of recurrence from 16 percent to 10 percent — roughly the same lifetime risk as for any other woman. "So I thought it was worth it." A year later, however, she was diagnosed with metastatic cancer. The radiation had been for naught.[28]

Although my experience with radiation wasn't nearly this dramatic I, too, was struck by the detached, sometimes insensitive behaviour of radiation staff. Yet I said nothing to protest the way the staff were treating me. Was it the fatigue induced by six months of chemotherapy and another eight weeks of radiation? I can't say, but Carole Jones also remembers being passive during the process of radiation. "I don't know whether you're still in a state of shock or if it's just such a new world, but when I think back to that time, what I picture is just going, day after day, for radiation, then coming home."

Later, during her chemotherapy treatments for metastatic breast cancer, Carole became friendly with several of the oncology nurses and she told them how surprised she was that she found radiotherapy more unpleasant than chemotherapy. "And they agreed with me. They said, as nurses, it's absolutely true. There's a different kind of atmosphere there. I wonder why?"

I think the death-ray machinery has a lot to do with it. Radiation therapy is a soulless process. Radiation technicians are at risk of exposure, as most of them undoubtedly know. The double doors, warning buzzes and flashing red lights designed to protect the staff create an atmosphere that, at best, is isolating. It's antithetical to the comforting touch of a physician's hand. At worst, the atmosphere is conducive to the outright abuse Carole experienced while in isolation.

In retrospect, I don't feel I made an informed choice about this aspect of my treatment. I was not aware of radiotherapy's limited function or possible harmful effects. I didn't realize how little firm evidence exists, either to support routine radiation or to permit anyone to assess the risk of long-term damage.

The dilemmas inherent in radiation shake my certainty that breast conserving surgery is a clear gain for women. For everyone — women, physicians and policy planners — the choices are harder and more complicated than I originally imagined. At first blush, irradiation of all women who have lumpectomies seems "safer," and for litigious-wary physicians, it may well be. But if the benefits do not translate into lives saved, the outlay of resources is enormous for a small gain or even harm. The reality is that post-operative radiation will not be practical for some women. For them, the drive to lumpectomies as an ideal treatment holds out a promise of choice in surgery which is more illusory than real — unless conservative surgery without radiation is developed as a practical alternative.

Radiation therapy's postwar legacy as "the sunny side of the atom" adds another complex layer of conflict to the treatment, at least for patients who are aware of it. For Vanessa Kramer, the ultimate irony was that her treatment ended on August 6. When the radiologist told her the date, Vanessa said, "Oh, that's Hiroshima Day." The doctor didn't make the connection. "I had to explain to her what Hiroshima Day was, and why it hit me the way it did."[29] Despite her difficult decision to go ahead with the treatment she suffered a recurrence in the area of her incision three years later and had to have a mastectomy.

Every medical intervention is a Faustian pact — we strike a bargain that we hope won't come back to haunt us. As patients, the regulations of our agreement reside in the informed consent procedure. With the routine use of radiation after a lumpectomy, once again a single treatment gains pride of place, despite unresolved issues in theory, practice and resource availability. The medical implications for the woman are not clear. A treatment that is high-tech and interventionist has been annointed the "recommended choice" in the absence of knowledge about the effects, both physical and psychological. Large resource expenditures are being made in our name. How many women would agree with these priorities?

Radiation as a post-operative "clean-up" carries a large weight of military history. More than with any other breast cancer treatment, large-P political issues complicate our assessment of radiation. An implicit agreement exaggerates radiation's small medical benefit, discourages controls that would limit radiation's harmful effects and blocks the dissemination of critical opinion. Patients, practitioners and researchers — we are all children of our age, and are all drawn into the bargain, usually unwittingly, but occasionally because we see no other option. As citizens, we do not have full access to the inner workings of this important industry. Anyone submitting to the embrace of a machine in the nuclear medicine arsenal hopes the equipment is the latest and the best (and that old equipment is disposed of safely), but how many of us are able to judge? The other Faustian pact of nuclear medicine is between the civilian and military sectors of western society. Its terms are top secret.

Notes

1. Susan Love with Karen Lindsay, *Dr. Susan Love's Breast Book*, (N.Y.: Addison Wesley, 1990), pp. 306-308.

2. Patterson, p. 195.

3. Patterson, p. 192.

4. Kushner, p. 262.

5. Kushner, p. 265.

6. Kushner, p. 263.

7. Vera Peters, "Wedge Ressection and Irradiation: An Effective Treatment in Early Breast Cancer," *Journal of the American Medical Association*, (Apr. 10, 1967), pp. 144-145.

8. Thomas Dao, personal communication, (July 28, 1994).

9. Richard A. Evans, "Selective Radiation Therapy in the Treatment of Breast Cancer," unpublished manuscript, (1993).

10. Richard A. Evans, "The 'Seed and Soil' Hypotheses and the Decline of Radical Surgery: A Surgeon's Opinion," *Texas Medicine/The Journal*, (Sept. 1990) 6:9, pp. 85-89.

11. Interview with Richard Evans, (July 29, 1993).

12. Ivo Olivotto, testimony to the House of Commons Subcommittee, (Feb. 11, 1992), [from transcript], p. 9:18.

13. Dawn Black, testimony to the House of Commons Subcommittee, (Feb. 11, 1992), [from transcript], p. 9:28.

14. Hazel M. Thornton, "Breast cancer trials: a patient's viewpoint," *Lancet*, (Jan. 4, 1992), 339:44-45.

15. John D. Boice, Jr., et. al., "Cancer in the Contralateral Breast after Radiotherapy for Breast Cancer," *New England Journal of Medicine*, (Mar. 19, 1992), pp. 781-785.

16. Described in Love with Lindsay, p. 162.

17. Ian MacKenzie, "Breast Cancer following Multiple Fluoroscopies," *British Journal of Cancer*, (1965), 19: pp. 1-8, cited in Rosalie Bertell, "Breast Cancer and Mammography," *Mothering*, (Summer 1992), p. 51; also A.B. Miller, G.R. Howe, G.J. Sherman et al, "Mortality From Breast Cancer After Irradiation During Fluoroscopic Examinations in Patients Being Treated for Tuberculosis," *New England Journal of Medicine*, (Nov. 9, 1989), 321:19: pp. 1285-9.

18. Love with Lindsay, p. 162.

19. Bertell, 1992, pp. 51-52.

20. Rosalie Bertell, in *Nuclear Witnesses: Insiders Speak Out*, edited by Leslie J. Freeman, (N.Y.: Norton, 1982), p. 27.

21. Bertell, 1982, pp. 28-29.

22. Telephone interview with Rosalie Bertell, July 29, 1993.

23. *American Journal of Public Health*, (Feb., 1979).

24. *American Journal of Public Health*, (Feb., 1979).

25. Constance Holden, "Low level Radiation: A High-level Concern," *Science*, (Apr. 13, 1979), pp. 155-158; and Jean L. Marx, "Low-level Radiation: Just How Bad Is It?" *Science*, (April 13, 1979), pp. 160-164.

26. National Coalition of Cancer Survivors National Assembly, Charlotte, N.C., (Nov. 1992).

27. A. Peck and J. Boland, "Emotional Reactions to Radiation Treatment," *Cancer*, (1977), 40: pp. 180-184.

28. Telephone interview with Carole Jones, Ottawa, (July 12, 1993).

29. Interview with Vanessa Kramer, Montreal, (Aug. 4, 1993).

Chemotherapy
Poison

... she had never forgotten that, if you drink much from a bottle marked "poison," it is almost certain to disagree with you, sooner or later.

— Lewis Carroll, *Alice in Wonderland*

I first read about the Alert in *Ms.* magazine's August 1988 issue.

"The National Cancer Institute [NCI] made history in May," the brief news item declared, "by announcing that all breast cancer patients should consider chemotherapy or hormone therapy after their tumours are removed, even if no cancer could be found in the adjacent lymph nodes."

The article went on to summarize three large studies which had shown that recurrences of early breast cancer were more common than previously thought, but that follow-up drug therapy could signficantly reduce the recurrence rate. "Before the announcement, early breast cancer was generally treated with surgery alone," explained the article. No more: "In one bold stroke, the NCI changed the course of treatment for early breast cancer."[1]

As well as sending the treatment Alert to major magazines and newspapers, the NCI put the Alert on the Physician Data Query System (PDQ), presented it at the NCI advisory board, published it in the *Journal of the National Cancer Institute*[2] and sent it to 13,000 cancer specialists and cancer institutions.

That fall, as I hurtled through the gamut of tests that would tease meaning from the small hard intruder in my breast, I went back to the *Ms.* article many times. The tone was reassuring. Maybe I had breast cancer, but I was just in time to ride the wave of medical history. Women who had been treated with surgery six or 12 months ago were not so lucky. Maybe they also should have chemotherapy, but the experts weren't sure.

In November, just before I entered the hospital for the lymph node dissection that would determine whether cancer cells had spread significantly, a friend brought me an article which put the Alert in a different perspective. The announcement had sparked consternation among cancer specialists, said *Consumer Reports*, because the studies it referred to had not yet been published in peer review journals. Here was the director of the all-powerful NCI urging physicians to make a drastic change in treatment practice before the details of treatment efficacy and side effects had been published.

Vincent DeVita, the director of the National Cancer Institute and the force behind the Alert, explained his departure from normal procedure in this way: "This was an urgent public health matter. Each year more than 60,000 women in [the United States] are diagnosed with node-negative breast cancer. We could not delay informing them and their physicians that additional treatment beyond surgery and/or radiotherapy might be beneficial." He went on to say that women with early stage breast cancer and their physicians "should consider adjuvant chemotherapy, hormonal therapy, or both following primary treatment."[3]

Many physicians refused to comply and met the wrath of their patients. Like me, the women had read popular accounts of the Alert; if their physician didn't recommend chemotherapy, they worried they were being offered less than the best.[4]

I awaited the results of my lymph node dissection with trepidation. If I was node-positive, my 10-year survival chances plummetted from about 85 percent to 50 percent or less. A positive lymph node status is a sign that the cancer cells have spread beyond the breast and are circulating through the lymph and blood system. The more positive nodes, the greater the spread and the worse one's survival chances. The results of my dissection showed cancer cells in one of my lymph nodes; I was labelled Stage II. That was terrifying, but at least I could go forward with the standard treatment, chemotherapy, believing that it would help my odds. Adjuvant chemotherapy is designed to kill as many of these marauding cells as possible, before they form a tumour in the lungs, liver, brain, or some other part of the body. For a premenopausal woman with even one positive lymph node, adjuvant (or "helping") drug therapy had been standard treatment for years.

The controversy over the Alert centred around the 20 to 30 percent of women whose lymph nodes are clear but who eventually develop metastatic disease despite their good prognosis. If chemo helps women who are node positive, the reasoning went, it might be even more effective in killing off the stray cells in those women with a circulating tumour load undetected by lymph node dissection. Opponents of this strategy contended that chemo was too harsh a treatment to be given to the 70 to 80 percent of node-negative women who would not eventually develop metastases.

Yet I eventually decided the controversy was not irrelevant to me at all. When I searched for the grounds for giving adjuvant chemo to women with Stage II breast cancer, I learned that the Alert was a mini-drama in a dispute that had been going on for decades. Defenders and detractors agree that chemo is an "aggressive" therapy; they differ on whether or not this is a good thing. The drugs have undeniable noxious effects, and not just the short term fatigue, hair loss, vomiting, digestive problems and lowering of the immune defenses. Long term effects can include leukemia and harm to vital organs such as the heart. How great were the benefits, I wondered, and when did any woman, or physician, decide they were worth the risks?

In theory, chemotherapy drugs work by a simple principle. The drugs kill cells that are dividing and cancer cells divide more rapidly than most normal cells. The bloodstream distributes the poisons to all parts of the body so they can attack cancer cells in distant sites, not just locally. Since all the cells won't be dividing at the same time, repeated doses hit the cells that were missed on previous rounds.

Some drugs may disrupt cell growth directly, others use up food that the cells need to grow. "Chemo cocktails" deliver combinations of drugs which attack the cancer in more than one way. As in any war, the civilian casualties are regrettable but inevitable. Fast-dividing normal cells are found in the bone marrow (where the blood is formed), the digestive tract, hair follicles, and the reproductive system.

Military language such as "bombarding" the cancer, and "mop-up" operation, are part of the chemotherapy lexicon. And, as in war, endless strategy debates fill the literature: whether a few big hits are better than many smaller ones; whether it's best to attack in the morning or late in the day (cell division slows considerably during sleep); whether to take the offensive before serious trouble develops, or to keep "the big guns" as a last resort.

Like radiotherapy, chemotherapy as a cancer treatment was an effort to turn war technology to peacetime use. In December 1943, an American ship carrying mustard gas exploded in a harbour on the coast of Italy. Some of the soldiers on board died from the toxic effects of the liquefied gas. Autopsies showed that the precise cause of death was anemia; the gas had blocked reproduction of white blood cells. Since certain cancers, notably leukemia and Hodgkin's disease, result from an excess of white blood cells, medical analysts reasoned that nitrogen mustards might control those diseases.

Research into poisonous chemicals as a cancer treatment began in secret during the war. Later the investigations were carried out openly, at Yale University, the University of Chicago, and at Memorial Sloan-Kettering Cancer Centre in New York. Cornelius "Dusty" Rhoads, head of Sloan-Kettering and chief medical officer of the Army's Chemical Warfare Division, zealously promoted testing of some 1,500 kinds of nitrogen mustard gas between 1945 and 1950.

Faith in drugs to cure diseases was at an all-time high thanks to the success of streptomycin against tuberculosis and the discovery of penicillin. When the nitrogen-based treatments produced remissions of acute childhood leukemia, cancer looked like the next disease to be conquered. "We can look forward to something like a penicillin for cancer, and I hope within the next decade," predicted Rhoads. The public showed its support with generous donations to cancer charities and political pressure to pour tax dollars into cancer research.

The National Cancer Institute began to invest heavily in chemotherapy research. The Food and Drug Administration (FDA), the Atomic Energy Commission and the Veterans Administration supplied back-up. "By 1957, the chemotherapy program was intense, absorbing almost half of the NCI's budget and testing thousands of chemicals a year," notes cancer historian

James Patterson.[5] With 400,000 drugs tested by 1970, critics dubbed it the "nothing-is-too-stupid-to-test" program.

Enthusiasts pointed to the 30 drugs which, by the early 1980s, saved the lives of about 3,000 young Americans with childhood leukemia, Hodgkin's disease and certain lymphomas (cancers of the lymph system). The trouble is, these cancer cases make up less than two percent of all cancer deaths. By comparison, chemotherapy showed only temporary regression in the solid-tumour cancers which killed over 400,000 Americans per year. Some patients, stripped of the immune system protection provided by white blood cells, died of anemia or infection.[6]

Chemotherapy as an adjuvant treatment for breast cancer entered this debate early on. Leading breast cancer surgeons recognized that surgery alone was not going to wipe out the disease. The infusion of funds into chemical research made oncology an increasingly powerful field of medicine. The American Cancer Society (ACS), which began to devote one-third of its campaign revenues to research and treatment, provided funds to many physicians specializing in breast cancer. As tax funding for cancer increased, these physicians splintered into groups based on geography and their specific cancer specialties. They gave themselves names like the South-West Oncology Group (SWOG), the Eastern Co-operative Oncology Group (ECOG), and — the largest — the National Surgical Adjuvant Breast and Bowel Project (NSABP). "Competition between the groups became apparent, and bitter rivalry sometimes occurred when conflicting results were published," notes sociologist Kathryn Taylor, in her study of breast cancer research. Although the core of several dozen oncologists "argued bitterly among themselves," she says, "[they] provided a united front to those who supported them."

In the mid-1970s, two research teams published early results of experiments using adjuvant chemotherapy with breast cancer. Bernard Fisher's NSABP group in Pittsburgh showed that women who were given a mustard drug after surgery had fewer recurrences than women who had surgery alone.[7] Even more dramatically, Gianna Bonadonna at the Milan Tumour Institute announced that women given a three-drug chemo cocktail after surgery had one-fourth the recurrence rate of women who had surgery only. An editorial in the usually circumspect *New England Journal of*

gs as of "monumental importance" and
ular."[8]

of the patients in these two studies
premature. But the excitement over the
that the chemotherapy program was
whole. Breast cancer is one of the most
d is a solid tumour cancer — even a hint
d large medical and political implica-

ed. The head of the National Cancer
Alert, was telling the world the
n hand — finally.

American studies, and a fourth from
ary 1989 in the *New England Journal of*
ed with three editorials. In a subdued
f Arnold Relman said, "all find small
e survival but, after follow-up periods
definite improvement in overall sur-
vi .... did not speculate about what this meant for treatment. Instead he cautiously posed a series of questions. "Do these
results warrant the routine use of adjuvant therapy; if not, which
if any patients should be treated, and with which agents?" He
urged physicians to "study the available evidence for themselves"
and tossed the ball to two writers with diametrically opposed views
— Vincent DeVita and William McGuire.

By now, DeVita was no longer the head of the NCI. In July 1988,
midway between issuing the Alert and the appearance of the
editorial, he resigned the post he had held for eight years with a
parting salvo: "If you want to fly with the eagles, you don't rot with
the turkeys."[9] He flew to a new nest at Sloan-Kettering Institute, in
New York, where he became physician-in-chief.

In his editorial, DeVita called the studies "the capstone of 32
years of clinical trials of treatment for breast cancer." He traced
the evolution of chemotherapy studies in breast cancer, from the
first clinical trials begun in 1957. These had led to a "marked
reduction in morbidity [i.e., medical symptoms]," and to the
development of "increasingly effective systemic adjuvant therapy"
for breast cancer. Expanding on this historical perspective, he
stressed that the outcome of the studies fits the theoretical model

of how chemotherapy works: the earlier the cancer, the more likely the treatment is to be effective, because fewer cancer cells are circulating in the system. He also endorsed the view that a heavy dose of chemotherapy is better than a mild one. Unfortunately, he said, clinicians often reduce the dose intensity of chemotherapy when treating patients with early stage cancer. The risk of mortality from chemotherapy treatment is "miniscule," he declared, compared to the 30 percent risk of a recurrence in node negative women, with the inevitable death from metastases. This reasoning went beyond the data of the studies, which had shown no survival benefit. The failure of the treatments to extend women's lives, explained DeVita, was "almost certainly a matter of timing."

In his opposing editorial, Texas physician William McGuire weighed the improvements in disease-free survival against the toxic effects and the financial cost per patient of treatment. One study found that with chemotherapy, four percent more women were disease-free after four years; in the other studies, the comparable percentages were nine, 15 and six. Thus, only four to 15 percent of the women benefited from treatments, while toxic effects ranged from mild to severe, including five treatment-related deaths. The per-patient costs of the four treatment regimens varied depending on the drugs and the number of treatments: $398 for cyclophosphamide, methotrexate, fluorouracil, and leucovorin; $5,920 for methotrexate and fluorouracil followed by leucovorin; $1,829 for cyclophosphamide, methotrexate, fluorouracil, and prednisone, and $4,745 for five years of tamoxifen.

If all 70,000 women diagnosed annually in the U.S. with node-negative breast cancer were to have one of these courses of chemotherapy, estimated McGuire, the direct financial cost would be $338,174,200 per year and 50 to 100 women would die from treatments. These figures did not include the cost of treating toxic effects or indirect costs, such as days lost from work. About 5,040 women would gain some disease-free time. "I would argue that the considerable cost outweighs the benefits of treating all node-negative patients, especially in the absence of a proved survival benefit," concluded McGuire.[10]

DeVita had bypassed the issue of cost and the lack of a survival benefit, and urged speedy action. Enter patients in clinical trials where possible, he exhorted, to accelerate research. While new research refined the results at hand, he called on clinicians to hasten the transfer of new treatments into general practice. He urged physicians to tell newly diagnosed women of their options and to offer each one some form of systemic treatment. He asserted, "we are now in a position to capitalize on this information ... to drive down mortality due to breast cancer."[11]

The editorials shattered any illustion of unity among oncologists — but what did the debate mean for women? I turned to Rose Kushner's book to get her view of chemotherapy's historical evolution. She painted a picture very different from DeVita's. After her diagnosis in the mid-'70s, and again when she had a recurrence in the early 1980s, Kushner took a hard look at this "spectacular" and "monumental" treatment for breast cancer. She discovered a strong pro-chemotherapy movement which was pushing to have the drug treatments adopted rapidly as the standard for all women diagnosed with breast cancer. Although the key studies supporting chemotherapy were done in Milan, the enthusiasm for chemotherapy was particularly strong in the United States, she noted. When she read the medical literature, Kushner noticed "a continuing war in foreign journals about the premature use of the Milan data in this country."[12]

Typical of the controversy was the response to the Milan team's 1976 report. The results showed that women with Stage II breast cancer had fewer recurrences after an average of 14 months if they had been treated with the drug combination CMF (cyclophaspamide, methatrexate and fluorouracil). For many physicians in the U.S., this was the cue to administer CMF to all women with Stage II breast cancer. Yet, Kushner pointed out, a survival time of 14 months is much too short to draw meaningful conclusions about the effects of a breast cancer treatment. A follow-up of 15 or 20 years is needed to determine the merits of a treatment, particularly since drugs like cyclophosphamide can cause leukemia down the line and create mutant strains of new drug-resistant cells that undermine the impact of later therapy. Despite calls for caution, an American survey showed that adjuvant chemotherapy for breast cancer had jumped from seven percent in 1976 to 22 percent in 1981. "But not in other countries," noted Kushner.

Kushner admitted her prejudice against adjuvant chemotherapy. She believed "the high-flying balloon of optimism about it would eventually pop," but was careful to stress that she could not know the future, any more than chemo's enthusiasts could. As a newly diagnosed node-negative patient in 1974, she took a wide pass on chemotherapy, despite the just-published results from Italy. As metastatic patient, in 1981, she chose again to pass on the cytotoxic drugs strongly recommended by three different oncologists. She opted for the hormonal drug tamoxifen, which was then experimental. At this point, Kushner's main reservations were about adjuvant chemotherapy used with women diagnosed after menopause. For premenopausal women with one to three positive lymph nodes (my own case), she was satisfied that research had shown chemo could extend life.

I wasn't surprised, therefore, when my surgeon told me the team of experts who had reviewed my case recommended chemotherapy. I was premenopausal and had one positive node. The recommendation was for six months of a combination dose known as CMF, a standard and relatively mild regimen, and "tamoxifen for the rest of your life." I wasn't crazy about taking any drug for the rest of my life. "Is it expensive?" I asked the nurse. She nodded. "But you'll get it from the hospital. All you pay is an administration fee of two dollars a month." I braced myself for the more immediate matter, the six months of "cell kill" drugs. I was relieved, at least, that the recommended treatment would improve my survival odds without subjecting me to the extreme toxicity of the potent anti-cancer drug Adriamycin.

When the oncologist, a week later, recommended that I enter a clinical trial, Adriamycin was part of the regimen. As a volunteer in the study, I would be randomly assigned to a standard, mild, or heavy dose of CAF, for either four or six months. My defenses dropped away. Adriamycin could weaken my heart, or even kill me. From reading Kushner, I had the impression the drug was used to treat women diagnosed with metastasis. I wondered what evidence supported the use of such an extreme treatment for someone with just one positive lymph node.

The oncologist cited the latest report on adjuvant chemotherapy, which had shown that premenopausal women with Stage II breast cancer lived three to five years longer, on average, if they had chemotherapy.[13] The women also had more disease-free years. Although the studies had not continued long enough to determine if any women would be completely cured by chemotherapy, the signs were hopeful. My odds of developing metastatic disease were high, stressed the oncologist, and chemotherapy could cut the risk in half.

As for Adriamycin's devastating effects, he would be monitoring me closely. I had my age and good overall health in my favour. I realized with a shock the peculiar perspective of an oncologist. For me, good health was a precious resource I wanted to guard; for him, it was a signal I could withstand greater devastation — like a forest that would grow back after levelling.

I also vaguely understood that oncologists still disagreed on whether one should use the most toxic chemo regimen possible, or opt for a milder treatment (with less harm to healthy tissue), perhaps over a longer period. The argument for aggressive therapy is that the heaviest dose of the most toxic drug the patient can withstand will kill the most circulating cells. The body's immune system then "mops up" whatever cancer is left and normal healing processes repair the damage to healthy cells. If one accepts the argument for aggressive therapy, part of the oncologist's job is to judge how much chemical devastation the patient can bear, lead her to the margin, then snatch her back. The risks in this game of brinksmanship include permanent organ impairment, secondary tumours, or death.[14]

The medical literature reflects the competing schools of thought within the oncology community. In 1981 the Milan team published an article in the *New England Journal of Medicine* advocating "more drug in a shorter time span." In the next issue of the same journal, the Pittsburgh-based team led by Bernard Fisher recommended "less drug, over a longer time span."[15]

I assumed that the change in my treatment plan reflected these disputes. Perhaps my oncologist was part of a minority faction at the tumour conference who wanted to take the "big guns" approach — aggressive chemotherapy. Before I began my treatments, the oncology nurse handed me a thick booklet describing the various side-effects of chemotherapy and advised me not to read it all at once: "It would be too depressing; besides, no one has all the side effects." Still unconvinced, I turned to my GP. From her vantage point outside the oncology fray, I felt she would be more in tune with my worries about chemical wastage. She was indeed sympathetic. In fact, one of her best friends had just been diagnosed with breast cancer so she had considered this very question in a personal context. Before making her treatment decisions, her friend had invited a number of female physicians she knew to breakfast and asked each one of them if they would have chemotherapy if they were in her shoes. They all said they would: "It gives you more time and a better quality of time," my GP explained.

I accepted the regimen. The most shocking effect came the day after my first treatment. I had just begun menstruating and my period abruptly stopped. A few weeks later, I noticed a small discharge of dried blood and phoned the oncology nurse in a panic. "The chemo is affecting your ovaries," she said matter-of-factly. Although I suffered all the classic effects of Adriamycin — hair loss, nausea and fatigue — none upset me as much as this sudden vault into menopause. The oncologist was sympathetic, but said hormone therapy was out of the question. Would I suddenly turn spindly-legged, grey and osteoporitic, I wondered? Or, since my tumour fed on estrogen, was the abrupt shut-down of my estrogen source a good thing? Nothing I had read so far about chemotherapy addressed this issue.

Several streams of thought feed the debate over adjuvant chemotherapy and one stream concerns the effect of the drugs on the woman's production of estrogen. The women who show the clearest benefit are those who are treated before menopause. Since chemotherapy can terminate ovarian function (and thus drastically reduce the supply of estrogen), the survival advantage may have little or nothing to do with cytotoxic ("cell kill") effects.

German biostatistician Ulrich Abel reached this conclusion in 1989, after reviewing chemotherapy trials from around the world. Nearly 10 years' work in clinical oncology left Abel puzzled by the faith in chemotherapy as a cancer treatment. At first he attributed his unease to a lack of understanding on his part. As he studied the evidence, he became increasingly sure that his misgivings were justified. Decades of intensive clinical research revealed little therapeutic success with chemotherapy regimens.

The studies that support chemotherapy, notes Ulrich Abel, suffer from methodological flaws. Patients must enjoy a fairly robust state of health to withstand high doses of chemotherapy; this stringent selection requirement opens the studies of dose-intensity up to a number of statistical biases.

The success of adjuvant chemotherapy for breast cancer presented a particularly intriguing puzzle, he said, because prophylactic use of chemo had failed with every other type of solid tumour. That chemo's benefit would be specific to breast cancer, and limited even more to a subset of women with breast cancer (that is, premenopausal women), is "somewhat strange" says Abel. He concluded that the action of adjuvant chemo in breast cancer could best be explained as a suppression of ovarian function. "Many oncologists, especially in Great Britain, now share this view," he says. The interpretation fits not only with much of the research findings, but satisfies simple logic and the results of studies with ovariectomies.[16]

Meanwhile, arrested menstruation, whether temporarily or forever, is typically presented as a negative consequence of chemotherapy. (In a woman under 40, the cessation of menses is more likely to be temporary than in a woman who is already close to her natural menopause. The strength of the chemotherapy also affects the likelihood that menstruation will be brought to a halt.) If the current opinion of contemporary British oncologists is right and chemo benefits women with breast cancer by stopping ovarian function and the flow of estrogen, this effect is to be desired; if the effect is what mediates longer life, it should be a primary goal of therapy, not a side effect.

Ironically, the operation known medically as oophorectomy, ovarian ablation, or castration, was the treatment for advanced breast cancer in premenopausal women before chemotherapy was introduced.[17] It was abandoned because physicians deemed the side effects (sterility and intense menopausal symptoms) too severe. Today, a woman who suffers chemo-induced menopause will have the same symptoms and the effects of toxic medication besides. When I read the ovarian ablation interpretation of chemotherapy I wondered why I wasn't offered the option of an oophorectomy. I also wondered why such an obvious explanation for chemotherapy's effect on breast cancer is only now being explored in clinical trials.

Another, practical question about chemotherapy, one which is vital to patients, is whether the treatment can be effectively administered in the "real world." Variability in treatment quality is an established fact of breast cancer surgery and a reality in radiotherapy as well. An assessment by an office of the U.S.

government suggests that chemotherapy may not be a readily transferable treatment, either.

In 1989, the General Accounting Office (GAO), the accounting arm of the U.S. government, examined the record of breast cancer survival for women with Stage II cancer. In a review of scientific studies up to 1985, the GAO concluded, "the question of whether chemotherapy has the potential to extend patient survival has been settled." Bonadonna's Milan studies had shown that chemotherapy extended survival in premenopausal node-positive patients, while Bernard Fisher's NSABP study had shown a benefit for premenopausal patients with fewer than four positive nodes.

Yet the agency's population study of survival rates for American women with Stage II breast cancer showed no improvement from 1975 to 1985. The GAO investigators used records from the official registries, which include 12 percent of the U.S. population. The stable survival figures puzzled the investigators because the percentage of American women receiving chemotherapy from 1975 to 1983 climbed from 23 percent to 69 percent.[18]

A number of explanations for this anomaly were possible, the report concluded. The GAO plumped for the middle ground — that the studies' conclusions were valid, but that somewhere between the controlled conditions of the clinical trial and the "real life" administration of chemotherapy in communities, the benefit of chemotherapy was lost. The report recommended research to determine why this might be. In a commentary, which was almost as long as the report itself, the Department of Health and Human Services (HHS) attacked the GAO study. The critique argued that the statistical power of the study was weak and the GAO had seriously underestimated the benefits of adjuvant chemotherapy. But, rejoined the GAO, the starting point of the study was a statement from the HHS that there was a "confirmed 25 percent improved survival for Stage II premenopausal women treated with breast cancer." If the gain was 25 percent, insisted the GAO, the study should have detected it.

The debate echoes the arguments over mammography screening. When the expected benefits of screening fail to materialize, adherents fault the studies and argue for more widespread screening, better equipment and better research. In the real world, however, technically tricky treatments will never be completely failsafe. From the patient's perspective, the GAO findings are a cautionary reminder that heroic treatments put one's life in the hands of the hero. Finding a competent breast surgeon is a daunting enough task. How many women facing chemotherapy are up to vetting the judgement skills of their oncologist?

A different set of disputes frames the use of chemotherapy with women who have advanced breast cancer. In 1981, as a patient with advanced disease, Rose Kushner was no more willing to undergo chemotherapy than she had been when her diagnosis was Stage I. More than a decade later, the utility of chemotherapy for women with advanced breast cancer is still under debate. While even chemotherapy's detractors acknowledge its effect as an adjuvant in premenopausal women, the doubters question whether chemotherapy can extend life in women of any age who have advanced disease.

My own scepticism about chemo's benefits for women with an advanced diagnosis was tempered when I learned the history of one famous breast cancer patient, Susan Sontag. Diagnosed with a virulent, metastacized breast cancer in 1975, Sontag was told she had only a 10 percent chance of surviving two years. That was the optimistic prediction. Doctors told her son she would likely live only six months. She had five operations, plus two-and-a-half years of chemotherapy and immunotherapy. Many vital and productive years later, Sontag credits her recovery to good treatment, including chemotherapy.

"Obviously some people do survive," she says, "and many more people would survive cancer if they were properly treated as I was." Her physicians at Sloan-Kettering simply call her a "medical miracle." Sontag disagrees. "I don't think I'm a medical miracle at all, I think I got very good treatment," she remarked in a radio interview. She criticizes doctors who discourage patients from taking chemotherapy by telling them it's agony. "Of course it's not," says Sontag. "It's perfectly bearable."[19]

Ulrich Abel, however, questions the use of chemotherapy for advanced breast cancer as a means to extend life rather than control pain. Cell-killing drugs can induce remissions, meaning the tumour shrinks or disappears, he says. When the goal is to reduce pain, the treatment is realistic, says Abel. In this case, chemotherapy is not expected to cure, but is considered a "palliative." Drugs used singly can give a response rate in 35 to 45 percent of breast cancer patients, he says, while combinations like CMF and CAF achieve response rates of 40 to 80 percent. The proportion of breast cancer patients who have complete remissions is almost always less than 20 percent.[20]

The fallacy, says Abel, is the belief that because cytotoxic drugs shrink some metastacized tumours, these patients will live longer. His review of the research showed no evidence, either direct or indirect, that remissions translate into longer survival. Despite the lack of hard evidence, he says, most clinicians are convinced, from their own observations, that certain patients do gain time from the treatments. The popular wisdom in oncology circles is that some subgroups of patients live longer; these might include patients with certain rapidly progressive tumours — for example, in the liver.

Studies comparing the survival of women with advanced breast cancer who were treated before 1970, in the era before chemotherapy became routine, with those treated after, found that patients treated in the 1970s lived about a year longer than those in the 1950s or 1960s. But Abel concludes that improvements in diagnosis account for much of this difference.

Finding metastases earlier gives the appearance of longer survival (just as early detection with mammography provides an illusion of longer life). Some studies which Abel reviewed showed worse survival rates in the chemo era than in the the pre-chemo decades. Two reviewers who surveyed randomized studies of chemotherapy with metastatic breast cancer concluded, "… these trials argue for a conservative approach to the management of this disease. There is no evidence that asymptomatic patients [with advanced disease] need any form of active treatment."[21] Abel concurs. He points out that polls of oncologists show that many would decline chemotherapy if they themselves faced terminal cancer.

Abel's analysis implies that treating women with advanced disease with chemotherapy is a desperate measure unless the treatment is simply a palliative for pain. A common rationale for using chemotherapy with metastatic breast cancer is the belief that the treatment improves quality of life. Oncologists usually interpret this "hazy notion" narrowly, to mean relief from tumour-related complaints, says Abel. For patients suffering from severe pain, the salutory effects are so evident they are unquestionable;

but chemotherapy is given to virtually all patients, many of whom have their quality of life reduced by the treatment's toxicity.

When Nina Docherty of Toronto was diagnosed with advanced breast cancer, she and her husband Neil understood that her physicians were administering chemotherapy because they believed the treatment could eradicate the tumour. When her situation worsened, Neil Docherty recalls, a doctor explained that the different drugs they were trying were simply causing the tumours (in her bones) to wax and wane. "That's a huge difference," he says bitterly.

Neil believes the doctors were well intentioned and wanted to do the best for his wife, but that the chemotherapy made her final months much worse, not better. In the light of Nina's experience, reading Ulrich Abel's analysis convinced Neil that chemotherapy should be abandoned as a treatment for advanced breast cancer. I told him what I knew of Susan Sontag's experience. If one person could recover so completely, "doesn't that suggest that the treatments could be effective for some women?" I asked him.

"For a very few, perhaps," he said. "But that doesn't justify using it for everyone — or that they keep on trying, when they haven't been able to improve their performance in two decades."

One of Neil's concerns is that other, more promising treatments are not being explored because chemotherapy is so dogmatically embraced. Ulrich Abel, for example, wanted to compare chemotherapy and immunotherapy. His proposals, and those of colleagues, were refused "for ethical reasons and without serious considerations."[22] Chemotherapy is so entrenched in the treatment repertoire that any research that would "deprive" patients of it is deemed unethical.

Nina Docherty's experience and her subsequent death prompted producers at *The Fifth Estate*, the investigative television program where Neil works, to look into the use of chemotherapy to treat patients who have advanced breast cancer. Their initial thesis was that oncologists were making the judgement to administer the drugs. After months of research, however, they concluded that many dying patients, in desperation, convince their oncologist to administer chemotherapy against the physician's better judgement. The physician, the logical messenger of the sad truth, is ill-equipped to resist these pleas.

"Doctors are not trained to handle an emotional scene," Marcia Angell, a physician and editor at the *New England Journal of Medicine*, told me, when I asked her why physicians would give chemotherapy to patients without evidence the treatment would help them. "It's so much easier to say, 'I'm going to give you this drug and this drug and this drug, and you try to think positively and be a part of the team. Your hair will fall out, you'll vomit and you'll feel terrible, but it might work.'" When the patient eventually dies, says Angell, the doctor has never really confronted the truth with her, and has never dealt explicitly with the particular fears of a dying patient, which are abandonment and pain.[23]

I question whether the patient in this situation is making an informed decision. In the 1970s, on very tenuous grounds, chemotherapy was declared a miracle treatment for breast cancer. Subsequent research has not borne out these predictions, and today many practitioners and researchers acknowledge that fact. The medical establishment does not, however, issue Alerts and press releases to retract excesses and announce failures. On the contrary. The public is fed a constant diet of stories about medical breakthroughs for breast cancer — of which the Alert I read was just one example. The dying patient and her family are ill-placed to discern the politics behind these bulletins.

Ulrich Abel's point that oncologists typically define quality of life more narrowly than do patients illustrates another gap between the realities of the physician or researcher and the patient. As with most cancer treatments, the question of negative effects — a vital one from the patient's perspective — gets less weight in the medical literature than the treatment's potential to extend life or reduce symptoms. Some of us indeed "tolerate treatments well" — I did with chemotherapy — but patients vary psychologically and physically. Frustration at the oncologist's tumour-centred view of the world is a common complaint when cancer patients exchange experiences.

One friend of mine, an artist with advanced multiple myeloma (a bone marrow cancer), refused to continue chemotherapy when the drugs triggered severe hallucinations. When she turned to a variety of dietary and underground alternative treatments she felt her physician became distant.

I had no such dramatic response to chemotherapy, but I was aware during my treatments that I had difficulty remembering names, telephone numbers or even maintaining a consistent train of thought. I assumed stress was taking its toll on my concentration until I spoke to Vicki Wells, a woman with breast cancer in San Francisco who co-founded a support centre for people with cancer. Memory impairment is very evident, she told me, in support groups with people who are all on chemotherapy. "We call it 'chemo fog' or 'chemo brains,'" she told me. "Someone will start a sentence and they won't be able to finish it because they don't remember what they started out to say. Now when it happens, the whole group will start laughing."[24]

Memory loss and hallucinations, both very large "quality of life" factors for the patient, are precisely the negative effects that medical researchers overlook because they are hard to quantify. Instead, oncology researchers look at the "quality of life" issues that are important and visible to them — delays in recurrences, which give the patient more "disease-free" years, or, more specifically, years free of breast-cancer.

Chemotherapy is at a crossroads. Oncologists react to the treatment's disappointing performance in one of two ways. Abel and McGuire are examples of those who say oncology should move on from cell-kill treatments and search for something more effective and less traumatic for the patient. Others, like DeVita, see great potential for chemotherapy as a treatment in breast cancer. They urge higher doses, given at an earlier stage of treatment, to more women.

As professionals continue the debate, women with the disease are left out of the discussion. As patients, we may be unwittingly harnessed to bolster the physician's firmly held beliefs — a pattern that has been documented in breast surgery. At the same time that critical reviews appear in the journals, more women than ever are having adjuvant chemotherapy, and many oncologists are upping dosages in the hope of gaining the hoped-for remissions.

Since the Alert appeared in 1988, adjuvant chemotherapy for breast cancer has become, in the United States, common for Stage I women.[25] For women with metastatic breast cancer, and even some Stage I or Stage II patients with poor prognostic signs (e.g., a very aggressive tumour in a young woman) "super-chemo," an extreme experimental treatment involving bone marrow or stem cell transplant, is the newest wave. At a cost of about $200,000 per patient, the treatment is patently impractical as standard treatment, even if it is shown to be effective. So far, results have been disappointing. From five to 40 percent of patients die during treatment, which involves removing the bone marrow and transplanting it back after a chemo infusion of 10 to 50 times the standard dose. Remissions of a year are considered good.[26]

Chemotherapy will probably not go gently into the good night of cancer treatments because heroic measures fit so well with North American values. Studies of American oncology show that hope is the dominant symbol of the profession. For physician and patient alike, this means pursuing treatment options to their limits, and until all possibilities are exhausted. The challenge of working with patients whose life is at risk draws oncologists to the field. As a profession, oncology is organized around the hope that, by working close to the limits, the oncologist can make a difference.

When I look back on my decision to have chemotherapy, I think my sense of living in an historic moment was accurate. The tide was indeed turning, but not in the way the Medical Alert suggested. The movement was going the opposite way. I believe the turmoil over the Alert was part of a coming to terms, by medical oncologists, with the failure of cytotoxic drugs to become breast cancer's magic bullet. Like the coming to terms with mammography's limitations, and with radical surgery's lack of benefit, this jockeying process could go on for decades. Meanwhile, women must continue to make treatment decisions.

In defending the record of chemotherapy for breast cancer, DeVita made much of offering women choice. "[A]ll women with newly diagnosed localized invasive breast cancer can and should be offered some form of systemic treatment," he asserted. Yet the rhetoric of patient choice can be a device to preserve the outward appearance of professional solidarity. The specialty's poor understanding of the disease, and the absence of a truly satisfactory treatment, are transformed into virtues which give the patient the privilege of deciding what is best for her.

In my own case, I regret that I made such an important choice believing that the "real" answer to my questions lay somewhere out in the never-never land of scientific studies not yet done. Power politics, fundamental world views and economics all play large roles in driving cancer research and treatment policies. These factors are as relevant to the patient's decision as her lymph node status. Only when we acknowledge these non-medical influences will women with breast cancer make truly informed choices about our treatments.

Notes

1. Robin Marantz Henig, "Breast Cancer News," *Ms.*, (Aug. 1988), p. 24.

2. News, "Treatment Alert Issued of Node-Negative Breast Cancer," *Journal of the National Cancer Institute*, (June 15, 1988), pp. 550-551.

3. News, *Journal of the National Cancer Institute*, p. 550.

4. "Is a Mastectomy Necessary?" *Consumer Reports*, (Nov. 1989), pp. 732-737.

5. Patterson, p. 196.

6. Blalock cited in Taylor, p. 231.

7. B. Fisher et al, "L-Phenylalanine Mustard (L-PAM) in the Management of Primary Breast Cancer: A Report of Early Findings," *New England Journal of Medicine*, (1975), 292:3, pp. 117-122.

8. G. Bonadonna et al, "Combination Chemotherapy as an Adjuvant Treatment in Operable Breast Cancer," *New England Journal of Medicine*, (1976), 294:8, pp. 405-410; and J.F. Holland, "Major Advance in Breast Cancer Therapy," *New England Journal of Medicine*, (1976), 294:8, pp. 440-441.

9. Jeffery Goodell, "Whose Cancer Is It Anyway?" *Seven Days*, (March 29, 1989), cited in Moss, p. 398.

10. William McGuire, "Adjuvant Therapy of Node-Negative Breast Cancer," *New England Journal of Medicine*, (Feb. 23, 1989), p. 526.

11. Vincent De Vita, Jr., "Breast Cancer Therapy: Exercising All Our Options," *New England Journal of Medicine*, (Feb. 23, 1989), pp. 527-529.

12. Kushner, pp. 30-35.

13. G. Bonadonna et al, "Current Status of Milan Adjuvant Chemotherapy Trials for Node-Positive and Node-Negative Breast Cancer," [monograph produced by the National Cancer Institute], (1986), pp. 65-69.

14. Taylor, p. 117, citing D.C. Tormey, "A Randomized Clinical Trial of Five and Three Drug Chemotherapy," *Journal of Clinical Oncology*, (1983), 1:138-145, p. 183.

15. G. Bonadonna et al, "Dose-Response Effect of Adjuvant Chemotherapy in Breast Cancer," *New England Journal of Medicine*, (1981), 304: pp. 10-14; and B. Fisher et al, "Treatment of Primary Breast Cancer with Chemotherapy and Tamoxifen," *New England Journal of Medicine*, (1981) 305: pp. 1-6.

16. Ulrich Abel, "Chemotherapy of Advanced Epithelial Cancer: A Critical Survey," *Hippokrates Verlag Stuttgart*, (1990), p. 53; Abbreviated version published in *Biomedicine of Pharmacotherapy*, (1992), 46, 439-452.

17. Love with Lindsay, p. 327.

18. "Breast Cancer: Patient's Survival," General Accounting Office Report, [PEMD-89-9, Washington], (1989), p. 21.

19. Susan Sontag interviewed by Robert Fulford, "In Her Own Words," *Ideas*, CBC Radio, (Jan. 1993); and by Eleanor Wachtel, *Writers and Company*, CBC Radio (Oct. 24, 1992).

20. Abel, p. 29.

21. V. McCauley and I.E. Smith, "Advanced Breast Cancer," *Randomized Trials in Cancer. A Critical Review by Sites.*, M.L. Slevin and M.J. Staquet (eds), (N.Y.: Raven, 1986), pp. 357-373.

22. Abel, p. 64.

23. Interview with Marcia Angell, Boston, (Oct. 13, 1989).

24. Telephone interview with Victoria Wells, (Apr. 3, 1990).

25. Sharon Green, House of Commons testimony, (Feb. 1992).

26. Deanna Hodgin, "Lethal Weapons," *Lears*, (March 1992), pp. 66-71.

Hormones
Frenzy

Sir Patrick: You mean to tell me you don't remember the woman with the tuberculosis ulcer on her arm?

Ridgeon: [enlightened] Oh, your washerwoman's daughter. Was her name Jane Marsh? I forgot.

Sir Patrick: Perhaps you've forgotten also that you undertook to cure her with Koch's tuberculin.

Ridgeon: And instead of curing her, it rotted her arm right off. Yes: I remember. Poor Jane! However, she makes a good living out of that arm now by shewing it at medical lectures.

Sir Patrick: Still, that wasn't quite what you intended, was it?

Ridgeon: I took my chance of it.

Sir Patrick: Jane did, you mean.

Ridgeon: Well, it's always the patient who has to take the chance when an experiment is necessary. And we can find out nothing without experiment.

— George Bernard Shaw, *The Doctor's Dilemma*

The crowded auditorium, mostly women, is primed for a clash between the two panelists. About an hour into the debate, the inevitable happens.

"There probably isn't a natural women in this room ..." says Richard Margolese, Montreal's most prominent breast cancer specialist.

There is a hushed pause, and he continues, "… because 100 years ago women had 14 children, of whom three survived. They started to menstruate at age 16 and they stopped at age 48. They probably had no more than 30 or 40 ovulations in their life. You have 400."

Physician Adriane Fugh-Berman of the National Women's Health Network, sitting next to Margolese on the podium, reaches for the mike.

"It's extremely unfortunate," she says, her voice icy, "that Dr. Margolese thinks women are defined by the number of their ovulations."

Spontaneous applause erupts in one part of the auditorium and gathers strength; but there are pockets of silence, too.

"I'm sorry you applaud that," rejoins Margolese. "It was a really silly remark. Because I don't define women by their ovulations. I define their physiology and its naturalness by their ovulations. And from the time human beings evolved, some hundreds of thousands of years ago, until the 20th century began, that's how many ovulations women had in their lifetimes: 30 or 40. Now you have 400. And I think that's not normal. I think we should learn about this and we should learn whether or not it's worth manipulating in some way, in order to protect women from diseases."

"Those women died at age 30," Fugh-Berman shoots back.

For those of us with breast cancer, and others who want to know how to avoid it, the word *manipulate* hits the core of the conflict. Female hormones are the essence of our physiological difference from men; manipulating them is being held out as the best prospect for controlling the disease that might kill me. I feel the frustration that always surfaces when I think about breast cancer and hormones. Estrogen, the hormone made by women's bodies and essential to our femaleness, seems undeniably linked to breast cancer. I have breast cancer, so my hormones have somehow betrayed me. In my gut, though, I can't accept that the alternative is for women to submit to experiments to change our hormonal balance. So I applaud Adriane Fugh-Berman, but I worry that Richard Margolese might be right.

As a "liberated" woman growing up in post-war North America, I expected to live well beyond my childbearing years, whether or not I had children. My generation enjoyed full reproductive choice for the first time and like many of my peers I took the Pill almost non-stop for 10 years; I did not have children. Now I am a statistic in the steady rise in the rate of breast cancer. If this relationship is cause and effect, women pay a high price for reproductive freedom — and the proportion of women with breast cancer could rise even higher as women like me move into the latter part of our lives.

I am at this debate today because I hope to see a way out of a vicious circle. If those of us with breast cancer could have done something to avert this disease, no one told us. If it is in our power to avoid a recurrence — a potentially fatal event for which every woman with breast cancer is at high risk — no one seems to know what it is. Our daughters, sisters and nieces are classified "high risk" because we, their mothers, sisters and aunts, have breast cancer. We would like to help them avoid the same fate. As the debate continues, women sitting next to their daughters or sisters exchange glances, grasp hands, or wipe away a tear.

The organization of breast cancer activists to which I belong has invited Adriane Fugh-Berman to the debate because she speaks our language. A feminist physician committed to preventive medicine, she shares our vision of a world in which medical treatment is an emergency measure. Richard Margolese, whom we have also invited to speak, is Montreal's best known breast cancer specialist. An internationally known researcher, he maintains an active practice — he is the oncologist of many of the women in the audience. He is also a passionate and articulate representative of the oncology establishment.

Much of the debate centres on the drug tamoxifen, currently the most frequently prescribed breast cancer treatment in the world. I've never taken it; I was given cytotoxic chemotherapy instead. Tamoxifen has been shown to be most successful with women who have passed menopause. I was premenopausal when diagnosed, although I began menopause the day of my first chemotherapy treatment. Sometimes I wonder whether that means I might benefit from tamoxifen, but I'm just as happy not to be on it. Other women attending the debate have been taking tamoxifen for five years or more — Carolyn, for example, who is chairing the discussion. When she asked her oncologist if she should continue taking the drug, he said they don't have the answer. The trials to test long-term effects have only been ongoing for five years.

The most heated part of the debate has to do with the use of tamoxifen as a preventative for breast cancer. Fugh-Berman has been outspoken in her opposition to this idea. Margolese is a leading proponent of the North American trial to test the drug with healthy women — in fact, he helped design it. His views are widely shared by other breast cancer specialists. The trial is actively recruiting women all over North America. Some women here tonight have volunteered to participate. Others have decided against it. To me, the trial is shocking. It's supposed to be for women who are at high risk for breast cancer, but the art of predicting who will get breast cancer is so primitive that the whole concept of being "high risk" seems artificial. I don't expect anything Margolese says will change my opinion, but I hope to gain a better understanding of his point of view.

Tamoxifen was discovered in the 1960s when the FDA was testing for a contraceptive; the drug proved to induce rather than inhibit ovulation. Pierre Blais, well known as a drug researcher who was ejected from the Canada's health protection bureaucracy when he spoke out about silicone breast implants, calls the tamoxifen story "the story of modern drug design, which produces garbage drugs. Good drug design ceased, unfortunately, in the 1930s." Tamoxifen, Blais asserts, "is a garbage drug that made it to the top of the scrap heap. It is a DES in the making."[1]

Blais is referring to diethylistilbestrol (DES), the first synthetic estrogen, created by British chemist Sir Charles Dodds in 1938. Soon after its debut in North America, DES was prescribed to women to treat a variety of gynaecological problems, including "menopausal symptoms," gonorrheal vaginitis, and the suppression of lactation. Prescribing estrogens as an all-purpose treatment for gynaecological problems, recalls Saul Cape, a pharmacist who began practicing in 1936, "was the mentality of the time."[2]

In this spirit, a Boston duo, gynaecologist George Smith and his wife Olive, an epidemiologist, decided to test DES to see if it would prevent miscarriages. They had observed that women who suffered spontaneous abortions had lower blood levels of estrogen than women whose pregnancies went to full term. After several studies, they concluded that pregnant women who took DES delivered babies that were not only healthy, but "grossly" more healthy than the babies of women who weren't given the drug. Millions of women took DES in the 1950s to prevent miscarriage.

Marketing DES to prevent miscarriage proved to be the "miracle" drug's undoing. A medical report described seven cases of young women, daughters of women who had taken DES, who developed a rare vaginal cancer.[3] Law suits followed. Manufacturers withdrew DES from the market in 1980 after a series of multimillion dollar court awards, although they continued to deny proof of a connection. Furious mothers organized, filed a class action suit and demanded more research into the drug's effects. One study of 3,029 women who took DES, published in 1993, showed that the mothers themselves have a 35 percent increased risk of breast cancer. The largest increase was found in DES mothers who were beyond age 60 at the time of the study.[4]

DES was just one piece of evidence in a slow but sure accrual of proof that estrogen could cause cancer.[5] Reason for suspecting estrogen medications ("exogenous" hormones) might *not* be safe came from research into "endogenous" hormones — those made by the woman's own body.

In the 1920s, having isolated the female principle through animal studies, researchers named it estrogen — "begin the frenzy," from the Greek words oistros and gen ("frenzy" and "begin"). The name itself says much about how scientists perceive the onset of womanhood. "Androgen," the name given to the comparable male hormone, denotes simply "the man begins" (ander="male person").

The ovaries produce two major hormones, the estrogen estradiol, and progesterone. During a woman's monthly cycle, the levels of the two hormones rise and fall in counterpoint; estradiol peaks sharply just before ovulation, falls, then rises more gradually after ovulation. Progesterone is absent in the two weeks before ovulation then surges just after ovulation. The breast responds to these hormonal changes. Before ovulation (the follicular phase), cells in the breast proliferate, but cell division appears to be even greater in the second (luteal) phase, when both hormones are in good supply.

The frenzy of being female begins when the pituitary gland stimulates the ovaries to produce estrogen: breasts appear and the young woman starts to menstruate. The body actually makes three forms of estrogen of which estradiol, secreted by the ovaries, is the most potent, and the most plentiful during the woman's reproductive years. The placenta and the outer covering of the adrenal glands also produce some estradiol, as do the male testes. The other estrogens are called estrone and estriol.

The connection between breast cancer and the reproductive system was made in the late 19th century. Experiments to remove women's ovaries began once anaesthetics and antisepsis made internal surgery practical. Removing the ovaries of breast cancer patients after a mastectomy became routine, although no one understood why an ovariectomy (also called an "oophorectomy" or "female castration") caused remissions or even tumour regression. Just as significant, in about half the cases, the operation failed to stop tumour growth. It was found that removing the ovaries of premenopausal women not only helped some women with breast cancer, the operation lowered the risk of breast cancer in women who did not have the disease. A woman in her 30s who has her ovaries removed has only one-fourth the usual chance of getting breast cancer. The effect is less dramatic for women who lose their ovaries in their 40s, but is still significant.[6]

As a breast cancer treatment, oophorectomy fell into disfavour in the 1960s. The results were deemed too unpredictable. A randomized clinical trial, begun by Bernard Fisher's group in 1961, ended the routine use of oophorectomy at first diagnosis in the United States. After three years, the trial showed that women who had their ovaries removed after breast surgery showed no advantage in recurrence or mortality over those who had only breast surgery. For advanced cancer, however, Fisher said "the worth of oophorectomy ... cannot be denied." The operation gives a remission rate of 25 to 30 percent to premenopausal women who experience a recurrence.[7]

The erratic effects of the oophorectomy and other hormonal manipulations suggested that some breast cancers were hormone dependant and some were not. A test called the Estrogen Receptor Assay (ERA), measures the number of estrogen-receptor molecules in the tissue of a breast tumour. The ERA, which came into experimental use in the early 1970s, classifies breast tumours at diagnosis as estrogen dependent (ER+) or estrogen independent (ER-). If a tumour has many receptors, estrogen will readily attach to the cancer and feed it. An ER- tumour has its own blood supply and grows without estrogen.[8] The ER- cancers are also more virulent, and are more common in premenopausal women.

Whether this means there are actually two types of tumours, or whether all tumours begin as ER+ and eventually develop to be ER-, is a hotly debated question. Evidence accumulated, however, that all breast cancers eventually become independent of estrogen. This conclusion came in part from animal experiments, in part from the discovery that even women with breast cancer who had their ovaries removed eventually recurred, with the tumour growing at the same rate as those whose ovaries were still functioning. This evidence that hormonal disruption only has a temporary effect further undermined the oophorectomy as a breast cancer treatment. Some researchers, however, continued to investigate the hormonal connection.

Even as one group of scientists puzzled over the connection between estrogen and breast cancer, others took the discovery of the female hormone in the opposite direction. They learned how to produce synthetic estrogen or "exogenous" hormones and thereby manipulate the hormones of healthy women. A frenzy of another sort began.

In 1929, estrone isolated from the urine of pregnant women became the first estrogen to be crystalized in a laboratory.[9] Within a few years, a dozen brands of estrogen injections were on the market, designed to assist women through menopause — which had already been pegged by the medical profession as "a physiological condition bordering on the pathological."[10] Menopause was just the first of many female conditions that ingenious researchers believed could be corrected by a dose of prescribed hormones. In her book *Estrogen and Breast Cancer: A Warning to Women*, medical journalist Carol Ann Rinzler writes, "The availability of purified estrogen, followed by the isolation of progesterone in 1934 and the male hormone in 1935, made it temptingly possible to manipulate a woman's hormonal balance."[11] The temptation became even greater with the discovery, in 1938, that synthetic estrogen could be made in an easily administered pill form.

In 1937, researchers at Pennsylvania State Univerity had discovered the contraceptive potential of ovarian hormones. In lab tests using rabbits, they found that natural estrogen and natural progesterone both suppressed the release of an egg from the ovary. Scientists dubbed the hormone "nature's contraceptive."[12] In the early 1950s, Boston professor of gynaecology John Rock began testing the efficacy of the same natural hormones for the opposite purpose, as fertility drugs in women. He found that the hormones inhibited ovulation but that some of his volunteers got pregnant after they stopped taking them; he concluded the pills had primed the reproductive pump.

Margaret Sanger, the founder of Planned Parenthood, was another key figure in the drive to manipulate women's hormones. Sanger was looking for a switch to turn off world overpopulation. She believed that a once-a-day pill was the elegant answer that would appeal to women in both the wealthy West and the under-developed world. In 1951 Sanger met with two Massachusetts biologists who were "working furiously" to create a chemical contraceptive.[13] She gave them seed funds for their research, as did another wealthy birth control pioneer, Katherine McCormick. The biologists came up with a pill made of progestins, which had been shown in animal studies to suppress ovulation.

By the end of the 1960s, millions of healthy American women were taking estrogen-based medications; the rate of breast cancer was also rising. Some breast cancer researchers worried that the two trends were linked. At the first National Conference on Breast Cancer in 1969, Harvard researchers Brian MacMahon and Philip Cole called the indirect evidence of estrogen's carcinogenicity "overwhelming."

No evidence linked the Pill directly to the rise in breast cancer, but human drug tests in the United States were geared to study short-term adverse effects. Roy Hertz of the National Institutes of Health (NIH) had tested a progestin-only Pill as early as 1952; he watched with concern as the combination estrogen/progestin Pill went to market in the 1960s. The absence of data linking the Pill to a rise in breast cancer offered no reassurance, he argued. Cancers from exposures to such carcinogens as X-rays, benzene, coal tar and radioactive paints take up to two decades to appear in statistics. What was known about estrogen and breast cancer in 1969, Hertz said, was analogous to what had been known about cigarettes and lung cancer before epidemiological data confirmed the causal link.

John Bailar, a statistician at the National Cancer Institute (NCI), concurred. "In my opinion," he wrote in a review of papers presented at the 1969 breast cancer conference, "there is no sound basis for assuring any woman that any dose of any estrogen, given for any reason, is safe."[14]

For the benefit of his audience at the debate with Adriane Fugh-Berman, Richard Margolese traces the progress of the research into tamoxifen.

Testing the drug's effect on breast cancer began in the early 1970s. Bernard Fisher's influential research group based in Pittsburgh conducted several large trials. The researchers theorized that tamoxifen could disrupt the symbiosis of estrogen in ER+ tumours by interfering with the protein synthesis. By this time, many had turned to cytotoxic drugs (chemotherapy) as the hope for breast cancer treatment. Others, however, still believed the promise for effective remedies lay in anti-hormonal remedies. The chief candidate was tamoxifen, a synthetic hormone with a structure similar to that of estrogen. Tamoxifen competes with estrogen for space in the tumour tissue and is often referred to as an estrogen-blocker.

"The first clinical trials were in advanced disease," recalls Margolese, who was a member of Fisher's research team. "We found there was a benefit." Next, they tested the drug in an adjuvant trial, that is, after breast cancer surgery, on women whose cancer was judged likely to recur or spread. "We took people with a poor prognosis and gave them tamoxifen in addition to other therapies like surgery, chemotherapy and so on. We found out that tamoxifen did help prevent some recurrence, and it helped prevent the spread of cancer." Encouraged by these results, researchers tested the drug on women with a good prognosis — for example, those with negative nodes. Again, those given tamoxifen had fewer recurrences than the women who did not take the drug. In particular, they were less likely to develop a cancer in the opposite breast.

Of seven trials around the world that have given tamoxifen to women with early stage breast cancer, all have found that the drug decreases the rate of cancers in the opposite breast from between 30 to 50 percent.[15] The difference is "not earth shattering, not dramatic," Margolese concedes. "But while we would like to have big gains, we are always content with gains, even if they are smaller."[16]

As tamoxifen gained credibility, Rose Kushner observed the emergence of two camps: those who favoured hormonal therapy for some patients, and cytotoxic drug advocates. She witnessed one head-to-head conflict at a conference in 1979. Among those promoting a shift to the hormonal or endocrine approach were William McGuire of Texas and her own physician, Thomas Dao. They argued that postmenopausal women with ER+ tumours should be given only tamoxifen as adjuvant therapy. The cytotoxic group pushed for adjuvant cell-killing therapy for all women, regardless of the tumour type. They downplayed the role of hormones and insisted the only difference between women with ER+ and ER- tumours was that the ER+ tumours were less aggressive.[17]

That round went to the proponents of cytotoxic drugs and combinations of cytotoxic drugs became routine. Physicians in the hormonal camp pursued a minority course, using the woman's estrogen-receptor status to determine her treatment. Premenopausal patients with ER+ tumours might have an ovariectomy, while postmenopausal women were treated with tamoxifen, an adrenalectomy, or both.[18] In 1981, Bernard Fisher's group published the two-year follow-up of a trial designed to evaluate tamoxifen as an adjuvant in women with positive nodes. Women given both chemotherapy and tamoxifen fared better than those given chemotherapy alone. The two-year results showed that adding tamoxifen particularly benefited one group of women: those over 50 who had ER+ tumours. Women younger than 50 did not benefit from tamoxifen.[19]

Kushner welcomed the study. The prestige and clout of Fisher's group, she believed, would reverse the trend of using toxic chemotherapy on women regardless of tumour type. She envisioned a future where treatments would be based on estrogen's role in breast cancer — where women with estrogen-dependent tumours would be treated differently than those who were ER-, and where post-menopausal women would have different treatments than those who were still menstruating.[20] Tests for estrogen-receptor status were becoming routine. "Progress is coming with the speed of light," Kushner wrote, optimistically. "When there is money to be made, changes come quickly."[21]

Although intuition told her that hormonal manipulation made sense as a breast cancer treatment, Rose Kushner had two concerns. She worried the tamoxifen pendulum might swing too far: that the drugs' champions would add it to all adjuvant treatments, regardless of the woman's age and estrogen-receptor status. This would be useless and expensive for women with ER- tumours, who would gain nothing from tamoxifen.[22] Her second concern was that there would be increasing, uncontrolled use of exogenous hormones in healthy women. Both concerns have proven to be prophetic.

Changes have come quickly, but progress — if it is measured in benefits to women — has not. By 1992, enough research had been conducted around the world to put both cytotoxic and anti-hormonal treatments in perspective. The British journal the *Lancet* summarized the results of 133 clinical trials involving 75,000 women given different kinds of adjuvant treatment for breast cancer. The anti-hormone treatment emerged the clear winner in women over 50. Regardless of how advanced the disease was, and even (surprisingly) whether the tumour tested ER+ or ER-, the treatments definitely increased the number of women who survived five years (about six more survivors out of every 100), with a more noticeable gain after 10 years (about 12 out of 100). Still, the majority of women on tamoxifen did not live longer. The cell-killing drugs showed a benefit only for women who had not yet had menopause, and was clearest for those with positive nodes. These results paralleled the benefits of removing the ovaries. The tables had turned. Proponents of cytotoxic treatments were on the defensive.

Compared to cell-kill cancer treatments, tamoxifen "looks like a vitamin," asserts Adriane Fugh-Berman, "but that's not to say it's a benign drug." Among the effects which are immediate and unpleasant, but not life-threatening, are menopausal symptoms such as hot flashes, depression and vaginal discharge or dryness. More worrisome are the carcinogenic effects, which include an increased rate of endometrial cancer, blood clots (more pronounced when tamoxifen is combined with chemotherapy), and vision problems. Researchers in Greece found that, among 63 people taking tamoxifen for either breast cancer or pancreatic cancer, many lost visual acuity and experienced retinal yellow dots. One showed corneal opacities. Most of the eye problems occurred after one year and were reversed when treatment ceased.[23]

Evidence of tamoxifen's long-term toxicity is sparse. Few women taking tamoxifen for breast cancer have been followed in clinical trials for more than five years, and researchers have not pursued the serious effects with great vigour. An example is liver cancer. "Tamoxifen is highly carcinogenic in the rat liver and causes hepatic changes in all species tested," notes Fugh-Berman. The changes are sudden. "Livers appeared normal until late in the rat's lifespan, at which point highly aggressive tumours developed." In humans, cancer of the liver can take up to 20 years to develop. Two cases of liver cancer were documented in a clinical trial in Sweden, but Fugh-Berman views this as a minimal figure. When women with breast cancer develop liver masses, these are usually assumed to be metastases and so are not routinely biopsied.[24]

Oncology's love affair with tamoxifen frustrates those women with breast cancer who do experience serious complications. Jan Morrow of Kelowna B.C. was hospitalized with a blood clot shortly after she went on tamoxifen and narrowly missed having her leg amputated. She is an avid swimmer and an oncologist told her afterwards that her swimming may have raised her risk of clotting from tamoxifen. A Montreal woman who experienced a stroke while on the drug was astonished when her oncologist assumed she would resume taking tamoxifen as soon as she came out of the hospital.

Although such serious complications are relatively uncommon and don't negate the benefits for node-positive postmenopausal women as a group, a dogmatic pro-tamoxifen stance patronizes women. A doctor prescribing tamoxifen should be aware that certain profiles have increased risk of complications, and patients should be told of these risks. Diabetes, obesity and endometrial abnormalities, for example, are known to increase the risk of endometrial cancer for women on tamoxifen.[25] Women who experience frightening effects need to know that they are not unusual and that going off tamoxifen is probably not a suicidal decision. Many women would welcome more research into profiles that increase risk.

Tamoxifen's enthusiasts use the same numbers argument as proponents of cytotoxic chemotherapy: give the drug to thousands and hundreds will benefit; give it to hundreds of thousands and thousands will live longer. These projections don't factor in the dismay of women who embark hopefully on a course of tamoxifen only to have recurrences. Indeed, all patients eventually become resistant to tamoxifen.

Paradoxically, during the two decades that tamoxifen gained dominance as a breast cancer treatment that works by blocking endogenous estrogen, Rose Kushner's second concern about the use of hormones came true: exogenous estrogens were increasingly prescribed to healthy women. She was appalled by the insouciant attitude of health watchdogs to this boom. Back in 1974, breast cancer was on the rise and so was use of the Pill.

She raised the subject with a Food and Drug Administration official, who snapped, "We have no evidence at all of a cancer risk with oral contraceptives."[26] Given what was known about the importance of estrogen to the development of breast cancer, Kushner thought that package inserts provided to patients should include a warning, especially to women with breast cancer or a family history of breast cancer. Obstetricians and gynaecologists, she discovered, were given a booklet with a long list of potential complications, from dizziness to epilepsy, and a warning against giving the Pill to women with breast cancer. Women were given no such information. Kushner was outraged.

Determined to know why the vital information was missing from the labels, where all women could read it, she tracked down bureaucrats at cancer registries and contacted researchers who had gathered figures on Pill use and and breast cancer. Despite studies that showed alarming numbers of breast cancer cases in women under 30 who took the Pill, everyone denied that the figures gave any cause for worry and no one seemed keen to follow up suspicious trends. Yet every breast cancer researcher she spoke to was certain, from the results of animal studies, that adding female hormones to a woman's body — especially a young woman's — was dangerous.

Kushner finally discovered an entry in the *Federal Register* for 1970; it was the explanation she sought. The text stated that organized medicine, speaking through various medical associations, opposed having a label on oral contraceptives to warn women of the risks, because package inserts would "confuse the patient" and "interfere with the physician-patient relationship." In short, doctors wanted to retain their power over patients. Kushner wanted the opposite — to give women the power to make their own decisions.

With this evidence that the FDA was looking after the drug companies and the doctors at the expense of women's health, Kushner pushed for a congressional hearing into oral contraceptive use and breast cancer. When her efforts failed, she filed a private suit against both the FDA and the Department of Health, Education and Welfare. Several years later, in 1978, she won a partial victory — a federal court ruled that all brands of oral contraceptives on the market should warn women with breast cancer not to take the Pill. Kushner had asked for more: that women with a family history of breast cancer be advised against taking oral contraceptives. This was not granted.

A congressional consultant told Kushner that the FDA had trouble dealing with the Pill because the agency was just too "business-oriented" to block the progress of a major money-making product. The problem wasn't chicanery or bribery, he told her, but "they have a business outlook in salvaging a product and making it work out."

The weight of the evidence now supports what Kushner's sources suspected 20 years ago: risk is increased when oral contraceptives are taken at an early age or for prolonged periods. In her 1993 book on estrogen and breast cancer, medical writer Carol Ann Rinzler elaborates on the medical establishment's protection of the Pill. Besides reflecting a business outlook, the pro-Pill bias matches the ideology of the contraceptive establishment. This powerful network is mostly liberal, mostly white, mostly upper-middle class — and well connected to health policy leaders. Physician Elizabeth Connell, for example, who wrote *The Menopause Book*, advised the FDA on the safety of estrogens, worked at the Rockefeller Foundation, chaired the national medical committee of Planned Parenthood World Population, and consulted for oral contraceptive manufacturers such as Ortho and Searle. The pharmaceutical companies, while they had a huge financial stake in promoting their product, also viewed themselves as humanitarians. Searle chairman John G. Searle described the company's contraceptive Enovid as "a positive answer to a world threatened by overpopulation, and the resulting poor subsistence, poor shelter and poor education that surplus people are forced to endure."[27] The American Cancer Society (ACS) is part of this network as well, says Rinzler, having among its benefactors John D. Rockefeller and many prominent physicians from the American Medical Association. Members of this influential community "had a philosophical and intellectual stake in defending oral contraceptives."

From the first trials of the Pill, carried out by Searle in Peurto Rico, researchers downplayed evidence of noxious effects. Nearly 20 percent of the women reported dizziness, stomach pain, headaches, diarrhea and stomach upset, either singly or in combination, but these complaints were put down to suggestibility. Although three women in the Peurto Rican trials died, the scientists did not ask for autopsies. The FDA didn't take the reports of side effects seriously either, until the product hit the market and reports of blood clots among Pill-users, some of them fatal, forced the issue.

In 1981, California biostatistician Malcolm Pike began to cut through the thicket of contradictory studies about the Pill. Since an early first full-term pregnancy reduces a woman's risk of getting breast cancer, he reasoned that the adolescent and early adult years might be a crucial time for establishing breast cancer risk. He hypothesized that the Pill triggers early breast cancers, which are relatively rare. He studied two populations of breast cancer patients who were under 35 at the time of their diagnosis. Both studies supported his theory. A single year on the Pill boosted a young woman's risk of early-onset breast cancer by 30 percent; eight years nearly quadrupled it.

Pike's findings were provocative but his sample sizes were small. In the late 1980s, however, a rush of new studies resuscitated Pike's hypothesis. The first two were large investigations done in Denmark and New Zealand. They confirmed that prolonged Pill use in young women increased the risk of breast cancer. Researchers then took yet another look at the American data and found that indeed, for a specific group of women, the Pill did increase the risk of early-onset breast cancer. The group comprised childless women who began to menstruate before age 13, began taking birth control pills before age 20 and stayed on the Pill more than eight years. In 1991, a meta-analysis compared the result of 29 previous studies. The analysts concluded that young women who use birth control pills for 10 years or more run an increased risk of early-onset breast cancer of 50 percent.

Links have also been established between estrogen replacement therapies (ERT) and cancer. When it was first introduced in the 1940s, estrogen replacement was prescribed for short-term use, to relieve menopausal symptoms. Unlike the birth control Pill, estrogen replacement was made from the urine of mares, a less potent formula known as conjugated estrogen. The first sign that ERT might be trouble was not with breast cancer but with endometrial cancer. A few cases in postmenopausal women on ERT were reported as early as 1966; evidence gradually accumulated that giving estrogen to postmenopausal women increased their risk of endometrial cancer — dramatically if the use was long-term. A study by Kaiser-Permanent Medical Center, for example, showed a 14-fold increase in the incidence of endometrial cancer among postmenopausal women who had taken ERT for seven years or more. The explanation seemed to be that estrogen, unopposed by progesterone, causes endometrial cells to proliferate. Far from being an aberration, this process is normal in the first two weeks of the menstrual cycle. Estrogen surges from the ovaries, stimulates cell-proliferation in the womb and creates a hospitable environment for a fertilized egg. After ovulation, the estrogen is opposed by progesterone, which triggers the thick accumulation of cells to shed — the menstrual period.

Harvard-trained epidemiologist Robert Hoover suspected early on that ERT might increase the risk of breast cancer, because of the evidence that breast cancer was a hormonal disease. A colleague who was very committed to ERT invited Hoover to study the records of his patients, women to whom he had prescribed conjugated estrogens between 1939 and 1972. Hoover jumped at the chance. The result, published in 1976, was the first epidemiological study to show an increased breast cancer risk from ERT. Hoover found that the increase in risk was related to both dosage and the length of time the woman took the hormones. These relationships have since been confirmed by eight solid studies. Other factors that increase risk are a family history of breast cancer and taking estrogen during, rather than after, menopause.

A meta-analysis of 19 studies, published in April 1991, concluded that ERT is a risk for breast cancer. The researchers placed the increase at 30 percent above normal after 15 years of use. With about 3.5 million American women now taking estrogen replacement therapy, the authors estimate that ERT caused 4,708 cases of breast cancer annually in the U.S. and about 1,468 of the 48,000 annual breast cancer deaths. Most American physicians now prescribe progestins along with estrogen for postmenopausal women who have not had a hysterectomy, a regimen referred to as hormone replacement therapy (HRT). Unfortunately this regimen, while it lowers the risk of endometrial cancer, may raise the risk of breast cancer.

The medical community remains subdued about exogenous hormones and breast cancer. In 1993, the ACS still did not include estrogens on its list of risk factors for the disease. In her book *Estrogen and Breast Cancer: A Warning to Women*, Carol Ann Rinzler points to a double standard. When a study of nurses in the Boston area showed a 30 percent elevation in the risk of breast cancer among women who consumed more than three drinks of alcohol a week, alcohol was declared a risk factor for breast cancer and the finding received wide press coverage. Leading researchers acknowledge that comparable data show ERT increases a woman's risk, but declare this level of risk tolerable.

The medical community deems ERT beneficial to women, while viewing alcohol as harmful. This defense of ERT rests on the assumption that ERT has real medical benefits — that the supplements protect against osteoporosis and heart disease, in addition to giving relief from menopausal symptoms and age-related cosmetic changes like dry skin. Most of the medical claims made for ERT are exaggerated, an expert advisory group of the U.S. National Institutes of Health reported. The drug is effective against osteoporosis for only a few years, for example. Furthermore, the National Women's Health Network argues that ERT promoters have convinced women that osteoporosis is the inevitable result of aging when in fact only 25 percent of postmenopausal women suffer from it. A package insert added in 1979, belatedly and only after considerable consumer pressure, notes a host of counter-indications for ERT, including a history of cancer, breast cysts, blood clots, and kidney, liver or heart disease.

Medical authorities are equally reluctant to declare the Pill a breast cancer risk factor or to pass on this judgement call to women. They stress the contradictory findings, or call oral contraceptives a "controversial" risk factor. Another obfuscation is to trade the risk of breast cancer off against the lowered risk of ovarian and endometrial cancer.[28] A report on the Pill issued by the Alan Guttmacher Institute in 1991, takes this tack. An off-shoot of Planned Parenthood, the Guttmacher Institute is an agency for research, education and policy development. Its report gave figures to support the argument that women who take the Pill have a lower incidence of reproductive cancers. True, says Carol Ann Rinzler, but an analysis that combines the risk of breast cancer, ovarian cancer and cancer of the uterus does not give a true picture of cancer risks. When the data for breast cancer is separated from the other two cancers, the figures show an excess of breast cancer cases among long-term pill users from age 25 to 44. Combining these figures with industry data on the numbers of women in the U.S. who take the Pill in these age categories, she estimates that at least 457 cases of breast cancer attributable to the Pill occur every year among American women younger than 45. "Now," says Rinzler, "even those who most vigorously defended the Pill have offered up proof of its dangers."

In the crowded auditorium, the debate centres once again on the prevention of breast cancer.

By 1992, tamoxifen use had been pushed even further than Rose Kushner had anticipated — into the population of women who do not have cancer. Those, like Richard Margolese, who believe tamoxifen is a reasonable breast cancer preventative hint that the drug may have other health benefits. "Not every side effect is a bad side effect," he comments as he points to some numbers on a slide. "Here you see the benefits on heart disease and the benefits on osteoporosis, which we suspect may be true."

Adriane Fugh-Berman catches him out. "This drug would never be approved to help bone loss or cardiovascular disease." She agrees that tamoxifen often lowers total cholesterol levels and that some studies — but only three out of eight — found an effect on bone loss. On close inspection, though, the findings offer scant hope that tamoxifen will alleviate those health woes.

"In women," explains Fugh-Berman, "the 'good' cholesterol (HDL or high density lippoproteins) seems more important in preventing cardiovascular disease than total cholesterol.

Tamoxifen has variable effects on HDL levels. In some studies, it seems to raise it, in others lower it, and in others it doesn't seem to make any difference." Only one study found a decrease in cardiovascular disease rates among women taking tamoxifen; since the comparison groups were not evaluated for risk factors such as smoking and high blood pressure, the results are unconvincing. In the three studies where tamoxifen affected bone loss, the effect was minimal. More significantly, no study has shown a decrease in fracture rates with tamoxifen, nor is there any reason for such a benefit to exist.

"I think we really need to look at methods of preventing disease that are health promoting, or at the very least non-toxic," says Fugh-Berman. "If you look at the side effects of a low fat diet, you also decrease your risk of cardiovascular disease, you reduce your risk of gall bladder and colon cancer, as well as some other cancers and obesity. All of the side effects are good. Tamoxifen just isn't in the same ball park."

Richard Margolese agrees fat is a problem, but he views changes in diet and other behaviours as complex and hard to achieve. "How many women in this room have eaten a doughnut, a pastry, a dessert with whipped cream, have put butter on toast or salad dressing on their salad in the past month?"[29] We need more research, he argues, to find out why dietary fat does not consistently correlate with breast cancer, and to find out how to encourage people to change their behaviour. This will take time. Meanwhile, "tamoxifen is now."

Margolese's reasoning is common among physicians: medication is a simple and immediate solution, while behavioural changes take longer to bring about. Physicians also describe widely used medications as so vital to our lives that they are an integral part of the culture. This rationale appears in an important review of breast cancer published in the *New England Journal of Medicine* in the summer of 1992. On the one hand, the authors say the use of oral contraceptives "appears to increase the risk of breast cancer by about 50 percent," while the use of postmenopausal estrogen "appears to increase the risk of breast cancer by about 40 percent ... Combining progesterone with estrogen replacement, which reduces the risk of endometrial cancer, does not appear to decrease the incidence of breast cancer, and may add to it." Here are two modifiable behaviours that could reduce breast cancer deaths in North America by several thousand women annually. Yet the same article plaintively concludes that "risk factors whose modification would be culturally acceptable have not been established, although efforts to identify them continue."[30]

The Pill and HRT, this argument goes, are part of a lifestyle that North American women voluntarily embrace. Yet health watchdog agencies steadfastly refuse to give women the information that would allow us to make a free choice. In January 1989, with mounting research evidence implicating the Pill in breast cancer, health activist groups carried on Rose Kushner's fight. They asked the FDA to add information to package inserts advising women about the potential risk of long-term use of oral contraceptives. The agency declined.

Encouraging judicious Pill and HRT use might reduce deaths by breast cancer by as much as three percent. But most of the hormones a woman are exposed to are produced by her own body. While the "frenzied" behaviour of endogenous hormones is usually thought of as beyond our control — except by medication — recent research has turned up leads on how women might lower the body's estrogen levels.

Endogenous estradiol levels vary across cultures. Asian women living a traditional lifestyle have estradiol levels 20 to 40 percent lower than western women and breast cancer rates that are four- to six-fold lower. Again, dietary habits are a possible explanatory factor, although this link has not been shown. Plant-derived estrogen found in soybeans, and some yams, may cut the body's own production of estrogen, says Fugh-Berman.

Reduced fat consumption is often proposed as a means of preventing breast cancer and it may also reduce the risk of a recurrence. A Swedish study found that women with ER+ breast cancer had fewer recurrences and lived longer if their diet was low- rather than high-fat.[31] Diet may also affect the onset (and cessation) of the menses. Age at first menstrual period is one of the breast cancer risk factors that varies across cultures. In wealthy countries like Britain, Canada and the U.S., which are world leaders in breast cancer, girls begin to menstruate, on average, at about age 12. In other countries, the average age at puberty can be as late as 17. A century ago, however, women in western countries began puberty at 17. Seattle epidemiologist Maureen

Henderson notes, "We have hardly studied the reasons that girls in North America mature so rapidly."[32]

"Most researchers don't believe in behavioural change," she adds. "Scientists prefer medical interventions." Henderson was involved in designing the large prospective study that will look at the effect of dietary fat intake on breast cancer. While the study was approved in 1992 by the National Institutes of Health, earlier proposals were repeatedly turned down over a period of 10 years.

Since the countries with the highest breast cancer levels also feature diets high in dairy foods and meat, a high-protein diet based on meat and dairy products has been postulated as the basis for cross-cultural variations in breast cancer. Dietary information that would lessen our consumption of these food products meets industry resistance, however. In 1992, new guidelines recommending low-fat dairy foods, fewer servings of meat and eggs and a reduced number of milk servings for teenagers were proposed for Canada's Food Guide. After complaints from the Beef Information Centre, the Dairy Farmers of Canada and the egg industry, the recommendations were reversed or modified.

Exercise is another modifiable behaviour that may affect the balance of hormones and breast cancer risk. "Physical exercise in pre-teen girls can actually delay menarch (onset of menstruation) and it's safe," says Fugh-Berman. Exercise has been proposed as a benign strategy to reduce breast cancer, on the theory that the number of menstrual cycles a woman has in her lifetime indeed affects her breast cancer risk. Several retrospective studies have in fact shown that women who were athletic during their teen years have a lower incidence of breast cancer.

Conversely, exposure to toxic chemicals such as DDT and dioxin, which have been introduced into the environment since 1940, may stimulate the body's production of estrogen. In early 1994, this theory was attracting enough attention to merit feature stories in science magazines and the popular press. Wildlife studies point to the feminization of a wide variety of species exposed to high levels of man-made chemicals that mimic the action of estrogen. Male alligators in a chemically contaminated Florida lake have abnormally small penises and are failing to reproduce. The Florida panther is also not reproducing, a longstanding mystery that now appears attributable to abnormalities in the male such as sterility, undescended testicles and deformed sperm. Male gulls on Santa Barbara Island are few in number and many are sterile, while the female gulls share nests and lay more than the usual number of eggs. Michael Fry, the toxicologist who discovered these unusual nesting patterns in the 1970s, concluded that the male gulls had been "chemically castrated" by DDT and other environmental pollutants and that their growing indifference to sex was one reason for the "lesbian gulls." Fry has recently observed similar nesting patterns among terns near a PCB-contaminated waste site in Massachusetts.[33]

In humans, too, there has been a rise in endocrine-related abnormalities. These include a 42 percent drop in sperm count in men between 1940 and 1990, an apparent increase in undescended testicles and urethral abnormalities in newborn males, and small penises in adolescent Taiwanese boys whose mothers unwittingly consumed PCB-contaminated rice oil in 1979. Endocrinologists view the effects of DES on women who took the drug as the model for problems that other synthetic estrogens might cause in humans. The rare vaginal cancers found in DES daughters are only the first of many abnormalities now documented. Others include structural deformities in the uteri that tend to make the women sterile and, in sons, undescended testicles, abnormalities of the scrotum, decreased sperm counts, malformed urethras and possible increased risk of testicular cancer. All the research on disrupted endocrine systems suggests that prebirth exposure is the most damaging. Lovell Jones of M.D. Anderson Cancer Centre told *Chemical and Engineering News*, "We are just beginning to realize the additional problems that the offspring of the women who took DES face."[34]

The evidence for chemically induced endocrine disruptions in both animals and humans lends credence to the theory that these same chemicals may contribute to the rise in breast cancer. At the same time, the new interest in estrogen has attracted attention to the cancer-fighting potential of naturally occurring estrogens in plants called phytoestrogens. Cincinnati researcher Kenneth Setchell gave rodents a chemical that induces mammary tumours and found that those on a diet of soy developed significantly fewer tumours than those on a soy-free diet. "Soy protein could be potentially equally effective as tamoxifen in preventing breast cancer," says Setchell.

Until the cultural and environmental determinants of endogenous estrogen levels are vigorously explored, they can't be dismissed as unmodifiable. The view often expressed in the medical profession, however, is that people can't or won't change their behaviour, while medication is a sure way to produce change quickly. Yet taking medication is a behaviour which pharmaceutical companies and physicians clearly understand to be amenable to change.

Meanwhile, of the hormone manipulation strategies proposed to prevent or control the spread of breast cancer, tamoxifen is just the first out of the gate. In the developmental stage are hormonal drugs to suspend ovarian function, to promote the changes in the breast cells that occur at pregnancy, and to control the menstrual cycle throughout all or part of the woman's premenopausal life.

Medicine's answer to the ovariectomy is a drug that simulates surgical removal of the ovaries. Ovarian function is controlled in part by a hormone secreted by the hypothalmus, called LH-RH. Drugs that hold the stimulating hormone in check are called LH-RH agonists. They have been used to treat endometriosis and metastatic prostate cancer and are now being tested as a breast cancer treatment. Women are given either the drug or a surgical oophorectomy. The drug treatment is reversible, a big advantage over the surgical intervention, says researcher Nancy Davidson of Johns Hopkins University. "One could effect an oophorectomy for some period of time, stop the drug and then the woman would be premenopausal again."[35]

Another hormonal intervention is the pseudopregnancy. The rationale is that an early, first full-term pregnancy protects against the development of breast cancer. A research team led by J. Russo proposes that this is because the proliferating cell pool in breast tissue decreases with a full-term pregnancy and terminal end bud cells in the lactation tree become more differentiated. Based on this theory, Russo and colleagues have come up with a hormone to simulate these changes. The hoped-for effect is to provide women who take the drug the protection achieved by a real pregnancy.[36]

An even more ambitious designer hormone has been developed at the University of Southern California, by Malcolm

Pike — the same researcher who found the estrogen-breast cancer link in young women — and his colleague Darcy Spicer.

Pike and Spicer developed a drug which they present as a disease-inhibiting contraceptive. It works by creating an "ideal" ovarian hormone profile. They are now testing it in a study using 21 women with a high-risk-of-breast-cancer familial profile. Fourteen of the women are on the drug. If it works according to plan, the hormonal injection will control fertility, breast cancer, endometrial cancer, bone loss, cardiovascular disease and menopausal symptoms caused by lowered postmenopausal estrogen levels. As if that's not enough, Spicer says the 14 women on the experimental drug feel better than the seven on placebo because the regimen eliminates symptoms associated with premenstrual syndrome. He also predicts that the breasts of a woman who uses the drug continuously for 10 years will always remain 10 years younger.[37]

The theory behind the formula is that breast cancer can be reduced by cutting back on the levels of progesterone and estrogen in the luteal phase of the menstrual cycle — the period when breast cell proliferation peaks. The injection administers about one-third of the estrogen dose of oral contraceptives, which Pike and Spicer believe is sufficient to hold a variety of female ills in check: loss of calcium from bone, symptoms of estrogen deficiency (e.g., hot flashes), cardiovascular disease, and abnormal effects on cholesterol. A complication is that while breast cells proliferate most when estrogen and progesterone are present in the system together, endometrial cells multiply under contrary conditions — when estrogen is unopposed by progesterone. If progesterone were removed from the formula altogether, the cost might be a rise in endometrial cancer. Pike and Spicer's solution is to administer progestin for approximately two weeks, but only every four months. To keep nature from throwing things out of whack, the formula blocks normal ovarian function, using the same LH-RH agonists that are being tested as a pharmaceutical oophorectomy.

An accepted principle of medicine is that any drug potent enough to have a desired effect will have unwanted side effects. Pike and Spicer have already discovered that women on their experimental drug lost two percent of their bone per year. Their answer is to add testosterone, a déjà vu strategy.[38] When the pioneers of ERT tried to counteract the effects of estrogen with the male hormone, they found even small amounts produced distressing masculinizing effects.

After the debate between Margolese and Fugh-Berman, a group of us exchange impressions. We all agree they were evenly matched as debaters: both defended their views with eloquence and passion. We are divided, however, in who we support.

"She blew it with that remark about the number of ovulations," says one woman. "She lost her cool."

"I disagree," says another. "This is an emotional subject. I liked the fact that she wasn't afraid to show her feelings. Why should we pretend these ideas don't upset us?"

"But I don't see anything wrong with the study. Taking tamoxifen is better than dying of breast cancer. We don't have any answers, so how can we oppose something that might work?"

The debate reinforces my gut level response to hormonal intervention, and helps me understand it. For me, the essence of the disagreement over tamoxifen is about control, not about whether an intervention is "natural" or not. Hormonal intervention strategies reinforce the control of medical professionals and pharmaceutical companies. A daily regimen of preventive medication hooks women into the medical system as permanent dependants. Such dependence should be a last resort, not a starting point.

I don't romanticize the "natural woman," whose life was an endless round of childbearing. She may have had a low risk of breast cancer, but she was in bondage to her physiology and to the sexual demands of her male partner. Hormonal medications shift our bondage to the medical profession.

In a narrow sense, proponents of the prevention trial are right — we cannot know with certainty the outcome of the trial without doing it. We can, however, predict the drug's likely utility, based on what we know of its history and the history of drug interventions in general. "World wide," says Fugh-Berman, "the most important public health measure in history has been clean water, a risk-free, low-tech intervention which does not require individual treatment and protects against a variety of diseases. In cancer prevention, the ideal is avoiding carcinogens."

For those of us with cancer, a romantic view of medicine is particularly seductive. Our fear and sense of urgency about the disease enhances the appeal of technological quick fixes. Our own experience with cancer treatments, however, can be the antidote to these nostalgic dreams. Many women who have taken tamoxifen have been forced to recognize that this is not a miracle cure for breast cancer. As a treatment drug, tamoxifen represents, as Margolese acknowledges, a "small gain." Why would its potential be other than small for women who don't have breast cancer?

Listening to Richard Margolese, I am struck by his sincerity and his frustration that many of us in the audience oppose using tamoxifen as a preventive. Ironically, within the context of breast cancer treatments, the hormonal camp played a progressive role by resisting the tide to cell-kill approaches. Tamoxifen's advocates envisioned treatments that would fight the disease more effectively and wreak less havoc on the woman's general health. Their tenacity benefited women with breast cancer.

I believe research that can help us understand how female hormones work will follow a different model than research geared to developing hormonal medications. We know from the human experiments of the past 50 years that various hormones act in concert to perform a myriad of functions. "The brain must intend the body to have a correct balance of all the hormones," Thomas Dao told Rose Kushner, when she asked him to explain the role of hormones in breast cancer. "We don't know exactly what 'correct' is." Given the extent of human variability, product-oriented drug research is unlikely to lead us towards this correct balance. Market economics don't work that way. "You can't treat every woman with the same drug," says pharmacist Saul Cape. But as soon as a pharmaceutical company finds a product that helps a few people, he asserts, "they assume that it will save the entire world."

Another impediment to useful research is the ingrained view that female hormonal activity is frenzied rather than purposeful. Women's cycles, during pregnancy, the monthly menstrual period, and menopause have long been viewed as barriers to good medical research, not incentives. The drive to force complex problems into a simple framework is market-driven. In this case, the market is the one that "buys" research ideas that are quickly published. To map the interplay between female hormones and breast cancer, we need more researchers who will approach the female body with wonder and respect for its difference from the male norm. Belief in the essentially purposeful workings of our hormones may provide some pleasant surprises.

Underneath the conflict over the best way to control breast cancer is a more fundamental difference of opinion. It has to do with how we, as women, can best assume control of our bodies and our lives. In the past, our attempts to purchase this control by taking drugs put us at the mercy of commercial interests and the medical profession. Ultimately, hormonal manipulation through medication does far more than control breast cancer, reproduction, osteoporosis or heart disease. These medications extend control over women and remove us even further from our understanding of ourselves.

Notes

1. Pierre Blais, "The Medicalization of Women's Lives," [conference sponsored by DES Action], Montreal, (Sept. 10, 1992).

2. Marie-Louise Gariépy, "Remembering DES: An interview with a pharmacist," *DES Action Canada Newsletter*, (Summer 1993) #35, p.1.]

3. Carol Ann Rinzler, *Estrogen and Breast Cancer: A Warning to Women*, (N.Y.: MacMillan, 1993), p. 85.

4. "DES and Breast Cancer Risk," *DES Action Canada Newsletter*, (Summer 1993), p.1.

5. Kushner, p. 136.

6. Crile, pp. 122-123.

7. Kushner, pp. 240-241.

8. Kushner, p. 199.

9. Rinzler, p. 8.

10. *Merk's Manual*, (1923), cited in Rinzler, p. 14.

11. Rinzler, p. 11.

12. Rinzler, p. 22.

13. Rinzler, p. 22.

14. Rinzler, p. 81; Hertz and Bailar, in *Cancer*, (Dec. 1969).

15. Breast Cancer Prevention Panel: "Best Guesses," [sponsored by Breast Cancer Action Montreal], Montreal, (Mar. 24, 1993), [from transcript], p. 13.

16. "Best Guesses," (Mar. 1993), transcript, p. 14.

17. Kushner, p. 252.

18. Kushner, p. 372.

19. Kushner, p. 251; Fisher et al, *New England Journal of Medicine*, (July 2, 1981).

20. Kushner, p. 253.

21. Kushner, p. 202.

22. Kushner, p. 253.

23. Reported in *Health Facts*, (July 1992), in citation from "Clear Evidence That Long-term, Low Dose Tamoxifen Treatment can Induce Ocular Toxicity," *Cancer*, (June 15, 1992).

24. A. Fugh-Berman, and S. Epstein, unpublished manuscript, (1993), p. 5.

25. Bruno Catuli, cited in "Tamoxifen Ups Risk of Endometrial Cancer," *The Medical Post*, (Apr. 6, 1993), p. 77.

26. Kushner, p. 128.

27. Rinzler, p. 40.

28. "Breast Cancer in Younger Women: Many Equivocate," Daling, pp. 37 and 95.

29. "Best Guesses," [transcript], p. 24.

30. Harris, Lippman, on oral contraceptives, *New England Journal of Medicine*, July 30, 1992, p. 322; on risk factors that could be modified, (Aug. 13, 1992), p. 478.

31. "Best Guesses," [transcript], p. 7.

32. Maureen Henderson, at the National Breast Cancer Forum, Montreal, (Nov. 14, 1993).

33. Bette Hileman, "Environmental Estrogens Linked to Reproductive Abnormalities, Cancer," *Chemical and Engineering News*, (Jan. 31, 1994), pp. 19-23.

34. Sharon Begeley with Daniel Glick, "The Estrogen Complex," *Newsweek*, (Mar. 21, 1994), pp. 76-77; also "PCBs Diminish Penis Size," *Rachel's Hazardous Waste News*, Number 372, (Jan. 13, 1994).

35. Nancy Davidson, "Ovarian albation in the Treatment of Breast Cancer," Breast Cancer in Younger Women Conference proceedings, (Bethesda, Jan. 29, 1993), p. 283; quote, page 280-81.

36. Richard Love, Breast Cancer in Younger Women Conference proceedings, p. 163. Also, Pike, in *Epid Reviews*, p. 30.

37. Darcy Spicer, Breast Cancer in Younger Women Conference proceedings, pp. 386-388.

38. Susan Rennie, "Breast Cancer Prevention: Diet vs Drugs," *Ms.*, (May/June, 1993), III:6.

Alternatives
The Cancer Underground

Advice to reduce an excess of black [cancer causing] bile.
Avoid the following foods: beef, the meat of goats, wild boars, asses and
camels, salted meats, snails, dolphins and tuna, cabbage, lentils, the
bran of wheat, heavy dark wine taken in large quantities, aged cheese.
Do not remain in a hot area after a heavy meal.[1]

— Galen, 2nd century AD

In the mid-'70s, Stanford psychiatrist David Spiegel and some colleagues carried out a study. Of 86 women with metastatic breast cancer, 50 were randomized into a treatment plan that involved weekly support groups — meetings of an hour and a half, with eight to 10 women per group. They also had meetings of family members every four to six weeks. The intent was to help the women face their fears of death and dying. In the jargon of cancer treatment outcomes, they hoped to improve the women's "quality of life."

"We called it 'detoxifying dying,'" Spiegel explained when I interviewed him by telephone. "We tried to break death down into a series of problems that can be addressed. Problems like fear of helplessness, fear of pain, fear of isolation and separation from loved ones and family members." He recalled one woman who compared this part of the process to being afraid of heights and standing on the edge of the Grand Canyon. "I still know that if I fell down there that would be the end, but I feel better about myself because I can look," she said.

Aside from this sense of strength, group members developed emotional bonds with one another which helped them overcome the isolation and stigma of having cancer. They visited one another in the hospital and wrote poems about one another if someone got sick or died. The sessions also taught the women to improve their communication with their doctors so that they felt more in control of their treatment.

The results of the study showed that the intervention was successful. "The women who took part in the groups had much less anxiety and depression, much less denial and discomfort with the illness, and about half the pain that the control group had," explains Spiegel. He and his colleagues published their finding in a series of papers in the early 1980s and forgot about the study for several years.

Two incidents that occurred during the study stuck with Spiegel, however. "One brilliant woman in the group who wrote books on computer programming had been to Dr. Carl Simonton's cancer centre and had learned to visualize her cancer cells being consumed by her white cells. When she came back she learned that she had a significant spread of the illness and she called her counsellor there, who said, 'Why did you want your cancer to spread?' This was a story I began to hear over and over again — the implication that you can control it, and if it spreads, why did you want it to happen? Which I think is a terrible thing to do to a cancer patient."

The second case that bothered Spiegel was a woman who stopped taking chemotherapy because she was sure she was visualizing well and the cancer was under control. "And she was dead within a year."

Spiegel hit on the idea of using the data from his study to debunk the philosophy that an improved emotional state would affect the course of the disease. He got a grant to follow up his study, to see what had happened to the women 10 years later. "By that time 83 of the 86 had died. And, much to our amazement, the treatment group had lived an average of 18 months longer than the control group. By the end of four years after entering the study, all of the control patients had died and a third of the randomized treatment patients were still alive. We were quite astounded by that and spent several years trying to see if there were some control variables, some differences between the two samples, that could account for it." Eventually the researchers concluded that the only difference between the two groups was that the group with women who lived longer had participated in the psychological treatment program.[2]

During the eight months after my diagnosis, as I rode the white-water course of surgery, chemotherapy and radiation, I was also initiated into the lore of cancer — the prejudices, the fears, and the many theories about who gets cancer, and why, and how to cure it.

At a party at my friend Jeannie's a young woman — a stranger — complimented me on the scarf I wore twisted around my head. After a brief hesitation (the word "cancer" can turn a conversation to stone), I took the risk and told her why the scarf. I was having chemo treatments and my hair had fallen out. In no time, a small group had gathered to question and advise. One woman told me I should eat garlic; a lot of it, every day. Another asked if I'd heard of a spa for cancer patients in Germany, known for a special diet. Cabbage juice was part of it. No one who went there ever died of cancer, she assured me. Other people probed me gently with questions like "Are you practicing visualization?"; "Have you made any changes in your life?"; "Do you have a good attitude?" They didn't come right out and say so, but the idea was clear: making changes in my life and thinking positively would help me get better. Welcome to the underground world of alternative cancer treatments.

The term "alternative cancer treatments" is used loosely to describe anything outside the orthodox circle of surgery, radiation and chemotherapy. This includes theories about dietary habits and behaviour patterns that might predispose one to cancer. It includes herbal remedies such as essiac, which was developed by Ontario nurse Rene Caisse in the 1920s. One of Caisse's patients said that a tea used for healing by a local Indian tribe had cured her of breast cancer 20 years earlier. Caisse obtained the recipe and began administering it to cancer patients, first as a tea and later as an injection or oral treatment. Essiac, which is Caisse's name spelled backwards, is still popular among cancer patients. Other herbal preparations are chaparral tea and Mistletoe — commonly used in Europe — and a formula called the Hoxey treatment (first offered by the late Harry Hoxey at his clinics in the U.S. but now available only in Mexico). Some alternative treatments are therapies developed by physicians and researchers with scientific training, but which have not been accepted by the mainstream medical profession. Among them are pharmacological and biological preparations, such as the antineoplastons developed by Texas biochemist Stanislaw Burzynski, and high-dose vitamin C, advocated by Nobel laureate Linus Pauling and his colleague Ewan Cameron. Then there are preparations designed to boost the immune-system, like Lawrence Burton's Immuno-augmentive therapy (IAT), and 714-X, developed by Gaeton Naessons of Quebec's Eastern Townships.

I soon learned that these alternative treatments numbered in the dozens, if not hundreds. Some were available only in far-off places, like Mexico or Switzerland. I was curious about them, but not to the point where I wanted to splurge my meagre savings on a visit to a foreign spa. After all, I didn't even feel sick. The "alternative" treatments I was most drawn to were accessible and inexpensive. They involved changes to my diet and such psychological changes as those studied by David Spiegel.

My oncologist seemed puzzled when I asked him what I could do to prevent the cancer from spreading. "You are doing something," he replied. "You're coming for treatments."

"What about my immune system?" I asked. "I need to build it up."

He gave a weary sigh and shook his head. Obviously he'd heard this one before.

Still seeking, I went to a public lecture at a local hospital, billed as "Non-conventional treatments of cancer." The lecturer, prominent breast cancer specialist Richard Margolese, opened his presentation with a discussion of quackery, then segued smoothly into a comparison of holistic and conventional treatments.

"Conventional treatments for cancer have not greatly increased survival, and this leaves room for holistic treatments," he explained. But, he argued, because holistic medicine is nonspecific, it can't be refuted. "The results of holistic medicine aren't held up to scrutiny the way conventional medicine is."

This was not what I had come for.

Margolese proceeded through a decade-by-decade description of major non-conventional cancer therapies: in the 1950s, the

Hoxey herbal tonic; in the 1960s, the toxin Krebiozen; in the 1970s, laetrile. Finally he came to imaging, and the psychological theories of cancer. These he had a bit more trouble with. "It's more sophisticated," he ventured. "We don't know what's going on. It's a mixture of common sense — a positive lifestyle and emotional support system — and bizarre visualization."

As Margolese spoke, I sensed a rising anger in the audience. Several people rose to attack him. I was as unprepared for this hostility as I was for the speaker's disparaging tone. Unconventional cancer treatments were a prickly subject, apparently. The drama, and the confrontation, piqued my curiosity. I still didn't know what to make of alternative therapies but I wasn't prepared to dismiss them because they weren't proven cures. Neither was chemotherapy, as far as I could tell, or radiation. I was especially baffled by the claims and counterclaims about visualization and techniques of "mind control" as a way of combating cancer.

Much of the debate over these techniques has arisen from within the community of people with cancer. When writer Susan Sontag was diagnosed with advanced breast cancer in the mid-'70s, she was surprised to encounter the widespread belief that painful emotions cause cancer and that certain people are cancer-prone by virtue of their personality or emotional experiences. She began to explore the beliefs and fantasies people have about cancer, and about illness in general. She came to the conclusion that these theories flourished when a disease is both dreaded and poorly understood. In *Illness as Metaphor*, Sontag set out to debunk the idea that cancer has emotional causes. "I had one insight which really gave me the key to the argument of the book," she explains. "I realized that people had, in the 19th and early 20th centuries, similar fantasies about tuberculosis, which we now regard as preposterous."

The prototype tubercular personality was the poet, someone consumed by passionate intensity. Cancer metaphors tend to be the mirror image of this romantic ideal, Sontag observed. The cancer patient is thought to suffer from repressed emotions, especially repressed anger and sexuality. The disease itself has become a metaphor for the evils of society that we don't know how to deal with: war is a cancer, pollution is a cancer, corruption is a cancer. Sontag was concerned with the potent effect these disease metaphors could have on the patient. "Psychological disease theories are a powerful means of placing blame on the ill," she wrote. "Patients who are instructed that they have, unwittingly, caused their disease, are also being made to feel that they deserved it."[3] And, she adds, "The people who have the real disease are also hardly helped by hearing their disease's name constantly being dropped as the epitome of evil."[4]

For months after my diagnosis, I was preoccupied by what cancer patients call the "mind-body question." Like Sontag, I was offended by the underlying implication of these questions: that some personal failing of my character had caused me to get cancer and that — if I really wanted to live — I would quickly perform the necessary major surgery on my life, if not my basic essence. The prospect was exhausting, even demoralizing.

Yet I couldn't reject completely, as Sontag did, the idea that cancer might have some emotional connection. I was curious about new research that suggested the immune system is affected by the emotions and that techniques like visualization and stress-reduction might improve my chances of survival. I also craved an answer to my own diagnosis. Something had caused me to get cancer; understanding it might help me survive.

At the top of my list of people to speak to was Carl Simonton, head of the Simonton Cancer Center in the Pacific Pallisades in California. As the reigning father of the contemporary mind-body healing movement, he takes the brunt of a lot of criticism about self-healing techniques, especially visualization.

Simonton was a radiation oncologist in Texas when he became interested in the role of the mind in cancer. He was struck that some of his patients with advanced cancer seemed to have given up: they weren't planning for the future or getting involved in things, they weren't buying new clothes. "They were dying, they weren't living," said Simonton. Others refused to accept their prognosis and maintained a very active lifestyle. Simonton concluded that motivation was an important part of getting well from cancer and began to search for ways to change his patients' attitude to their disease.

He was married at that time to Stephanie Matthews Simonton, a psychologist whose specialty was business and sales. Together they worked on adapting techniques from motivational psychology. One currently popular book, by Napoleon Hill, was called

Think and Grow Rich — "A terrible title for just a wonderful book," recalled Simonton. "Hill was looking at why successful people are successful and his conclusion was that it was largely a mental process."

By this process of cross-pollination, *Think and Grow Rich* became "think and get well": imagine yourself recovering from cancer and maybe you will. The Simontons adapted guided imagery techniques to cancer. The patient is encouraged to visualize her body overcoming the cancer in some way, such as imagining white blood cells as huge sharks devouring weak little cancer cells, or the powerful rays of radiation zapping the cells to smithereens. "If you think back on your own situation, once you are told your diagnosis and the possible outcomes and the possible treatments, what you're left with is the working of your imagination," Simonton explained.

Yes, the nighttime terror of awakening, drenched in sweat, monitoring twinges and aches. Cancer everywhere.

"Our imagination is working in all of us at all times," he continued. He tried the idea with a patient who had advanced throat cancer and who also happened to have a deep belief in the power of the mind. "He had a very miraculous, dramatic recovery," said Simonton. From that point on, Simonton saw no turning back. He ignored the ridicule of colleagues and wrote *Getting Well Again* with Stephanie Matthews Simonton and collaborator James Creighton.

Simonton's interest in the mind-body issue is personal as well as professional, he told me. He has had skin cancer on his face twice, the first time when he was 16 years old. "I'm working out my own salvation," he said of his theory. "I was a strongly cancer-prone person who tended to react to stressful situations with an excessive amount of hopelessness, bottled up emotions, and difficult relations with one or more parents. All those things fit me classically." Rhyming off this dismal list of attributes, he seemed unabashed.

"It's not a very appealing personality," I offered.

"It's not flattering, is it!" he laughed. "It's not like the heart attack-prone personality, which is prized in our culture. With Type A behaviour, it's 'rah, rah, ya! Get out there and win, hurry up, overachieve.' That's one of the reasons there's been no great difficulty in getting it accepted. But you don't want to say, 'I have a cancer-prone personality, a flawed personality.'"

So why do it? I asked, thinking of Sontag.

Blaming and guilt are pitfalls of his holistic approach, Simonton readily agreed. Such feelings can be easily resolved if you have good counselling, he said. "But if you have inferior counselling, or you're doing it on your own, or you're not particularly attuned to deal with those problems when they arise, you can get into very great difficulty and disrupt your quality of life. People can die earlier and more miserably as a result of exploring in this area, because they are using the information against themselves.

"If the evidence weren't so overwhelming, I wouldn't feel so strongly about moving ahead. So what if it's an undesirable personality? It's very changeable. And as I change, it improves the quality of my life as well as impacting the course of my disease. I don't want to focus primarily on my cancer-prone personality when I'm looking at getting well from cancer," Simonton concluded. "That needs to change. The focus needs to be on what's right with me. What are some of the things that are strong that can help me change the way I view the world, my universe?"

In the 1980s, news stories began to appear claiming that researchers had found scientific evidence that the mind does in fact affect the immune system. This "hard-wired proof" came from a new specialty, psychoneuroimmunology, or "PNI." The awkward tag conveyed its multi-disciplinary nature, comprised of psychologists, neurologists and immunologists — to name a few.

University of Rochester neurologist Robert Ader, who coined the term PNI, is one of the pioneers of the field. Using classical conditioning techniques, Ader and his colleague Nicholas Cohen showed that the immune system can learn to respond in different ways. When Ader and Cohen gave mice an immune-suppressing drug and a placebo together, they found the immune system continued to respond to the placebo alone after the drug was discontinued. This experiment was replicated by others, and along with other research, demonstrated a definite biological link between the immune system and the central nervous system.

The immune system turned out to be much more complicated that had been assumed. Different cell types in the body's defense system were identified. Natural killer (NK) cells in test tube experiments destroyed tumour cells; cytotoxic t-cells fired lethal proteins on virally infected cells. Macrophages destroyed foreign intruders by engulfing them like pacmen. Other cells sent signals, telling the immunological troops when to attack, and when to back off so as not to turn against the body. But the key discovery, from the standpoint of the mind/body debate, was that cells in the immune system could communicate with the central nervous system and the endocrine system.

Self-healing advocates like Simonton, editor Norman Cousins and surgeon Bernie Siegel heralded a new era in which all sorts of questions that had been dismissed as lore, anecdotes and speculation could be — had in fact now been — validated scientifically. If the immune system had biologically observable links to the central nervous system (the mind) and the endocrine system (which governs the emotions), the link between thoughts and emotions and illness was real.

At this point, however, scientists in the PNI trenches hedged, qualified and disclaimed. Ader told me emphatically that his research had "nothing to do with the popular theories that you boost your immune system and cure yourself of cancer. One is science, the other is religion." The issue was obviously an irritant.

University of Ohio Immunologist Ronald Glaser was less categorical, but agreed, "we're not there yet." Glaser, with his wife, psychologist Janet Kiecolt Glaser, had begun to study people whose lives would be termed unusually stressful. They had looked at students facing exams, couples who had been through the trauma of divorce, and people living with the long-term stress of being the principal caregiver to someone with Altzheimer's disease. The Glasers took immune-system measures, administered psychological tests, and followed their study groups over time to see whether they came down with more diseases than control groups. Their early results supported the commonsense idea that these stressful life events depressed certain immune responses. They also had preliminary evidence that the older people with depressed immunity got sick more often (the youngest study group, the medical students, didn't often get sick even when pre-exam jitters depressed their immunity). But Glaser wouldn't speculate about cancer.

"We don't know a great deal about the pathophysiology of cancer," he told me, "and we don't know a great deal about the significance of the immune response and its ability to either prevent or control cancer." Some people with extremely depressed immune systems, because of an organ transplant or the AIDS virus, have a higher-than-average risk of certain cancers. So — at least with some cancers — this suggests the immune response is important in controlling the risk for cancer and its progress. To study the question in a carefully controlled way would take years and a huge study population, he emphasized, because even a common disease like cancer doesn't afflict all that many people in a given time period.

Another PNI researcher, Nicholas Hall of the University of South Florida, has studied the immunological effect of guided imagery done by women with breast cancer. In a pilot project, he found that the t-cells cells of the women who did guided imagery showed a greater ability, in a test tube, to duplicate themselves and their natural killer cells were more effectively able to fight a tumour. Hall told me he considered his research results provocative but hardly proof that guided imagery is effective in combating breast cancer. "There are so many checks and balances in the immune system," he explained, "that it is possible that a depression in one cell type would be compensated for by an increase in another cell type." The cell samples he was able to measure had uncertain meaning for another reason. "We take our samples from blood cells, but at any given time only about three percent of the total white cell population is coursing through the blood stream. The rest of the time they're lodged in organs deep within the body that really aren't accessible to study. So what does it mean when you see a change in immunologic function based on a test tube analysis using a very miniscule sampling of the total population of white cells?"

Beyond seeing his research as very preliminary, Hall had observed negative effects of guided imagery in some patients. This worried him. One patient became so regimented in doing guided imagery, he ignored family, friends and activities that in the past had been rewarding; others suffered feelings of guilt for (they believed) bringing the cancer on themselves, or were angry at someone else who had precipitated feelings of depression which they believed must have triggered the cancer.

The bottom line for Hall, as for the half-dozen PNI researchers I spoke to, is that the scientific evidence has not demonstrated that cancer onset or progress is affected by the mind or emotions, much less that people with cancer can change the course of their disease. "People shouldn't be told that this intervention has been proven to be beneficial," said Hall. "They shouldn't be told that by engaging in this they are going to get better. The message communicated should be that not enough studies have been done to prove that the intervention is beneficial. A lot of claims are being made in the popular press, but we don't have enough data to warrant drawing any fine conclusions, and certainly not to go out and start profiting from this." Scientists are very conservative, he reminds me, "and we have to be, because we depend on very conservative organizations to get our funding."

David Spiegel's article on the life-extending potential of breast cancer support groups caused a sensation when it appeared in the *Lancet* in October 1989.[5] In the broad sense, Spiegel's finding seemed to support Simonton's point of view, that is, a non-medical treatment makes a difference to length of life. ("They were trying to refute the study that I published, and instead they found almost exactly the same results," Simonton told me, with satisfaction.) Spiegel rejected the comparison. "At no time did we ever have them do imagery about their white cells killing their cancer cells. We didn't in any way convey to them that this would have an impact on the course of the disease. In fact in some ways we were doing the opposite. We were saying, 'Look, you have an illness that is likely to shorten your life. How do you want to revise your life values, your life goals in the face of that?' And the sad fact is that all but five of the women in the study eventually did die of metastatic breast cancer. So in no way did we wish away the illness."

Although he ruled out imagery and hope of recovery as explanations, Spiegel was not sure what made the difference to length of life between the two groups in his study. One possibility is medical: the women in the support group may have received more vigorous medical treatment, suggested Spiegel, because their doctors saw they were less depressed and decided they could take that extra dose of radiation or chemotherapy. Or, because they were less depressed, they may have followed a better diet and exercised more. "It's also possible that there was some other mechanism either via handling stress better so the body had to respond to fewer stress hormones, or there could be some psychoneruoimmune mechanism."

The explanation Spiegel seemed to favour, however, is that the social support and connectedness that came from being in the group was beneficial. "There's a whole line of research on social networks and health. People who are socially connected have lower rates of age-adjusted mortality than those who are isolated. It's a rather strong effect, as strong as the smoking and death by emphysema effect. So while in some ways it seems like a radical and new thing, it is consistent with other research on social support and health."

When I was first diagnosed with cancer, I could not accept that I might actually sicken and die. I was drawn to the implied promise that I could cure myself by practicing mind-body techniques. Later, as I became more familiar with the realities of the disease, I reframed my dilemma. Having breast cancer meant living with enormous uncertainty. Whatever treatments I had, the disease could come back. I began to regard imaging and similar techniques as useful primarily on the psychological plane. Having breast cancer meant enlarging my view of life — specifically, it meant allowing an awareness of life's finiteness to be part of my everyday existence. I was pleased to discover a pair of articles in the *New Age Journal* that reflected some of my thinking on this issue.

In 1984, a San Francisco woman named Terry Killam learned she had breast cancer. Terry (she later changed her name to Treya) had just married writer, psychologist and fellow-meditator Ken Wilber. The Wilbers combined their experience of Terry's illness with their understanding of spiritual philosophies and produced a devastating critique of New Age theories of illness, epecially the idea that we make ourselves sick. Spinning theories about why people we know got sick can cause them a lot of pain, wrote Terry. When dealing with the crisis of her cancer, she said, the people she needed to be around were "people who loved me as I was, not people who were trying to motivate me or change me or sell me on their favourite idea or theory."

In the companion piece that appeared in *New Age Journal*, Ken Wilber was more emphatic. New Age theories kill people, he said, by encouraging people to cure diseases like cancer with visualization, meditation and psychotherapy alone. Central to his analysis was the idea that diseases differ in their primary level of origin: physical, emotional, mental or spiritual. The primary course of treatment should be a same-level procedure. New Agers were mixing levels, he contended. With a disease like cancer that is mostly physical, spiritual and emotional approaches could be important adjuncts to physical treatments, but never a cure.

Like Sontag, Wilber highlighted the guilt issue as an added cost of the idea that we can "visualize" disease away. On the other hand, you could still use a disease as a metaphor for the things about your life that you wanted to change anyway. Cancer could be a spur to changing your diet, your exercise program, your mental outlook and spiritual relationships. You can use the disease this way without believing these factors caused the disease.[6]

The articles brought one of the largest responses in the history of the *New Age Journal*, most of it sympathetic. But, wrote Wilber later, "the hard-core New Agers reacted with rage, saying things like, if Terry and I thought that, she deserved to get cancer. She was bringing it on herself with these thoughts."

Few of my close friends would ever have made a statement like "you create your own reality." Still, I felt strengthened by Terry and Ken Wilber's account because it made the feelings of the person with cancer paramount. Their analysis helped me order some of my own confusion. In the months after my diagnosis, I sometimes found visualization a useful relaxation method on nights when I was gripped with terror and unable to sleep. Most cancer patients I've met learn not to be dogmatic about using visualization. They adapt the techniques to their own needs and seldom proselytize to patients who choose a different approach.

"I think that visualization for some people is a helpful tool," says Vicky Wells, who worked with hundreds of people at the Cancer Support Community, a centre she and Terry Wilber started in San Francisco. "I think that meditation is a helpful tool, biofeedback, exercise, a good diet. And just as I don't want people throwing their theories on me, I don't believe I have any right to say to somebody that visualization will or will not work for them — because I don't know."

My initial exploration of the cancer underground was limited primarily to dietary and psychological techniques — relatively simple changes I could make myself. Most women I know with breast cancer respond to their early diagnosis by exploring dietary changes and self-healing techniques such as meditation and visualization. We review crucial aspects of our everyday lives and change as many things as we can that we don't like — work, relationships, our own attitudes and ways of dealing with the world. We then concentrate on living, as intensely as possible, hoping the cancer will not return.

A recurrence, or a diagnosis of metastatic breast cancer, often stimulates a renewed interest in alternative treatments. The woman has to face the reality that she has a chronic condition, and perhaps a fatal one. Since I have not yet had to face this phase of living with breast cancer, I've learned what I know about it by talking to other women and reading written accounts. One of the most memorable published accounts appears in a book by Ken Wilber called *Grace and Grit*, which includes copious excerpts from the journal his late wife kept in her five-year struggle with breast cancer.

After I read the Wilbers' articles in *New Age Journal*, my friend Karen, who lives in San Diego, told me she had just read *Grace and Grit*. Would I like to read it, she asked. She was hesitant about sending it to me. "You know she died," she said carefully.

"Yes. I know. I want to read it. Please send it."

Terry Killam was 36 when she was diagnosed with breast cancer. Only months before, she had met Ken Wilber, through mutual friends. They fell in love and decided to marry. The diagnosis of cancer was confirmed just days after their wedding. They cancelled a planned honeymoon in Hawaii, and instead booked into a hospital in San Francisco, where Terry had a segmental (partial) mastectomy followed by radiation. Her husband slept next to her on a cot in the hospital room.

After a great deal of research into both conventional and alternative therapies for cancer, Terry decided to follow a course of orthodox treatment, combined with "a full spectrum of holistic auxiliary treatments." A big factor in her decision was the fact that the pathologist characterized her tumour cells as extremely aggressive — grade four on a scale of one to four. Thus, although she was a big fan of holistic treatments, and was aware that many advocates of these treatments oppose radiation or chemotherapy because they depress the immune system (and thereby make the job of alternative treatments more difficult), she could find no evidence that alternatives, such as the Simonton approach, the Gerson diet or Burton treatment, could successfully combat a grade four tumour. "These tumours are the Nazis of the cancer crowd," was how Ken Wilber put it, "they are not terribly impressed with wheatgrass juice and sweet thoughts. You have to nuke these bastards if you're gong to have any chance at all, and that's where white man's medicine comes in."

Once Terry had made her decision, she was able to face the surgery and radiation with equanimity. She described feeling "excited about the discipline/regularity of the [radiation] process." Her oncologist agreed with the medical treatment she chose. Of 20 lymph nodes that were removed, all were negative — a good sign, although she was classified as Stage II because the tumour was intermediate in size, not small.

She began seeing two holistic doctors, and developed an alternative treatment regimen of daily walks, megavitamin therapy, meditation, exercise, acupuncture, dietary changes, keeping a journal ("part of the cure") and simply enjoying life with her husband ("his unoffical job is to keep me laughing"). She adopted a philosophy that balanced "take charge" — control and responsibility — with surrender and letting go. This latter task was an ongoing lesson, which deepened as her medical prognosis worsened. She described it as "balancing the will to live with the acceptance of death."

The first turning point came when she was diagnosed, a year later, with a recurrence. While taking a shower she discovered five small bumps under her breast — at the very spot where a drainage tube had been inserted to remove excess fluid after her partial mastectomy. She asked her oncologist if the cause could have been stray cancer cells from the drainage tube which got caught in the skin when the tube was removed and somehow escaped being "nuked" by the radiation. He agreed this was probably what had happened. Other experts agreed her case was very unusual and very unfortunate. "I just happened to be the person lying on that particular table when the odds caught up to the surgeons."

Once more she reviewed her orthodox and mainstream choices. This time she decided to have a full mastectomy. Her doctor told her the recurrence was odd and he could not be sure if it was local, and therefore treatable by surgery, or a sign of metastases — which would call for chemoptherapy. Two of her doctors believed the recurrence was local; they recommended against chemotherapy.

She began to expand and intensify what she and Ken called the "core curriculum" of alternative treatments: a low-fat, mostly lactovegetarian diet, high in carbohydrates with absolutely no social drugs; daily megavitamin therapy, emphasizing antioxidants (A, E, C, B-1, B-5, B-6), zinc and selenium, and the animo acids cysteine and methiorine; daily or twice-daily meditation; visualizations and affirmations, varied daily; daily journalkeeping, including a dream journal; and regular jogging or walking.

To this basic regimen Terry added various "elective or adjuvant" alternative treatments. The Wilbers began to research the various programs available at different healing centres, including an immune-boosting anti-viral treatment offered at the Livingstone-Wheeler Institute in San Diego. Both Terry and Ken felt, however, that the mastectomy had taken care of the cancer. The future looked bright.

Terry continued to confer with oncologists about the significance of her recurrence, however, and eventually concluded that the weight of the evidence pointed to the "bumps" being a sign of metastatic disease. As the opinions accumulated that she had had a chest wall recurrence, the advice of the experts shifted from no chemotherapy, to a moderate regimen of chemotherapy, to the most aggressive course of chemotherapy possible. She took stock of the bad signs: her tumours had recurred within a year of the first treatment, the cancer had come back in the area that had been radiated, it was ER- (the first tumour had been classified ER+), and the cells were again grade four. "Slowly, ever so slowly, I am convinced it would be foolish not to do chemotherapy," she wrote, at this point.

As she began to veer towards accepting the recommendation of chemotherapy, she weighed the recommendations of two oncologists that she have a moderate regimen (CMF) against the advice of a specialist in Texas ("generally regarded as the finest oncologist in the world") that she follow an Adriamycin regimen. She balked. Only when the pathologist told Ken that he had never, in his career as a pathologist, seen a meaner cancer cell, did she decide on this course of action. The prospect of taking Adriamycin upset her profoundly. Losing her hair, having her white blood cells die, developing sores in her mouth, possible damage to her heart — all these disturbed her, but most of all she worried about the 50 percent odds that she would become sterile. She still had dreams of having a child. Against these fears, she weighed the prediction based on her pathology report — 50 percent odds of a lethal recurrence in nine months. Physically she managed the chemotherapy fairly well, however, resuming her normal activities between treatments. At first the main impact was psychological and spiritual. Several months later, her periods ceased, she developed painful mouth sores and often had painful bowel movements.

In the next year her periods came back, but new crises arose. The strain of her disease almost ended her marriage, and the couple went through a painful — but successful — reconciliation period. Terry learned she had diabetes and would have to follow an even stricter diet than the one she was on. And two weeks after her oncologists decided the cancer was unlikely to recur, she discovered a hard lump under her arm.

At this point, she underwent a profound change. She faced this recurrence — which almost certainly meant the cancer would eventually metastacize to her lungs, liver or brain — with an equanimity that unnerved her husband and friends. She experienced an inner shift in which she redefined herself as a less masculine person. She had grown up wanting to be the eldest son, and had striven to succeed through accomplishments that would be valued in the male world. Now she decided to embrace her power as a woman. Rather than trying to force herself into "a profession with titles," she would work on projects that inspired her. She would bring people together, network, and use her hands to create. Working with another women who had breast cancer, Vicky Wells, she founded the Cancer Support Community. The centre itself would have a feminine approach, she said, "with less emphasis on fighting cancer, or recovering from cancer, and more emphasis on quality of life during the whole process." On her 40th birthday, she sent her friends a letter saying she no longer wanted to be known by the name Terry ("a masculine, independent, no-nonsense kind of name"). Her name was now Treya, short for Estrella, the Spanish word for star: she described the name as "softer, more feminine, kinder, more subtle, with a bit of mystery to it."

Despite the pleas of her doctors, she would not pursue any more orthodox therapies. The only treatment the oncology world had to offer was radiation to the spot of the recurrence, but the failure of her first round radiation convinced her that her tumour was not responsive to radiotherapy. Far from feeling despair, Treya saw this juncture as "a wonderful opportunity. Here is the perfect impetus to explore other modes of cancer treatment, a kind of postgraduate course in experimental therapies. I intend to explore alternatives ranging from metabolic therapies to low-fat, raw-food diets, to immune system stimulation to psychic healers to Chinese herbs."

Her first stop was psychic healer Chris Habib, in Del Mar, California. One week of treatment cost her $375 and she said she felt better about spending that money than most of the money spent on her cancer care. "I don't dare tell my orthodox doctors I'm doing this," Treya wrote. "To choose a psychic healer over radiation? How subversive." Yet, she said, the decision felt, "fully healthy and life-affirming." The healer worked in a relaxed, casual atmosphere, with several patients in the room at the same time. She moved her hands to different places on Treya's body, working different spots, shifting energy around. She told Treya that cancer is caused by a virus and did some work to keep the virus from moving from one spot to another in Treya's body. Treya liked her.

Treya and Ken argued about Chris Habib. To Ken, she was "wild, fabulous, insane, lovable" and "wacked-out," but he remained sceptical about her explanations for what she was doing. Eventually, he decided that the role of a "good support person" is to express any scepticism about treatments at the time the other person is struggling to make a decision. Once the decision was made, "shelve your scepticism and get behind them 100 percent."

Some months later, Treya experienced waviness in her left visual field. Tests showed she had brain and lung tumours. The cancer had metastasized. At this point she and Ken began a furious search for any treatment that might be able to handle such an advanced and aggressive cancer. They considered two chemotherapy treatment plans available at the time in the United States ("standard" and "aggressive"). They also considered almost two dozen alternative approaches, and eventually opted for a "very aggressive" treatment of short-term, high-dose chemotherapy offered at the Janker Klinic in Germany. Although the Klinic boasted a remission rate of about 70 percent, American doctors argued that the remissions were extremely short-lived and the cancer, when it returned, was quickly fatal. The Wilbers left for Bonn, where Treya spent four months being treated simultaneously with radiation and chemotherapy. The Klinic was run by a doctor Treya described as "full of energy and vitality and jolliness." He gave her a drug called ifosfamide, a treatment that had not been approved for use with breast cancer in the U.S., but which Herr Professor Doktor Scheef had been using for 10 years.

Despite the rigour of the treatments, Treya found them less "soul-destroying" than Adriamycin. Scheef agreed and said the drug was also "much, much stronger" than Adriamycin. Treya was impressed that Scheef had books by Burzynski, Gerson and Kelley on his shelves — all proponents of well-known alternative cancer therapies. Ken liked the fact that he kept a beer dispensing machine in the clinic. While she was still undergoing treatments, however, tests showed that Treya's brain tumour had not gone into complete remission as hoped; furthermore, she had two new lung tumours and two spots on her liver. At that point, she and Ken both understood she might well die within the year.

They prepared to return to the United States in a changed, but far from pessimistic mood. With little expectation for long term survival, Treya savoured the present. She went to an acupuncturist who treated her with needles, an herbal tea and acupressure; she took an herb called echinacea that supposedly boosts the immune system; and she consulted with her inner guides and had a "very satisfying but throat-tearing session of screaming."

On the way back from Germany they stopped in New York City so that Treya could visit Dr. Nicholas Gonzales, whose rigorous individualized dietary program included taking oral megadoses of pancreatic enzymes. The Kelley/Gonzales regimen is a variant of a program developed in the 1960s by a dentist named William Kelley, who believed he had cured himself of metastatic pancreatic cancer. He wrote a book about his dietary theory which sold well but, as Treya and Ken Wilber learned, eventually went "rather bonkers." Far from upsetting them, wrote Ken Wilber, "we found that part of the story strangely reassurring. We had tried all the treatments that sane men had come up with."[7]

Ken Wilber described Nicholas Gonzales ("Nick, as we knew him") as a highly intelligent and knowledgeable physician with a medical degree from Columbia, training from Sloan-Kettering and a practice that complied with all the laws of medicine in the United States. Among the thousands of case histories compiled by Kelley, Gonzales found 50 that he judged to have ironclad medical documentation. The cases impressed him enough that he tracked

Kelley down and spent eight months studying with him while he was still lucid. When Treya began treatment, Gonzales had been working with Kelley's ideas for about eight months. Treya had been diagnosed as having about 40 lung tumours, three brain tumours, at least two liver tumours and possible lymph involvement. Using a test of his own devising, Gonzales estimated her total tumour activity on a 50-point scale as 38; he considered a score of 45 or above to be incurable. Treya embarked upon the program.

She and Ken were now living in Boulder, Colorado. She described her daily routine, of which the seven daily doses of pancreatic enzymes (six capsules) — including doses at three AM and seven AM — were just one component. She continued her meditation and visualization, spiritual reading, acupuncture, "judicious consultations and tests with the local oncologist," yoga, exercise, coffee enemas (to stimulate the release of stored toxins and waste from the liver and gallbladder) and work with a psychologist.

The disconcerting part of the Kelley/Gonzales regimen, explains Ken Wilber, was that it created changes in the body that were indistinguishable from increased cancer growth. When enzymes attack tumours and begin dissolving them, the tumours flare up, and the flare-up, seen on a CAT scan, looks identical to a tumour that is growing. Similarly, a tumour marker called the cancer embryonic assay (CEA), which measures the amount of a protein released into the blood by cancer cells, goes up when tumours grow, but the breakdown of tumours by enzymes also causes the CEA measure to rise. And so, in what Ken Wilber called "by far the most nerve-racking, anxiety-inducing leg of this journey," Treya's orthodox doctors told her she had what looked like massive tumour growth, while Gonzales assured her that her cancer-activity score was decreasing. The oncologists wanted her to either go on continuous chemotherapy or have high-dose chemotherapy with bone marrow transplant. Treya confronted Gonzales with her dilemma. "What if you are wrong, and what if we decline orthodox treatment based on your recommendation, and then I die? Can't my family sue the daylights out of you?" Gonzales replied, "Yes, they can." But the reason his program was still operating, he said, was that it had a high success rate. "If not, then both me and my patients would be dead!"[8]

At the beginning of her period on the Gonzales regimen, Treya underwent another psychological and spiritual shift, which she summed up with the phrase "passionate equanimity." She envisioned this as passion, minus its usual baggage of clinging to something or wanting someone. As an idealized state of being, passionate equanimity meant "to be fully passionate about all aspects of life, about one's relationship with spirit, to care to the depths of one's being but with no trace of clinging or holding."[9] She viewed the first part of her life, the "doing" years, as a period guided by passion, while her life after cancer, the "being" period, had forced her to learn equanimity. Now she felt she was bringing the two types of learning together, "to work passionately for life, without attachment to results." Applied to her treatment regimen, living with passionate equanimity meant she was making every effort to stay alive, without desperately pursuing a cure.

Looking back over her treatment choices, and forward to her possible death, she concluded that she would feel more at peace at the time of death if the choices she made along the way were her own, not unduly influenced by the beliefs of others around her. "My main advice," she wrote, "is always to beware being knocked off center by what doctors say (they can be terribly convincing about what they do and terribly close-minded about non-traditional approaches), to take the quiet time to be clear about what you want and what you are intuitively drawn to, and to make a choice you feel is yours, a choice you can stand by no matter what the outcome. If I die, I have to know it is by my own choices." The Scheef program in Germany, and the Kelley program definitely felt like her own choices, she said. In retrospect she felt she would have chosen a mastectomy rather than segmental surgery at first, if she had listened to her own voice rather than various doctors. The other choice she felt she would have made was to go to the Livingston-Wheeler Clinic in San Diego. This clinic, established in 1969 by physician Virginia Livingston-Wheeler, provided a treatment plan based on Dr. Livingston-Wheeler's theory that cancer is caused by a common infective agent. The treatment involved a vaccine made from the patient's own culture, as well as laxatives, cleansing enemas, and a special diet, low in carbohydrates and high in well-cooked proteins, fresh fruits, raw vegetables, and vitamin and mineral supplements. Livingston-Wheeler died in 1990. In February the same year,

California health authorities ordered her clinic to stop prescribing and administering the vaccine portion of the treatment.[10]

After two-and-a-half months on the Kelley/Gonzales program, Treya's tumour score was down from 38 to 28 on what Dr. Gonzales called his "funny little test." Gonzales estimated Treya had a 70 percent chance of either stabilizing or going into remission, while her orthodox oncologists said she had two to four months to live. To Ken Wilber, it was "a Twilight Zone atmosphere." Psychologically, he split into two segments: one believed Gonzales, the other believed the oncologists. "I could find no completely convincing evidence that either side was definitely right or definitely wrong. Neither could Treya."

Shortly thereafter, Treya's symptoms multiplied. She had difficulty breathing and had to go on portable oxygen. CAT scans showed (according to the oncologists) a 30 percent growth in all her tumours; Dr. Gonzales described this as a normal inflammatory reaction. She went blind in her left eye and had surgery to have a large mass in her brain removed. After the surgery, she had virtually no vision. On New Year's Day, 1989, she told Ken she had decided not to go on — even if the enzymes were working, they weren't working fast enough to avert the rapid deterioration of her body. She gave herself one more week, and then died an ecstatic death, surrounded by family and friends.

Treya Wilber's journey through the confusion of orthodox and unorthodox treatment decisions encapsulates for me all the essential issues about alternative cancer therapies: quality versus quantity of life, questions about the relationship between mind and body, the tension between orthodox and unorthodox healers, and the question of who controls decision-making. She also introduces the concept of masculine and feminine value poles in responding to a cancer diagnosis, defining quality of life as the more "feminine" value — concerned with being, rather than doing, with the subjective evaluation of one's own experience, rather than the objective goal of achieving a longer life.

The conscious way in which she researched and chose her treatment plan belies the image painted by the medical community of a cancer patient driven into the arms of exploitive quacks by fear and desperation. Clearly, she wanted to live and hoped to find some treatment, whether conventional or unorthodox, that would keep her from dying of breast cancer. Equally important, however, was the spirit of an existential adventure that she brought to her pursuit of treatments. The most essential requirement was not whether the treatment "worked," but that undergoing it was a choice freely made. Whether a different strategy would have had a better outcome is an unanswerable question.

Free choice is an issue that cuts across orthodox and alternative treatment worlds. Just as Treya's doctors pressured her to undergo treatments she doubted could help her (and tried to dissuade her from the Janker and Kelley treatments), she met alternative healers who told her she must have violent emotions "eating away at her insides." These unsolicited judgements from well-intentioned people aroused feelings of guilt, confusion and increased vulnerability. She learned to reject them and encouraged others with cancer to do the same. In both cases, the point of tension was power: hers versus the healer's. Undoubtedly, however, some people are exploited by alternative healers.

The past few years have seen a slight shift towards a detente between mainstream medicine and the world of alternative cancer treatments. In 1986, a committee of the U.S. House of Representatives asked the Office of Technological Assessment (OTA) to examine the question of unconventional cancer treatments. The immediate stimulus for the request was the closing of a popular clinic in the Bahamas run by biologist Lawrence Burton. Clinic patients wrote to their government representatives requesting an investigation. Another contributing event was an historic court ruling against the American Medical Association (AMA) in 1987, which gave legitimacy to chiropractors as health care providers and thus weakened the control of the AMA over non-physicians engaged in health care activities. Critiques of mainstream cancer treatments from within the medical community also lent impetus to the investigation.

The OTA's 300-page report, entitled *Unconventional Cancer Treatments* and published in 1990, was a first step in bringing alternative cancer therapies up from the underground. Hundreds of reviewers, mainstream and alternative, contributed to the investigation. The acrimony between the two communities "reaches well beyond scientific argument into social, legal, and consumer issues," say the reports' authors in their introduction. They admit, however, that the process of discussion that led to the document "did not bridge the gulf between two highly polarized positions." Historically, both the American Medical Association and the American Cancer Society have defined the limits of orthodoxy in cancer treatments and discouraged the use of unorthodox treatments. The division of treatments into mainstream and unconventional rests legally on the concept that "the average consumer cannot be expected to make informed choices in a complex scientific field" and so requires legal protection against ineffective treatments. (Ironically, the multiplication of conventional treatments means the cancer patient is just as vulnerable to exploitation by mainstream doctors.) The contrary view is that the individual should be free to choose a treatment, following his or her own judgement. Mainstream cancer treatments recommended by a physician are usually covered by medical insurance, while unorthodox treatments are not.

The OTA report has symbolic importance, even if it doesn't solve any of the problems faced by the cancer patient trying to make a treatment decision. In the months after my diagnosis, the illicit aura of alternative treatments added considerably to the anxiety of trying to get my bearings. Once I made my diagnosis public by writing about it, I began to receive phone calls and articles about alternative treatments, sometimes anonymous, sometimes with tentative "I hope this helps" notes enclosed. The hush-hush atmosphere about unorthodox treatments seemed part and parcel of the perception of cancer as a shameful and secret disease, so I'm pleased to see that alternative cancer therapies are now discussed a little more openly.

More recently, the concept of alternative treatments has even gained the trappings of legitimacy. In January 1993, the National Institutes of Health (NIH) in the U.S. opened an Office of Alternative Medicine and invited proposals from researchers who wanted to explore the merits of therapies outside the mainstream. The new office has a shoestring budget — $2 million in 1993, out of a total NIH budget of $10.3 billion — and it is not specifically devoted to cancer treatments (let alone breast cancer treatments); but questions about such treatments can now be posed in an open forum.[11]

In Canada too, the medical mainstream is paying attention to this once-taboo topic. The Breast Cancer Initiative, a government-initiated fund set up in 1993 to do research in breast cancer, chose as one of its first projects to develop a catalogue of alternative treatments. Since the fund is administered by the National Cancer Institute of Canada, which in turn is affiliated with the Canadian Cancer Society, the newly struck Task Force on Alternative Therapies springs from the centre of Canada's cancer establishment.

A tolerant atmosphere for the open discussion of cancer treatments is long overdue. Some alternative therapies are biomedical in nature and have the potential to be evaluated in clinical trials, according to conventional medical criteria. For these treatments, the benefit of opening up the system to review would be to gain a hearing for regimens that have been rejected because they don't fit current theories. I have some qualms, though, about the "mainstreamization" of other alternative therapies, especially those designated as "soft." One reservation is the possibility that these treatments will be evaluated according criteria irrelevant to the people using them. For medical researchers, the bottom line in assessing a treatment's efficacy is whether or not it extends life. What will these researchers make of approaches that alleviate symptoms, reduce anxiety, provide a feeling of control, deepen the patient's spiritual understanding, or teach her something about herself? I also wonder if self-care "home remedies," like visualization, diets and herbal teas, will become the purview of professionals and thus lose their main cachet — accessibility.

David Spiegel's study of support groups illustrates the unequal value medicine puts on quality of life vs extra time lived (which may be only a few months). On the first go-round, his study demonstrated ways that women with advanced breast cancer could alleviate some of the the stresses they face when death becomes a likely outcome of the disease. The study received almost no attention and would have been forgotten altogether if Spiegel had not discovered that the women in the support groups lived many months longer than those in the control group. Suddenly the study was international news. Support groups had a "real" benefit. The study challenged entrenched views about the separation of mind and body, and about cancer as a wholly organic disease. The fact that participation in the groups had added to the women's quality of life was never considered an important finding.

Yet attention to quality of life is precisely what many women complain is missing from cancer treatment plans. When I first heard of David Spiegel's study, I felt envious of the women who had participated in it. The fact that they had gained more months of life was not what impressed me most deeply (at that time, I had the perspective that 18 months was a disapppointing gain). Rather, I wished I lived in a community where women with breast cancer could meet with one another and have professional assistance as they confronted the emotional devastation of a cancer diagnosis, ranging from conflicts with medical professionals, through social stigma, to the fear of standing "at the edge of the canyon."

After speaking to Spiegel I was intrigued, also, by his suggestion that the benefits in longer life might be related to something as basic as social relationships. A large part of the appeal of this thesis was that women with cancer might learn to cope by improving personal networks of friends and other supporters — a low-tech solution available, in theory, to anyone at no cost. I was dismayed, therefore, to read in mid-1993 what had become of Spiegel's idea. He was several years into an attempt to replicate the study. He had formalized his protocol in a 100-page manual which he attempted to distribute widely, hoping professionals at other cancer centers would adopt it. Other investigators were cool to the idea, sometimes because they were sceptical that the program could extend life, but also because they found the procedures too formidable. The carefully structured program required extensive training and planning. Patients had to commit to 90 minutes of intense "dredging" dialogue, once a week for a year. In order to verify that the program extended life, women would also have to be randomly assigned to a test or control group — an ethically problematic procedure.

These developments illustrate the downside of pushing to have once-alternative treatments accepted into the inner circle of orthodoxy. The very procedure of making the process quantifiable and methodologically rigorous may destroy what is most valuable about it.

A year or so after my diagnosis, I was surprised to find I had lost all interest in the question of whether emotions cause or affect cancer. I had been obsessed with understanding why I got cancer and how I could stop it. Suddenly, the obsession was spent, a fever burned off. For me, the appeal of the mind-body theory had been in the promise that I could return to a state of pre-cancer innocence, an ideal of perfect health. This dream now seems almost childish. The cancer underground lost its allure.

My obsession with ferreting through orthodox treatments diminished as well. This search had as its premise the assumption that a cure for breast cancer, being desirable, was also possible. I began to entertain a different view: that curing breast cancer might indeed be a mere wishful fantasy. Although it was frightening, this thought was also liberating. It freed me from a search that had been largely sterile, and enabled me to think about realistic alternatives: ways of living fully with breast cancer and dying of the disease — if it came to that — without the immobilizing fear that leads us to deny the possibility altogether. Turning away from the treatment marketplace also freed me to join others engaged in the search for preventive strategies. But first I wanted to examine medicine's new frontier — genetic research.

Notes

1. Rudolph Siegel, *Galen on Psychopathy and Function of the Diseases of the Nervous System*, [Part III of Galen's *System of Physiology and Medicine*], (Switzerland: S. Karger, AG 1973), p. 196.

2. Telephone interview with David Spiegel, Mar. 22, 1990.

3. Susan Sontag, *Illness as Metaphor*, (N.Y.: Farrar, Straus, and Giroux, 1978), pp. 56-57.

4. Sontag, p. 85.

5. David Speigel, Joan R. Bloom et al, "Effect of Psychosocial Treatment on Survival of Patients with Metastatic Breast Cancer," *Lancet*, (Oct. 14, 1989), pp. 888-891.

6. Ken and Treya Wilber, "Do We Make Ourselves Sick?" *New Age Journal*, (Sept./Oct. 1988), pp. 50-54 and 85-91; also in Ken Wilber, *Grace and Grit: The Life and Death of Treya Killam Wilber*, (Boston: Shambhala, 1991).

7. Wilber, p. 337.

8. Wilber, p. 351.

9. Wilber, pp. 338-9.

10. U.S. Congress, Office of Technology Assessment, "Unconventional Cancer Treatments," OTA-H-405, (Washington, D.C.: U.S. Gov't Printing Office, Sept. 1990), pp. 107-111.

11. Natalie Angier, "U.S. Opens the Door Just a Crack to Alternative Forms of Medicine," *New York Times*, (Jan. 10, 1993), p. 1.

Heredity
Gene Hunters

*"It is but sorrow to be wise
when wisdom profits not."*
— Sophocles, *Oedipus Rex*

When Kay Dickersin learned she had breast cancer in 1986 she had no reason to believe her genes had anything to do with her diagnosis. She was 34, the oldest of four sisters, all of them healthy. Five years later her sister Gail, the second oldest, was diagnosed — at age 38. The following year Leslie, the third sister, learned that she, too, had breast cancer at 38. By now the Dickersons fit the pattern considered indicative of familial breast cancer — two or more close relatives diagnosed before menopause. Amy, the fourth sister, was 35 and still free of cancer.

The Dickersin sisters became part of the hottest story in medical science, the hunt for the breast cancer gene. When *Science* magazine cited their case in an article, prominent gene hunter Mary-Claire King saw it and contacted Kay Dickersin to ask if the family would be part of King's research program. They agreed. Participation meant submitting blood samples from three generations of the family to King's lab in Los Angeles for DNA analysis. Using a research technique called linkage, which compares the inherited material of family members who do not have the disease with those who do, King and her colleagues determined that Kay, Gail and Leslie very likely carried the yet-to-be-discovered gene, dubbed BRCA1 (for "Breast Cancer 1"). King estimates that women who carry the gene have an 83 percent chance of getting breast cancer before age 70. The youngest sister, Amy, appeared to have escaped. Her chances of getting breast cancer were probably no higher than the American average.

Of the various known risk factors, family history is the one that best predicts the disease. But what constitutes family history? When I was diagnosed, I immediately thought of my aunt, who had died of breast cancer when I was in my 20s and she was in her 60s. Was Min's death a harbinger I had chosen to ignore? My mother had sailed into her 70s, vigorous and active. I preferred to believe I had inherited her genetic robustness.

"I've always worried that it might be in the family," my mother confided, when I raised the subject. She had some cousins who had breast cancer, and then her sister Min was diagnosed. With my premenopausal diagnosis, my two younger sisters were now considered high risk. Although I knew the reaction was irrational, I felt vaguely guilty about this, as if I were some kind of tainted seed, fouling the family bloodline. The thought of my five nieces also stirred queasy feelings. Three were adolescents, the other two had the innocent vulnerability of childhood; if Aunt Min was my early warning, was I theirs?

But further investigation showed me that having a sprinkling of female relatives with breast cancer doesn't mean the disease is in the family. Researchers long ago concluded that only a small number of cases have a hereditary component — estimates range between five and 10 percent. Since breast cancer is relatively common, many families would have more than one "sporadic" (non-hereditary) case, either by chance, or because members share cultural risk factors. Some families would even have many cases, simply by bad luck or because members had been exposed to the same carcinogenic environment.

It was precisely this "well-known, but unidentified family link" that drew geneticist Mary-Claire King to breast cancer in the mid-1970s. "I was intrigued, and then I got hooked," says King. "I wanted to do something in basic science that was constructive, that I could apply to a big problem right away." King had already distinguished herself in genetic circles. A product of Berkeley in the '60s, she dropped out of graduate school to join Ralph Nader's consumer advocacy movement. She went back to university and completed her doctorate, a ground-breaking piece of work which showed that humans and chimpanzees have more than 99 percent of their DNA in common. Still the idealist, in the early 1970s she moved to Chile where she helped set up medical research programs for Salvador Allende's socialist government. After Allende's assassination in 1973, she returned to the U.S. For 15 years she slogged away at the breast cancer puzzle.

She spent over a decade compiling family trees of women with breast cancer and analyzing the coded pattens in their genetic material. She combed the 23 pairs of human chromosomes to find a distinctive inherited pattern of genetic components known as a marker. A marker that is consistently inherited along with a disease shows the approximate region where the gene linked to the disease will be found. King, whose maternal grandmother died of cervical cancer, hopes her research will eventually do for breast cancer what the pap test did for cervical cancer.

In October 1990, at a genetics meeting in Cincinnati, King carved a moment in scientific history that colleagues describe with envious relish. Late in the evening, she stepped to the podium to make an unscheduled announcement: she had found the rough location of BRCA1. Until King presented her data, few scientists believed a single defective gene could account for a substantial proportion of breast cancer cases. Even if such a gene existed, the odds of discovering it through the type of conventional family linkage studies King had performed were miniscule. The sceptics now agree, however, that a gene on the long arm of chromosome 17 runs in many breast cancer families and may be implicated in up to five percent of breast cancer cases.

By the end of 1993, King's quest had become a race and was garnering media attention more typical of celebrity sports events than the mental sweat of scientific achievement. Between rising breast cancer rates and the growing activist movement, the public hungered for a good news breast cancer story. The BRCA1 story fit the bill. *Glamour* magazine put King on its Women of the Year list, *Newsweek* ran a cover feature and Time soon followed with a cover dossier on genetics, including a prominent insert highlighting BRCA1.[1]

The immediate practical application of finding BRCA1 could be a simple blood test of genetic susceptibility which can be performed on any woman or man, of any age; on fetuses; and on unfertilized sperm and ova. Such tests now exist for rare diseases but the breast cancer gene promises to be the first linked to a common cancer. If widely used, the test could be lucrative. King and others predict that identifying the gene or genes linked to breast cancer could pave the way for a "molecular mammogram" — a genetic early detection marker that would replace breast X-rays.

These applications are hypothetical and will remain so until BRCA1 is identified, or "cloned." In the meantime, we can glimpse the direct effects of testing through the experiences of women like the Dickersins, who have taken part in research projects. Kay Dickersin, an epidemiologist, worries about genetic testing for breast cancer — especially for women with no family history of the disease. I notice, as she presents her views during a panel discussion of the ethics of genetic testing, that she is markedly less enthusiastic than co-panelist Mary-Claire King. "We have nothing to offer women who test positive," she says simply.[2]

Her statement recalls Maureen Roberts' comment about mammography — that early detection of a disease is always second best to prevention or treatment. Detecting mere susceptibility to breast cancer is the ultimate early detection. If a test for BRCA1 were available tomorrow, the choices for women who tested positive would be variations on the same unpalatable and unreliable treatments now available to women who are diagnosed with the disease: removal of both breasts, removal of the ovaries, experimental use of tamoxifen or other hormonal manipulations, and intense surveillance with mammography or other unreliable methods.

Objections to genetic testing go far beyond its limitations as a medical tool, however. The Privacy Commissioner of Canada viewed the potential harms of genetic testing as so devastating that he compares unlocking the gene in the 1990s to unlocking the atom in the 1940s. "In both cases we allowed scientists to unleash forces which can alter life as we know it, paid for their efforts with public funds and, at least initially, set few ethical or legal controls on the enterprises."[3]

Loss of medical insurance is the potential harm of genetic testing that is most often cited. Kay Dickersin suggests others. "Interventions, such as prophylactic mastectomies or tamoxifen, could be mandated. Childbearing could be prohibited." Dickersin concludes, "For most women, the harms of testing probably outweigh the benefits."

The hunt for the breast cancer gene is part of a larger scientific undertaking, the Human Genome Sequencing Project. By the year 2005, the international scientific community hopes to have mapped the entire human system of genetic information, the complex nucleotide sequence for all the human genes.[4] Guided by this map of a "normal" human being, scientists will look for the abnormal genes — the ones with proteins that are out of whack — and try to find ways to normalize them. An estimated 4,000 human diseases have an inherited basis and gene hunters believe that finding the genes could lead to the discovery of genetic therapies.

Medical geneticist Francis Collins, who directs the Human Genome Project in the U.S., compares locating a gene from scratch to "trying to find a burned-out light bulb in a house located somewhere between the East and West coasts without knowing the state, much less the town or street the house is on."[5] Every cell carries an identical set of the body's estimated 50,000 to 100,000 human genes, except for the sperm and egg cells which have only one set. The genes are organized into larger units, called chromosomes. Twenty-three pairs of chromosomes are found in the DNA, one pair inherited from the mother, the other from the father. King's achievement was to map the gene BRCA1 to a region of the chromosome 17. By pooling their families, an international consortium of gene hunters narrowed the region to an area which could include 100 or more genes.[6]

Several other genetic links to breast cancer have already been identified. A very rare family pattern of multiple cancers known as Li-Fraumeni syndrome may be present if a woman has early onset breast cancer and has relatives with certain childhood cancers. In 1991, a mutated cancer gene called p53 was discovered in families with Li Fraumeni syndrome. Breast cancer is the most common cancer in p53 carriers, but they are also susceptible to bone cancers, leukemia, brain tumours, lung cancer and adrenocortical carcinoma.[7] Only a tiny proportion of women who get breast cancer have Li-Fraumeni syndrome — less than one percent. The p53 gene generated considerable interest, however, when cancer patients with no family history of the disease were found to have acquired mutations of p53. The implication was that women born with a normal p53 could suffer a mutation to this gene later in life which would make them susceptible to the same complex of cancers that make up the Li-Fraumeni syndrome.[8] This finding suggests an explanation for sporadic breast cancers — the 90 percent that have no hereditary component. The "multi-hit" theory proposes that two or more mutations must take place before cancer develops. Those born with a mutated gene have a head start in the process because they have already suffered the first "hit."

The inherited or "germline" DNA mutation appears in every body cell. A somatic, or non-hereditary, mutation could appear in the same gene, but will occur at first in only one cell of an organ (such as the breast). The mutation then shows up in all descendants of that one cell.[9] Some researchers speculate that BRCA1 will also be crucial to sporadic cancers. If this proves to be true, a BRCA1 test could predict sporadic breast cancer. Rather than being a simple blood test, the test for somatic cancer would be performed on breast tumour tissue or cells in fluid aspirated from the breast.

Early onset of breast cancer signals that the disease may have a genetic component. In their search for a BRCA1 marker, King and her colleagues turned up no promising markers until one member of the research team suggested they line the families up by age of diagnosis. "Everything fell into place," she says.[10] Her research shows that 40 percent of women who are diagnosed in their 20s carry BRCA1. The percentage decreases with age: 20 percent of cases when the woman is diagnosed in her 30s, 10 percent of women diagnosed in their 40s, seven percent of those diagnosed in their 50s, and so on. Only one percent of cases diagnosed at age 80 or beyond test positive for BRCA1. While this pattern supports the multi-hit theory, her data does not, King emphasizes, show that most early onset cancers have a genetic component: "There is no age at which the majority of cases are genetic."

After King's announcement of her linkage findings, other geneticists from around the world joined the race to identify BRCA1. In France, Gilbert Lenoir and Steve Narod had already gathered data on women with a family history of both breast and ovarian cancer. Eventually the two joined with King and a select group of breast cancer researchers in England and the United States to form a consortium. To speed up the search for the gene, members pooled their information. Altogether they had DNA from 214 families with a history of either breast cancer alone, or breast and ovarian cancer. Out of this collaboration came the discovery that BRCA1 was linked to ovarian cancer. The pooled data showed that most cases in the 57 families with breast and ovarian cancer were linked to BRCA1, compared to only 45 percent of the 153 families with breast cancer alone.[11]

One sceptic of the gene mapping plan is Harvard biologist R.C. Lewontin. In his view, a quest for wealth, not health, drives the project. The U.S.-based Human Genome Project and its international counterpart, the Human Genome Organization, constitute a half-billion dollar endeavour, money that has been diverted from other potential investigations. To justify and maintain this investment, molecular biologists need to convince governments and the public of the project's potential. "Great careers will be made. Nobel Prizes will be given. Honorary degrees will be offered. Important professorships and huge laboratory facilities will be put at the disposal of those who control this project and who succeed in producing thousands of computer discs of human genome sequence," says Lewontin.[12]

Superlatives are indeed the rule when genetic explorers talk about the potential of molecular biology for breast cancer. James Watson, co-discoverer of the double helix, says of the search for BRCA1, there is "no more exciting story in medical science." Prominent surgeon Susan Love is equally enthusiastic. "[T]he discoveries being made now by cancer researchers are so vast, and their potential to virtually eliminate the disease so great, that the real excitement is in the future, not the present," she asserts in *Dr. Susan Love's Breast Book*. "Surgery, radiation and chemotherapy are all gross ways to deal with disease. The real answer is on the molecular level."[13] Love depicts a science-fiction future in which genetic discoveries will open the door to prevention, diagnosis and treatment of breast cancer. To prevent breast cancer, women with a family history could have their DNA tested for mutant genes: "we could do genetic engineering, with a virus or something like it, to alter the nature of the DNA and normalize it, so the person would never get that cancer."[14]

As aids in diagnosis, Love envisions designer antibodies, tagged with a scannable substance, that would replace the lymph node surgery now used to determine whether the cancer has spread to distant sites: "The antibody could be injected into the bloodstream where it would search for a cancer cell and, if it found one, attach itself to it. A scan could then detect the presence of cancer cells."[15] As for treatment, picture instead of chemotherapy an antibody that would carry the molecule of a powerful drug into the bloodstream, like "a little kamikaze pilot that attaches to the cancer cell and blows it up on contact. Only the cancer cell will be harmed ..."[16]

Lewontin contends that a deep knowledge of cellular processes won't necessarily lead to useful therapies. The discovery of genetic mutations leading to extremely high cholesterol levels has not aided the understanding of most cardiovascular disease, he says. Nor does the discovery of cancer genes linked to specific cancers mean "the causes of cancer lie in DNA."[17] Mutations in the oncogenes make cell division less stable and more likely to occur at a pathologically high rate, but "In no sense of simple causation are mutations in these genes *the* cause of cancer, although they may be one of many predisposing conditions."[18] Lewontin predicts a hangover of public disillusionment when the gene-mapping project is completed. "The public will discover that despite the inflated claims of molecular biologists, people are still dying of cancer, of heart disease, of stroke, that institutions are still filled with schizophrenics and manic depressives, that the war against drugs has not been won."[19]

In January 1994, I attended a meeting sponsored by the National Cancer Institute of Canada (NCIC) to discuss how the discovery of BRCA1, when it occurred, should be presented to the Canadian public. The molecular scientists at the meeting were divided in their opinions. Some wanted to highlight the discovery as an important scientific advance that would raise public money for cancer research; others urged a more tempered approach. And the scientists disagreed among themselves about the significance of locating the gene. One researcher was certain that finding the gene would point the way to effective therapies and move breast cancer treatment out of the dark ages. Another was pessimistic about the potential of the gene to lead to new therapies, but optimistic that the discovery would suggest ways to prevent the disease. A third, a scientist who had published a number of important papers on BRCA1, foresaw both preventive and therapeutic possibilities. On the other hand, he said, "It might not make any difference at all." None of them, however, wanted the public to view discovery of the breast cancer gene as primarily a problem.[20] As the consumer advocate on the committee, my own tendency was to highlight exactly that possibility.

In the search for BRCA1, ethical dilemmas are tightly entwined with the promise of financial gain. Under existing laws, DNA sequences are interpreted as patentable resources. Legally, explains Lewontin, anything defined as "natural" cannot be patented, so "if a rare plant were discovered in the Amazon whose leaves could cure cancer, no one could patent it. But, it is argued, isolated genes are not natural, even though the organism from which they are taken may be. If human DNA sequences are to be the basis of future therapy, then the exclusive ownership of such DNA sequences would be money in the bank."[21]

The first major newspaper piece about the hunt appeared in *The Wall Street Journal* in December 1992. The winner of the race, declared the front page story, "will reap the biggest payoff yet from the Human Genome Project." An estimated one in 180 American women carry the gene, James Watson told the *Journal.* "Suddenly, we've had to realize that breast cancer may be the most common [inherited] disease there is."[22] (The one-per-180 figure may well be an overestimate. As researchers narrow the number of potential genes, they have determined that the gene is not present in many of their high-risk families. Stephen Narod estimates the number of carriers in the population at between one per 500 and one per 1000. Lower probabilities could dull the allure of a commercial test considerably.)

The business of molecular science creates serious conflicts of interest. Most molecular biologists are positioned to reap the profits of their genetic discoveries, says Lewontin. "No prominent molecular biologist of my acquaintance is without a financial stake in the biotechnology business," he notes. "Many have founded biotechnology firms funded by venture capitalists. Some have become very rich when a successful public offering of their stock has made them suddenly the holders of a lot of valuable paper. Others find themselves with large blocks of stock in international pharmaceutical companies who have bought out the biologists' mom and pop enterprise and acquired their expertise in the bargain."[23]

The head of the Human Genome Project at the National Institutes of Health (NIH) is Francis Collins, whose work at the University of Michigan made him another leader in the hunt for BRCA1. *Time* magazine depicts Collins in a romantic pose astride his Honda Nighthawk 750 — a "relentless hunter of disease genes" who sticks decals on his motorcycle helmet to keep a running tally of every gene he and his collaborators have tracked down. He is also a devout Christian with a "passionate conviction that the new genetic discoveries bode more good than ill and that a reasonable society will curb abuses."[24] When asked, in mid-1993, if commercial exploitation of BRCA1 would "overturn the best intentions of all the ethicists and scientists," Collins predicted that the "moral authority" of the Human Genome Project would prevail over the greed of any overenthusiastic company.[25]

Yet, the lure of financial exploitation had already enticed entrepreneurs. In mid-1993, prominent gene hunter Mark Skolnick of the University of Utah set up a company called Myriad that would enable him to patent and market a test if he was the first to find BRCA1. A competing researcher remarked, "If Mark Skolnick clones this gene I worry a little about what will happen, because there will be a commercial interest attached to seeing as many people screened as possible."[26]

A readily available test has great financial and ethical implications for the public. Breast cancer costs insurance companies dearly because it is one of the most common cancers, the most expensive one to treat, and currently has no reliable predictors. In 1993, the vice-president of the Canadian Life and Health Insurance Association, Charles Black, stated bluntly: "The position of the industry is that since insurance is a good-faith contract, the insurer must have access to all the information that the individual has." Nor did Black rule out mandatory genetic testing, although he said that wouldn't become an issue until the genetic tests for cancer are actually developed.

John Golenski, an American bioethics consultant in Berkeley who spoke on the panel with Dickersin and King, made a similar assessment of the situation in the U.S.: "Insurers are hell-bent on any information they can get, as early as possible, to reduce their risk," he said. Golenski argues for stringent, statutory assurances of confidentiality.

Canadian Privacy Commissioner Bruce Phillips has urged that laws be created to prohibit mandatory genetic testing by the state, employers, and the private sector, except in criminal investigations. Our laws — including privacy laws, the Canadian Charter of Rights and Freedoms, medical ethics and laws governing medical confidentiality — offer some protection, said Phillips, "But let no one be fooled; existing laws will not prevent realizing our worst fears about privacy abuses through genetic testing."[27]

In the U.S., the Institute of Medicine (IOM), a policy body made up of scientists, issued a report that expressed similar concerns about the potential effects of widespread testing and screening, and underscoring the need for special legislation. The IOM also raised particular concerns about the emotional impact of testing for breast cancer: "The psychosocial consequences of receiving such loaded information have not yet been fully evaluated, nor has the effect of such information on insurability." Intensive counselling is provided to participants in BRCA1 research protocols, but, the report pointed out, "This process is very costly and may not be feasible economically or in terms of available trained personnel if large-scale screening interventions in breast cancer or other forms of cancer are designed."[28]

Financial issues aside, the hunt for disease-related genes raises basic questions about disease causality, science and, ultimately, human nature. The genome project rests on a model of biological determinism, says Lewontin. Although leading scientists deny they accept this simplistic view of human life, Lewontin finds in their language a world-view that places biological causes far above social and environmental ones. "With straight faces and no quotation marks," he says, molecular biologists call the human genome The Code of Codes, and describe the Human Genome Project as a search for the Holy Grail. Molecular biology, he concludes, is a religion and molecular biologists are its prophets.

Many molecular biologists are wary of preventive approaches to cancer. John Galloway, head of public relations for Britain's

Cancer Research Campaign, laments, "The idea has spread that most cancers are preventable, and as a consequence that research into the genetic roots of cancer is a waste of time and money, which would be better spent preventing cancer." Galloway says the need for treatment will be with us for a long time and "studying cancer genes probably still represents the best hope of progress."[29] Mary-Claire King told *Science* magazine, "If there were something we could do to prevent breast cancer, I would not be doing genetics, I would be focussing on that." She believes breast cancer is an inherent affliction of affluent societies. "If we can't eliminate the disease," she says, "then we should be able to eliminate mortality from it."

In their book *Dangerous Diagnostics*, Dorothy Nelkin and Lawrence Tancredi critique the machine metaphor of mind and body that underlies the new diagnostic tests. Tests like gene probes assume that machinelike systems can be discovered, understood by deciphering a code, and imaged on a computer screen. Defective genes are seen as replaceable parts and cellular proteins are "chemical building blocks" which can be rearranged. Such metaphors, Nelkin and Tancredi argue, objectify the person tested, who becomes "less an individual than a set of mechanical parts or chemical processes that can be calibrated and well defined."

Indeed, the immediate promise of genetic discoveries in breast cancer seems to stop abruptly at diagnostic testing. Authors of a 1992 review of medical progress in breast cancer concur that "gene therapies based on repairing an identified defect do not appear close to clinical reality," despite the fact that "a variety of genetic changes have been described." Among the changes are an overproduction of the protein produced by such oncogenes as p53. The pathogenetic importance of these changes "has not been fully elucidated," notes the article.[30]

To fix or replace defective copies of a gene like BRCA1, explains *Newsweek*, "You would have to remake millions of cells in the breast and ovaries to give high-risk women any protection." No one sees this type of application over the horizon. Instead, imminent therapies might include drugs that synthesize a protein produced by the missing or defective gene.[31]

A common rationale for genetic testing is to identify women at risk for breast cancer so they can be followed more closely or given a treatment such as tamoxifen that might prevent the cancer from occuring. To anxious women, this sounds like the ultimate in early detection. "Could we screen every woman for the breast cancer oncogene when she's 20? Or when she's 35? Or 50?" asks Susan Love.[32]

Yet increased medical surveillance has limitations. Familial cancer is very different from other inherited diseases, notes p53 researcher Stephen Friend of Massachusetts General Hospital. The gene for Down's Syndrome, for example, predicts with 100 percent certainty that the child will be born with the disease. The genetic tests for mutant genes like p53 show predispositions: "There are no examples of people being born with a *fait accompli*, no bad genes that make them destined to develop cancer or some other disease," says Friend. Instead there are "bad genes sittting around waiting for other events to occur that will turn a predisposition into a reality."[33]

One of these events might be medical X-rays, according to Michael Swift at the University of North Carolina. Swift and his colleagues have studied the Ataxia-telangiectasia (A-T) gene, which they estimate contributes to between seven and 14 percent of breast cancer cases. The A-T gene gets its name from a rare recessive disease that produces uncoordinated movements (ataxia) and red skin splotches (telangiectasia). People with A-T are predisposed to lymphomas, leukemias and many other cancers including breast cancer, although few women with A-T survive to an age when breast cancer occurs. While A-T only afflicts one person per 100,000, between 1.2 and 1.8 percent of the population carry the gene, according to Swift's estimates.[34]

The Swift team found that a history of diagnostic X-rays increases the likelihood of breast cancer in women with a family history of A-T. Of the women in their study who got breast cancer, more than half had chest or abdominal exposure to X-rays. In a matched group of women with a family history of A-T who didn't develop breast cancer, only 19 percent had had equivalent X-ray exposure.

For women who suspect they might carry the A-T gene, the finding creates a Catch-22. If they have frequent mammograms to detect breast cancer early, the tests themselves may promote the cancer.[35] Says Swift, "the amount of radiation that can trigger cancer in gene carriers is appallingly low."[36] He wonders about the effects of X-rays on all women, whether or not they are A-T gene carriers.

The dilemma of whether or not women with a familial pattern of breast cancer should have frequent mammograms is on my mind as I listen to Mary-Claire King present her research at the panel discussion on the ethics of genetic testing for breast cancer. The mammogram option should be offered to women in a breast cancer-prone family, says King, with mammography beginning at the same age as the first diagnosis in the family.

"Isn't it possible," I ask her, "that a woman with the breast cancer gene is more susceptible to radiation-induced breast cancer than a woman who doesn't have the gene?"

"That's an incredibly good question," she replies. "We don't know the answer. When the gene is cloned, the biology of that gene will give us some clues. We may not have to do the long-term epidemiological work to get the answer."

In an article on BRCA1, King, Susan Love, and Sarah Rowell (a young epidemiologist who has been a King collaborator since she was 18), outline the choices for women with inherited breast cancer. Aside from intensive surveillance — with mammography, clinical breast exams and breast self-exams — other proposed strategies are preventive: the double prophylactic mastectomy (preventive removal of both breasts), a prophylactic oophorectomy or participation in the tamoxifen prevention trial (provided the woman is older than 35).

The effectiveness of these interventions in preventing breast cancer in a carrier of BRCA1 is not known. The main preventive treatment for women who test positive will likely be the double mastectomy, an even more drastic treatment than that faced by most women actually diagnosed with breast cancer. Surgical removal of the breast still leaves some breast tissue, since breast tissue is not so identifiable that a surgeon can be sure it has all been removed. Some reduction in risk is assumed, but not necessarily proportional to the amount of tissue removed. "There have been anecdotal reports of breast cancer following prophylactic subcutaneous mastectomy," say King, Love and Rowell in their article, "and animal models have shown no preventive effect of such surgery."[37]

The evidence on removal of the ovaries, or long-term use of tamoxifen are no more informative. The authors go on to discuss the woman's "choices": "A woman's decision will be highly individual and may change over time. That is, a woman choosing surveillance without surgery at one time in her life retains the option of surgery at a later date."

These are choices only in the narrowest sense, however. Having to make them, in the absence of information about the likely outcome, will produce enormous anxiety. The broad choices are tied up in our vision of a humane society and our concept of human identity.

With the BRCA1 gene hunters in the final throes of their search, the likely public response to finding the gene is difficult to predict. The general public knows little about genetic testing and appears "ambivalent" and "confused" about confidentiality measures, says the Institute of Medicine.[38] More than eight out of 10 respondents polled by the National Opinion Research Center (NORC) opposed genetic screening tests by employers to make hiring decisions and said an insurance company was not justified in refusing to insure a person based on test results that show susceptibility to a disease. But another poll, taken by Louis Harris Associates for the March of Dimes, found that 57 percent of Americans believed someone other than the patient had a right to know that the person had a genetic defect. "Of those who answered positively, 98 percent said a spouse or a fiancé had the right to know, 58 percent said the insurer had the right to know, and 33 percent said an employer deserved to be so illuminated."[39]

The concept of genetic testing taps into deeply held ideologies about what it means to be human, and what sort of society people want to live in. Ethicists and social scientists warn that genetic research is the cutting edge of a new eugenics movement. The first eugenics movement began in the 1860s, and the idea of improving the human race through controlled breeding worked its way into social policy. Canada and the U.S. enacted laws to sterilize those deemed to be mentally or physically "unfit." Nazi atrocities brought the movement into disrepute. The post-war revival, say Dorothy Nelkin and Laurence Tancredi in *Dangerous Diagnostics*, has prominent scientists encouraging parents to "produce a healthier society," or to "assure the quality of all new babies" by planning their families with the aid of prenatal testing.

Geneticist Margery Shaw, for example, argues that parents may be held liable if they have children despite information about potential genetic disorders. Shaw proposes that the police powers of the state could be used to prevent genetic risks. In an article in a medical law journal, she writes "The law must control the spread of genes causing severe deleterious effects, just as disabling pathogenic bacteria and viruses are controlled."[40] Such proposals have not had wide potential for application, since genetic tests have been available only for rare diseases. When BRCA1 and genes linked to more common diseases are identified, testing for these diseases could be a focus for advocates of eugenic purity.

Geneticists who are searching for BRCA1 doubt that there would be much demand for fetal screening, says one science magazine, given that breast cancer is not an inevitable outcome of the disease, is often successfully treated, and does not strike until adulthood.[41] Once a test is available, however, prospective parents will be a natural target for commercial marketing.

Even used as it is now, in a research setting, testing for breast cancer susceptibility is raising new ethical dilemmas. Francis Collins reports that counselling family members who have been tested for the gene is one of the most "fascinating and disturbing" experiences of his career. The unfolding life dramas of the women who are being studied can force an issue, such as whether and when to give subjects their test results. Early in the research, a woman who had taken part in the research decided she was going to have her breasts removed. She had seen her mother and sister die, another sister had been diagnosed and she could no longer stand her dread of getting the disease. The researchers were 98 percent certain the woman did not have the gene. They decided to tell her so, and she cancelled the surgery. Even good news can have an emotional cost, however. The woman who cancelled her surgery was initially ecstatic. She danced around the oncologist's office, laughing and crying. A few days later she was overcome by survivor guilt, similar to that experienced by Nazi concentration camp survivors. Others have documented a sense of ostracism from affected family members, or simply disbelief.[42]

Genetic counselling is not without risks for the woman, who puts herself in the hands of a professional to help her interpret her situation and make decisions. "When the interpretive boundaries are fluid, they can easily be cloaked in the neutral garb of science," Nelkin and Tancredi warn. "Assumptions about scientific objectivity enhance the power of diagnosis and conceal the values embedded in many tests." Health care institutions, for example, which may employ genetic counsellors, have an enormous stake in discouraging the birth of children with a condition that might require expensive medical care.[43]

One conflictual issue already identified is the age at which someone could be tested or, if tested, told they have the gene. The Michigan researchers decided that teenagers in their study should not be told their status until they were 18, the age at which they can give informed consent for a medical intervention. "Informing minors seems to be breaking the rules," said Collins.[44] The potential psychological effects are the reason Mary-Claire King worries about teenagers being tested once a test becomes widely available. "The idea of young girls living with the fear of drastic intervention disturbs me," she says.[45] As well, the concept of planning for a future in which breast cancer is a high probability is a daunting one. A woman who learned, at 19, that she was a gene carrier, told *Newsweek* she had decided she wants to have and breast feed children by the time she is 25, then have both a double mastectomy and an ovariectomy.[46]

The odds that I inherited the BRCA1 gene are slim. My mother's vibrant health suggests she doesn't have the gene, so she couldn't have passed it on to me. The age at which my aunt developed breast cancer suggests she didn't have the gene either. I know of no one in my family who has ever had ovarian cancer (which has also been linked to BRCA1), and not many have had breast cancer. And only about 10 percent of women who are diagnosed with breast cancer in their 40s, as I was, are believed to carry BRCA1. The gene can travel invisibly through families for several generations if there are relatively few females, or if the women die young of another disease, but I doubt that this is true in my case. But even if BRCA1 is not in my family, I could carry some other inherited gene, such as A-T, or a less potent gene than BRCA1 that has not yet been studied. Even if the odds are against my being "tainted" by a defective gene, the idea of this type of labelling makes me uneasy. I recall the vague sense of guilt I felt when I was diagnosed and how I worried that my sisters and nieces were fated to follow my lead.

I can understand why women who have lost a series of relatives to breast and ovarian cancer are riveted by the search for BRCA1. If I thought the applications would be limited to testing and counselling these families, and finding treatments for them, I would vicariously share their hope. But BRCA1 has been prepackaged and presold on the basis of as-yet-unrealized potential. In its politics, the gene hunt resembles the earlier searches for chemotherapy drugs and radiation treatments.

The effort to translate BRCA1 into useful knowledge will take a long-term commitment to the genetic research project. Genetic researchers want that commitment from the public. I worry about all the resources, all the hope, that will be harnessed to develop marketable high-tech tests and interventions. We've been this route before. Even when the interventions proved useful, market forces drove the technologies to overuse — helped along by professionals attracted by the rewards of promising careers. Miracles have not materialized, yet the techniques are applied to more women, not less. Past technologies linger, even when they disappoint.

Genetic therapies reinforce the narrow view of illness as a bio-medical phenomenon. But biology is not destiny even for those with the breast cancer gene. The focus on breast cancer genetics deflects our attention and resources from the search for the roots of the disease in our culture.

The most astonishing argument put forward for the BRCA1 search is that its discovery will empower women. As investors, geneticists, counsellors, employers and insurers prepare for the cloning of BRCA1, I remember Lewontin's codicil on the knowledge-is-power maxim: knowledge, he says, further empowers only those who have, or can acquire, the power to use it.[47]

I hope women will be able to use the power of genetic knowledge to our benefit, but I don't believe we can assume others will solve the problems on our behalf. Women pondering the pros and cons of testing need to hear the stories of women like Kay Dickersin — women who have glimpsed the brave new world of breast cancer genetics. As participants in a research protocol, Kay and her family have already felt the emotional impact of being genotyped. When she explained the hereditary aspect of her disease to her two teenaged sons, one asked, "Does this mean my daughter will get breast cancer?" He hasn't been tested, but males can carry BRCA1 and pass it on to their offspring. "What a burden for children," says Kay. When her sister Gail was diagnosed, Leslie decided to leave her unhappy marriage because she thought she would be next in line. "It was a mixed blessing," explains Kay Dickersin. "A year later Leslie was diagnosed and she was a single mom with two kids, no insurance of her own, and a former partner who lived hundreds of miles away." Another sister does have her own insurance but worries that she could lose it.

As the breast cancer gene story unfolds, I will look to women like the Dickersin sisters to keep the issues in perspective.

Notes

1. Geoffrey Cowley, "Family Matters: The Hunt for a Breast Cancer Gene," *Newsweek*, (Dec. 6, 1993); and Philip Elmer-Dewitt, "The Genetic Revolution," *Time*, (Jan. 17, 1994).

2. Kay Dickersin, "Just Research: Women and the Ethics of Genetic Testing for Breast Cancer," [talk at the APHA Annual Meeting, San Francisco], (Oct. 25, 1993).

3. Bruce Phillips, *Genetic Testing and Privacy*, (Ottawa: Officer of the Privacy Commissioner of Canada, 1992), p. 3.

4. R.C. Lewontin, *Biology as Ideology*, (Toronto: Anansi, 1991), p. 48.

5. Philip Elmer-Dewitt, "The Genetic Revolution," *Time*, (Jan. 17, 1994), pp. 40-47.

6. Leslie Roberts, "Zeroing in on a Breast Cancer Susceptibility Gene," *Science*, (Jan. 29, 1993), p. 623; and Phillips, pp. 5-8.

7. Roberts, p. 629.

8. C. Ezzell, "Cancer Gene May be Relatively Common," *Science News*, (May 16, 1992), vol. 141, p. 324.

9. Lori B. Andrews et al (eds), "Assessing Genetic Risks: Implications for Health and Social Policy," (Washington, D.C.: National Academy, 1993), [IOM report], p. 28.

10. Roberts, p. 623.

11. Roberts, p. 623.

12. Lewontin, p. 52.

13. Love with Lindsay, p. 377.

14. Love with Lindsay, pp. 380-381.

15. Love with Lindsay, p. 381.

16. Love with Lindsay, p. 383.

17. Lewontin, p. 51.

18. Lewontin, p. 36.

19. Lewontin, p. 52.

20. Meeting of the Ad Hoc Committee of the NCIC to Discuss BRCA1, (Toronto, Jan. 27, 1994).

21. Lewontin, p. 38.

22. Michael Waldhole, "Stalking A Killer: Scientists Near the End of Race to Discover Breast Cancer Gene," *Wall Street Journal,* (Dec. 11, 1992), p. A1.

23. Lewontin, p. 37.

24. Lewontin, p. 49.

25. Phyllida Brown, "Breast Cancer: A Lethal Inheritance," *New Scientist,* (Sept. 18, 1993), p. 38.

26. Brown, p. 37.

27. Phillips, p. 3.

28. Andrews et al, p. 26.

29. Leslie Roberts, "Zeroing in on a Breast Cancer Susceptibility Gene," *Science,* (Jan., 29, 1993), p. 622.

30. R. Jay Harris et al, "Medical Progress: Breast Cancer," *New England Journal of Medicine,* vol. 327, no. 7, pp. 477-478.

31. Geoffrey Cowley, "Family Matters," *Newsweek,* (Dec. 6, 1993), p. 52.

32. Love with Lindsay, p. 380.

33. Trisha Thompson, "Medical Fortune Telling," *Harper's Bazaar,* (Nov. 1991), pp. 123, 166-167.

34. M. Swift et al., "Breast and other Cancers in Families with Ataxia Telangiectasia," *New England Journal of Medicine,* (1987) 316: pp. 1289-1294.

35. *New England Journal of Medicine,* reported in *Breast Cancer Action Newsletter,* (Apr. 1992), p. 4.

36. M. Swift et al, "Incidence of Cancer in 161 Families Affected by Ataxia-Telangiectasia," *New England Journal of Medicine,* (1991), 325: pp. 1831-1836; Quoted in Norma Peterson, "X-ray, Breast Cancer Link in Some Women," Breast Cancer Action Newsletter (Apr. 1992), #11, p. 4.

37. Mary-Claire King, Sara Rowell, and Susan M. Love, "Inherited Breast and Ovarian Cancer: What are the Risks? What are the Choices?" *Journal of the American Medical Association,* (Apr. 21, 1993), pp. 1975-1980.

38. IOM Report, pp. 3-4.

39. Natalie Angier, "Many Americans say Genetic Information is Public Property," *New York Times,* (Sept. 29, 1992).

40. From Margery Shaw, "Conditional Prospective Rights of the Fetus" in the *Journal of Legal Medicine,* 63 (1984), 63-116, cited in Dorothy Nelkin and Laurence Tancredi, *Dangerous Diagnostics: The Social Power of Biological Information,* (N.Y.: Basic Books, 1989), p. 13.

41. *New Scientist,* (Sept. 18, 1993), p. 38.

42. IOM Report, chapter 4, p. 2.

43. Nelkin and Tancredi, p. 66.

44. *Science*, p. 624.

45. *New Scientist*, (Sept. 18, 1993), p. 38.

46. Cowley, p. 52.

47. Lewontin, p. 38.

Prevention
Making Connections

In nature nothing exists alone.

— Rachel Carson, *Silent Spring*

"If the world were run by women, we would work on prevention,"[1] Rose Kushner used to tell male researchers and politicians.

In my first dives into the murky waters of breast cancer prevention, I came up with this detritus:

- My GP's wry comment that there was no way I could have prevented myself from getting the disease — except maybe by choosing different parents or having a baby at 16.

- My oncologist's bewildered "What for?" when I asked if he would refer me to a dietician: "You're stuck with your risks. Eat what you enjoy."

- An epidemiologist's statement that he had excluded women from a large study of workplace carcinogens. So few of women's cancers were occupational in origin, he said, that studying women wasn't worthwhile.

Pitiful as they seemed, they were a fair sampling of what was being said about preventing breast cancer in the late 1980s. Heredity and age of first childbirth were accepted as factors, but useless from the standpoint of control. Anti-cancer diets were assumed — at least by physicians — to be the realm of faddists and quacks. And the environment was simply irrelevant to breast cancer (except for radiation, too touchy to mention).

I was puzzled that breast cancer would have no environmental causes. Other common cancers clearly did and I couldn't see why breast cancer would be so different. Yet all the sources I could find alluded vaguely to a black alchemy between female hormones and fat in the diet. One way or another, if this theory were true, I had inadvertently conspired to turn my own biology in on itself simply by eating a normal (read "varied" and "rich") North American diet.

In Rose Kushner's post-diagnosis investigation, she quickly found that breast cancer mortality rates in the U.S. were highest in the urban corridor between Washington and Boston, the industrialized area around the Great Lakes, in San Francisco-Oakland and Los Angeles, and in individual counties in otherwise low-risk states like North Dakota, Wisconsin, Minnesota and Maine. When she tried to make sense of this map her sources reminded her that geographical clues to cancer mortality rates were unreliable in a mobile society like the U.S. The environment a woman inhabits when the cancer begins may be far away from where she lives during her last years.

Shortly after I learned I had breast cancer I discovered that Montreal, my home since 1981, has the highest incidence of breast cancer mortality in Canada. Two successive cancer mortality maps have been published in Canada. One showed deaths from 1966 to 1976 and the other covers the period 1980 to 1986. Both maps show Montreal as a bright red "hot spot" for breast cancer mortality. Granted, I had been fairly mobile in my life and I was not yet a mortality statistic, but I couldn't help wondering about the city's high breast cancer mortality rate. Yet no one seemed to have looked beyond the bright red blotches except to remark that they appeared mainly in urbanized areas.

I felt a nagging malaise about the the experts' stance on prevention. Was there really no more to say than that? It was June 1989, while I was in the throes of radiotherapy treatments, that my prevention antenna went rigid. I read a series of articles in the *New Yorker* suggesting that low-level electromagnetic fields emitted by power lines could cause a variety of cancers. Most of the evidence linked the mysterious emissions to childhood leukemia, but the articles cited some evidence that breast cancer might be caused by the low-level emissions. Not only had a number of men who worked on power lines been diagnosed with breast cancer (which is very rare in men), but some clusters of breast cancer had been documented in offices where large numbers of women worked on computers. Other sources of electromagnetic radiation included common household products like electric blankets and waterbed heaters, whose users would have extended exposure to the radiation fields. '

The articles shocked me. I had never read anything about electrical power fields before, but I realized that on a typical day I was probably exposed to them almost around the clock. I had been sleeping on a waterbed for eight years. For the past four years I had worked all day on a computer at the office, and often spent hours in front of my home computer evenings and weekends. Shaken by the thought that I might have unwittingly created a cancer-inducing environment in my own home, I unplugged the heater on my bed and moved my computer to the far corner of my desk.

What was equally disturbing about the *New Yorker* account was that the researchers who had been working in this field were blocked systematically from carrying out and publishing their research. Scientists and government agencies, particularly those involved in defense and hydroelectric projects, discredited their work. The links between cancer and electromagnetic radiation, if they bore up under further study, clearly had enormous importance for the prevention of cancer. They also had staggering implications for the companies that sell hydro power, for the military, for the manufacturers of certain consumer products, and for our way of life.

Prevention has never been the central preoccupation of cancer researchers. Biological scientists want do the basic biological research they are trained in. They're cool towards prevention, which involves the alien (to them) machinations of public education and social policy change. They argue that diseases can't be prevented or cured unless their biological processes are understood. Prevention advocates contest this: "Potable water remains the most important public health measure in history," says Adriane Fugh-Berman.[2] Sanitation works as a method of disease control; the reasons why matter less than the practical benefits.

Canada has officially had a prevention-oriented health policy since 1973, but in the 1980s, virtually all of the federal "prevention" funds spent on breast cancer research went to the National

Breast Screening Study (NBSS) to evaluate early detection methods.[3] As a nod to prevention, the NBSS had a dietary fat study tacked onto it. Beginning in 1982, Geoffrey Howe and his associates at the University of Toronto had 57,000 healthy women who took part in the NBSS fill out a dietary questionnaire. The researchers compared the diets of women who were later diagnosed with breast cancer to those of 1,182 women who did not have breast cancer. When the dietary reports were analysed and divided into quartiles, on a continuum from low to high fat, the data gave weak support for the hypothesis that fat had a dose-related effect on breast cancer. The women who reported very fatty diets had higher rates of breast cancer than those in the middle, but the women who reported a low-fat diet also had a somewhat elevated risk of breast cancer.[4]

Norman Boyd, head of epidemiology at the Ontario Cancer Institute, began pilot work for a much more exacting study on dietary fat and breast cancer in 1981. Ten years later he was still trying to raise enough funding to meet his goal of a sample size of 9,000 women. Boyd's study involved assigning women at random to a control group that would follow the conventional diet set out in Canada's Food Rules, or to a test group whose members would receive individual counselling on how to achieve and maintain a balanced carbohydrates-based diet of only 15 percent fat. The pilot work showed that 45 percent of the eligible women who attended mammography screening centres were willing to volunteer ("a remarkable number compared to treatment trials," says Boyd). A serum blood test verified that the women were sticking to the diet; those in the treatment group were able to reduce their fat intake from the national baseline of 35 percent to 15 percent and keep it there, while those in the control group stuck with their original diets. Very few women dropped out of the study.

Funding, not recruitment or compliance was the sticking point for Boyd when he decribed his research before the Parliamentary committee on breast cancer. He knew that he could recruit two to three times the number of women needed. At the time, the study was the only one of its kind in the world, but he had been able to raise only 40 percent of the funds he needed to achieve the necessary sample size.[5]

In the U.S., a similar dietary fat study had been proposed to the National Cancer Institute (NCI) as far back as the early 1980s and was repeatedly rejected. In its rejections, the NCI cited the study's high cost, design difficulties and the belief on the part of peer review panels that women wouldn't be able to maintain the low-fat diet. "Paternalism," accused journalist Susan Rennie in *Ms.* magazine. The study now has promised funding of $625 million over 14 years, but the money comes from the newly established Women's Health Initiative, not the NCI.

American critics of the NCI have decried the lack of prevention research since the agency's inception. In the 1950s, basic lab work squeezed out epidemiological studies and investigations into environmental and occupational carcinogens.[6] With the rise of the pharmaceutical giants, the NCI's research emphasis shifted to treatment, mainly testing of chemotherapy regimens. In 1990, the NCI funded 900 studies on treatment and only 27 on prevention.[7] A U.S. government report the next year concluded that the absence of a clear strategy for improving survival "argues for the importance of prevention." The report held out little hope for a successful prevention program, however, "until we have a better understanding of the factors that cause breast cancer."[8]

Public pressure encourages treatment research, says cancer historian James Patterson. The taxpaying public wants cures and is easily seduced by images of white-coated scientists fine-tuning gigantic hunks of machinery or peering at test tubes. Scientists regard the magic bullet approach as naive, but an essential part of the game they must play to finance the basic research they believe in.

By the end of 1990, though, preventing breast cancer was suddenly "the next frontier," as an article in *Vogue* magazine put it. *Harper's Bazaar* went further, with the cover come-on, "Breast Cancer: The Avoidable Killer." Other popular magazines followed with features boldly headed, "Preventing Breast Cancer" and "How to Reduce Risk."

How, how? I wanted to know. The breakthrough to prevention, it turned out, was mainly in the rhetoric. *Self* magazine's advice to readers was typical: women could minimize risks "by examining your breasts every month and having regular mammograms, by making a few sensible dietary changes and by lobbying for more money for research." The real strides in prevention, all the articles stressed, were about to happen.

What drew my attention was the loose use of the word prevention. High resolution mammography, blocking estrogen with tamoxifen and GnRH agonists, and genetic testing followed by a preventive double mastectomy went holus-bolus into the mix with research on dietary fat, reducing alcohol consumption and eating broccoli. And still no mention of environmental contaminants.

"Prevention," it seemed, had been rescued from research oblivion and revamped in the image of treatment. In '90s parlance, preventing breast cancer could mean anything from having two healthy breasts removed to having your entire hormonal system shut down and replaced. Prevention's "new frontier" looked suspiciously like treatment's old frontier, but scarier.

In the cancer lexicon, "prevention" has been co-opted before. Screening for cancer is commonly called "secondary prevention" while virtually any treatment that might control some of the effects of cancer weighs in as "tertiary prevention." Adjuvant chemotherapy, given to patients with no sign of distant metastasis, is called preventive chemotherapy — its purpose is to prevent lethal tumours, which may or may not be forming. "Primary prevention" is mainly considered a hypothetical concept, a heading where strategies to keep people from getting cancer might be listed, if anyone, by some fluke, ever tripped across one. When biostatistician John C. Bailar III argued the case for cancer prevention in the *Journal of the National Cancer Institute*, in 1979, he felt obliged to point out that he was not talking about screening and treatment programs.[9]

That plea for a preventive approach to cancer "didn't get much of a play," Bailar told me when I asked him about it, but a paper he published in 1986 with colleague Elaine Smith certainly did. "Progress Against Cancer?" a statistical analysis of cancer deaths in the United States from 1950 to 1982, probably did more than any other single article to push cancer prevention into the forefront of scientific and policy discussions. The sum of Bailar and Smith's numbers was that three decades of heavily financed cancer research hadn't slowed cancer's death toll.[10] It was time, they argued, to try a different approach.

Reaction to the paper came from all around the world — the Japanese called it "The Bailar Shock." Bailar recalls three different waves. "The first response was immediate, and it was just absolute blind rage on the part of people who had devoted their lives to the study of cancer." The second wave of reaction, says Bailar, came from epidemiologists, who shrugged and said they knew all along that treatment research wasn't having an effect. Then came "a kind of deep reflection, that maybe there was something here and we ought to give more attention to prevention," says Bailar. "And I think within a year or a couple of years the whole thing had been absorbed into people's thinking."

For the public, the statistical shock therapy came a few years later. News that the odds of a North American woman getting breast cancer in her lifetime had slipped from 1-in-10 to 1-in-9 shattered the illusion that breast cancer was under control. The 1-in-9 statistic became official in the United States in 1991 and in Canada in 1992. In both countries, just 30 years earlier, the odds had been 1-in-20. Unless strides were made in prevention, it looked like breast cancer would become the legacy of every woman in North America, perhaps within a generation.

Women with breast cancer began to speak out and their message was what Kushner had predicted: prevention. "Hold the line at one in nine," cried activists at a Boston rally in 1992. The Women's Community Cancer Project of Boston/Cambridge demanded that the NCI and the U.S. government direct research to focus on prevention, the environmental causes of cancer, and new, non-toxic therapies.[11] When I called together a small group of women with breast cancer to meet in my home, with the goal of forming an activist group, we found that we all agreed on one thing: prevention should be a top priority. From San Francisco to Berkeley, from Halifax, Nova Scotia to St. Catharines, Ontario, groups of women with breast cancer wanted a prevention-focussed policy.

In the U.S., particularly, cancer research responds to public pressure. Some kind of highly visible prevention research initiative was probably politically inevitable. Waiting in the research wings were two opposing visions of breast cancer control: Maureen Henderson's randomized study to test the dietary fat hypothesis and a pharmaceutical assault on estrogen.

Maureen Henderson's Seattle-based team proposed to randomly assign 160,000 postmenopausal women into two groups. Half the women would continue eating a typical North American diet, the other half would be taught to achieve and stick to a diet that was only 20 percent fat. Breast cancer would be one, but not the only, health effect tracked. The group had done years of methodical pilot testing. The study seemed an ideal candidate to show that the NCI was serious about understanding how to prevent breast cancer. In the summer of 1990, though, the National Cancer Institute Advisory Board vetoed spending the money, despite recommendations to go ahead by scientific advisors and by the NCI itself. The rejection only served to highlight the NCI's acceptance, in principle, to fund a another study: the Tamoxifen Breast Cancer Prevention Trial, which would administer tamoxifen to 8,000 healthy women.

The tamoxifen trial fit current medical values, says medical journalist Susan Ince, and had a boost from political theatrics. In the summer of 1990, a California surgeon named Phillip Bretz told the FDA he wanted to test tamoxifen for 10 years on 7,100 postmenopausal women who had never had cancer. Ince notes that political brashness helped Bretz, a research neophyte, gain an FDA hearing. "… Bretz grabbed global attention for his proposed study by signing an agreement with Soviet health authorities to offer tamoxifen to Soviet women, including some exposed to radiation during the Chernobyl nuclear accident."

The FDA didn't approve the specifics of Bretz' plan, but endorsed the idea of a large-scale preliminary trial using tamoxifen with healthy women. For those seeking to hasten prevention, concluded Ince, "there may be a lesson in the contrast between years of methodical pilot testing by the dietary fat study team and the flamboyant politics that quickly gained the tamoxifen trial an FDA hearing."

The strongest opposition to the tamoxifen prevention trial came from the feminist National Women's Health Network, which opposed it entirely. Physician and board member Adriane Fugh-Berman said the trial was "premature in its assumptions, weak in its hypotheses, questionable in its ethics and misguided in its public health ramifications."[12]

Fugh-Berman's critique put my own reaction into medical terms. The tamoxifen trial seemed to make a mockery of the whole concept of prevention. When the Parliamentary committee on breast cancer invited me to testify in the fall of 1991, I spoke of my concerns about giving a drug with known toxic effects to healthy women, many of whom would only be at moderate risk for getting breast cancer. Those of us who already had cancer were not being monitored adequately for the long-term toxic effects of chemotherapy, radiation and tamoxifen treatments, I said. Our physicians couldn't answer our questions. How could researchers justify extending such treatment to a healthy population?

Adriane Fugh-Berman defines the tamoxifen prevention trial as a watershed in at least three ways. "It marks the first time (except in the case of correcting nutritional deficiency) that a treatment for a disease is being touted as a preventive agent for the same disease." Second, "The tamoxifen trial also marks the first time that a drug with known severe adverse effects is being given to a healthy population." And third, says Fugh-Berman, "The tamoxifen trial heralds a new era in preventive medicine: where previously we battled external sources of harm, we have now turned our sights towards internal enemies. The war against normal physiology has begun.

"Disease prevention and disease treatment are two completely different fields, and that's the way it should be," says Fugh-Berman.[13] She calls the tamoxifen trial a dangerous precedent because it blurs a definite and necessary boundary between prevention and treatment. "Risks acceptable for the sick are not risks acceptable for the well," she emphasizes.

That the trial crosses a boundary is alarming to women and public health officials alike. Most women don't know as much as we might about breast cancer, but we feel familiar with preventive medicine. As the traditional keepers of the family health, women are the ones who pack an apple in their child's lunch, put soap in the bathroom and a childsafe latch on the medicine cabinet. We understand that the whole point of preventive medicine is to prevent having to take medicine. To many women, proposing tamoxifen to prevent breast cancer is an affront to common sense. Public health workers (who are mostly women) view the trial as an infringement on their terrain. When Helen Rodriguez-Trias, President of the American Public Health Association, came back from an international meeting on breast cancer prevention held in Europe in March 1993, she wrote with dismay that tamoxifen prevention and similar chemoprevention schemes dominated all discussion. At a time when even affluent countries were staggering under health costs, she said, how much sense did it make to test "disease prevention" strategies that entail daily expensive medication, constant medical surveillance and a costly medical infrastructure?

Breast cancer is no stranger to intervention-style prevention. "Preventive" or prophylactic mastectomies are performed annually on an unknown number of women, sometimes on the grounds of a strong family history, but more often on the basis of weaker indicators that they might be "susceptible" to breast cancer. Paradoxically, while those doing the research see nothing Draconian about delivering a potent, hormone-altering drug to thousands of healthy women, many of them do cringe at the use of mastectomies as a preventive measure, except in rare instances where a woman's family history suggests she is at exceptionally high risk for breast cancer.

Feminist surgeon Susan Love says of preventive double mastectomies: "In very few other parts of the body do we suggest removing an organ to prevent a disease from occurring." She once suggested, on a TV show, removing men's testicles and replacing them with Ping-Pong balls to prevent testicular cancer. "Somehow," she recalls, "the men in the audience didn't think this was as good an idea as preventively removing breasts."[14]

Love says both the tamoxifen trial and the dietary fat study are important, "because they represent the first time that federal money is going into trying to prevent this killer." If the tamoxifen trial prevents 65 breast cancers in the 8,000 women in the test arm of the trial, as projected, she explains, "this is only a drop in the bucket but it's a start."[15] In her testimony before a government committee that marked the 20th anniversary of Nixon's War on Cancer, Love continued, "It certainly would be better to truly prevent breast cancer with lifestyle changes than to try and turn it around at a later stage with drugs. Still, drug prevention is better than having to treat a potentially fatal disease."

In tandem with drug prevention studies using tamoxifen, retinoids and RU 486, Love said, "we must pursue ... studies of dietary and lifestyle changes if we are really going to make any long term difference in incidence and mortality."[16] Love advocates research on the diets, exercise activity, sleeping habits, and other modifiable behaviours of adolescent girls. She also broaches the issue of environmental carcinogens, and the hormones used in beef and chicken. "Maybe it isn't our high-fat diets themselves that are at fault, but the contaminants of the fat. We can't be satisfied with limited research in prevention — the area that is ultimately the most important."[17]

Love's proposals to investigate environmental carcinogens and a broader range of dietary questions are refreshing, but her acceptance (albeit lukewarm) of "drug prevention" perplexed me. Fugh-Berman explains the oncology community's intoxication with tamoxifen in terms of oncology's skewed world view. "Supporters of the tamoxifen trial are cancer doctors and their patients all have cancer," she says. "In oncology, which uses more toxic medications than any other specialty, tamoxifen is the most benign substance going ... When you compare it to vaccinations, iodized salt, and vitamin D enriched milk, it doesn't look so great."[18]

Another hypothetical explanation is that tamoxifen's advocates see the drug as more high-tech than the alternatives. Double mastectomies are probably more effective than tamoxifen but the crudeness of the operation offends a community that views itself as progressive and scientific. Medication seems more sophisticated, even if its efficacy is likely less and physical side effects are systemic rather than local. The public wants a prevention strategy, and a drug of dubious safety also seems preferable to admitting that prevention is beyond current medical knowledge.

Since much of the public pressure for a preventive strategy comes from the alarming rise in the incidence of breast cancer, we need to consider what incidence figures mean. In their statistical analysis of cancer, Bailar and Smith argue that a good bit of the apparent rise of breast cancer is an artificial creation of mammography programs. After early detection programs for breast, lung and prostate cancer were introduced, survival rates for these cancers improved, but mortality did not, said Bailar and Smith in their analysis. This suggested that more sensitive detection methods were picking up benign lesions which were being classified and treated as if they were cancerous. This interpretation of breast cancer incidence rates undercuts the claims of progress attributable to mammography and breast cancer treatment. If many of the cancers detected by mammography are actually benign lesions, the net impact of those cases is a broader definition of cancer, not lives saved.

This reading of the figures suggests that the rise in breast cancer incidence is less alarming than the public assumes. A conservative treatment policy would label those women with pre-cancers "high risk"; they could be closely monitored rather than treated. Instead, the dogma of early detection and the oncology norm of aggressive treatment shapes the public response. *In situ* cancers are celebrated as the ultimate in early detection.

The logic behind the tamoxifen trial is the same as that behind detecting and treating pre-cancers, but the diagnostic circle is drawn larger. To be eligible for the trial, a woman has to have a risk of breast cancer at least equal to that of an average, healthy 60-year-old woman — that is, a risk of a cancer diagnosis of just under two percent within five years. Put another way, a woman could have a 98 percent chance of not getting breast cancer in the five year trial period and still be classified as "high risk" for study purposes. Younger women had to have one or more risk factors besides age to elevate their risk, such as a previous biopsy for suspected breast cancer, one first-degree relative (mother or sister) with breast cancer, or early menarch (defined as before age 12). If the trial had included only women at very high risk, Fugh-Berman says she might not have objected to it. "In order for the researchers to get enough volunteers, they've cast their net very broadly. They are including women who are not at very high risk, but essentially healthy women."[19]

The idea that "high risk" groups of women be targeted for medical interventions simply underscores how little we know about predicting who will get the disease. Seventy to 80 percent of the women who get breast cancer have none of the known risk factors except for age. Fugh-Berman's critique of the tamoxifen trial casting too wide a net would apply to any prevention-intervention project for the simple reason that we don't have the knowledge to identify women who are truly high-risk except for those in presumed "breast cancer families."

Some researchers, to their credit, have begun to propose potential risk factors that merit further study. Lists include diagnostic radiation in adolescence, smoking (including second-hand smoke), alcohol, lactation,[20] attention to the types of fat consumed, prolonged use of hormone replacement therapy at high doses, prolonged use of oral contraceptives before first pregnancy, stress and exercise patterns, and exposures to pesticides and other fat-seeking synthetic organic chemicals that can bioconcentrate in fat.

In 1993, a report that some vegetables seem to have active ingredients that actually cause cancers to regress made waves. Fiber, anti-oxidents (green-yellow vegetables), calcium and vitamin D are now getting serious attention as useful routes to cancer prevention. The alleged cancer-fighting properties of vegetables like broccoli, cabbage and carrots was nothing new. Food writer Jane Brody had been pushing them for years; after reading her *Good Food Book* I took to eating broccoli almost daily. The news that scientists had isolated the active ingredient for the effect and christened the new field "chemoprevention" — the same term used for tamoxifen — cast a pall, for me, over the new direction in dietary research. While the public awaits concrete advice on how to improve diet, researchers are off on a search to transform everyday vegetables into high-priced pharmaceuticals.

A common response to the confused picture over dietary links to breast cancer is to say that women should eat less fat and more vegetables anyway, and a sensible diet will probably help reduce breast cancer risk even though no one has proven it. In 1981, prominent British cancer epidemiologists Richard Doll and Richard Peto declared that U.S. breast cancer rates could probably be cut in half by dietary measures. By the end of the decade, Doll conceded his belief in the dietary hypothesis was more a matter of faith than scientific knowledge.[21] Still, women's magazines, and even doctors, have now taken to saying that a low-fat diet for breast cancer will do no harm and probably some good — even if the research data is confused and incomplete.

Even as I changed my own diet to virtually eliminate beef, alcohol, nuts, butter, cheese, avocados, any milk products other than skim, and to include a daily hit of broccoli or some other "cancer-fighting" vegetable, this argument struck me as hollow — like going to church every week, just in case God was really up there keeping a scorecard on me. A few months after I began my low-fat regimen, I shed the 15 pounds I'd gained on chemotherapy. For that I was glad, but I felt no less susceptible to cancer. I also resented the pang of guilt whenever I succumbed to a slice of cake or a few buttery nibblies at a party. I'd look around the room at all the people quaffing gobs of goodies and my hair shirt would begin to itch. Something was wrong here — none of them had cancer. Indeed, mounting evidence shows that women who get breast cancer before menopause tend to be tall and thin.

The first person I heard state, unequivocally, that *environmental* contaminants caused breast cancer was San Francisco activist Judy Brady. Judy was diagnosed with breast cancer in 1980. Ten years later she was compiling a book about women and cancer and wanted to include my newspaper polemic against the ethos of facing breast cancer with stoic cheerfulness. She described the theme of her book as cancer and the environment. "But breast cancer has no environmental causes," I protested. I wondered if she was some kind of environmental extremist.

She sighed, then explained, very firmly, that breast cancer most certainly did have environmental causes. "Benzo(a)pyrene has been conclusively linked to breast cancer," she said. "So has butadiene [emitted in the manufacture of synthetic rubber]. With breast cancer, these connections are indirect," she said, "but they are certainly there."

Judy Brady's search for an explanation of her breast cancer diagnosis took her to the office of the National Association of Radiation Survivors. There she came across a scientific report on the effects of low levels of ionizing radiation that stated, "The female breast is one of the organs most susceptible to radiation carcinogenesis." She read about the breast cancer cases among Japanese women who survived the bombing of Hiroshima and Nagasaki, then found another report that hit home. It showed the distribution throughout the U.S. of sites that produce ionizing radiation. They included nuclear energy and fuel production plants, weapons production and research plants and toxic waste dumps. California had more of these sites than any other state. For Judy, who had lived all her life in California, this was the explanation she was looking for. She joined the National Association of Radiation Survivors on the spot. "I was one of them and I knew it."[22]

From that first epiphany, she went on to develop an analysis that frames breast cancer, along with all other cancers, as a social and political issue. Her cancer and its treatment, with radiation and toxic chemicals, are a price paid, she says, "for being born in a time and place where polluting the world is more profitable than protecting it."[23] While some of the links between specific carcinogens and cancers are well documented — asbestos to lung and stomach cancer, vinyl chloride (used in the manufacture of plastics) to liver cancer, benzene (produced in oil refineries) to leukemia, benzo(a)pyrene in cigarettes to lung cancer — Judy argues, "it doesn't take a particularly imaginative mind to make some connections [to breast cancer], even if those connections haven't been 'proven.'" Benzo(a)pyrene, which is present in fossil fuel emissions as well as cigarettes, has been linked to breast cancer, she learned; animal studies show that it tends to attach itself to fat cells, and excess weight is linked to breast cancer. If definitive proof was lacking, Judy pointed out — still making connections — what did you expect when the heads of chemical companies were often one and the same as the heads of major cancer agencies? Her analysis led her straight to political activism aimed at eliminating carcinogens from the chemical and nuclear industries. Of course she says, there will be "cries of bankruptcy from the industries which must be shut down." We will have to ignore them.

Brady's book, *1 in 3: Women with Cancer Confront an Epidemic*, appeared in 1991. Within a few years, scientific reports trickled in that lent credence to her ideas about the links between cancer and chemical pollutants. "The Israeli Breast Cancer Anomaly" published by Israeli researchers Jerome Westin and Elihu Richter, is a study of breast cancer mortality rates in Israel. The anomaly was that Israel stood out as the one western country where the disease had actually loosened its grip, by an impressive eight percent, in the decade from 1976 to 1986. That was all the more surprising, said Westin and Richter, because a number of key breast cancer risk factors (such as dietary fat consumption and reproductive patterns) would have predicted a continuing increase.

Another anomaly in the Israeli data, the researchers pointed out, was that breast cancer mortality in Israel had been especially high among younger women compared to other countries with equivalent levels of fat consumption. The drop in mortality had been dramatic (30 percent) in women under 44 years of age. Death rates of premenopausal women are usually relatively constant from year to year and one country to the next; the variability is typically among women over 50, and correlates highly with the country's level of fat consumption. To Westin and Richter, all the signs pointed to an especially potent environmental factor which was selectively hitting younger women in Israel, and was then removed.

The most plausible explanation, they suggested, was the country's ban, in 1978, of three potent carcinogenic pesticides: benzene hexachloride, lindane and DDT. For at least 10 years before, Israeli milk and dairy products had been highly contaminated by these products. These pesticides had estrogenic properties which might be expected to interact strongly in the bodies of premenopausal women. The data fit their theory elegantly.[24]

When a small American study found that women with breast cancer had higher residues of DDE (a DDT by-product) and PCBs stored in their breast tissue than did those with benign breast lumps, the chemical carcinogen theory made newspaper headlines. Chemist Mary Wolff, of New York's Mount Sinai School of Medicine, followed up with an NCI-funded study of DDE and PCBs in blood samples taken from women who had breast cancer and a matched group who did not. This study found no link between breast cancer and PCBs, but women with the highest levels of DDE (the top 10 percent) had four times the breast cancer rate of women in the bottom 10 percent. The study's publication in the *Journal of the National Cancer Institute* exposed the most mainstream cancer researchers to what had been, a few years earlier, a fringe theory.

Although DDT was phased out in 1972 in the U.S., "we're all exposed to it through diet," said Wolff. DDT is stored in the body for decades, so most adult North Americans still carry residues, while children are exposed through their mother's milk.[25]

Wolff's findings held a poignant irony for environmentalists. The U.S. ban on DDT was a direct result of Rachel Carson's book, *Silent Spring*, published three decades earlier. "The most determined effort should be made to eliminate those carcinogens that now contaminate our food, our water supplies, and our atmosphere," wrote Carson, "because those provide the most dangerous type of contact — minute exposures, repeated over and over throughout the years."[26] Carson died of breast cancer in April 1964, two years after her book appeared.

In 1957, Carson had covered a trial on pesticide spraying as part of an article on pesticides she was writing for the *New Yorker*. The citizens of Nassau and Suffolk counties sought a court injunction to stop state and federal government officials from spraying their land with DDT to control the gypsy moth. The protesters lost their lawsuit, but the testimony Carson heard then about the potential dangers of DDT for people and wildlife grew into her classic indictment of pesticide spraying.

Long Island today has one of the highest incidence rates of breast cancer in the United States. But activism in Long Island has proven to be as stubborn as pesticide residues. When women on the island learned, in the mid-1980s, that Nassau and Suffolk counties had breast cancer rates 13 to 14 percent higher than the state average, they organized. The island was once New York's vegetable garden and spraying, in particular, was routine. The women suspected the environment was involved in some way, "or at least you need to study it and rule it out," said one member of the activist group, which called itself "One in Nine."[27] The women demanded a prevention-based research program.

In November 1993 the federal government committed money to long-term, wide scale studies analyzing a range of environmental factors, from drinking water, the dust in home carpeting, and radiation emissions from household appliances. The study is probably the most ambitious research project ever into breast cancer prevention.

Suddenly it's not wildly speculative to discuss breast cancer and environmental contaminants — and to talk about actually trying to prevent breast cancer through changes to the way we live. The theory that fat-soluble synthetic chemicals mimic or amplify the cancer-causing effects of estrogen is so frequently discussed it now has a name — the xenoestrogen hypothesis. Middle-of-the-road scientists are sceptical. "It hasn't gained in credibility," said one researcher to *Scientific American*, "The people who are pushing this feel they want to make a contribution, and they are simply responding to public fear by trying to identify a removable cause."[28]

Despite the condescension of sceptics, however, in a few short years a genuine prevention perspective has found a niche in breast cancer theorizing. Occupational research in breast cancer is rare, but the few studies that have found links are consistent with the environmental research. Women chemists, hairdressers and golfers (who spend hours at a time striding over chemically maintained greens) have all been found, in scattered studies, to have elevated rates of breast cancer. A well-documented report by Greenpeace proposes that dioxins, the chemicals used to bleach paper, may contribute to rising rates of breast cancer, especially in the Great Lakes communities contaminated by industry.

Communities fed by the Great Lakes include my home, Montreal. In its 1992 report, the Parliamentary committee studying breast cancer noted that Montreal was still a breast cancer hot spot, along with Toronto, the manufacturing centre of Brantford, Ontario, and the steel industry town of Sydney, Nova Scotia. The report recommended investigations into chemical contaminants and breast cancer and a few have already received funding.

Intervention is still the preferred "prevention" route among oncologists. For many women, however, the tamoxifen prevention trial stimulated a process of making connections. I think of us as the spiritual daughters of Rachel Carson, women who read her nearly banned book as high school or university students. After learning, with a shock, that she died of "our" disease, we discover in her writing a clear exposition of the principles that separate true prevention from the prevailing culture of intervention-prevention.

The war on cancer that has been waged with so little effect for the past 40 years bears the same hallmarks as the war on insects waged in the 50s with pesticides. The aggressive and blanket approach to combating breast cancer with radiation, drugs and mammography has significant parallels with the mass spraying with DDT that was promoted as the answer to agricultural pests and, by extension, to world starvation. Both strategies arise from the same scientific philosophy, geared to domination, control and financial profit.

Spraying with poisons was promoted as a quicker and more effective solution to crop devastation than trying to solve the political and economic problems behind starvation. Carson ended her book with an appeal that we follow what she called "the other road," a new direction in science and technology. Rather than using science to control living organisms, she urged that it be used to understand those organisms and the "whole fabric" of life to which they belonged.[29]

As women with breast cancer begin to gather under a common banner, we are urging that the same shift in ideology be applied to the disease. We question treatments with success rates that are hailed as statistically significant but which, on close scrutiny, benefit only 10 or 12 percent of those who endure them; treatments which come brightly packaged with undisclosed short- and long-term harms to body, mind and spirit. We question why "alternative" treatments — ranging from unorthodox biological approaches, to diets, meditation, and support groups — are actively denigrated by the medical community when so many patients report they are helpful. We question treatment and research policies that bolster and promote these narrow tumour-focussed treatments while ignoring the adverse effects that breast cancer has on the "whole fabric" of our lives — our emotions, spirit, sexuality, personal relationships and financial security. We question the millions spent on treatments and biological research at the expense of a long-term strategy to understand how women can live our lives without ever getting breast cancer.

We are beginning to understand the answers to our questions. Environmental engineer Patricia Hynes immersed herelf in Rachel Carson's epic work and produced her own feminist reading of it, titled *The Recurring Silent Spring*. In it, Hynes lists four guideposts by which we can recognize technologies descended from the atomic bomb — "the midcentury touchstone of male dominance, with nature as the instrument of destruction."

- First, a mythology encases the technology to make it necessary and acceptable. Once it becomes technically possible, it becomes inevitable;
- Second, regulation and policy are used to protect the technology, to ensure that it can profitably survive conflict, public distrust, and even failure;
- Third, public policy, ethical analysis, and analysis of the technology's risks lag behind the technology's development;
- And fourth, the new technology is not presented as one among many solutions to a problem but as the dominant one. The alternatives to the technology, "the other road," are shut out.

Just as pesticides fit this pattern, says Hynes, so do agricultural policies based on genetic engineering; so do the new reproductive technologies.

Current breast cancer treatments can also be characterized as descendants of the bomb, part of the recurring pattern of a control-oriented science. Radiation and chemotherapy are literal offshoots of wartime technology. Chemotherapy, like the bomb, was developed in secret and research into radiation — even medical uses of radiation — is closed to public scrutiny.

Consider Hynes' four guideposts:

1. *A legitimizing mythology.* The mythology that surrounds orthodox breast cancer treatments is that harsh, aggressive attacks are effective and indeed the only way to combat cancer, even though evidence of progress is a will-o'-the-wisp. Promoting the technology are the two slogans, "early detection is your best protection" and "cancer can be beaten." The dozens of chemotherapy combinations, strengths and schedules, the increasing precision of radiation and mammography have not fulfilled their promise, but science presses further along the same path with inventive hormonal intervention schemes and the impending genetic technologies. The limits of surgery are now well established, yet elaborate schemes to "improve" breast surgery through breast implants and tram flap breast reconstruction and more precise post-lumpectomy radiation continue apace.

2. *Regulation and policy ensure profit and acceptance.* Regulations and policies protect orthodox treatments and discourage the use of treatments termed unorthodox or alternative. The medical associations work closely with such agencies as the Cancer Societies and the cancer research institutes, and with government regulatory agencies. Radical mastectomies, breast implants, chemotherapies and post-mastectomy radiation all were launched into standard use as breast cancer treatments without evidence of long-term safety and all survived long after their effectiveness was called into question. Mammography was rushed into mass use before it had demonstrated a utility in saving lives and continues to flourish, without adequate quality controls. The hormonal and genetic treatments now in development are getting advance promotion with the same promises and with the same regulatory support as the established treatments.

3. *Policy analysis lags behind technical development.* The tamoxifen prevention trials dramatically illustrate that risk evaluation, and debate about ethics and policy, lag behind the development of

breast cancer treatment technology. The trials were approved by government agencies in a half-dozen countries before ethical and policy issues had been addressed and before long-term risks of the medication in cancer patients had been assessed. Public health workers who, on the whole, do not support the trial and were not partners in its development, will confront unprecedented decisions about administering the drug if the trial outcome shows tamoxifen has preventive potential. Genetic applications to cancer, similarly, have galloped ahead of discussion about the non-medical effects. Policy papers on the likely impact of genetic screening for cancer are just beginning to appear, a year after scientists announced the discovery of the breast cancer gene could be imminent. Although analysts generally agree that genetic testing poses daunting practical and ethical problems, social and ethical implications take a back seat to technological research.

4. *Technology is presented as the dominant approach.* For four decades, the single dominant approach to controlling breast cancer has been aggressive, and increasingly technical, treatment. By combining treatments and moving them back to ever-earlier stages of disease and, finally, to women with no sign of disease, the numbers of women treated are increased, independent of whatever real increase in incidence may be occurring.

"The other road," which has been closed off, is to aim to prevent breast cancer through an understanding of the female body and its relation to the environment. This approach would seek to limit exposure to carcinogens and non-toxic ways to enhance the body's resistance to breast cancer. David Spiegel's research on support groups (see "Alternatives" chapter) is one prototype of a benign treatment method; dietary changes are another.

Like most people I know, I once believed that mammography unerringly found cancerous breast lumps years before they could be felt, that existing treatments would cure the disease, that women who got breast cancer soon put the disease behind them and went cheerfully on with their lives. The gap between these beliefs and reality still takes my breath away. How could such a distorted view be entrenched and sustained for so long?

The mythology is powerful and has been constructed over a period of decades: it sustains the belief that an arsenal of sophisticated biotechnical weaponry has breast cancer virtually beaten. The information that reaches the public is groomed not only by the medical profession but by a variety of powerful interest groups: cancer charities, multinational companies and the media. Each filters the truth in a way that complements the others and serves its own needs.

Notes

1. Susan Ince, "Health: Breast Cancer Prevention," *Vogue*, (Oct. 1990), p. 284.

2. Adriane Fugh-Berman, *The Medicalization of Prevention*, unpublished manuscript, (1994), p. 6.

3. Subcommittee on the Status of Women [Barbara Greene, M.P., Chair], *Breast Cancer: Unanswered Questions*, [Report of the Standing Committee on Health and Welfare, Social Affairs, Seniors and the Status of Women], (Ottawa: House of Commons, June 1992).

4. G. Howe et al, "A Cohort Study of Fat Intake and Risk of Breast Cancer," *Journal of the National Cancer Institute*, (Mar. 6, 1991), pp. 336-340.

5. Norman Boyd, *House of Commons Proceedings*, (Nov. 26, 1991), p. 6:32-6:41.

6. Patterson, pp. 184-5.

7. Ince, p. 280.

8. General Accounting Office, *Breast Cancer: 1971-1991*, (Washington, Dec. 1991), p. 4.

9. John C. Bailar III, "The Case for Cancer Prevention," *Journal of the National Cancer Institute*, (Apr. 1979), vol 62, no 4, p. 727.

10. John C. Bailar and Elaine Smith, "Progress Against Cancer?," *New England Journal of Medicine*, (May 8, 1986), pp. 1226-1232.

11. Rita Arditte with Tatiana Schrieiber, "Breast Cancer: The Environmental Connection," *Resist*, (May/June 1992), p. 7.

12. Adriane Fugh-Berman, "Tamoxifen in Healthy Women: Preventive Health or Preventing Health?" *The Network News*, (Sept./Oct. 1991), pp. 3-4.

13. "Best Guesses" transcript, p. 9.

14. Love with Lindsay, pp. 150-151.

15. Love in Wadler, p. 169.

16. Susan Love, Testimony before the Human Resources and Intergovernmental Relations Subcommittee of the Committee on Government Operations, (Dec. 11, 1991), [from transcript], p. 4.

17. Love in Wadler, pp. 169-170.

18. "Best Guesses," pp. 8-9.

19. Janet Raloff, "Tamoxifen Quandry," *Science News*, (Apr. 25, 1992), p. 268.

20. Richard Love, Breast Cancer in Younger Women Conference, (Feb. 1993), [from transcript], pp. 150-151; Devra Lee Davis, Canadian Breast Cancer Forum, Testimony before the U.S. Hearing on Breast Cancer, (Dec. 11, 1991).

21. Cited in General Accounting Office, p. 41.

22. Judith Brady, ed., *1 in 3: Women with Cancer Confront an Epidemic*, (Pittsburgh: Cleis Press, 1991), p. 8.

23. Brady, p. 14.

24. Jerome B. Westin and Elihu Richter, "The Israeli Breast-Cancer Anomoly," *Annals of the New York Academy of Sciences*, (1990), pp. 269-279.

25. AP story "Women's Exposure to DDT Tied to Breast Cancer in Study," reported in the *Globe and Mail*, (Apr. 21, 1993), p. A6.

26. Rachel Carson, *Silent Spring*, (Boston: Houghton Mifflin, 1987), p. 242.

27. Quote from "Dirty Business," hosted by Lynn Glazier, *Centrepoint*, CBC Radio, (Fall 1993).

28. Tim Beardsley, "A War Not Won," *Scientific American*, (Jan. 1994), p. 137.

29. Carson, p. 244, cited in Hynes, p. 16.

THREE

Filters

*The raw material of news must pass through successive
filters, leaving only the cleansed residue fit to print.
They fix the premises of discourse and interpretation,
and the definition of what is newsworthy in the
first place and they explain the basis of operation of
what amount to propaganda campaigns.*

— E S. Herman and Noam Chomsky, *Manufacturing Consent*

"Perfect People"
Cancer Charities

Some readers may be startled to learn that the overall mortality rate from carcinoma of the breast remains static. If one were to believe all the media hype, the triumphalism of the profession in published research, and the almost weekly miracle breakthroughs trumpeted by the cancer charities, one might be surprised that women are dying at all from this cancer.

— Editorial, *Lancet*, Feb. 6, 1993

The ad in the London newspaper was in large type, like a child's reader. The text encircled a hand mirror, face-up with an open tube of lipstick resting on the glass:

What use is a lipstick to a woman who is dying of cancer? There once was a woman who wore bright red lipstick because it made her feel optimistic and confident. She wouldn't have dared leave the house without it on. Then one day she found she had cancer. It was serious, she didn't have long to live. Suddenly she didn't feel like wearing her lipstick anymore. She didn't want to face the world again. She just wanted to be at home with her husband and family and to be left alone. Soon she retreated into a shell where no one could reach her. Then one night a Marie Curie nurse came and she sat with the woman and she gently drew her out until she was able to talk about her grief and fears. In the morning the nurse handed the woman her bright red lipstick and said, 'Why don't you put some on?' The woman hesitated, but then she took it. And when she looked at her reflection, she smiled. Suddenly she felt better. She was ready to face the world again. Now there are others who need your help. Please help us to help them. Send your donation to Marie Curie Cancer Care, 28 Belgrave Sq., London SWIX 8QG. For credit card donations Tel: 071-823 1907.

— *The Daily Telegraph,* March 11, 1992

The period of my cancer treatments was an intensely inward-looking time. I counted the days to the end of my chemotherapy and radiation treatments, and watched my athletic looks give way to pallor, weight gain and ghoulish baldness. I struggled with my fear of death. And I wondered: how could I have been so oblivious to a disease that claims the lives of so many women — 5,500 in Canada and 45,000 in the U.S in 1992; 570,000 world wide in 1980. Breast cancer claims women at an age considered young in industrialized countries; age 62, compared to age 82 for women who die of cardiovascular disease. Many who die are women like me, who believed themselves healthy, well informed, and somewhere in the mid-region of their life. When I learned these facts, I felt tricked, as if I had stumbled into a chamber of horrors kept secret behind a veil of cheerful platitudes. *Do breast self-exams. Have regular mammograms. See your doctor at the first sign of a lump. Breast cancer can be cured!* I needed to know where these slogans had come from.

As I sat with my friend Jeannie watching the TV special Destined to Live, still hairless from chemotherapy, this feeling of deception came into sharp focus. The one-hour documentary profiled American women with breast cancer, many of them well known (Nancy Reagan, Gloria Steinem, Jill Eisenbury and the late Jill Ireland), all looking vibrant and happy. Each spoke movingly about her terror at the moment of diagnosis, but each had conquered her fear of cancer. Pithy bright messages dotted the testimonials. "When life kicks you, let it kick you forward," advised a woman who had survived a year and two months. "Cancer was the best thing that ever happened to me," said another. "I laughed at it and I beat it, that's all," proclaimed a man, still alive 11 years after his diagnosis. A syrupy theme song gushed, *Brand new dreams, I've got brand new dreams! They're not just dreams, they're coming true!*

Courage is all very well, I thought, as the credits rolled, but the broadcast was one-sided in the extreme. The sick were not mentioned and the dead were not mourned. Nowhere in the broadcast was any suggestion that the public should be concerned about breast cancer. I looked at the list of sponsors — a veritable who's who of America's cancer establishment — the American Cancer Society (ACS), the American Medical Association (AMA), etc., etc. What purpose was served by misrepresenting breast cancer, I wondered. If I could answer that question, I felt I would better understand my own naive assumptions.

The sponsors of Destined to Live represent the interest groups James Patterson calls "the Alliance against Cancer." A political historian at Brown University, Patterson turned his eye to cancer after his wife died of the disease. His book, *The Dread Disease: Cancer and Modern American Culture* is a thorough analysis of cancer politics in the United States, seen through an unsentimental lens. The "Message of Hope," says Patterson, is the most prevalent theme running through cancer educational campaigns in the 20th century. More specifically, it is the message that cancer can be attacked by a strategy available to all Americans: early detection.[1]

The origins of the message date to the early part of the century, when an elite corps of doctors began a campaign to challenge popular pessimism about cancer as a disease that was invariably fatal and about which nothing could be done. They recruited as allies optimistic and progressive professionals like themselves, including statisticians, philanthropists and influential people in the press. Their basic goals — to overcome the cancerphobia that kept the disease in the closet and to advance medical knowledge — were a potent mix of the laudable and the self-serving. They wanted to get patients into their offices. They wanted funds for research. They were painfully aware that they didn't know how to cure most types of cancer or to explain the origin of its many forms. With the Message of Hope as their central theme, they launched a campaign against cancer that continues, with only slight variations, into the 1990s.

The first drafts of the message were prepared by the American Society for the Control of Cancer (ASCC), precursor to the American Cancer Society. The inspiration of Mrs. Robert Mead, daughter of a New York gynaecologist, the ASCC was part of a larger trend in which progressive-thinking wealthy people took up the cause of various diseases. The *New York Times* headlined the 1913 story: "Rich women begin a war on cancer." One of Mead's friends, John D. Rockefeller Jr., became a major benefactor to the Society, urged on by his medical adviser, who told him: "Here is the outstanding disease, not only in this country, but the whole world ... I cannot think of anything that would be more *popular* for Mr. Rockefeller to do than to become vitally interested in this cancer field."[2]

Doctors, particularly surgeons, dominated the ASCC in the early years, says Patterson, and their central message to the public was "to see their doctors at the slightest hint of trouble." Of special concern was the shame that kept women from the doctor's office if they had a symptom of cancer in their "secret parts." Working through women's organizations, the Society tried to overcome the stigma of breast, uterine and cervical cancers. The ASCC had other reasons for focussing on women. Early on, a Prudential Insurance executive named Frederick Hoffman joined forces with the Society and became its chief statistical expert. Hoffman found that deaths from cancer killed twice as many of the company's female policy holders as male policy holders (10 percent versus five percent in 1912). For 30 years, pamphlets, speakers and magazine articles directed at women stressed the value of early detection and trusting the doctor.

At the outset, the ASCC had scant contact with women outside the elite circle of the wealthy founders. That changed in the 1930s, when an enterprising ASCC president hatched an idea called the Women's Field Army, envisioned as a cadre of women volunteers headed by a radiologist, Marjorie Illig.

"Illig took over as National Commander," says Patterson, "leading the 'war' against the 'stubborn foe' and issuing orders to state commanders and captains dressed in brown uniforms. Posters and handbills listed Eleanor Roosevelt and other national figures as honorary supporters and featured the ASCC's symbol, a flaming sword that glowed with spirit and determination. 'There shall be light!' these proclaimed: enlist in women's field army! Thus armed, the officers hoped to build an army of foot soldiers who would carry the message of early detection and medical intervention into every home in the land."[3]

The Field Army brought middle-class women into the alliance, forming a triangle with the doctors and the rich women. Their place in the order of things was definitely unequal, however. As the name implied, their role was to carry out orders from above.

Despite its blueblooded connections and the outreach of the Women's Field Army, the ASCC was a relatively small, struggling charity, concentrated on the east coast, until the mid-1940s. In 1944, a group of business people led by Mary Lasker, the wife of an advertising tycoon, swept into the modest New York office of the ASCC and took charge. They changed the organization's name to the American Cancer Society, added leading businessmen to the board, and applied their aggressive techniques of advertising and fundraising to the cause of cancer. The Society's budget — only $102,000 in 1943 — ballooned accordingly. By 1948 Lasker and her team had raised $14 million.

Doctors were alarmed by the power grab, which threatened for a while to split the Society in two. The businessmen, complained the Society's physician-president to a colleague, had taken up cancer control as "a civic interest which is in no way comparable to the relationship of the professional men in the field." The group, he complained, was developing an "unjustifiable, troublesome, and aggressive attitude of 'knowing it all.'"

Nevertheless, Lasker's team stayed at the helm for decades, growing in influence and moving cancer, and other diseases, into public awareness. They effectively worked their contacts, not just among the very wealthy, but among federal politicians whom Lasker's critics dubbed "Mary's Little Lambs." One key to getting federal money, they realized, was to tie research allocations to specific diseases. That way congressmen could be seen as backing research into the very diseases of which their constituents were dying. The Lasker group lobbied to bring huge sums of money to the National Cancer Institute (NCI), a government-funded research agency set up in 1937.[4]

The gush of money overcame most of the reservations medical people had about Lasker's team. The collaboration was made more comfortable by a mutually agreed upon division of labour that gave the ACS responsibility for charitable fundraising and education while the NCI got its money from taxes and spent it on research. Early concerns that the public would balk at the double hit on their wallets proved groundless. Beneath the word "cancer" was a bottomless well of fear, ready to be tapped. There was more than enough for everyone.

In the 1950s, the optimistic tone of American Cancer Society advertising became relentless. Before that, fundraising pamphlets and speakers sometimes hammered its messages home with frightening statistics. "Every Three Minutes Someone Dies of Cancer ... Give to Conquer Cancer." People began to accuse the Society of fanning cancerphobia. Why not a helping hand as a symbol, one suggested, instead of a flaming sword entwined with snakes? The progressive surgeon George Crile Jr., one of the early crusaders for conservative breast surgery, argued that the Cancer Society was driving people to demand unnecessary tests and surgery. "People who have never had cancer have died of operations done in cancer's name," said Crile. Soon, direct appeals to fear virtually disappeared from the Society's propaganda arsenal.

Under the new regime, grass-roots volunteers were no longer needed for either fundraising or public education. The Lasker group was contemptuous of the Women's Field Army ("a Ladies Garden Club style" operation composed of "do-good amateurs") and soon disbanded it. Slick campaigns in leading popular magazines were more effective.

Reach to Recovery brought "ordinary" volunteers back into the organization. The Cancer Society's signature program for women with breast cancer, "R2R," was based on a concept developed by mastectomee Therese Lasser in 1952, back when the Halsted radical was standard treatment. Lasser's idea was innovative for the time. She believed that someone who had personally experienced cancer could provide invaluable emotional support to other cancer patients. With perseverance, she eventually gained enough acceptance for her idea in the medical community to have it officially adopted, in 1969, as an ACS program. After her surgery, a woman is visited in the hospital by a woman who has herself recovered from the operation. The Canadian Cancer Society set up a Reach to Recovery service in 1972; similar programs have been set up in Britain and Japan.

In packaging Lasser's concept of visits from someone who's "been there," the Cancer Society lost most of the goodness at the core: emotional support. The visitor, who had to pass muster with the Society as someone who had "adjusted" physically and emotionally to her own surgery, was recast as a walking testimonial to medicine's ability to cure breast cancer. The woman's surgeon had to approve the visit. If the doctor gave the OK, the volunteer

arrived with a kit designed to aid the newly recovering woman —
a piece of string, an elastic band and a rubber ball for exercises
and a puff of lambswool to stick in her bra until she had healed
well enough to be fitted with a "real" form. Many emotionally
loaded areas central to the woman facing this major trauma
(family relationships, doctors and other hospital staff, the scar)
were off limits for discussion.

Society fundraisers also maintained an upbeat tone. Lavish
luncheons and galas for the wealthy were no place to talk about
dying women or the long-term distress of those who had been
"looked after" by their physician. One of Canada's most
celebrated breast cancer fundraisers is Toronto socialite Nancy
Paul, wife of a wealthy developer whose first wife died of breast
cancer. Paul is one of an elite group of Toronto women profiled
by society chronicler Rosemary Sexton in her book *The Glitter
Girls.* Paul put in more than a decade volunteering for the
Canadian Cancer Society (CCS), organizing an annual CCS
fashion show sponsored by the exclusive clothing store Creed's. In
1986 she wanted to stage a charity lunch for Italian designer
Valentino with the proceeds to go specifically to breast cancer, but
she hit a snag. Cancer Society rules wouldn't permit the money to
be earmarked for one type of cancer. The enterprising Paul set up
her own fundraising group, the Canadian Breast Cancer Foundation (CBCF).

Paul's model for a breast cancer charity was the Susan Komen
Foundation, founded by the American socialite Nancy Brinker.
Nancy Paul and Nancy Brinker met in Palm Beach. Brinker set up
her charity in memory of her sister, who had died of breast cancer.
She was subsequently diagnosed with breast cancer herself. Inspired by Brinker, Paul staged her first gala in honour of Valentino. The black-tie dinner for 260 in the basement of her
12-bathroom mansion raised $35,000. The event was so grand,
Paul told Rosemary Sexton, *Women's Wear Daily* pronounced it the
most spectacular on the designer's North American tour.[5]

While Nancy Brinker was Nancy Paul's immediate inspiration,
the extravagant style harks back to Mary Lasker. Lasker knew how
to reward her lambs, both political and scientific. Compliant
politicians of either party received generous campaign donations,
while the annual Albert Lasker Awards in Medical Research
stroked scientists' egos. Of more than 200 Lasker award

recipients, an astonishing 42 later received Nobel prizes.[6] At the Canadian Breast Cancer Foundation's second awards luncheon, the focus was "an awards ceremony at which various doctors and generous benefactors were paraded down the long raised platform amid the guests. Each one was presented with a medal as his or her respective virtues were lauded to the hilt." Celebrity guests from television, politics, opera, ballet and sports accompanied the winners down the runway. Although critics called the luncheon excessive in its display, Sexton says, "the success and the large profits being raised for the CBCF could not be denied."

When the federal government earmarked $25 million for breast cancer research, Sexton says the allocation was "largely due to the hard work and lobbying done by Nancy and her successors." This is a contentious claim, since a large grass-roots lobbying effort had been mounted by women with breast cancer; however, the statement again points to ambitions reminiscent of Mary Lasker. Lasker and her cronies exercised a control over American national health policy that was probably unparalleled. "We're not second story burglars. We go right in the front door," bragged a cohort, lobbyist Mike Gorman. He attributed Lasker's success to "a high class kind of subversion, very high class." Lasker's clout in Washington was such that the amount of money going into cancer research began to trouble even researchers. The grant-hungry scientists were putting a "cancer angle" in their proposals and Congress was throwing more money at the problem — especially at chemotherapy — than researchers could use wisely.[7]

As well as bringing fame and influence, fundraising for worthy causes lends weight to pursuits that would otherwise appear frivolous, says British journalist Nicholas Coleridge in his book on the fashion high life. "Charity work underpins the Shiny Set," says Coleridge, referring to the well-dressed, well-travelled wives of oil magnates, bankers and real estate high rollers. "[Charity] provides both a purpose and a justification for buying couture dresses." Given a cause, members of the Shiny Set can throw themselves into staging charity fashion shows (where they view the clothes they later acquire) and charity balls (to which they wear them).[8]

Women who are called "the no-names" by Nancy Paul's friend Catherine Nugent help organize the Foundation's glittery events. No-names are also the target of the Breast Cancer Foundation's educational outreach. Paul told the Parliamentary Committee on Breast Cancer that while a "small, dedicated, high-profile group of people" started the Breast Cancer Foundation, the organization "very quickly trickled down into the community ... We felt strongly," said Paul, "that our goal over the five years that we've existed was to get the trickle down to the grass-roots, to get the message out as broadly and widely as possible." The CBCF message is that "early detection is your best protection." The CBCF also promotes standardized breast-screening programs and "wellness not illness."[9]

After my diagnosis I became very curious about the Cancer Society. What I had assumed was a worthy organization devoted to aiding people who had cancer took on the appearance of an extremely odd beast which lumbered in incomprehensible ways. As a cancer patient, I was struck most of all by the Society's absence in my time of need. No volunteer had visited me in the hospital. After my surgery, in the long hours of waiting for chemotherapy treatments and check-ups, I sometimes perused the the stacks of brochures in the hospital waiting room. Most were published in the U.S. and simply reprinted with a Canadian Cancer Society logo. For the most part they gave the standard advice on breast self-exams and explained the conventional treatments. One that caught my eye was titled "The Woman with Breast Cancer as a Single Woman." I picked it up, wondering why we singles needed our own special leaflet. Inside, a text that would do Ann Landers proud explained that a woman does not have to mention her cancer surgery to a man on a casual first date, but she would want to tell him soon, "if he is someone she cares about."

A few years later, I got another glimpse of the Cancer Society at a meeting of the National Coalition of Cancer Survivors (NCSS) in Denver. I joined the American advocacy group because I wanted to meet others with cancer and no Canadian organization existed to give a voice to our concerns. The conference had a slot set aside for networking and a group of about 12 of us with breast cancer squeezed into someone's hotel room to exchange experiences.

Elaine Hill, a slender Black woman in her early 50s, gave a frank account of her frustration with the American Cancer Society. Her first disappointment with the Society had come shortly after her diagnosis. She decided she needed something more than her conversations with doctors, friends and family could provide. "I'd reached the point where I wanted to talk to another woman who had the disease." She called the American Cancer Society in her Tennessee community and explained her situation. The receptionist told her about Reach to Recovery. She could send Elaine a visitor, but she needed a doctor's referral.

Elaine was incredulous. "You mean you don't believe I have breast cancer?" she asked.

"Oh, no," said the receptionist, "You just have to have a doctor's referral."

At that point Elaine was looking for another surgeon. She didn't want the same doctor who had done her biopsy to perform the rest of her surgery and she had no physician who could make the referral. "So I struggled along without another woman to talk with, until I finally pinned down a neighbour and said to her, 'You've lived here all these years, surely you must know *one* woman with breast cancer I can talk to!'

"And that was my first experience with Reach to Recovery."

I considered Elaine's experience little short of emotional abuse, but it wasn't the first disturbing story I'd heard about Reach to Recovery. Rose Kushner waged a long battle with the American Cancer Society over its Reach to Recovery program. The problems started in 1974 when Kushner, who was convinced that women who had mastectomies suffered long-term physical and psychological trauma, asked the Society to help her document women's reactions to breast surgery long after the operation. No way, said a Reach to Recovery rep in the ACS' Washington office. Kushner's idea ran counter to the whole philosophy of Reach to Recovery, namely, "to convince women they do not have a disabling handicap." When setting up the program, the Cancer Society had explicitly rejected the idea of a "mastectomy club" although such long-term support groups exist for people who have had bowel, bladder and larynx operations. "Having a mastectomy is not a permanent handicap," the woman informed Kushner, "and even the worst of scars can be hidden by a well-fitting prosthesis and the right clothes. So we decided we would help the woman for just a few weeks and then leave her to her own psychological recovery."[10]

This made no sense to Kushner. "What good was a 'recovery' program that left women stranded after a hospital visit and a few weeks of telephone service?" she asked. Her own mastectomy, although expertly done and not a radical, left her numb for five months in the area around the incision, and so tender in other places that "any fondling from the waist up was simply out of the question." Anywhere near the left arm was "strictly no touch." And a day of Caribbean sun left her with a temporary case of lymphedema — her arm "began to develop strange swollen curves and to twist and grind."[11] As for her psychological adjustment, she firmly believed for several years that she had no hang-ups about being one-breasted, until a fire in a hotel where she was staying forced her to admit that she could not venture out in public looking lopsided, even if her life was in danger.

I had also read an essay by the poet Audre Lorde about her encounter with a Reach to Recovery volunteer. Lorde felt "outraged and insulted" after the woman's visit to her hospital room, and "even more isolated than before." The volunteer, says Lorde, was "quite admirable and even impressive in her own right." But she did not speak to Lorde's concerns, which were not about "what man I could capture in the future, much less whether my two children would be embarrassed by me in front of their friends." Lorde's questions had to do with her chances of survival, the effects of a possibly shortened life upon her work and her priorities, whether the cancer could have been prevented, and how she could keep it from recurring. As a 44-year-old Black lesbian feminist, she did not expect the woman to be a role model but she did attempt to discuss with her the task of integrating the experience into the whole of her life. The woman glossed over her questions, chided her for not looking "on the bright side of things" and gave her a lambswool puff to fill out her bra.

The volunteer's response gathered resonance when Lorde went to her doctor's office 10 days later. This was her first trip out since coming home from the hospital and she had groomed and dressed herself carefully. She felt beautiful and glad to be alive. She was surprised when the nurse, rather than complimenting her on how well she looked, remarked instead ("a little anxiously and not at all like a question") that she was not wearing a prosthesis. "No," said Lorde, "It doesn't really feel right."

The nurse, usually sympathetic, continued to press the point. Even if the temporary prosthesis didn't look exactly right, it was "better than nothing" and would do until she was ready for a "real form." She informed Lorde that she would "feel so much better with it on" and that they really would like her to wear something when she came for her appointments, "otherwise it's bad for the morale of the office."[12] Lorde was outraged by this "assault on my right to define and to claim my own body."

In a newspaper article, I'd read about a Canadian Cancer Society volunteer named Darlene Betteley in Waterloo, Ontario. Darlene's story was so odd I made a detour to her modest bungalow in the community outside Toronto, to hear her full account.

After Betteley's cancer diagnosis in 1986, she had both breasts removed. A few years later, she became a Reach to Recovery volunteer. When one of the convenors (the woman who matches visitors with patients) discovered that Betteley did not wear breast prostheses, Betteley was advised that she would have to get a bustline or give up her visits. "We like our volunteers to look normal," the convenor explained.

Betteley has all the letters and newspaper clippings from the dispute neatly organized in a big blue binder. The opening page has two full-length, colour photos of her, standing erect in her back yard — Before and After Surgery. "Now I ask you, Sharon," she prompts me, "Do I look normal?"

An unlikely rebel, Betteley is in her mid-50s, a mother of grown children and a devout believer. She loved making hospital visits. She enjoys people and when she recovered from her two operations she was so happy to be alive that she wanted to share her zest for life with others. She had modelled as a teenager and she still loves clothes. She took pride in her ability to dress becomingly after the two mastectomies. She had been a Reach to Recovery volunteer for over a year when her convenor, who knew she didn't wear a prosthesis, called her to "talk things over." It happened that the head convenor for Ontario had called the local convenor in search of a suitable visitor for a woman who was having a double prophylactic mastectomy. Darlene's name was suggested. Did she wear a prosthesis? the Ontario convenor wanted to know.

"No."

"Well," the provincial convenor said, "We like our volunteers to look normal."

The local convenor, a woman Betteley knew well, presented her with the senior convenor's verdict. Faced with the prospect of losing her volunteer status, Betteley almost capitulated, but something in her rose up in protest. "Why should I have to go against something I really believe?" she asked. "I am happy with myself. You have to like yourself before you can share your happiness and your love with other people."

In that case, the convenor said, Betteley could no longer make hospital visits.

"Well, there were tears and there was anger," explained Betteley, "because visiting was very important to me." She began asking question that had never occurred to her before. "I thought, 'does the Cancer Society have anything to do with all these companies that make prostheses? And what do they do with the money they raise?'" Betteley's daughter Cathy was particularly incensed by her mother's dismissal. Cathy worked as a personnel officer and she urged her mother to complain to the Human Rights Commission. Betteley demurred. She would rather put the whole thing behind her. "There'll be another door opening," she said, with her characteristic aplomb.

Cathy wrote a letter to the chairman of the volunteer unit at the local Cancer Society office. Betteley also wrote to the Society, explaining that "after discussions with my doctor and my husband, I decided, for my own physical comfort, not to wear a prosthesis." Cathy sent yet another letter to the editor of the local newspaper and the paper decided to run a story. At a nearby university, a sociology student was so indignant when he read the article, he fired off letters to every major newspaper in the country. The first to pick up on it was the *Globe and Mail.* By now, Betteley had lost her reticence about speaking out. A male volunteer, she pointed out in the front page story, "is not required to shove a golf ball down his pants before meeting people." The policy, she said, was sexist ("a word I didn't even have in my vocabulary until these students brought it to mind.") "I'm wondering how many men sit on the board of the Cancer Society who need to see a woman with a bustline," she told the reporter. The *Globe and Mail* story opened the media floodgates. First the Toronto *Star* phoned for an interview, then a Florida tabloid, which ran its version of the story under the headline, "Whatta Bunch of Boobs!" The same day, reporters from her local TV station crowded into her small living room with lights and cameras while another TV crew waited in the driveway to get in. Next Betteley guested on a noon hour radio phone-in program from Montreal. "It was awesome," she recalls.

The Canadian Cancer Society's public response did little to shed light on the organization's thinking. "There is a lot of misinformation and confusion about our policy," said the local convenor, Maryann Istiloglu. "Women who are about to undergo breast surgery, or who have just had the procedure, don't want to be reminded of how they are going to end up looking," she said.[13] Mark Sikich, co-chairman of patient services for Betteley's local unit explained that breast cancer patients are usually emotional after surgery, "Most patients are very concerned with body image and looking so-called normal. It's best to send someone in wearing a prosthesis." An Ontario representative said that since one aspect of a volunteer's visit was to provide a temporary prosthesis, and information about purchasing a permanent prosthesis, "To be not wearing a prosthesis herself would appear to be a contradiction of the message she is bringing." Not all Society personnel agreed. One said the policy made her angry and she would never enforce it.[14] Most of the eight volunteers working for the Society's Kitchener-Waterloo office resigned after the incident.

Wear casual clothes. Must be well-fitted over the bustline. Darlene Betteley points to the offending line in the handbook she was given when she trained as a Canadian Cancer Society volunteer. In later editions the grooming instructions were changed (*Be nicely groomed and dressed. Don't wear heavy cologne or jangly jewelry*) but the policy stood as an unwritten rule, at least in the minds of some Cancer Society officials. Other rules clearly circumscribe the volunteer's scope for discussion. "*Never* give medical advice or interfere with the patient's relationship with the doctor," says one; "Do not be persuaded to show your scar, or look at the scar of the person you are visiting," instructs another. Among the qualifications for volunteers is "a positive attitude toward conventional treatment methods." As well, the volunteer "does not promote unconventional therapies."

Needless to say, the Cancer Society was stung by the publicity over the Betteley incident. After she sent her own letter to the Society, she asked if she could volunteer for Cansurmount, a one-on-one visitation program for terminally ill patients. No, she was told, the Society hadn't appreciated the letters and public criticism.

Lost in the hubbub was the woman who triggered it, the one scheduled to have the double mastectomy. She never had a visit.

"The local doctor who sits on the board of the Cancer Society said 'this is not cancer, this is a precautionary measure, so we don't need to send out a visitor,'" says Betteley. "To this day," she adds, a little wistfully, "I would love to meet her."

Elaine Hill's second experience with the Cancer Society in Tennessee was a variation on the same theme. Elaine's surgery left her with lymphedema ("milk-arm"), a permanent and debilitating result of breast surgery which is not uncommon. Both surgery and radiation can damage the circulatory system of lymph fluid in the arm so that the fluid flows down the arm but not up. One result is a lowered resistance to infection in that arm; another is swelling which can be extremely painful and impair movement. An elastic post-mastectomy sleeve is one method of damage-control, while severe cases may require a lymphedema pump.

Elaine wears a lymphedema sleeve. When I met her in Denver, she described a rejection not unlike Darlene Betteley's. People at the local branch of the ACS knew that Elaine had worked as a social worker and approached her about working as a Reach to Recovery visitor. She agreed, she says, "because I thought it was a very good thing."

Shortly before the training session started, Elaine developed lymphedema. She decided she should let the Cancer Society know about this development before the training started. "In the back of my mind," she says, "I guess I thought they would say, 'well gee, you're so great, come on and do it anyway.' Instead, they said they would get back to me." Three weeks passed without a word, so Elaine called the office. "After hemming and hawing," Elaine recalls, "the lady told me they couldn't use me because of the sleeve. They needed 'perfect people,' people with no sign of cancer to go to talk to the women. That was their policy."

"Well, lymphedema *is* a common side effect of breast cancer surgery," Elaine responded. The woman wouldn't bite on that one, but suggested perhaps Elaine could take off the sleeve, or come in when the lymphedema got better. "I have no real hope that I can ever go without the sleeve," Elaine told her, "and I can't do exercises without the sleeve on."

Elaine didn't let on how hurt she felt. "I assured them I had no hard feelings — though I really did feel badly. I said, 'I understand, I certainly don't want to frighten anyone or raise their anxiety level.'" In fact, she felt rejected. "First I had surgery, then three months later they found cancer in the other breast so I had surgery again. This seemed like another knock in the face — and from the American Cancer Society!"[15]

Far from overhauling its "get-on-with-it" view of breast cancer recovery, in recent years the American Cancer Society has redefined the cosmetic problem. In 1988, the ACS launched a new initiative called Look Good, Feel Better (LGFB), in collaboration with a charitable foundation set up by cosmetics manufacturers and people employed in the beauty industry. Women having treatment are now invited to come to their local hospital for a group makeover "workshop" where they receive tips on beauty techniques and a package of free cosmetics. The idea caught fire in the U.S., spread to Australia, and soon had its copycat program in Canada, sponsored by the Canadian Cancer Society and a similar consortium from the beauty industry.

"The undertaking fits like a glove for us in the industry," said Normand Pitre, president of Chanel in Quebec. "It's a perfect way for our industry to help women and give something back to the community." Pitre described Look Good, Feel Better as a win-win opportunity for everybody. "Undertaking the Program, underwriting the substantial costs involved, is a marvelous way for member companies to play an important Canadian societal role while simultaneously building consumer confidence in the industry."[16]

Like Reach to Recovery, Look Good, Feel Better has grass-roots origins. Diane Noyes was a Seattle sales representative for a women's fashion and accessories firm when she was diagnosed with ovarian cancer in 1986. Her treatment included "industrial strength" chemotherapy which caused total hair loss, nausea and fatigue. Determined to keep on working, she began to experiment with make-up and head wraps. Along the way she made some mistakes — such as the purchase of a wig before her hair fell out, which no longer fit when she needed it.

Noyes decided to write a how-to book of appearance tips for women undergoing cancer therapy. She teamed up with an oncology nurse in Los Angeles and they wrote *Beauty and Cancer*, which Noyes and her husband self-published out of their basement. A mixture of sensible advice about diet, making and tying headwraps, protection from the sun, and traditional dogma ("all women who have had a mastectomy should wear a breast form"), the book was a surprise success. Soon the beauty industry and the medical profession adopted it as their own.[17]

The PR and marketing appeal of LGFB for the beauty industry is fairly straightforward, but the gusto with which medical professionals have taken up the cause of make-up for cancer patients warrants scrutiny. Oncology is, after all, the same specialty that rains scepticism on meditation, visualization, support groups, and other "soft" feel-good adjuncts to medical treatment. Yet in no time, with funding from the cosmetic industry's Foundation, Yale University's Comprehensive Cancer Center undertook a two-year study "to evaluate the effectiveness of Look Good, Feel Better on quality of life for women breast cancer patients undergoing chemotherapy treatment."[18]

The intense romance between medical experts and cosmeticians is less bizarre than it seems at first glance. The same magnet that pulled surgeons to Reach to Recovery now has oncologists stuck on Look Good, Feel Better. In the days of the Halsted radical, surgeons used to worry that terror of surgical mutilation would keep women from having a lump investigated. Bedside visits by "perfect people," they hoped, would soothe fears about surgery. These fears were firmly rooted in reality — the operation was sexually devastating, often caused permanent physical disability and frequently failed to arrest the disease — but that was of no matter. Reach to Recovery was tailored precisely to deflect these fears, not to meet the woman's deep emotional needs. Part of Reach to Recovery's current crisis stems from the fact that the Cancer Society can't figure out how to adapt the program to women who look no different after surgery than before.

Enter Look Good, Feel Better. The treatment that most often affects a breast cancer patient's appearance today is chemotherapy. Now it's the oncologist who frets that a patient might not show up for her appointment. Chemotherapy's most dramatic effect is hair loss, but the circulating poisons can also cause weight loss or weight gain and turn glowing skin into a splotchy mess. In the early stages of the disease, when most women are diagnosed, the illness itself is much less likely to affect the woman's appearance than are the treatments. Radiation, which is standard therapy after breast conserving therapy, has some of the same effects on one's looks. Reach to Recovery gained entrée as a

Cancer Society's program in the late 1960s, just when the Halsted radical was going down for the last count. Now, with chemo cocktails on the ropes, make-up companies are welcomed in many leading cancer centres.

Coincidence or not, both programs have the timely effect of diverting our attention from the main drama being played out in the medical arena. In the current debate over chemotherapy, as in the earlier debate over radical surgery, critics within the profession are asking defenders of an orthodox treatment whether the benefits really justify making the woman Look Bad, Feel Worse.

Audre Lorde faulted Reach to Recovery for encouraging nostalgia in women with breast cancer. While the urge to go back to the pre-cancer state is a natural reaction (Lorde felt its pull herself), it is regressive, she says. Rather than facing the the full dimensions of the diagnosis, Reach to Recovery encourages the woman to concentrate on breast cancer as a cosmetic problem, "one which can be solved by a prosthetic pretence."[19]

Rose Kushner also deplored Cancer Society policies that forced women to go underground with their pain. She welcomed the famous coming-out of Betty Ford and Happy Rockefeller in 1974, but was uneasy that the women and the media coverage steered away from the subject of physical and emotional aftereffects. "Pain? Swelling? Not a word. The only problems either woman would admit to were some fatigue and discomfort. As far as the psychological aspects of losing their breasts were concerned, neither woman admitted having any emotional problems whatsoever." Mrs. Ford was quoted as saying the mastectomy involved only a "little foam rubber." She had no patience with women who said they would rather lose an arm than a breast, "I can't imagine such talk," she said, "It's so stupid." Her advice to women was the classic, "Once it's done, put it behind you and go on with your life."[20] Mrs Rockefeller wrote in Reader's Digest that she, too, was "putting breast cancer behind her." In the coverage of the Ford and Rockefeller diagnoses, Kushner complained, "the grim side of breast cancer was somehow understated. The media seemed to concentrate only on the cosmetics of breast cancer."

When Kushner revised her book in 1984, she reported that a whiff of reality appeared to have seeped into the American Cancer Society. Several women she regarded highly had risen in the Society's hierarchy. Kushner predicted "new and valuable programs" would be put in place and "archaic traditions" would be abandoned. She was particularly eager to see the ACS abandon a long-standing philosophy that all information must reach patients through their physicians. "The words M.D. no longer stand for Medical Deity in the minds of women today," she declared. "While menfolk may still be timid and trusting about their medical/surgical problems, we women want to know. What's more, we want to have more than a tip of our fingers in deciding our own destinies. Current ACS standards prohibit giving women anything other than predigested information that has been approved by a board of physicians."[21] Kushner, of course, was a leading fountain of "non-approved" information. In addition to writing a popular book, she set up a non-profit information hotline and mail service, the Breast Cancer Advisory Centre, which she ran with a nurse.

My assessment, in the early 1990s, is that the changes Kushner hoped for have not occurred. If anything, the Cancer Societies, both Canadian and American, are more removed than ever from women's desire to know and to control their destinies. Incidents like Darlene Betteley's expulsion (in 1990) and Elaine Hill's exclusion (in 1991) dramatize the attitudes that make Reach to Recovery an object of anger and ridicule among women with cancer. They are not isolated incidents, but part of the underground lore now developing among women with breast cancer who are speaking out.

A longtime peace activist named Miriam told this post-mastectomy story to the *Village Voice* in 1991: "A smiling woman in a Lana Turner sweater, with long fingernails and teased hair, floated into the room right out of the 50s. I thought I was dreaming of my childhood in Brooklyn." Of course, the apparition was a Reach to Recovery volunteer, who proceeded to demonstrate "how a lambswool puff in a cotton bra could help Miriam go back out into the world 'without anyone ever knowing your little secret. With a good prosthesis,' the woman gushed, 'you can even wear a strapless evening gown!'" Miriam recalled, "We had a long talk. I don't think it did her much good."[22]

Pat Kelly of Burlington, Ontario, had a mastectomy in 1987. She called the Canadian Cancer Society to find out what support and information they could offer her — a 35-year-old mother of two pre-school-aged daughters. A Reach to Recovery volunteer soon called her back. Pat's pleasure turned to disappointment, then anger, when she learned that the volunteer was in her 70s and her only advice was not to lift anything with the arm on her affected side. As the woman spoke, Pat was standing at the phone holding her 18-month-old baby in the arm on her "affected" side. The conversation was one of the jolts that prompted her to begin a support group with another woman in her community and to become an outspoken activist.[23]

The Canadian Cancer Society has scheduled a review of its Reach to Recovery program for 1994, an exercise that the American Cancer Society completed two years ago. As a chance to overhaul the Society's signature service to women with breast cancer, the ACS review was an opportunity missed. The report acknowledges that the service has problems, that it needs to be updated and strengthened, but the focus of change is to align the service with the "new medical technology" in treating breast cancer. The phase-out of the radical mastectomy and the increasing number of women now having lumpectomies with radiation plus chemotherapy means that women now spend less time in the hospital and their treatment experience differs from that of the older cohort of volunteers, explains the report. Increasing cultural heterogeneity (or awareness of its importance) gets a nod and the surgeon-referral system is recognized as passé. Self-referrals and referrals by social workers and nurses are discussed as valuable ways of linking women with volunteers.[24]

Nowhere does the report address the fundamental criticism that Reach to Recovery falsifies the breast cancer experience by packaging it as a cosmetic mishap, only slightly more serious than a broken fingernail. The emotional support function of R2R, says the report, comes from the patient "interacting with a woman who has experienced what she has experienced and survived as a fully functional person," and the expected benefit is that the woman "will feel supported and will respond with hope and courage to get on with her life."[25] Look Good, Feel Better, like big sister R2R, makes a fetish of looking "normal." When you are having chemotherapy treatments, sallow skin, a bald head and facial puffiness are as normal as a flat chest after a double mastectomy. Rather than put on make-up, a women might well prefer to stay home and sleep. Or she may want to halt her treatments.

"Suggesting these makeovers to sick women is just public relations," says Sacramento activist Helen Hobbs. At a Mother's Day demonstration in 1991, Hobbs held up her breast prosthesis and cried out to the crowd, "They gave me this and said it would make me feel better. But I don't feel better." Next, she pulled off her wig and held it aloft beside her bald head. "Then they gave me this. They said it would make me feel better too. But I don't feel better and I won't feel better until more research is done into this horrible disease."[26]

Hobbs won't hide the signs of her disease from her four children because she feels they have a right to the truth about her illness. "Women have been expected for centuries to conceal how bad they feel and get on with it." Like mammography, she says, the cover-up programs present breast cancer as a "nice" disease. "Your mammogram finds it real early. Then you can have reconstruction, put on a wig, and every thing's hunky-dory. Well, that's not true."[27]

In their book *Manufacturing Consent*, Noam Chomsky and Edward Herman present a "propaganda model" to explain how the mass media mobilize support for the special interests that dominate state and private activity. In their model, these special interests manage public opinion by ensuring that information that reaches the public passes through a series of filters. The "cleansed residue" creates a systemic bias in what the public ultimately accepts as "objective facts." This analysis helps clarify why the public's understanding of breast cancer diverges radically from the reality experienced by women who have the disease. The filters have done their work.

Cancer charities hold up the Rosy Filter to breast cancer. "The future for women who develop breast cancer has never been more promising," asserts a CBCF brochure.[28] "Looking better gave me the energy to carry on," says the Susan G. Komen Foundation's Nancy Brinker. "I wanted my family to feel better about who they saw when I was sick, and frankly I wanted to like what I saw too."[29]

But noblesse oblige exacts its price. Fundraising by the privileged bolsters the status quo and in breast cancer that means promoting the interests of the very rich, on the one hand, and the medical community on the other. The business behind the glittery galas works to consolidate connections between wealthy interest groups. Thus, fundraisers and their husbands sit on hospital boards. Drug companies donate money for a lavish dinner, and their executives in turn are invited to give prizes to researchers at an awards luncheon. The fundraiser and her family gain intimacy with leading physcians which stands them in good stead when they get sick. The glow of good works discourages anyone from looking too closely at the mutual payoffs.

"I don't see anything wrong with the socialites doing what they do," a friend with breast cancer told me. "Raising money is what they're good at, so why not let them raise the money?" The unstated assumptions were that the money had materialized at no cost to women with cancer and would be spent to our benefit.

The philanthropists' logic is that the prosperity of the rich has a trickle-down benefit for the rest of us. Nancy Paul looks back on the 1980s as good years for the poor. "The 80s consisted of some of the most positive growth years concerning gains for the poor, relating to their economic well-being," she told Rosemary Sexton. "It's wrongheaded to think of those policies as bad economics. I can't take pride in the fact that we're no longer wearing mink and diamonds. Wealth is a sign of a healthy economy — it's not bad."[30]

When Lasker's group took over the leadership of the ACS, its members introduced a few biases into the way cancer was presented to the public, says James Patterson. Understanding their dependence on very wealthy contributors, they reinforced messages that would appeal to this group: that the disease hit the rich as well as the poor, young as well as old. In fact, certain industrial cancers were much more common among the blue collar classes. The disease overwhelmingly hit the aged, and cancer caused great suffering among needy people who were less connected to the medical system. Under Lasker's leadership, the Society didn't obscure the role of social class, says Patterson, but "neither did it play it up." Rather the new leaders strengthened the Society's links with private practitioners, urging people who suspected cancer to see doctors and stay away from quacks. The ACS welcomed federal aid for medical research and opposed government interference in fee-for-service private practice.

What the cancer charities offers those of us outside the charmed circle are optimistic platitudes disguised as "education." The research may eventually be beneficial or it may not, but the reassuring slogans encourage us to trust in the system, rather than to ask questions that might reveal weaknesses. When our experience runs counter to the reassurances, we doubt our senses. Women need to know that mammography frequently fails to detect a cancer, that early-detected cancers can be lethal, that women die from breast cancer despite all the proscribed treatments, that five years of survival do not mean you are "home free."

When your life is at risk, play-acting that you are well exacts an emotional price. It creates barriers of communication between the woman with cancer and those she loves. Attempting to look "beautiful," "normal" or "perfect" drains money from our bank accounts at a time when we may be unable to work. Most important, these tricks to keep surgery and baldness secret make us invisible to each other and to society at large. Astonishingly, it took activists speaking out in large numbers to alert the North American public that the "advances" of modern medicine have not lowered the death rate of women in our most prosperous societies from breast cancer. Women, and the public at large, had swallowed the lie that breast cancer is a piffling disease, easily treated and relegated to one's past.

Naomi Wolf argues that the idea of an objective quality called "beauty" is a myth that is not about women at all. "It is about men's institutions and institutional power."[31] The experiences of Audre Lorde, Darlene Betteley, Rose Kushner and Elaine Hill illustrate how the beauty myth is used against women with cancer to reinforce the power of the institutions of medicine and medical technology. Inner confidence in her own beauty allowed each woman to buck the coercion. Rather than conforming to the norm of silence, they spoke out. The same assurance permits a growing number of women, like Ellen Hobbs, to live with breast cancer on their own terms, and to challenge these oppressive institutions.

The changes in my appearance when I was having cancer treatments affected me in a way that was not trivial. My altered appearance was an integral part of a profound change in my life. Just after my diagnosis, I recall glimpsing myself in the washroom mirror at the office and observing a woman with dishevelled hair and wild eyes. The Madwoman of Shallot, I thought with a shock … and I continued out into the office without bothering to comb my hair. I was a madwoman at that moment and if it bothered my co-workers, so be it. As the months wore on, I lost my hair and became increasingly fatigued. When my friend Jeannie commented that I looked tired, I snapped in anger that I was not at all tired, I'd just been to the gym. Later I admitted to myself that her remark, meant caringly, was extremely threatening. Maybe the treatments weren't doing me any good. Maybe I was dying. My appearance was an imperfect barometer to my prospects of recovery but it was more real to me than a blood test. I also remember shocks of pleasure, like examining the contours of my bald head in the mirror and marvelling at its shapeliness. These experiences, and many more, were part of reconciling myself to the changed person I was — no longer a woman whose health was "perfect."

The beauty myth subverts women's power, says Naomi Wolf.[32] A woman with cancer who confronts the world with her baldness or breastlessness has tremendous power to effect change. Audre Lorde captured this in her oft-quoted image, "What would happen if an army of one-breasted women descended upon Congress and demanded that the use of carcinogen fat-stored hormones in beef-fed cattle be outlawed?" Gradually women with cancer are beginning to harness the power Lorde held out to us. Artist Matushka used it when she revealed her mastectomy scar on the cover of the *New York Times Magazine*. With one unforgettable image, she obliterated the pretence that women look "normal" after breast surgery.

Seeing my own photo, hairless, in the newspaper gave me strength. I had faced my own human vulnerability and exposed my tenuous grip on life to others. I felt the power of my act when I arrived for a doctor's appointment and learned that a nurse had posted the article in the staff room. Again, when a stranger who heard me say my name in the post office accosted me to tell me that she had given my article to a newly diagnosed friend. And once more when a shy woman approached me at a public meeting holding the crumpled three-year-old clipping in which I had voiced her own feelings.

"There is nothing wrong, per se, with the use of prostheses, if they can be chosen freely for whatever reason after a woman has had a chance to accept her new body," says Audre Lorde.[33] Nor is there any reason why a woman with cancer shouldn't wear make-up or a wig. I know women who thoroughly enjoyed a Look Good,

Feel Better session, who were happy to have a free bag of expensive cosmetics to take home. (Not the least of their pleasure came from the opportunity to meet with other women with cancer.) But the intense promotion of prostheses and cosmetics, coupled with the coercive tactics used on those who eschew them, signal that these accessories are not really meant for our benefit.

The myth that medical treatments transform women with breast cancer back into "perfect people" nurtures a dependence on the medical profession and related technologies. We turn their inadequacies against ourselves, believing that if we die of the disease, it is because we failed to do breast self-exams the "right" way; or we didn't have mammograms often or soon enough; or our uncooperative bodies "failed to respond to treatment." If each woman with breast cancer understood medicine's limited ability to control the disease, our reliance on physicians, tests and medical interventions would be enormously reduced. The power of these institutions over us would dwindle accordingly. Without the Rosy Filter, women with breast cancer would gain the right to map our own futures, within the very real constraints imposed by a life-threatening disease.

Notes

1. Patterson, p. 76.

2. Patterson, pp. 69-70; 71-73.

3. Patterson, p. 122.

4. Patterson, p. 183.

5. Rosemary Sexton, *The Glitter Girls*, (Toronto: MacMillan, 1993), pp. 159-173.

6. Daniel Greenberg, "Whatever Happened to the War on Cancer?" *Discover*, (Mar. 1986), p. 55.

7. Patterson, p. 184.

8. Nicholas Coleridge, *The Fashion Conspiracy*, (London: Heinemann, 1988), p. 56.

9. Nancy Paul, Testimony before the Parliamentary Committee on Breast Cancer, Ottawa, (Oct. 29, 1991), [from transcript], pp. 2:17 and 2:23.

10. Kushner, pp. 314-315.

11. Kushner, p. 325.

12. Audre Lorde, p. 59.

13. Robert MacLeod, "Cancer Society Aide Attacks 'Sexist' Policy," *Globe and Mail*, (Dec. 6, 1990), p. A1.

14. Margaret Mironowicz, "Ex-cancer Patient is Eager to Share Gained Confidence," *Kitchener-Waterloo Record*, (Aug. 24, 1990), C1.

15. Interview with Elaine Hill, Tennessee, (Jan. 4, 1992).

16. Barbara Aarsteinsen, "Don't Make Do ... Makeup: The Look Good, Feel Better Program," 40-page insert in *Chatelaine*, (Oct. 1993), p. 8.

17. Telephone interview with Diane Noyes, (Dec. 18, 1991). Also, Diane Doan Noyes, written with Peggy Mellody, R.N., *Beauty and Cancer*, (Los Angeles: AC, 1988).

18. Aarsteinsen, p. 8.

19. Lorde, p. 55.

20. Patterson, p. 258.

21. Kushner, pp. 380-381.

22. Alisa Solomon, "The Politics of Breast Cancer," *Village Voice*, (May 14, 1991).

23. Juanne Clarke, "Burlington Breast Cancer Support Services," unpublished manuscript, (Oct. 1993), pp. 8-9.

24. M. Kreuter et al, "A National Assessment of Reach to Recovery: A Report to the Nursing and Patients Services Department," American Cancer Society, (Dec. 15, 1992), pp. 15-16.

25. Kreuter et al, p. 28.

26. Sue Woodman, "Breast Cancer Cover-up," *Allure*, (Oct. 1991), p. 44.

27. Woodman, p. 45.

28. "Breast Cancer: Your Best Protection ... Early Detection," Canadian Breast Cancer Foundation [Ontario Chapter], Toronto, (1989), p.3.

29. Woodman, p. 44.

30. Sexton, p. 172.

31. Naomi Wolf, *The Beauty Myth*, (Toronto: Vintage, 1991), pp. 12-13.

32. Wolf, p. 46.

33. Lorde, p. 63.

Cancer Consumerism
The Win-Win Filter

Tremendous progress has been made in treating breast cancer. Many women no longer have to lose a breast to this disease. And those who do may be able to have immediate plastic surgery, allowing them to leave the hospital with essentially the same silhouette. There are many new drug therapies that can help control the spread of breast cancer. But the key to taking advantage of this progress is finding breast cancer as early as possible.

— National Breast Cancer Awareness Month brochure, published by Zeneca Pharmaceuticals, 1992

At an international meeting of cancer scientists in 1981, Rose Kushner noticed a disturbing change. People who had gladly given her preliminary results of studies in the past were now "mysteriously silent."

"I've applied for a patent on that," one told her.

"I've granted a license to a drug company to produce a test kit, and I can't go into detail about that yet," said another.

In 1979, the U.S. government began cuts to cancer research (meanwhile pumping more money into Defense). Kushner discovered that, in response, American scientists had turned to the private sector for research money. Data once shared at scientific symposia and in journals were now industrial trade secrets, "locked in corporate vaults until they can be exploited commercially." Kushner did not believe most of these scientists were motivated by a lust for personal wealth. Rather, selling their ideas to the highest commercial bidder was the only way they could continue their basic research. She also felt that most subscribed to the principle that a free exchange of ideas and data was the only way scientific progress could be made. "Unpublished trade secrets, by definition, result in duplication, overlap, and in a waste of time and resources. Yet this unprecedented situation has begun and is spreading with the speed of light."[1]

In Canada, despite our public system of health care, the 1980s were also a period of commercialization. Montreal medical reporter Nicholas Regush noticed the shift in his dealings with the federal Health department's Health Protection Branch. "The branch had begun its decline during the late 1970s," he recalls. "Tough economic conditions led to government cutbacks. Programs that reviewed the safety of drugs and medical devices did not broaden according to plan … By the early 1980s, government safety reviewers were under increasing pressure from their managers and industry representatives to speed up pre-market evaluations."[2] One result, which Regush documented in a series of newspaper stories throughout the 1980s, was the marketing of the foam-covered breast implant called the Même. Like other breast implants, this model was originally developed as an internal prosthesis for women who had had a mastectomy. But in the intensely consumerist climate of the 1980s, the implants were marketed chiefly as a commercial product to increase bust size. Governments went along, knowing that safety data on breast implants were non-existent.

In Canada as elsewhere, says Regush, "government and industry are developing a familial bond … The multinational drug companies are looking to the day when they will no longer be required to jump through different regulatory hoops before their drugs are approved for market. They had been nagging Canada and other nations to agree on a single standard for drug-safety review. This, the companies claim, will save them bushels of money, which they will then shovel into research and investment. That will grow more jobs and better drugs."

This is the win-win theory of consumerism and health: spend money on medical equipment, drugs and research and watch the economy and our health flourish in tandem. It's an appealing theory. Those of us raised in the post-war consumer culture have learned to equate societal prosperity with progress, individual choices, and the good life — which includes health. As children of a culture whose economy is market driven, we habitually measure our freedom by the number of choices available to us. Since 1950, breast cancer treatments have indeed multiplied. At mid-century, the standard was a radical mastectomy plus radiation. We now have a plethora of treatment options: radical and conservative surgery; post-operative radiation and boosts; a wide range of realistic-appearing external prostheses; implants and complicated surgical reconstructions that transplant stomach flesh to the chest; multiple drug regimens, both cyctotoxic and hormonal; drugs to combat the side effects of the drugs that combat the cancer; and the promise of the 1990s — genetic therapies.

When baby boomers like me get breast cancer, learning that the mortality rate from breast cancer has remained constant over the past 40 years comes as a rude awakening. We feel bewildered rather than privileged by the treatment choices we face. A second shock is the discovery that breast cancer — unlike most other cancers — is a disease of affluent countries. The getting and spending of money neither protects us from getting breast cancer, nor offers us a sure cure if we are striken.

Breast cancer activists have, nonetheless, led the lobby for increased spending on breast cancer research. Before we go any further, we need to look closely at the information that passes through the consumerism filter — and examine what gets left behind.

Three profitable industries related to breast cancer are mammography, drug treatments and genetic research. In mammography, the commercial winners are the manufacturers of the machines and the film, and the people who operate the machines and read the film. The putative health winners are the women whose lives are saved by early detection of breast tumours. Cancer drug treatments constitute a profitable industry that boomed through the recent recession, providing jobs and investment opportunities. In return, says a TV ad from the American Pharmaceutical Manufacturers Association, "... pharmaceutical company research provides the best hope for conquering diseases like cancer and dramatically reducing health care costs." Genetic research is also a hot investment sector. "The biotech field is to the next 20 years what the computer industry was to the last 20," says economic forecaster Nuala Beck, author of *Shifting Gears: Thriving in the New Economy*.[3] Current health policy thinking is that biotech research will bring us predictive tests in breast cancer, new therapies, and a better understanding of breast cancer's basic biology.

Consumerism's win-win filter looks forward. Much of what it filters out is our understanding of the past.

Mammography

Mammography illustrates how the consumer filter operates when a technology or practice becomes entrenched.

When the results of the National Breast Screening Study (NBSS) were published in late 1992, Vancouver surgeon Charles Wright predicted, "What we are going to see here is a massive attempt to discredit this study. And the attack is going to come from the huge multi-billion dollar industry that has developed around screening, which includes the manufacturers, the radiologists and the technicians."[4]

For those poised to benefit, anthropologist Pat Kaufert calls mammography a classic win-win paradigm, a combination of doing good while making profits. The manufacturers of mammography equipment and film are the most obvious in a line of beneficiaries that includes radiologists and technicians, surgeons and cancer charities.

A mammography machine costs between $110,000 and $184,000 in 1984 U.S. dollars. A tally of dedicated mammography machines in the U.S., published in 1990, showed an exponential increase in the number of machines available in the 1980s. In 1982, for example, only 134 units were installed. By 1988, the successful promotion of mammography — led by the American Cancer Society (ACS) — and aggressive marketing techniques by the industry had pushed new installations up to 8,000. The result, the authors concluded, was an oversupply of equipment. The estimated need in 1988 was only 2,600 new machines, even if all women in the target age groups went for regular screening. The overabundance held in all geographical regions and applied even if the more liberal screening guidelines (beginning at age 40) were used.[5]

The surplus, said the authors, was coupled with an estimated surplus of 6,450 diagnostic radiologists and an undersupply of trained technicians. For the woman users, the authors point out, these figures translated into inflated mammography charges, as centres with machines tried to recoup their capital investments. Apart from the inefficiency of having thousands of costly, under-used machines, quality standards are more likely to be met in centres that have high volume and low prices. The shortage of trained technicians is also worrisome for women seeking competent mammography.

Rather than cautioning women about the poor quality and inflated prices and trying to rectify them, ads paint mammography as an unqualified advance — a "breakthrough." In fact, the same machinery that created the problems, created the climate for the mammography hype.

The ACS launched the first in a series of campaigns to promote mammography in 1983. In 1986, the Society announced its Breast Cancer Awareness Program. In the local and national campaigns that followed, says Kaufert, "the Cancer society became increasingly skillful at using the tactics of mass advertising to publicize mammography. The result is that most North Americans have become familiar with messages promoting mammography screening carried on television, in newspapers, in women's magazines and even on billboards along American highways."[6] These ads promote mammography as an unqualified good. No mention of false positives and their sequel, the biopsy; or of false negatives, which lead the woman with a cancer undetectable by X-ray to believe she is fine. No hint that a lump detected while microscopic can still metastasize. Nothing about lumps (like mine) that are palpable but not visible on a mammogram. Nothing about price gouging and the lack of enforced standards — this vital information is filtered out.

In 1992, a grass-roots group called the Women's Community Cancer Project, based in Cambridge Massachusetts, prepared a report on screening mammography called "What the Cancer Establishment Never Told You." The authors of the report examined the ACS' mammography screening media campaign and decided to look at the logic behind one particularly disturbing example of the ACS' media advertising. The ad featured a photograph of two young women in their mid- to late-20s, and one young man. The text claimed that early breast cancer detection through mammography would result in a cure, "nearly 100 percent of the time." The researchers asked the local ACS director of Professional Education about the 100 percent claim, which she acknowledged was not strictly correct. Nonetheless, she defended the ad, explaining, "When you make an advertisement, you just say what you can to get women in the door. You exaggerate a point ... because advertising people do that." The logic behind the ad, she said, was that mammography's purpose is to look for premalignant cancers. For the subset of patients with these cancers, she said, the cure rate "is 100 percent. Mammography can find many of these patients — but only if women get regular mammograms. The reality is, however, that you don't cure."[7]

Breast cancer awareness campaigns are designed to cut a wide swath. Instructions to participants advise involving community groups: hospitals, mammography facilites, physicians, nurses, local heath departments, churches, businesses, rural social groups, associations for retired persons, and offices on aging. These campaigns "combined shrewd marketing with elements of evangelism," says Kaufert. And the sponsoring agency, the American Cancer Society, stood to profit, as well as those in the mammography business. Early detection campaigns are more than simply public service announcements, Kaufert points out. A successful breast screening campaign also has great fundraising potential.

The filter of consumerism explains some of the public misunderstanding about the age at which women are most apt to benefit from mammography. Ads tend to target younger women, not the older women who could benefit from mammography, argues Maryann Napoli of the Centre for Medical Consumers in New York. She says one reason is because younger women have more money. The report by the Women's Community Cancer Project found that full-page mammography ads placed by Dupont (a major manufacturer of mammography film) in 1989 apppeared in upscale publications, such as *Newsweek, Time* and the *Smithsonian*. They did not appear in more popular publications such as *True Story, Family Circle* and the *National Enquirer*. Other mammography ads featuring young women were sponsored by film manufacturer Eastman Kodak (an ad in the television coverage of the 1988 Summer Olympics) and General

Electric (an ad shown during the Academy Awards in March 1989).

Early detection by mammography is the main message of National Breast Cancer Awareness Month (NBCAM). In 1984, the pharmaceutical giant Imperial Chemical Industries (ICI) co-founded NBCAM, a pro-mammography PR campaign that takes place every October. The campaign's co-founder was the support group Cancer Care Inc, although ICI remains the sole financial sponsor. Other powerful interests endorse the project, including the American Academy of Family Physicians, the American Cancer Society, the American College of Radiology, the American Medical Women's Association, the American Society of Clinical Oncology, the Susan G. Komen Breast Cancer Foundation and the National Cancer Institute (NCI).

Many women participate in runs and community-based events that are planned under the NBCAM banner. Few of these women know, however, that the ICI has power of approval over every poster, pamphlet and advertisement used by NBCAM. Endorsement by the National Alliance of Breast Cancer Organizations (NABCO), the New York-based umbrella organization of breast cancer groups, adds enormously to NBCAM's credibility with women. So do the high-profile political names listed. The 1992 list was headed by Susan Bales Ford, daughter of Betty Ford and former President Gerald Ford, with support from Marilyn Tucker Quayle, Julie Nixon Eisenhower, Luci Baines Johnson, Pat Nixon, Nancy Reagan and Linda Johnson Robb. NBCAM promotes the month, supplying its members with a package of posters and pamphlets every fall. The ICI logo appears on the promotional material, with the note that the month is "made possible by an educational grant from ICI Pharmaceuticals Group, a business unit of ICI Americas Inc."

NBCAM sponsor ICI is one of the world's largest pharmaceutical companies, with annual sales exceeding $26 billion in 1991. Detroit journalist Monte Paulsen, who wrote an exposé of Breast Cancer Awareness Month in 1993,[8] points out that the British-based multinational manufactures the breast cancer drug tamoxifen, via its subsidiary Zeneca Pharmaceuticals, and also makes chlorine- and petroleum-based products, including plastics, explosives and paint. In Quebec, an ICI paint subsidiary singlehandedly dumps one-third of the toxic chemicals into the

St. Lawrence River. These are precisely the kind of estrogen-mimicking toxins now suspected of promoting breast cancer. "Not surprisingly," says Paulsen, "carcinogens are *never* mentioned in NBCAM's widely distributed literature." Instead women are told, "Early detection is your best protection. Don't be an easy target — get a mammogram *now*."

With this annual blitz, it's little wonder that the slogan "early detection is your best protection" is as familiar to most North Americans as the Golden Rule, while the three steps to early detection (regular mammograms, monthly BSE, regular breast examinations by a physician) seem as inviolable as the Ten Commandments. A camera-ready article, titled *News on Health: Do You Know These Facts About Breast Cancer?* assures the reader: "There is no need to be afraid to learn about breast cancer. The facts are encouraging and reassuring. If you remember only one thing about breast cancer, it should be this: your best protection is early detection."

Breast Cancer Drugs

The drug industry is shrouded in secrecy. The U.S. government, says Ralph Moss, routinely hides sales figures on drugs to avoid disclosing figures for individual companies. He cites a government report on pharmaceutical preparations from the U.S. Department of Commerce, which says, "Data on new prescriptions are compiled privately for drug manufacturers by a company that copyrights its figures. Thus, they rarely work their way directly into public hands ..."

Adriamycin, the highly toxic breast cancer treatment drug my GP jokingly dubbed "The Red Killer," hit the market in 1974. That first year, reports Moss, it sold "an impressive $10 million." The development of Adriamycin illustrates how the American public pays once for the development of cancer drugs, and again at monopoly prices to purchase the drugs from private companies. Adriamycin was developed by an Italian conglomerate, Montedison, under an arrangement with the National Cancer Insitute and the Sloan-Kettering Cancer Centre in New York, which permitted the company to test the drug on animals and humans. "U.S. researchers did much of the work to develop the drug in this country and even obtained permission from the Food and Drug Administration to market it," says Moss.[9]

Another popular breast cancer drug, and part of the chemo cocktail I was prescribed, is 5-fluorouracil or 5-FU. Hoffman-La-Roche held the patent for 17 years with the American Cancer Society (who owned 25 percent) says Moss. "Perhaps by coincidence," he adds, "one of the founders of the American Cancer Society, Elmer Bobst, is a former president of Hoffman-La Roche."[10] Bobst was one of the high-profile businessmen Mary Lasker brought onto the ACS board when she took charge of the Association in the 1940s.[11]

The sales of chemotherapeutic agents more than doubled in the four years from 1983 to 1987, from $270 million (U.S.) to over $564 million, reports Moss, adding that these drugs are only part of the total American picture. Not included in the figures are "pharmaceutical preparations affecting neoplasms, the endocrine system and metabolic diseases, or the radioactive immunoassay market, diagnostic and detection kits, or painkillers, antibiotics and antiemetics that are used by cancer patients."

The market for cytotoxic drugs began to plateau in the 1980s, says Moss, partly because of the toxicity of traditional chemo drugs and partly because the regimens have not had a high success rate. The pharmaceutical companies therefore have pinned their hopes on biotechnology, "on such exciting new products as tumour necrosis factor, monoclonal antibodies and interleukin-2." The biotech companies were originally in competition with the pharmaceutical giants. After the 1987 stock market crash, however, the drug companies began to buy up the innovative core of these small competitors. At the same time, they reinvented some previously approved drugs with slight modifications and marketed them as new entities. Leading the list of large companies producing breast cancer drugs were Adria Labs (Adriamycin/ doxorubicin), ICI Pharmaceuticals (Nolvadex/tamoxifen) Hoff-mann-La Roche (Efudex/5-FU) and Bristol Meyers (Cytoxan/ cyclophosphamide).[12]

That directors of several major pharmaceutical companies producing cancer drugs also sit on the board of Memorial Sloan-Kettering Cancer Center does not imply, says Moss, that they are doing something illegal or immoral. "On the other hand," he says, "it must be said that their drug company positions certainly predispose them to direct research in a manner consistent with the interests of the profit-making sector."[13]

For the public, and for women making treatment decisions, the impact of these "connections" on recommended treatments is impossible to assess because the process is so opaque. If chemotherapy is given in cases where the benefits seem marginal or nil, patients can only wonder what weight these commercial interests play in influencing research directions, physicians' thinking and the setting of recommended protocols. "The drug industry is a kind of silent partner in the cancer research enterprise," writes Moss. "It has managed to invest relatively little in the cancer problem yet stands to reap tremendous benefits when and if a breakthrough is found."[14]

Just such a breakthrough was announced in December 1985. The director of the National Cancer Institute (NCI), Vincent DeVita, trumpeted dramatic results from "lymphokines," elements of the body's natural defense system. The new treatment involved removing white blood cells from patients, culturing them with an immune system activator (either interferon or interleukin-2) and reinjecting them back into the system. According to the theory, the new "killer cells" would then attack the cancer. When DeVita hailed the treatment as "the most interesting and exciting biological therapy we've seen so far," *Fortune, Newsweek*, and the national TV news broadcasters ABC and NBC quickly packaged stories on the "cancer breakthrough."[15]

Interferons are "fabulously expensive" says Moss. Human cells produce them in minute quantities — the conventional production method required 65,000 pints of blood to produce 100 mg of interferon.[16] In the late 1970s, one ounce of interferon was worth $1.8 billion. When clinical trials in Sweden showed that a rare and virulent type of bone cancer could be controlled by interferon, the scramble was on to test the drug on more common cancers.

The ACS put up $2 million for a "crash program" to test European interferon in the U.S. on 200 patients with four kinds of cancer, including breast cancer. The cost of clinical trials carried out in Sweden in the mid-1970s, and in the U.S. in 1979, ranged from $500 to $5,000 per patient per day, depending on the dosage. The profit potential was obviously vast. Drug companies flocked to a 1979 international workshop sponsored by the American Cancer Society, Memorial Sloan-Kettering, the National Cancer Institute and the National Institute for Allergy and Infectious Diseases.[17]

Media hype raised hopes and incited public pressure to pour more money into interferon research. By 1981, the American Cancer Society had spent nearly $6.8 million to buy interferon and the National Cancer Institute had spent about $11 million. Several commercial firms were awarded contracts to develop different types of interferons. "Only members of the New York Stock Exchange and the Internal Revenue Service know how many private dollars were bet on this 'magic bullet,'" says Kushner.[18]

Optimistic early reports of the four clinical trials involving breast cancer appeared in the business press, including *Forbes, Business Week* and *The Wall Street Journal,* but when Kushner attended an international conference in May 1980 she found "the mood was all cynicism and scepticism." Under cover of anonymity, an interferon project director at the NCI told Kushner, "There are a lot of people making fortunes overnight on interferon as a cure for cancer." While he allowed that "maybe, someday" interferon might be effective against colds, shingles, pneumonia, or malignancies caused by a virus, he asserted, "Interferon is emphatically not going to be any magic bullet against breast cancer." He blamed the press reports for the deluge of pathetic pleas he was getting from women who wanted access to the "miracle drug."

Kushner, too, was inundated with calls from desperate women. When a medical-writer friend asked her what she thought of the drug's potential, Kushner replied, "according to my sources, a woman with breast cancer would be better off buying stock in any of the companies jumping on the bandwagon than she would be by taking interferon." But the official stance remained one of hopeful persistence. In February 1981, the senior vice-president of research at ACS told a group of science writers, "I never thought interferon was a magic bullet for cancer treatment, but you've got to go for broke ... The jury is still out." That month, the NCI began testing 150 patients with advanced breast cancer to determine minimum safe doses. "Again," wrote Kushner, "we women must wait for the development of technological know-how, this time to solve the puzzle of interferons."

A few days after Vincent DeVita's 1985 announcement of interferon's promise, a patient taking the drug died. Others suffered a range of side effects, including chills, fever, jaundice, confusion, breathing problems, and significant retention of fluids. While interferon has since been approved by the FDA, it is only used for a few very rare kinds of cancer, including kidney cancer and melanoma (a type of skin cancer). A 1987 NABCO fact sheet on interferon and interleukin-2 for breast cancer treatments says, "Unfortunately, none of the interferons have been effective against breast cancer. Nor have other immunological substances that have proved effective against various malignant diseases succeeded in destroying breast cancer cells." Studies continue, although "some scientists believe this lack of success is evidence that breast cancer is not a disease caused by a weak or deficient immune system."[19]

Viewed through the win-win filter, cutbacks on spending for profitable treatments and tests appear as the abandonment of suffering cancer patients. U.S. President Clinton discovered this in early 1994 when he attacked the pharmaceutical industry for price gouging. The drug companies struck back with a multi-million dollar ad campaign aimed at the public. The industry also invested in campaign contributions to members of Congress, then began intense lobbying to the recipients of these donations.

The campaign used language laden with numbers and words like "cure," "progress" and "hope." One TV ad in response to Clinton's attack said: "To Trena Brown, whose family has a history of breast cancer, the search for a cure has a special urgency. Drug companies are currently testing 73 medicines for cancer in women, including 52 for breast cancer. Progress like this from pharmaceutical company research provides the best hope for conquering diseases like cancer, and dramatically reducing health costs."[20]

The Gene Hunt and Consumerism

The consumer angle of the much-touted, but yet-to-be-discovered, breast cancer gene BRCA1 has to be understood in the context of the Human Genome Sequencing Project. This project emerged from the three-way union that Rose Kushner observed in the early 1980s, which comprises government, biomedical researchers and drug companies. During the Reagan-Bush era, several important pieces of legislation were passed to promote "technology transfer," by which universities and corporations can own patents on inventions developed with public money. The idea is to funnel public research money into medical industries to create jobs and wealth. The Genome Project is a politically attractive umbrella under which federal funds can be directed to high-tech Research and Development. It's the '90s counterpart to bomb testing in the 1950s and the space race of the 1970s.

The hush-hush aura that Kushner complained about marks genetic research. Harvard biologist and genome critic Richard Lewontin says of the conflict-of-interest now arising at university biotech labs, "In some cases graduate students working under entrepreneurial professors are restricted in their scientific interchanges, in case they may give away potential trade secrets. Research biologists have attempted, sometimes with success, to get special dispensations of space and other resources from their universities in exchange for a piece of the action. Biotechnology joins basketball as an important source of educational cash."[21]

Writing in the *New Yorker*, John Seabrook says that the technology transfer policies "helped to create the biotech industry, and made the health sector the engine of growth that it was throughout the [last] decade." A measure of their success was that drug companies took in $67 billion in 1990. He refers to the same subsidy system that has benefited companies making anti-cancer drugs. The policies also meant "that in some cases the public was paying for medicine twice — once in the form of taxes, to develop it, and the second time in the form of medical bills, to buy it back from a private company that the government had transferred the patent rights to."[22]

The Human Genome Project is designed to serve two constituencies Seabrook calls irreconcilable: the money culture of technology transfer and health, and the "public-spirited venture devoted to relieving human misery."

During the Bush Administration, Washington's policy was to "make science into technology and economic power." As part of this plan, the federal government applied to patent the gene sequences turned up under the American Genome Project. James Watson, whom the National Institutes of Health (NIH) had proudly recruited to head the project, publicly opposed the patent applications, arguing that gene sequencing should be an international cooperative effort that would create a free data base. He said patenting would make the Human Genome Project a land grab, with different nations rushing to patent different segments of the genome. Watson resigned when the applications went ahead.

James Watson's successor at the head of the American Genome Project, Francis Collins, is a leading BRCA1 gene hunter. He has already made his mark by helping to find the gene for cystic fibrosis. His mandate, presumably, is to reconcile the two irreconcilables that felled Watson.

In a feature article in *Time* magazine, Collins comes across like a sincere and idealistic scientist who believes in the win-win formula. "These are exciting times, and the consequences for clinical medicine will be dramatic," he told *Time*. The same article pointed out Collins' concern about possible abuses. "He is worried that private genetic information will be too readily available to insurance companies and employers."[23]

We should not be surprised that gene hunters dream of using their high-tech expertise for the social good. Public support for their work depends on it. As well, social analysts Nelkin and Tancredi point out, "Scientists are oriented to the present." The warnings against win-win thinking are clear and they lie in the past.

"That any sane nation," observed George Bernard Shaw, "having observed that you could provide for the supply of bread by giving bakers a pecuniary interest in baking for you, should go on to give a surgeon a pecuniary interest in cutting off your leg, is enough to make one despair of political humanity."[24] Shaw could have used a different example. When he wrote this, in 1906, surgeons in North America and Europe were vaulting to the top of their profession, largely on the strength of the Halsted radical.

The history of breast cancer treatment is one of successive interventions that primed the economic pump with scant health benefit for women. The scientists charging off into the genetic frontier hail the potential of BRCA1 as somehow different from its predecessors, but the rhetoric echoes predictions of breakthroughs past. Referring to the interferon dead end of the 1980s, James Patterson comments, "The episode repeated with specific clarity a very old pattern: implied claims for a cure, exaggerated coverage in the media, desperate hope among fearful people, cruel disappointment when the predictions proved to be premature. The more things changed, the more they seemed to stay the same."[25] Richard Lewontin predicts the same hangover 30 years from now, when history takes stock of the Genome Project. "The rage for genes reminds us of Tulipomania and the South Sea Bubble in McKay's *Great Popular Delusions of the Madness of Crowds*," he says.[26]

The win-win system is designed to build careers, create jobs and stimulate profits. Health benefits simply follow, the model predicts, as surely as interest follows a bank deposit. The filter is designed to obscure all evidence that the model doesn't work. Mammography and chemotherapy both demonstrate that health deficits can also follow from increased medical care. Yet advocates of mammography and chemotherapy balk at efforts to ration these interventions to those most apt to benefit. Instead, they target women of financial means. While molecular tests and genetic treatments for breast cancer are largely in the future, we know they will be costly. We also know they will pose excruciating treatment dilemmas and social problems with which we are not ready to cope.

Britain's National Health System was set up with the idea that the country had a fixed amount of morbidity. If the population was treated for these illnesses in an equitable way, the reasoning went, the amount of sickness would decline and health costs would go down as therapy reduced the rate of illness. No one expected, said Ivan Illich in his 1977 analysis entitled *Limits to Medicine*, that the redefinition of health would broaden the scope of medical care and that only budgetary restrictions would keep it from expanding indefinitely.[27] "Attempts to exercise rational political control over the production of medical health care have consistently failed," he explains, and the reason "lies in the nature of the product now called 'medicine,' a package made up of chemicals, apparatus, buildings, and specialists, and delivered to the client. The purveyor, rather than his clients or political boss, determines the size of the package."

Those of us with breast cancer are good examples of the medical dependants Illich describes. Consumer movements in medicine can only be effective he argues, if they move beyond the control of quality and cost — that is, demands for technical improvements in the wares offered — to the defense of "unfettered freedom to take or leave the goods." Our dependence on institutional health care, he says, "soon turns into an obstacle to autonomous mutual care, coping, adapting and healing, and, what is worse, into a device by which people are stopped from transforming the conditions at work and at home that make them sick."[28]

The idea that women with breast cancer should work towards autonomy from the medical profession challenges win-win thinking. Pleas to examine costs in medicine are unpopular. "We have a tremendously well-funded health-care industry in Ontario (and Canada)," says family physician Gary Gibson, who teaches cost-effectiveness in medicine at the University of Western Ontario. "Only the United States spends more on health care than we do ... And we waste enormous amounts of money on useless services, tests and treatments — obscene amounts when compared to the medical resources available to most of humanity on this planet."[29]

Check-ups of women with breast cancer could be added to the list of wasteful expenditure, say two American analysts. In "A Minimalist Policy for Breast Cancer Surveillance," David Schapira and Nicole Urban challenge the practice of routine surveillance to detect a recurrence early. "Clearly, patients receiving adjuvant therapy require observation during therapy," they say, "but the value of follow-up of patients after therapy and of patients who have never received adjuvant therapy has not been established." Intense surveillance in the first three years after therapy, when 60 to 80 percent of recurrences are detected, rests on two assumptions: first, that most recurrences are detected at an early stage by the surveillance visits, and second, that early treatment of recurrences offers a better chance of cure or longer survival. The data, Shapira and Urban say, contradict both. Studies show, for example, that patients discover 75 to 95 percent of breast cancer recurrences between follow-up visits. Chest X-rays, bone scans and blood chemistry studies rarely detect metastases in asymptomatic patients. NSABP data showed, for example, that of 7,984 bone scans, only 52 (0.06%) found bone metastases in asymptomatic patients. Another study found that only 17 (19.5%) of 87 patients who suffered a relapse after breast cancer surgery were asymptomatic and only one of those had an abnormal chest X-ray. Standard follow-up tests, furthermore, have poor specificity. Of patients whose bone scans came back abnormal (as mine did), only one in nine have bone metastases.

The authors estimate that annual follow-up costs in the first three years after treatment could be reduced from an average of

$5,735 in 1990 U.S. dollars, to $1,025 (the cost of a physical exam and mammogram). The annual estimated savings in the U.S. would have been $636 million in 1990, rising to $812 million in 1995 and $1,036 million in the year 2000. Many women with breast cancer would no doubt resist the idea that our follow-up care should be a target for cost-cutting; but Illich's point is that the public gains health, in both the narrow and broad sense, by achieving autonomy from the medical complex. If these visits and tests really don't improve our health, we would indeed gain autonomy while saving money. We would be spared the anxiety caused by false positive scans and consciously assume greater responsibility for detecting signs of metastases ourselves.

Despite spiralling health costs, politicians are hard-pressed to advocate such cost-cutting measures. Some are committed to the win-win credo, but even those who are not are ill-placed to challenge it. The Honourable Monique Bégin, Canada's Minister of Health throughout the 1970s, confronted this problem in a 1989 essay called Redesigning Health Care for Women. "I fully understand, intellectually," she wrote, "Illich's thesis that it is necessary, as a first step in dealing with iatrogenesis (physician-induced disease), to investigate the global inefficiency and the dangers of our expensive health care system. But I, when I was Minister of National Health, increased the budgets of medical research programs and protected existing provincial health care budgets ... In other words, I was unable to translate my intellectual understanding into political action." As she explained her dilemma, "To this day, I am incapable of reconciling the following contradiction: how can we accept only the positive elements and reject the negative elements of modern science when the internal logic of biomedical research insists that all things must be explored in an eclectic fashion and in total freedom, and when the internal logic of the health care system is to use to the utmost the practical applications and the technology of bio-medical research?" When she tried to convince herself of the need to cut budgets, said Bégin, "A part of me would not cooperate. And that part corresponds to the thousands of women, children and men who live in hope of being saved by medicine and by science."[30]

Emily Dickinson called hope "the thing with feathers, that perches in the soul." This wordless songbird is precisely what enslaves us to the win-win cheerleaders. Fearing for our lives, we are wooed by technology's easy promises of imminent cures and breakthroughs. But a moment's reflection should convince us that technology cannot deliver "the thing with feathers." Cancer technology is already so expensive it is virtually impossible even for our wealthy societies to treat all the afflicted. American women know this first-hand. In Canada, our health coverage has, so far, kept the skyrocketing costs of treatment from our view, but the illusion can't last. Celia Felipe, a woman who came to Canada from the Phillippines to work as a nanny in 1990 learned this when she was ordered to leave the country because of a breast cancer diagnosis. Admitting her to Canada as a citizen, a letter from the immigration department said, "would cause, or might reasonably be expected to cause, excessive demands on health or social sevices."[31] As treatments become ever less affordable, governments and private insurers will step up their search for ways to drop more women through the trap door. Insurance companies have their eye on the breast cancer gene hunt for this precise reason.

High-dose chemotherapy with autologous bone marrow transplant, costing up to $200,000 per treatment, is the high-tech procedure presently being held out to breast cancer patients as the thing with feathers. The procedure has not been demonstrated effective with breast cancer in clinical trials — indeed, the death rates both during and after treatment are extremely high. Attempts to test the efficacy of super-chemo regimens are thwarted because so many doctors, already convinced that more is better, promote bone marrow transplants to women outside clinical trials.[32] Who can we hold accountable for such escalation? The physicians and the pharmaceutical companies will proclaim they are trying to help the woman who has made a "choice." The woman, failed by all other treatments, decides she has nothing to lose. She wants the right to choose any treatment that gives her hope. The record suggests most of the women will lose both their money and their life. Nonetheless, a risky, high-cost treatment is moving into widespread usage without ever proving its value for women. Once entrenched, it will be difficult to dislodge.

Visiting my friend Mary one afternoon, we fall into one of our wide-ranging conversations and I mention the win-win filter. Her eyes brighten.

"Exactly!" she says, "It's like the nudibranchia."

I demand, laughing, that Mary explain the nudibranchia connection. "I have no idea what you're talking about," I confess.

She begins her explanation with a special relish. "The nudibranchia is a beautiful sea animal, all rainbow colours that change constantly," she says. Now I understand her enthusiasm. Nature and beauty are two themes that animate Mary's soul.

"It feeds on jellyfish tentacles, which are sometimes poisonous," she continues. "If the nudibranchia sucks up poison from another animal, it becomes poisonous itself. It squirts poison out, and poisons other animals."

"The poison of the postwar era is consumerism," she says. "It infects our society and distorts every promising idea. What's frightening," she adds, "is that even the best-intentioned can be poisoned by it."

The marriage between government and industry, far from being a winning proposition for the consumer, often amounts to lose-lose, as we pay twice for new developments — once through taxes for development, then again to purchase the product. When a product falls short of the expectations the hype creates, we pay with dashed hopes and alternatives missed.

Our best hope, and the one that will give us power, is to see past the illusion of the win-win filter. Only by rejecting the false promise of health consumerism will we discover what conditions in our life give us cancer and find ways to transform them.

Notes

1. Kushner, p. 391.

2. Nicholas Regush, *Safety Last: the Failure of the Consumer Health Protection System in Canada*, (Toronto: Key Porter, 1993), pp. 2-3.

3. Interview with Peter Gzowski, *Morningside*, CBC Radio, (Jan. 14, 1993); see also, Nuala Beck, *Shifting Gears: Thriving in the New Economy*, (Toronto: Harper-Collins, 1992), pp. 76-79.

4. Patricia Kaufert, "Mammography and the Misplacement of Faith," paper presented at the American Anthropological Association, p. 16.

5. M. L. Brown, L.G. Kessler, and F.G. Rueter, "Is the Supply of Mammography Machines Outstripping Need and Demand? An Economic Analysis," *Annals of Internal Medicine*, (1990), 113 (7): 547-552.

6. Kaufert, p. 11.

7. Kate Dempsey et al, "Screening Mammography: What the Cancer Establishment Never Told You," *Cambridge: Women's Community Cancer Project,* (May 1992), p. 33.

8. Monte Paulsen, "The Politics of Cancer," *Metro Times,* (May 19, 1993), reprinted in *Utne Reader,* (Nov./Dec., 1993).

9. Moss, p. 90.

10. Moss, p. 91

11. Patterson, p. 173.

12. Moss, p. 75-76.

13. Moss, p. 93.

14. Moss, p. 94.

15. Patterson, pp. 295-6.

16. Kushner, p. 279.

17. Moss, p. 88-89.

18. Kushner, p. 280.

19. "Interferon, Interleukin II and Other Biological Response Modifiers for the Treatment of Breast Cancer," *NABCO Fact Sheet* 1/8702, (1987).

20. Neil A. Lewis and Robert Pear, "Clinton Gets a Dose of His Own Medicine," [NY Times Service], *Globe and Mail,* (Mar. 11, 1994).

21. R. Lewontin, "The Dream of the Human Genome," *New York Review of Books,* (May 28, 1992), pp. 37-8.

22. John Seabrook, "Building a Better Human," [review of *The Gene Wars,* by Robert Cook-Deegan], *The New Yorker,* (Mar. 28, 1994), pp. 112-113.

23. Madeleine Nash, "Riding the DNA Trail," *Time,* (Jan. 17, 1994), p. 49.

24. G. B. Shaw, *Preface on Doctors,* (London: Constable, 1906), p. v.

25. Patterson, p. 296.

26. Lewontin, *New York Review of Books,* p. 37.

27. Illich, p. 224.

28. Illich, pp. 238-239.

29. Gary Gibson, "Doctors Must Choose the Way to Go," *Globe and Mail,* (Jun 18, 1993).

30. Hon. Monique Bégin, "Redesigning Health Care for Women," (Ottawa: CRIAW, 1989), pp. 28-29.

31. Shawn Ohler, "Cancer Risk Means Nanny Must Go," *Edmonton Journal,* (Jun 23, 1993), p. B1.

32. Gina Kolata, "Boosting Chemotherapy May Prove Ineffective," *New York Times,* (May 1994).

Scoops
Fear & Cheer

Cancer is eating at every bone in my child's body. Why does Congress allow federally sponsored fundraisers and researchers to parrot Madison Avenue slogans — like "promising breakthroughs" and "tremendous strides"? Strides? What strides? Come on, let's tell it like it is.

My daughter is only 39. Her breasts are gone. There's a shunt in her chest to feed in the chemo because her veins are shot. There are three metal bars in her leg to avoid amputation. They're attached to a disintegrated hip. The leg is useless. It's in her ribs. It's in her spine and it hurts …

— Betty Wooten, *San Francisco Chronicle*, Sept. 5, 1991.

"**B**reakthrough," read the front page headline, "local researchers develop skin cancer treatment. Quick cheap method could help thousands."

I was in Kingston, Ontario for a week, at a writers' workshop. Members of the small class knew I had cancer and that I was writing about it.

"Did you see the paper this morning?" one woman exclaimed. "They've had a breakthrough — you must be very excited!"

She was far more excited than I was. In two years of scanning the headlines for any news about breast cancer, I had become increasingly irked by cancer stories in the media. The phenomenon was something I was trying to understand, as a journalist, and as an ordinary reader of newspapers.

I don't recall reading many stories about breast cancer before I was diagnosed, but afterwards, any headline with the words "cancer" or "breast cancer" jumped out at me. And the stories reassured me. All over the world, they said, scientists had found incredible new approaches to fighting cancer. STOPPING CANCER CELLS IN THEIR TRACKS, a large illustrated feature from the National Cancer Institute (NCI) in Bethesda, told how malignant cells from breast tumours recognize the blood vessel lining inside certain organs. "As they are whizzing around in the circulation, they recognize these signposts and know where to get off," a researcher explained. This research, claimed the article, would "block cancer's spread within the body." From Britain, a story titled TINY CANCER KILLERS said that a Nobel-prize winning chemist had learned how to program little "molecular robots" so that cancer drugs would hit their target with unprecedented accuracy. In France, researchers were "cracking a major obstacle to cancer chemotherapy," said a story headed, CANCER: ELECTROCHEMOTHERAPY OPENS THE DOOR. Another American story, headlined CANCER-FIGHTING MOLECULES SEEK AND DESTROY TUMOURS, was about synthethic molecules of a powerful anti-cancer agent. "We are really excited about these compounds," said a spokesman for the Scripps Research Institute. Like Trojans in the legendary horse, "The molecules enter the cell intact and upon activation, destroy the genetic material."

For a year or so, I eagerly clipped these stories. If had to have breast cancer, I thought, how fortunate to have it at a time when the answer to the riddle was so close. As the clippings accumulated, however, I noticed a pattern. Beyond the breathless headline, somewhere towards the end of the story, were qualifications. One new treatment had only been shown to work with a rare form of leukemia, and the cells soon became resistant to it; another had been tested on rats — showing that it worked with humans would take many years. The genetic engineering experiment appeared only to have a temporary effect, but the scientists "hope to build on their findins in future research." And so on.

I kept on clipping, but for a different purpose. I wanted to understand the filtering process by which the media shapes the public's beliefs about cancer.

In his cultural history of cancer in America, James Patterson discovered two consistent themes in cancer coverage: fear and cheer. Cancer stories listed in the *New York Times* index from the beginning of the century show the dual face the media gives to cancer.

"One type [of story] emphasized the Message of Hope," says Patterson. In 1907, for example, the *Times* wrote, "the cancer problem may be likened to an impregnable citadel," but, "professional opinion sanctions the belief that it will ultimately fall." Several articles described experiments by a Scottish doctor who had injected animals with a digestive juice of the pancreas. "The most amazing thing I have ever seen," remarked a visiting American physician. Two years later experts prophesied, "the beginning of the end of the cancer problem is in sight," in a report about dogs vaccinated with slow-growing tumours to render them immune to malignancy. In 1910, Patterson notes, the *Times* "lauded the work of a scientist who was injecting fluid from a recovered cancer patient into another victim, and described the experiment as 'one of the most important ever made in connection of the treatment of this dread malady.'" Three years later, a page-wide headline in the paper announced, CAUSE OF CANCER FOUND AT LAST. The cause, revealed the sub-head, was "Not a germ but an inorganic chemical poison, isolated from malignant tumours after many experiments ..."[1]

The reporting behind these stories, says Patterson, "regularly reflected an entirely uncritical and breathless regurgitation of preliminary research." The misrepresentation and exaggeration in cancer reporting appalled cool heads in the medical community. Dr. Charles Childe, for example, wrote a book about cancer published in 1906 in which he complained, "A doctor ... has only to read a paper before one of the medical societies, ... and we see immediately in the columns of some of the daily papers a sensational article under the heading, 'Cancer Cured at Last,' 'The Death Blow to Cancer,' or something of that kind.'"

The second type of coverage wallowed in cancer's shadow side. "Scare stories in lurid language followed headlines like BIG INCREASE IN CANCER DEATHS," says Patterson. "The *New York World* reported that cancer 'may well be called the living death, for it creeps upon its victims insidiously, and drags them down to desperation before they realize the meaning of its deceptive early signs.' Not to be outdone, another journalist branded cancer 'a living thing ... a veritable Frankenstein's monster, bent on the destruction of its host.'"

Founders of the American Society for the Control of Cancer (ASCC), whose goal was to promote an awareness of the disease, recognized the horns of a dilemma soon after the ASCC's birth in 1914. Whatever strategy they adopted to publicize the message of early detection, they risked criticism. Sober messages might bore the audience; but the dramatic "Chicken Little" approach opened them to charges of using scare tactics. Some early ASCC pamphlets, posters, and stories tilted to excess — especially the messages designed to highlight the rising death rate. These occasional appeals to fear, Patterson says, "dramatized the horrors of cancer in order to deliver the moral: seek medical help before it was too late." More often, however, they plunked for the Message of Hope, designed to bring cancer out into the open and to "soberly overturn the conspiracy of fear and silence" surrounding the disease.[2]

As the ASCC gained strength, its leaders became more adept at using the media to get its message out. By the mid-1930s, the group had a leader, Clarence Little, with a coherent strategy to publicize cancer. In 1935 he created the Women's Field Army. Next, he hired a publicity director, who saw the potential of using recruitment for the army as a publicity hook. He called the campaign "United States Cancer Week." The plan worked. In 1937 a burst of stories about the the menace of cancer and the enlistment drive appeared in major magazines and on radio broadcasts from coast to coast.

Little's greatest coup was to get stories in *Time, Fortune* and *Life.* Some articles featured Little himself — a Harvard graduate who had been president of several universities and was an authority on cancer genetics — heading a laboratory in Maine that bred mice for research. For its feature story, *Life* posed Little with a dramatic photo of laboratory mice. Another photo showed an imposing 1,250,000-volt X-ray machine at Columbia University, described as "the biggest gun in the war" against cancer. The same story broke journalistic ground by including graphic photos of very sick cancer patients, but the overall theme was one of hope from science. *Time* featured a pipe-smoking Little on its cover. *Fortune* prophesied continuing increases in cancer mortality for the next 35 years, but affirmed that society had the power to "finance the brains and equipment by which [light] might be called forth." All in all, says Patterson, the stories managed to have it both ways.

Cancer was "both a looming threat to civilization and a disease that brilliant scientists were beginning to conquer."[3]

These magazines would not have joined the official voice against cancer, unless their editors believed the stories would have mass appeal. The response from readers was telling. *Life's* photographs of visibly ill people sparked outrage: ("I burned up my copy. I can't imagine anything more repulsive"; and, "horrible and revolting ... fortunately I was able to clip them before the issue reached my wife, who is particularly sensitive to such gory specimens.") The exaggerated promise of technology, on the other hand, brought pitiful pleas for help from sick people: "Let me know what your terms and rates are ... I think I need help have a lump in my left brest [sic], if it is not too expensive"; and "I have a breast cancer and would like to know more about this type of treatment [radiation]. I haven't any faith in operations as so many who have had an operation for this live a short while."[4]

After the war, cancer stories became a press staple. The 1950s were a time of optimism in America and most articles beamed forth the confident mood. "More than in previous decades," says Patterson, "the magazines and newspapers extolled the researchers and predicted eventual success — especially if people gave money to the cause." The word that best captures the flavour of these stories, says Patterson, had not yet been coined: Hype. A 1949 *Time* magazine story, for example, featured on its cover the head of Memorial Sloan-Kettering, Cornelius Rhoads, who, in Patterson's words, "wore a white coat and looked confidently forward, his sharp, keen eyes gleaming behind his glasses. Next to him was a glowing sword, symbol of the Americal Cancer Society, smashing through a fierce-looking crab." Inside, the story described the work being done at the Sloan-Kettering ("a tower of hope"). Rhoads spoke about making "a frontal attack with all our forces." All but buried beneath the paragraphs of positive thinking was the staple reminder that a cure for cancer was nowhere close to being found.[5] *Reader's Digest, McCall's, Look,* and *Life* were other popular vehicles that delivered the message of hope into American homes.

A few serious publications, including *Harper's, The Nation* and *Saturday Review* tried to put things in perspective, says Patterson, "by pointing out how little the scientists really knew." Their reasoned analyses did nothing to restrain the mainstream press. In a 1958 story in *Life*, the head of the NCI declared, "We are on the verge of breakthroughs." The same year, *Reader's Digest* heralded an experiment in which Ohio prison inmates were injected with cancerous cells to test their immunity. The *Digest* called the experiment a "history-making research project that could lead to a breakthrough in the struggle to understand this dread killer."

Another significant change in the postwar years was that the ASCC metamorphised into a more media-conscious organization, the American Cancer Society (ACS). Patterson found two key changes in the media strategy. First, the society relied more heavily on the advertising methods familiar to the business executives who had joined its new board. Second, in the late 1950s, the ACS dropped the appeals to fear almost entirely.

The revamped charity, blessed with unprecedented wealth, "distributed an ever bigger stream of pamphlets, radio scripts, and advertising materials to magazines and newspapers," says Patterson. The agency started a scholarly journal, *Cancer*, and a magazine *Ca*, for physicians and medical students. It made expert use of contacts with writers, publishers and celebrities. Enthusiastic ACS backers included *Reader's Digest*, *Time* and *Life*, which carried stories in support of the society's goals and ran calls for contributions during the annual April fund drive. In 1947 the society began sponsoring "cancer seminars" which brought leading science writers on tours of ACS-funded research organizations. "Impressed," says Patterson, "many writers responded by publishing stories on the need for more money to fight cancer." When the tours proved popular, the ACS expanded the plan to include meetings for large numbers of reporters and magazine writers. The format encouraged uncritical reporting and the timing was geared to solicit donations. Many of the meetings, says Patterson "took place in March in well-appointed facilities of warm southern resorts, where the writers were treated to reports of the latest research. Scientific peer responses — standard at regular meetings of researchers — were uncommon at these programs. Optimistic stories about cancer research then appeared in America's magazines and newspapers on the eve of the annual April drive for funds."[6] Journalists in the 1950s "never tired of promoting the technological marvels of radiation," says

Patterson. In the two decades that followed, chemotherapy inherited the mantle of the imminent breakthrough.

In the 1980s, newspaper and magazine articles about cancer had reached record numbers: in one 40-day period in 1981, the NCI charted almost 1,500 stories. In part, the volume reflected a greater openness about the disease. This notable change, says Patterson "helped any number of patients deal better with the disease," but the articles didn't necessarily lessen public fear. Many raised the spectre of "cancer towns" and widespread environmental dangers, while an analysis in *Cancer News* showed that television dramas and films "often wallowed in mawkishness and awe." The NCI's announcement, in 1985, that the immune-system activator interleukin-2 was "the most exciting biological ther-py we've seen so far," generated the usual enthusiastic coverage from the national media, hailing the treatment as a "cancer breakthrough."[7]

The American Cancer Society's promotional strategies are only part of the media story. As a journalist and editor, I wondered why media professionals — who take pride in being sceptical and informed — were so easily seduced by these overtures. In my own experience prior to getting cancer I had seldom covered medical stories, but as editor of a consumer advocacy magazine I recalled with some embarrassment a story on external breast prostheses that I edited before my diagnosis. The article, entitled "Buying a breast prosthesis," struck me at the time as a straightforward and helpful service piece and I passed it through the process with minor editing.

Only after reading Audre Lorde's discussion of breast prostheses, months later, did I understand that the article had not posed the type of questions that are standard in a consumer protection magazine — obvious questions that I, as an editor, also failed to ask, about price, misleading sales practices and — most basic of all — whether the potential consumer needed the product. Lorde pointed out that breast prostheses are often chosen "not from desire, but in default," because conforming to the expectations of others is easier than facing disapproving looks, or fashioning clothes that look attractive on an asymmetrical body. She described a marketing scam which promoted a breast form, supposedly custom-made and attached by a special adhesive.

Women had paid up to $600 for the product, which got national publicity on a popular morning TV show, but the forms bore no relation to the women's bodies and failed to adhere. Although the forms made by reputable makers are of acceptable quality, said Lorde, even these prostheses are "outrageously overpriced." Lorde's analysis made me realize how vulnerable women with breast cancer are to exploitation and how readily others, including journalists, offer dubious support "in much the same way that candy is offered to babies after an injection."[8]

The lax professional standards in cancer coverage have not entirely escaped the notice of journalistic watchdogs, I discovered. In 1975, Washington-based science policy analyst Daniel Greenberg wrote an article for the *Columbia Journalism Review* (CJR) called "A critical look at cancer coverage." He examined American expenditures for research into cancer cures over the previous two decades ("several billion dollars"), and the five-year survival rates over the same period ("approximately the same ... as ... before any of that research took place") and observed "certain gruesome and curious parallels" between the early reporting of the War on Cancer and the war in Vietnam. Like Patterson, Greenberg identified optimism as the hallmark of cancer reportage.

To uncover the reason for the upbeat official reports issued by the National Cancer Institute (NCI) and the American Cancer Society, Greenberg visited the NCI and two other, unidentified, cancer-related bureaucracies. "Why," he asked various employees, "issue optimistic reports in conflict with the harsh facts?" Three people — a health economist, a cancer statistician and a physician in a top administrative post — spoke frankly but were not willing to have their views attributed. "It just doesn't serve to rock the boat," said a scientist at NCI. "Look, when you've got 10,000 radiologists and millions of dollars worth of equipment, you give radiation treatments, even if study after study shows that a lot of it does more harm than good." The physician-administrator said, "I'm convinced that for some cancers, the survival rates were better decades ago, but don't tell anyone I said that. The official line is that we're making a lot of progress." Greenberg reported that his interviews pointed to this consensus: "there is no conscious intention to mislead the public. Rather, there is a desire to sustain public support and federal appropriations by conveying a picture of an immensely difficult problem that will slowly yield if we spend on it and work at it."

No harm in that, Greenberg told one researcher, if it was the only way to get the necessary support.

"There's a good deal of harm," the other replied, "because as long as the establishment is persuading the public that results are being achieved, there isn't going to be any pressure for supporting alternatives to these dead-alley lines of research that dominate the program."

The implicit Vietnam parallel convinced Greenberg. A sceptical view of public policy seems cruel when directed at well-intentioned efforts to cure a dread disease, he acknowledged, because such questioning brings no solace to those afflicted with cancer. "But if the war is going badly, as it is, recognizing the truth may be a step toward making it go better."[9]

In the next issue of the CJR, the science director of the American Cancer Society took Greenberg to task for using anonymous sources and challenged his overall assessment. Almost 20 years later, though, Greenberg's evaluation rings truest. In breast cancer, for example, the ACS source agreed that mortality showed no significant reduction in 35 years, but he predicted the cure rate would "soon improve as more women benefit from new detection techniques" — specifically, the mammography, thermography and clinical breast exams that were then part of the Breast Cancer Detection Demonstration Project. The mortality rate in fact has not declined.

Knowing the journalistic community had been put on alert about cancer coverage by the premier journal of the trade simply added to my puzzlement. The article seemed to have had no effect. The clippings in my collection, begun almost 15 years later, contained examples that were interchangeable with examples Greenberg cited. Not only that, at least two additional critiques had since appeared in the CJR. "The Gene Craze," published in late 1980, chastized the profession for promotional reporting of genetic research. From 1974 to 1978, said the author of that article, the press conscientiously covered genetic engineering as a political issue and ritualistically balanced its reports to include risks vs benefits, critics vs proponents, and potential harms to society as well as hoped-for benefits. But when scientific leaders and DNA researchers banded together to lobby against restrictive legislation, coverage went flaccid. In the same vein, a 1985 article on coverage of new pharmaceutical drugs found that reporters for the general press (unlike the medical trade press) neglected to tap readily available information on adverse drug reactions and simply regurgitated the contents of press kits supplied by the drug companies.[10] Something was rotten in the state of journalism, I concluded, and it was apparently chronic.

When the journalists' organization to which I belonged put out the word that it needed someone to organize a panel on medical reporting for the group's next annual meeting, I seized the moment. I assembled as speakers Eve Savory, a prominent TV journalist who specialized in medical and science stories, Varda Burshtyn, a writer with a bent for social analysis, and Margaret Somerville, a medical ethicist known for her frequent media commentaries. Ten days before the panel, the *Globe and Mail* obligingly provided fodder for my opening remarks by running a front page story titled "Study Links Diet, Breast Cancer." As the journalist told it, a Canadian research team had proven, for the first time, a link between breast cancer and a high fat diet. It was a classic "breakthrough" story. Ten days later, less typically, the paper's science columnist ran a critique of the same scientific study. The study hadn't shown any link at all, wrote Stephen Strauss in his back-page column. Of the 56,837 women in the study, those who ate the least fat (the bottom quarter) were just as likely to get breast cancer as those who ate the most fat (the top quarter). The conclusion that the study showed a fat-cancer link could have been drawn only by the "most tortured finessing of the statistics," said Strauss.

Strauss was more critical of the medical journal than of his own newspaper. But if the study was that inconclusive, I asked the panelists, how had the story describing it made the front page of the paper, claiming proof of a link?

Eve Savory had first-hand insights into the coverage of this particular story. When the dietary fat article appeared on the front page of the Globe and Mail, the Canadian Broadcasting Corporation (CBC) decided the story was so important they called Savory in to do a TV report that night, even though she was on holiday. "I came home from my fitness walk to find a message on the machine, absolutely frantic. They asked me to call in right away, and when I did they read me the first two sentences of the story. The first was, 'Scientists at the University of Toronto have found a link between breast cancer and fat.' The second was, 'Scientists have long suspected such a link but this was the first study to prove it.'"

Savory tore in to the office and began making phone calls, only to find the research was a retrospective study of the type that asks participants to complete a diet-history questionnaire where they have to remember how often they ate root vegetables or chicken with skin on it. The questionnaire listed 86 food items common to the Canadian diet. Savory had covered enough stories about fat and breast cancer that she wasn't impressed. "These studies don't prove anything," says Savory. "If you put a group of women on a low fat diet, and have a control group, and follow them to see how many get breast cancer later on — now that can prove."

She explained this to the producer, but the *National* still wanted the story, "because it was on the front page of the *Globe.*" Problem number one: media outlets play follow-the-leader, so a morning story in the major newspapers can set the agenda for the rest of the day, even when the story doesn't merit the concentrated attention. The media also like a local angle. When I spoke to him by phone, Strauss defended the *Globe and Mail*'s decision to give the story front page play because the researchers were Canadians, and the article had been published in the *Journal of the National Cancer Institute* in the U.S. Like the story about Kingston researchers that appeared in the Kingston newspaper, this one had a subtext: Local Boys Make Good. Savory handled the situation by doing a story that summarized the ongoing efforts to link diet and breast cancer; she discussed the limitations in the new study and concluded that dietary fat *might* be a cause of breast cancer.

Savory looks out at the full room of 60 or so reporters. "How many of you are medical journalists?" she asks. One or two hands go up. One of the problems for journalists reporting medical stories, she points out, is that so few specialize in medical reporting.

"Very few of us get the beat full time," she says. "I do environmental science and technology as well. Often we don't get to stick with the medical beat either — the turnover's really rapid. A few have been around a long time and are doing a superb job, but they are only a tiny number and therefore the stories seldom have the context." For example, she says, a reporter might write up a study that sounds important, without realizing a lot of other studies have been published, sometimes showing exactly the same thing and sometimes finding absolutely no link.

"My observation," remarks a man in the audience, "is that as medical reporters get lucky enough to develop contacts and have continuity and be a name in their field, this process has within it the seeds of destruction. Because the more they get into it, the more they see the forest instead of the trees, the more they start reporting things that may upset the sources that give them the best stories. And after a while, if they're true to their conscience, they become persona non grata. They begin to compromise for the 'greater good' of keeping alive their access to their sources."

"I think that's true," concedes Savory. "And it makes me really sad to say it's true." She cites one instance where she herself failed to do an important story because she could not find a way to do it without compromising her source. The same pressures apply in political coverage, she points out. "I covered the Hill for four years and I think it's worse there. Everyone hangs around the National Press Gallery. It's a problem of reporting — of a beat."

Another real lack in medical reporting, says Savory, is that most journalists are arts graduates and don't know how to read statistics. "I don't," she admits frankly. "I can't talk to you about confidence levels, I have to get someone to interpret them. We don't know how to read and analyze research literature, and so we get sucked in." To get around the problem, journalists will often ask someone to interpret the study. "And if it happens to be the guy who did the study, and he says it's a breakthrough, we say it's a breakthrough. We don't know, we can't figure out what it says.

"It's been said that fear sells papers, so does hope," says Savory. "So we deal in fear, and we deal in hope, and we don't analyze. We're very intimidated by scientists. Can you imagine us treating scientists the same way we treat politicians?"

In 1990s medical reporting, industry promo kits are alive and well. "Why do the big pharmaceuticals spend hundreds of thousands of dollars on fancy-packaged videos? And press kits?" asks Savory. "Because far too many of us take those stories and just almost rerun them the way they are. Nice little bit of free advertising for the drug companies. Nice way for us to be lazy. All the work's done for you!" The drug companies prefer free publicity to paid advertising not only because it's cheaper, reports the CJR, but because patients are more likely to demand a drug from their doctor if it appears in an article.

"An analyst, writing in the British magazine *New Scientist*, once complained that we don't report science and medicine," says Savory. "We don't investigate our subject the way other reporters do, we retail it. He said that readers want positive news and we supply it. And it's true — generally speaking, we are far too quick to accept the medical line, and far too slow to realize that these are people with their own ambitions and problems, just like any one else. So these tiny advances and tentative findings, and corroborative studies are trumpeted as major breakthroughs.

"One reason we tend to be almost advocates of science and medicine," continues Savory, "is because it's the only way to get print or air time. Our quote is better if we have that enthusiasm. We want the researchers to be very enthusiastic, and if they're not, we squeeze them until they get that way. I heard one reporter ask, 'Just tell me how you felt at the Eureka Moment. Couldn't you *feel* it?' We really don't go outside enough to get other people's views about what's going on. And I'm talking here about medical reporters. When a generalist gets assigned to a medical story, they're even less sceptical."

"Deference to doctors is extraordinary," says Varda Burshtyn. "Doctors deal with life and death and they seem to be able to perform magic." Our deference to doctors, she says, goes beyond the intellectual. "Doctors benefit from a deep emotional need to be taken care of. So when medicine proposes that it has a solution to a problem, we're drawn by the emotional and ideological poles to believe this claim. We want to believe it, we need to believe it, we're told to believe it. And so we believe it. We see doctors as saviours."

The journalist, Burshtyn adds, may feel above this deference to medicine. "But we all partake of this in one way or another and it's one of the things that makes it harder to be critical when we write our medical stories."

Margaret Somerville agrees that medicine has taken over the roles that previously were fulfilled by religion. In this other role, "medical stories represent our collective search for hope, optimism, and immortality," says Somerville. "As a religion substitute, medical stories reflect us. They tend to be 'good news' stories and I don't think there's anything wrong with them playing that role."

Reporters do have to ask, however, what their obligations are regarding the downside of modern medical technology, she adds. "There is some obligation. You cannot always do what I call Modern Medical Miracle Hype. You do have to issue some warnings because people generally believe that medicine is going to do them good. People find it extremely difficult to believe that medicine is going to harm them, even when you go to great lengths to tell them that could happen. So if they don't get any of that as part of their normal diet, it's very difficult. We have a very strong tendency in our society to medicalize societal problems. A lot of things that may not be medical problems get turned into medical problems and get handled in medicine. One reason that occurs," she says, "is partly because we still believe medicine is a safe forum, in that, more than politics, more than business, more than some other areas, it is fundamentally governed by altruism."

Somerville also contends that the medical reporter is not detached from the content of his or her stories. "A reporter is never going to be a politician ... but every single person in our community identifies with medicine. There is practically no other institution that that's true of. Everyone thinks that they could be sick, their parents could be sick, their baby could need care. They identify."

Polls asking what kind of stories people want covered in the media show that medical stories are among the most in demand, and one reason for their popularity is that people are seeking control of their lives. Editors therefore feel pressured to print medical stories that are helpful and not too complicated. This creates problems for the medical reporter.

"I believe the public has a right to information," says Somerville. "I also believe the public is going to have to live more comfortably with uncertainty, because part of this information is going to raise uncertainty and with it accompanying anxiety."

Eve Savory agrees that control is the hook behind many medical stories. "We all want to be in control, and when disease strikes, you feel like you're out of control. We're desperate for information that can help us feel we have some control in what happens in our lives, and if we can change our diet and avoid breast cancer, that's great."

While stories about breakthroughs in medical technology appeal to our awe of science, dietary studies and other prevention research tap into our fantasies of control over our lives. These stories quickly gain a mythological status. As an example of this, surgeon Susan Love cites the myth that cutting caffeine from the diet will help prevent fibrocystic disease and, in turn, reduce the risk of breast cancer. The term "fibrocystic disease" is a waste-basket designation used to describe just about anything unusual in the breast that isn't cancer, says Love. Clinicians refer indis-criminately to lumps, tenderness, swelling and breast pain as fibrocystic disease. Pathologists who examine biopsied tissue refer to non-cancerous microscopic lesions as fibrocystic disease. Radiologists call the dense breast tissue characteristic of younger women fibrocystic disease. When Love looked at the published medical literature, she found that the term could be traced to a small number of poorly thought out studies. One group, for example, analyzed the breast tissue of women who had had mastectomies for breast cancer and discovered that most of these breasts showed evidence of fibrocystic disease — "so the re-searchers brightly concluded that fibrocystic disease was linked to cancer ... They might as well have decided that, since all the cancerous breasts had nipples, nipples cause cancer."[11] The term fibrocystic disease, however, entered the lexicon both in the medical journals and the popular media. Here was a new disease of the breasts which was not cancer, but which women could take steps to prevent.

Love traced the origin of the alleged caffeine link to fibrocystic symptoms to a study that got enthusiastic media coverage. An Ohio surgeon named Dr. Minton decided to test his theory of a link. He told 40 women who had clinical symptoms — pain, lumpiness, swelling and so on — to stop all caffeine intake. Half the women ignored his advice and of the remaining 20, 13 said their breasts felt better as a result of cutting caffeine from their diets. Minton did no objective testing, and the study did not employ a randomized design or double blinding procedure to keep the subjects and researcher from knowing which group they were in. Minton's article appeared in the *American Journal of*

Obstetrics and Gynaecology in 1979. "In spite of its glaring inadequacy," says Love, "Minton's research got a lot of press and it wasn't long before it was extended in the popular imagination to include cancer prevention." The myth promoted a double fallacy. Since caffeine doesn't cause the symptoms associated with "fibrocystic disease" and the symptoms don't lead to breast cancer, cutting caffeine from the diet won't prevent breast cancer.

Subsequent studies, with better designs, did not show any relationship between reducing caffeine intake and breast symptoms such as pain or lumpiness either. Yet the myth persists, perpetuated by both physicians and the media. Love says that physicians sometimes defend telling women to give up caffeine as a method of reducing breast symptoms, even though they admit the evidence linking the two are non-existent. They reason that coffee isn't good for you anyway, it's easy to give up, and the woman will feel better if she is given a diagnosis and a cure. Love disagrees. "This is extremely insulting to an adult woman, who is entitled to honesty from her doctor, and it also ignores the social importance of caffeine in our culture."[12]

A few years ago, when prevention became the buzzword in breast cancer, magazines began to package stories with the promise that readers could control their risk of breast cancer. Of course none of the articles could explain how to prevent breast cancer. They described recent research in diet, family history, hormones and the Tamoxifen Prevention Study, but couldn't deliver what no one knows — how to reduce breast cancer risk — which was the anxiety-reducing information the headlines promised.

Publishers of medical journals have their own grievances about the way the media covers medicine. The medical establishment's method for curtailing irresponsible reporting is the peer reviewed journal article. In 1981, when Arnold Relman was editor of the *New England Journal of Medicine*, he wrote an article called "The Patient and the Press" for the *Bryn Mawr Alumnae Bulletin* which explained how this system works. The popular press, he acknowledges, has played an increasingly important role in medical education since the war. Medical research burgeoned, along with a new popular consumerist attitude towards health which encourages patients to be informed and sceptical towards the medical establishment. The popular media broadened its coverage of health issues according-ly. A result that Relman deplores is that, given the demand for medical stories, the media often responds by publishing research results prematurely, that is, when they are reported at a con-ference, or when an over-zealous researcher decides to discuss unpublished findings in an interview.

Medical research news, Relman argues, differs from the news material generally published in newspapers because research is not an event that occurs at a particular moment. The who, what, where, when and how of a typical news story does not suffice when reporting research, which typically has "a long and uncertain gestation period." A preliminary step is for the researcher to present tentative conclusions before colleagues at a scientific meeting, "where discussion and criticism may indicate the need for still more work or for further modification of the hypothesis." When the evidence finally seems secure enough, perhaps six months or several years from the outset of the project, the re-searcher submits the paper to a scientific journal which then sends the manuscript to be read by two or more experts. A consultant statistician and other members of the journal's staff also critique the paper and may send it back to the authors to collect more data, re-analyse the data presented, or modify their discussion and conclusion. This process takes another six months to a year. The eventual publication of research in a journal, says Relman, is the news event which the media ought to report.

Only rarely, says Relman, is medical news of such import that it should bypass this "leisurely and orderly process." He cites, as an example of such an emergency, the sudden outbreak of "toxic shock syndrome" among young women and its apparent relation to the use of tampons. Most medical developments are not like that, says Relman. The *New England Journal of Medicine* warns would-be authors against premature disclosure of their work to the press, believing that the public does not benefit from media reports that arise from uncorroborated statements made in an interview, at a conference, or in a press release.[13]

Relman's critique no doubt applies to some of the flagrantly promotional stories about breast cancer that appear in the popular press — what James Patterson calls the "breathless regur-gitation of preliminary results." Appearance in a peer review journal offers one yardstick which journalists and readers can use to size up a potential research story; but research served up prematurely to the public doesn't explain the consistently promotional tone of cancer stories. Many such stories — the dietary fat article described in the *Globe and Mail*, or the mythical caffeine link to breast cancer, arose from articles that appeared in established medical journals. The very cachet of having successfully cleared all the barriers to peer review publication prompts researchers to revel too much when their papers finally reach the finish line. Journalists, on the other hand, take too secure a refuge in the fact that a researcher has published a paper and is therefore a peer-certified "expert" in his or her field. And the "article-publication-as-news-event" mentality is what is wrong with many journalistic stories. They provide no context to inform the reader about where this particular article fits in the breast cancer research gestalt.

Medical emergencies present another interesting dilemma, since this designation is clearly subjective. Recent events in breast cancer research offer striking examples of press statements issued or publicized on the grounds of medical "emergencies." Vincent DeVita chose to issue a Medical Alert about the use of chemotherapy for Stage I breast cancer patients prior to an article's publication, arguing that women's lives hung in the balance. Many media outlets considered this story, issued by the head of the National Cancer Institute, to be newsworthy, and did not seek the opinion of others. When the *London Times* chose to feature a pre-publication conference report of excess deaths in screened women from of the National Breast Screening Study, the newspaper apparently concluded that lives were at stake. Journalists cannot be expected to ignore such potentially important stories, although they could certainly handle them better than they do.

The sacredness of publication in a peer review journal can be used to delay politically awkward scientific findings. When four women in one NSABP trial testing tamoxifen as a breast cancer treatment died of endometrial cancer, the deaths contradicted information in consent forms for the NSABP's Tamoxifen Prevention Trial. The deaths were reported in a peer-reviewed journal several years after the fact, in April 1994. This finding was, arguably, an emergency, or certainly something that women taking tamoxifen would like to know, but senior investigators insisted they were right to keep the results from the public because they needed to be properly validated and presented in the context of a peer reviewed article.

The process in which Relman takes pride is also part of the competitive system that concerns ethicists. "One of the problems is fraud in medical research," Margaret Somerville reminded journalists at the panel discussion. "There's an enormous concern about that at the moment, precisely because of the publish or perish situation." As Somerville spoke, in March 1991, fraud committed by Dr. Roger Poisson at Montreal's St. Luc hospital was under investigation (see Part Four of this book). Her remark is a reminder that the peer review process cannot detect fraud and is part of a system that may contribute to it. When fraud was discovered in already-published breast cancer data, researchers argued that the sacredness of the "leisurely and orderly process" of peer review was a reason for delaying a revised analysis.

The media screens messages about breast cancer through the filters of fear and (its flip side) hope. The first fans cancerphobia, the other spins magical solutions of research breakthroughs and idealized schemes for early detection. In this double barrelled appeal, media coverage of cancer bears no small likeness to religious propaganda. On the one hand, fire and brimstone that will consume the careless or nonbelieving; on the other, a promised land, accessible to the good women who perform breast self-exams, go for mammograms, and comply with medical treatments. The reassuring stories I clipped after my diagnosis gave me transient comfort but that comfort turned to anger when I realized the false impression they gave. Faced with a reality that was dramatically at odds with what I had read, I felt confused and powerless.

In their propaganda model of the media, Edward Herman and Noam Chomsky charge that the American mass media fails to perform the responsibility entrusted to it, namely to provide the public with the information necessary to act intelligently as citizens. Rather than searching for the truth, independent of authority, the media serves a "societal purpose," inculcating and defending the economic, social and political agenda of privileged groups. Cancer coverage bears out this model. The press routinely publishes upbeat stories about breast cancer shaped by cancer charities, medical organizations, research agencies and commercial interests. The impact is to create the impression of a disease under control and about to be eliminated.

A myriad of forces nurture the media's habit of presenting breast cancer as a disease that science will inevitably conquer via early detection and research. Cancer charities have honed their optimistic messages over the decades, working the media to maximize donations. Cancer research agencies have also flourished by endorsing the public's naive dream of an impending medical miracle. Hooked on their annual injection of funds from the public largesse, no one in the research community wants to upset the myth of "an immensely difficult problem that will slowly yield if we spend on it and work at it." The media counts on the cancer research community to supply a stream of good news stories of continued advances and periodic breakthroughs. The naiveté of these stories is attributable in part to the public's deep-seated belief that medicine and technology can solve societal problems. Journalists, like most middle-class North Americans, view medicine and cancer institutions as benevolent. Factored into the equation is the journalist's own fear of cancer. She or he needs to believe as much as anyone that "Cancer Can be Beaten."

The public eagerly accepts the optimistic promises. Everyone wants to keep the faith that breast cancer is preventable and curable. Seeing these statements in print makes the hope tangible. Sheltered from reality, however, we are denied the option of exercising politically responsible judgement towards the medical and cancer agencies. Nor can we act in our own best interest if we get cancer. Researchers and physicians recognize the potential for backlash when the reality of a cancer diagnosis penetrates the media hype. "In many ways we've led the public to expect miracles and conveyed the impression that progress in cancer was more advanced than it really is," a physician told the Parliamentary Committee on Breast Cancer. He continued, "... we are still relatively in the Dark Ages when it comes to understanding the mechanism by which cancer cells behave. Slogans like the Canadian Cancer Society's 'Cancer Can Be Cured' ... may be interpreted, particularly by the vulnerable cancer patient in whom the diagnosis has just been made, that her cancer can be cured. The gap between what is expected and what is realistic is wide ... Disappointment leads to anger, fear, and distrust."[14] Confronted with vulnerable patients, these professionals are trapped by the images they know are unrealistic. At the same time, they want money to do their research.

The flip side of cheer, the filter of fear, keeps women from confronting our immobilizing dread of breast cancer. The hyperbolized terror associated with the disease helps neither those who might get it, nor those currently living with it. In the current rash of genetic stories, the breasts of women with a family history of breast cancer are frequently called "time bombs about to go off." Paradoxically, journalists perpetuate cancer's mythic horror in such alarming metaphors while denying, by omission, the real pain of women who live with the disease and sometimes die of it. Cheerful stories about survivors abound, but I can't recall ever seeing a frank media story depicting what a woman terminally ill with breast cancer goes through. While death by breast cancer is not pretty, it is real in a way that metaphors about "the living death" or "a veritable Frankenstein's monster" are not. Real pain demands real solutions. Inchoate dread invites fantasy answers like miracle breakthroughs. The real stories of women who die of breast cancer, if told, would force the public to question the facile promises of progress. We might, as a society, move beyond phobia and fantasy to assess what medical research can realistically do and which problems are beyond its scope.

The research community can be expected to resist the curtailment of its powers that would necessarily follow such an assessment; but realistic expectations by the public would ultimately free researchers to do their work more effectively. Our wish for total control of our health, for example, is not a problem that medicine can solve. Nor is our fear of death. These anxieties reflect the spiritual malaise of a secular, progress-driven society. Yet we project these spiritual dilemmas onto medicine, which in turn responds by devising consumable answers: costly tests and treatments which can't possibly provide the hoped-for results. Cancer charities, the bio-medical industry, the state and the media all benefit materially from these measures which, despite their ineffectiveness, create jobs, foster unrealistic optimism, and supply advertising revenue. In moments of candour, however, cancer researchers admit to feelings of failure. "It's really very depressing," an epidemiologist for the American Cancer Society told the

New York Times in 1986. "After all this work, we don't know much more about the causes of breast cancer than we did 20 years ago."[15]

In the wake of organizing the panel on medical reporting I recall imagining that, at least in the short run, an enlightened corp of journalists would flood the Canadian media with accurate medical articles. Instead I felt assailed by ever more upbeat stories about breakthroughs and imminent cures. The article in the *Kingston Whig-Standard* about the new skin cancer treatment cream was just one example. The following day a second, more telling, front page story appeared, titled "Breakthrough cancer cream attracts firm." It featured a prominent Canadian entrepreneur, whose company was "on the verge of purchasing the rights to the breakthrough cancer cream ..." Overnight, the medical miracle had metamorphized into its true identity, a business venture that promised to boost stock prices and pump money into the local university. Everything that ails cancer reportage, I realized, is deeply rooted in our culture. Simply exposing the problem to well-intended journalists is not going to bring about change.

Meaningful social change, Herman and Chomsky argue, will come about through the networking and activism of community groups. The organization and self-education of such groups, they say, are fundamental steps towards democratizing our society. "Only to the extent that such developments succeed can we hope to see media that are free and independent."[16]

If an independent media wrote truthfully about breast cancer, our society would have to summon the emotional resources to deal with its devastating toll. If we recognized medicine's limited powers, we would be forced to recognize the causes of breast cancer in our way of life. We would then have to face the most fundamental choice of all about breast cancer: will we change the way we live, or will we accept the disease as the price of life in a western industrialized society?

Notes

1. Patterson, p. 84.
2. Patterson, pp. 76 and 86.
3. Patterson, pp. 124-5.
4. Patterson, p. 125.

5. Patterson, p. 146.

6. Patterson, pp. 172-177.

7. Patterson, p. 194, p. 307, p. 295-6.

8. Lorde, pp. 63-68.

9. Daniel S. Greenberg, "A Critical Look at Cancer Coverage," *Columbia Journalism Review*, (Jan./Feb., 1975), pp. 40-44; Alan C. Davis, "ACS Defends 'Cautious Optimism,'" *Columbia Journalism Review*, (Mar./Apr. 1975), letters.

10. Rae Goodell, "The Gene Craze," *Columbia Journalism Review*, (Nov./Dec. 1980), pp. 41-45; and Jim Sibbison, "Pushing New Drugs — Can the Press Kick the Habit?" *Columbia Journalism Review*, (July/Aug. 1985), pp. 52-54.

11. Love with Lindsay, pp. 75-79; also, Susan Love et al, "Fibrocystic 'Disease' of the Breast: A Nondisease," *New England Journal of Medicine*, (1982), 307: 1010, 16, pp. 81-87.

12. Love et al, pp. 81-87.

13. Arnold S. Relman, "The Patient and the Press," *Bryn Mawr Alumnae Bulletin*, (Fall 1981), pp. 2-5.

14. Dr. E. Sterns, Parliamentary Testimony, (May 4, 1992), [from transcript], p. 16:22.

15. Cited in Patterson, p. 303, from the *New York Times*, (June 23, 1986).

16. E. S. Herman and N. Chomsky, *Manufacturing Consent*, (N.Y.: Pantheon, 1988), p. 307.

FOUR

From Silence to Language & Action

And, of course, I am afraid — you can hear it in my voice — because the transformation of silence into language and action is an act of self-revelation and that always seems fraught with danger.

— Audre Lorde, *The Cancer Journals*

Stolen Conflicts:
A Feminist Revisioning

Conflicts as Property

Norwegian social philosopher Nils Christie has an unusual theory about conflicts as precious resources. To participate in the fundamental conflicts of one's daily life, Christie argues, is to be fully alive. He deplores the tendency in western societies for professionals to "steal," or take over, confrontations that rightly belong to others.

Christie, a criminologist, writes about justice. Within the justice system, lawyers are particularly adept at stealing conflicts. In a criminal court case, for example, lawyers have all the fun. Citizens who have been robbed, assaulted or defrauded are called by the lawyers as mere witnesses, to answer questions that are irrelevant to how they feel; or they may not be called at all. The wronged individual never has the opportunity to confront the accused to ask essential questions, such as, "Why did you do that to me?" and, "How will you compensate me for what you put me through?" Instead, the lawyers transform the conflict into a debate that is gibberish to non-lawyers; they are the ones who feel the adrenaline rush of the courtroom drama, who come out of the courthouse having "won" or "lost" the case. Whatever the outcome, the victim-turned-witness loses the main prize — participation.[1]

When I first encountered Christie's theory, about 10 years ago, I was struck by its aptness to women who had been sexually assaulted. The state justice machinery focusses on the aggressor and shunts the victim aside. A sexual assault victim may not even be asked to testify, because our system of law divides justice into two components, public and a private. The criminal system addresses the public portion and the civil system the private. Under criminal law, the state is the wronged party in a sexual assualt, not the woman. Under civil law, someone who feels wronged by an asssault has the right to pursue a private law suit to obtain redress.

While, in theory, nothing prevents a sexual assault victim from pursuing her aggressor in a civil suit, few assaulted women pursue this option (or are even aware of it). Christie's point, however, is that they should not have to. He questions the very separation of crimes into public and private components. The victim, in his terms, owns the conflict that is at the heart of the crime and should not be assigned a peripheral role in the state proceedings.

Breast Cancer As Property

When I was diagnosed with cancer I often felt disconnected from the medical proceedings. What impressed me about AIDS activists was precisely their personal involvement in the public process. They refused to parcel AIDS into public and private components. When I decided to speak out publicly, in a newspaper article, the process was exhilarating. I felt engaged in a personally meaning-ful struggle, not just as a "woman fighting cancer" but as a citizen ready to take part in a larger societal battle with the disease.

In the past five years, increasing numbers of women have decided to "go public" about having breast cancer. Often, they describe their encounter with the medical system in terms of estrangement. They liken medical treatment to being on a conveyor belt. They seek vital information in vain. They don't understand what the doctor is talking about. When they try to articulate their fears, those around them urge a "chin up" attitude.

The cancer patient's alienation can be framed in personal terms — you are in shock, facing a new situation, terrified of death — but this is a too-easy out. Of course every woman with breast cancer suffers personal trauma. But equally important, the institutionalization of our "problem" distances us from our lived reality. The state system, designed to "control" cancer, in reality controls the woman — and particularly her conflict with cancer — more effectively than it controls the disease. We are labelled "patients." We are thrust ("no time to waste!") into a medical system governed by undisclosed rules. Here, "compliance" gains approval. Physicians speak to us in the private jargon of medical science, or with an infantilizing "there, there dear" paternalism. "Recovery" programs encourage us to "look normal" and "get on with life." Soon charities descend, urging us to "fight cancer with a check-up and a cheque." The money goes into "support" programs in which we have no say, or to researchers studying questions unrelated to our own.

Cut off from the vital action, the woman with breast cancer struggles to gain control through personal life changes. Diets, religious quests, the renegotiation of personal relationships — those are means to take back the conflict by putting it in subjectively meaningful terms. When professionals ridicule such self-help regimens as medically useless, they not only miss the point, they marginalize the woman still more. Most "alternative" treatments are not primarily bids to beat the disease. Whether we survive the cancer or not, active engagement draws us into the fray. We claim a piece of the action, however small.

Involvement in personal projects, however, will not release women with breast cancer from the doll's house that confines us. Like crime victims, we confront a conflict that has private and public meaning. If we are to really participate, we must also take on the institutions that are society's response to the disease, and reshape them so that they are meaningful to us. If we limit our quest for involvement to the private sphere, we abandon a large part of the conflict that is ours as well. We will continue to feel that others are doing things *to* us, rather than *for* us. A feminist revisioning of breast cancer will break down the wall between the public and private definitions of the disease. Through this process, the woman with breast cancer will assume her rightful place at the centre of the conflict as a whole.

From the moment of diagnosis, we are protagonists in a drama which may end in our death. If ever we should feel fully engaged, it is now.

Other Owners

The concept of breast cancer as stolen property challenges the popular perception that cancer agencies exist to serve our needs. At first blush, the theory seems an affront to professionals in the cancer field, most of whom are hard working and honest. Generally, cancer researchers toil in good faith to answer difficult questions. Physicians work long hours to save or prolong lives. A theory of stolen conflicts does not impugn the integrity of these other parties. The challenge is to the system that separates the conflict neatly into private and public domains. By extension, the theory challenges the rationale for this separation: that women with breast cancer have neither the ability to engage in the public conflict, nor the will.

We live in a society that values expertise. In every sphere, we divide the world into professionals and the lay public. Professionals engage in the work of problem-solving in their own sphere. They own those problems. If we challenge the strict separation of breast cancer into public and private property, we are saying professionals will have to cede some of their ownership of the disease.

As a property, breast cancer is vast. No one agency lays claim to the whole. In the past century, various groups have divided up the turf and set mutually agreed-upon boundaries. Treatment is one parcel and the main owners are oncologists. Research is another parcel, and medical researchers stake the largest claim here. Fundraising is a third parcel, owned by the cancer charities and the state. A fourth large chunk, encompassing support and educational services, is owned largely by the cancer charities. The private anguish of breast cancer is a separate turf. That belongs to the woman with the disease and her loved ones.

In the past five years, increasing numbers of women with breast cancer have rejected their traditional place in this tidy schema. Inspired partly by the AIDS movement, breast cancer activists have moved into each of the public spheres. The reaction of the professionals to this influx of collaborators is telling. If the fight against breast cancer is an onerous burden, one might expect those who have borne it on our behalf to welcome our involvement. If, however, the conflict is a property with intrinsic value, women who cross over the line from the personal sphere can expect to meet some resistance.

In the analysis that follows, I examine each of four public turfs to see how the present owners gained title and what the conflict means to them. Of particular interest is the non-monetary value of the property. As a group, breast cancer turf-owners have ample professional options. Why did they choose breast cancer? I also examine the reasons activists have ventured onto each section of public property and the reaction we have met upon arrival.

The Treatment Turf

Medical practitioners, specifically oncologists, own cancer treatment. Oncology gained official status as a medical specialty in 1973, when the first certifying examination was given. Breast cancer specialists had been organizing for about two decades before that, via professional meetings, journals and cooperative treatment research groups like the National Surgical Breast and Bowel Project (NSABP). Through these professional activities, oncologists developed a strong power base. They acquired the authority to define how breast cancer is treated and by whom.[2]

On the face of it, the appeal of treating breast cancer is not obvious. The treatments are unpleasant for the patient and often don't work. If professional gratification hinges on feeling one's work has done some good, the incentive for becoming a breast cancer specialist is puzzling.

A study of oncologists at Harvard teaching hospitals explored the reasons why these physicians chose oncology. The researchers found that the physicans described their commitment to the field in terms of "challenge." A radiation oncologist said, "We have a superb program ... it is dangerous ... we are right up to what we can get away with. It's exciting, but it's a different brinkmanship."

Another, a medical oncologist, explained, "the diseases [various cancers] are very threatening to patients and you are really dealing with important stuff. And I like that ... I didn't want to deal with zits. Or people who couldn't sleep, or have low back pain and are depressed. *Everyone who walks into my office might die.* And although I don't wish them all to die, I ... get more of a buzz out of dealing with something."[3]

What these oncologists value, then, is precisely the "buzz" of confronting a potentially fatal disease. The opportunity to engage in the patient's battle against death is a plus, not a deterrent. From this perspective, treating breast cancer, with its uncertain odds, offers an even greater challenge than a cancer that is either very treatable or almost invariably fatal. The danger for the patient is that the physician may take over to the extent that the woman feels like an object.

The rivalries between specialists who use different treatment and detection modalities is further evidence that physicians covet the breast cancer property. Sociologist Patricia Kaufert sought to understand the bitter disputes that erupted over mammography screening for women under 50. The anger expressed by radiologists when results of the National Breast Screening Study (NBSS) were published could not simply be explained as loss of face or loss of profits, she concluded. "Radiologists take seriously their own role as protectors of women against breast cancer and death. They are convinced young women will die. The NBSS [which found no benefit in extended life for screening women under 50] has committed the equivalent of heresy."[4] Screening radiologists, radiation oncologists, chemotherapists and surgeons have all fought hard to gain a piece of the breast cancer turf. Members of these specialities all want to believe their work is more than just a living. Unless their intervention is vital to the woman's welfare, they are mere pretenders in her struggle.

Women with breast cancer have entered the treatment turf largely because they question the current treatments. Many are angry to learn that punishing treatments which had been promoted as cures have uncertain and limited benefits. They are shocked to discover how little mortality rates have changed in 50 years. They wonder if other treatments, particularly less toxic ones, might not be just as beneficial as the "slash/burn/poison" trilogy — or more so. Women also seek to expand the definition of treatment into the psycho-social sphere. Medical treatments don't begin to address our subjective experience of cancer, which reaches to every area of our lives. In fact, many women are medically asymptomatic except for a painless lesion in their breast. Treatments transform them from well to sick. For these reasons, women who stake a claim on the treatment turf are not content to be simple partners with their oncologist, waging the same struggle of medical technology vs the tumour. Rather, they want to redefine the conflict in a way that drastically reduces the oncologist's significance in the drama.

"Oncology nurse tells me patients do massage, yoga, herbal stuff, etc. 'on the side' like bad children," journalist Jeannette Matthey wrote in her diary, "because doctors frown on it — I think, wouldn't it be wonderful if the two worlds came together!"[5]

Diagnosed with breast cancer when she was 36, Matthey, like many women in her situation, sought the best of both treatment worlds — orthodox and alternative. She began a conventional medical program of aggressive chemotherapy because the cancer had spread to her lymph nodes. She also designed a "soft" healing regimen consisting of macrobiotic food, anti-oxident vitamins, Chinese herbal medicines, shark's cartilage, meditation and visualization. Matthey deplored the "brick wall" between practitioners of conventional medicine and non-conventional therapy. "I realize I am the lonely traveller between two solitudes," she wrote.

Even women like Matthey who commit to aggressive conventional treatment feel the resentment of oncologists if they try to renegotiate the terms of their conflict. The hostile reaction takes patients by surprise. They are following a recommended treatment, so what has the doctor lost? If the main prize is ownership of the contest, the oncologist forfeits a good deal.

Matthey's writing leaves no doubt that she wanted control of the struggle. "Don't like his manner terribly," she wrote of a doctor who failed to explain the meaning of a white blood count reading while she was on chemotherapy. When her oncologist in England gave her a lower dose of chemotherapy than was standard in America, she instructed him to up the dose. She flung herself into the fight for her life, reading and experimenting with treatments. She did not survive breast cancer, but those close to her believe she won a different battle. "She ... showed us that we must never stop living and must never let somebody else control our most valuable possession — our own lives," her partner, Thomas Ginsberg, wrote after her death.

Women with breast cancer want more than the much-touted partnership of shared decision-making in medical treatments. This would be relatively easy to negotiate. The more contentious ownership questions involve redefining the treatment terrain — moving the boundaries beyond the medical. Oncologists resist this because their primacy in the treatment struggle is questioned. Evidence that support groups and dietary changes may extend life undermines oncology's ownership of breast cancer, even when these approaches are proposed as complementary to medical ones. Similarly, long-term preventive approaches pose no immediate threat to the oncologists' patient load, but they do reduce the oncologists' role in the societal struggle against the disease.

The Research Turf

Researchers own the enigma of breast cancer. As custodians of the intellectual conflict with the disease, they engage in the search for understanding that could eventually solve the puzzle. In this struggle with the unknown, they define what questions are important.

Biological researchers occupy most of the research turf. Since the postwar years when cancer research began to boom, treatment research has predominated, particularly clinical trials to compare the different treatments and treatment combinations. Chemotherapy trials continue, but currently the "hot" area is molecular research: the hunt for genes related to breast cancer and for genetic markers that would predict the course of disease. Early detection research has abated as the value and limits of early detection become clearer. Prevention and psycho-social issues continue to be relatively less studied.

Medical scientists jealously guard their ownership of the breast cancer puzzle. The mechanism for maintaining control of the process is peer review. Researchers whose ideas challenge the current model of breast cancer complain that this reliance on well-established experts keeps the ownership of research in the hands of a relatively small number of people with similar ideas. Dr. David Horrobin, an Oxford-trained medical researcher engaged in breast cancer research in Nova Scotia, testified to the Canadian

Parliamentary Committee on Breast Cancer, "I have sat on researcher panels and repeatedy have observed that what we get is support for mainstream research. And, repeatedly, the oddballs, the strange people who are proposing research projects out of the mainstream, are not funded and do not get any response." Throughout the western world, noted Horrobin, medical research consists of large numbers of very similar projects. The "experts" in breast cancer, he argues, "are not real experts who know how to do things but failed experts who have thought about the problem and not produced an answer."[6]

Horrobin went on to propose that substantial control of research funds be handed over to lay people. He argued, "... it is important to understand that lay people do not have a vested interest in the outcome of research, other than in seeing practical results." While the interest of the public is to find answers to practical questions, he said, the scientists' self-interest is, paradoxically, to maintain the state of puzzlement so they can continue doing research. These attitudes are not malicious, or wrong, he stated, "but one has to recognize, as happened with polio and TB when they were conquered, that the experts in the field will lose authority, respect and many of the things they hold dear if somebody else comes up with an answer."[7]

In the researcher-driven process, scientific peer review panels explicitly exclude members of the public. A place on the research turf, however, is one of the the demands advocates have pressed hardest for. As with treatment, women with breast cancer seek involvement on a changed turf, not the one that currently exists. We ask different questions. Medical rearchers most often ask which medical treatments will help extend the woman's life or what basic biological processes are involved in the development of the tumour. After a breast cancer diagnosis, a woman's first question is why she got the disease. She then wants to know if exercise or certain foods can prevent its spread or onset or lower the risk for her daughters. She asks how the recommended treatments will affect her quality of life — her sex drive or her employability, for example. She seeks ways to minimize the toxic effects of treatment in both the short and long term. Physicians are usually unable to answer these questions and researchers don't seem very interested in them. They don't fit the current model of "good" science.

Members of the 1992 Canadian Parliamentary Committee on Breast Cancer challenged the system of peer review: "… we believe it is outdated, in 1992, to adopt an approach that suggests that only physicians and scientists are equipped and qualified to evaluate the efficacy of research proposals and to make policy decisions on the nature and direction of cancer research," they wrote in their report.[8]

Medical researchers respond with horror to the suggestion that lay people, and particularly women with breast cancer, should share ownership of the research "property." Breast cancer advocacy groups "desire to permeate and ultimately disrupt the entire scientific establishment," said Dr. Henry Pitot, Professor of Oncology and Pathology and a member of the President's Cancer Panel in the U.S. In the same vein, Frederick Becker, research chief at the M.D. Anderson Cancer Research Center in Houston warned that "a tidal wave of advocacy … may wash away certain bulwarks of basic science that have been the greatest contributors toward the potential for cancer prevention and cure."

Even a woman with breast cancer who happens to be a scientist may be judged unfit for a peer review panel. By the norms of the scientific community, her personal vested interest in the research outcome undermines her credibility. She is not "objective." One researcher who has breast cancer explained to me that she has chosen to remain in the closet because she believes she can have more effect in the breast cancer research milieu if other researchers aren't aware of her medical status. She cited a colleague who had come out as a breast cancer survivor and said, "I notice she's no longer invited to some of the important meetings." A scientist with breast cancer who supports the prevailing view may not face the same conflict. Ann Flood, director of policy studies at the Centre for Evaluative Clinical Sciences at Dartmouth College, agrees with the mainstream scientific view that earmarking money for breast cancer results in "micromanagement of science that doesn't result in the best spending of money." Flood, 12 years past a breast cancer diagnosis, said she has herself studied breast cancer but "I still strongly feel that it's overstudied."[9]

In San Francisco, the group Breast Cancer Action has lobbied for advocacy representatives on breast cancer research committees at all levels. Their goal was "a say in the research process based upon the real life experience of people living with cancer." They were determined to be engaged in the process, ideally in a collaborative relationship with scientists. "We can be adversaries or partners in accelerating research," they said. "We would prefer to be partners." After eight months of negotiations with the head of the local cancer centre, the activists had the beginnings of a working partnership. Dr. Craig Henderson, who described the women as "surprisingly intelligent, bright and verbal," granted a seat for an activist on scientific committees, participation in the review of grant proposals for new projects, and input into the research process for large clinical trials.[10]

Despite such concessions, patients' desire to participate in the research arena will not be easily accommodated. The strongest resistance does not arise from researchers' fears that they will lose funding. In the U.S., breast cancer activism has dramatically increased the amount of money available for breast cancer research in a short period of time. This very increase in funding has drawn criticism from researchers. The nub of the resistance is to our wish to redefine the puzzle.

The Fundraising Turf

Cancer fundraising was first owned by the American Society for the Control of Cancer (ASCC). The first cancer fundraising turf war took place in the mid-1940s when Mary Lasker took over the ASCC and transformed it into the American Cancer Society (ACS). Lasker was the wife of advertising tycoon Albert Lasker, who pioneered a campaign urging women to smoke, using the slogan, "Reach for a Lucky Instead of a Sweet." She added leading businessmen to the board and applied corporate advertising and fundraising techniques to cancer charity work. Lasker also cultivated links with influential federal politicans and drove the lobby to expand the National Cancer Institute into a major research institute. Doctors who had called the shots in the old ASCC initially resisted Lasker's coup, but her genius as a fundraiser overcame their opposition.

When the tax-funded National Cancer Institute began to boom in the late 1940s, the American Cancer Society worried that the American public would let their donations flag. "We're going to be skunked," said the scientific director of the ACS. "People are going to say, 'if we're giving all this money in taxes, why do we have to give it out of our philanthropy?'"[11] The two agencies agreed to divide the turf: the NCI would use its funds, raised from taxes, for research; the donations-dependent ACS would have jurisdiction over services and education. The ACS lobbied the government for NCI appropriations and in return the NCI let the ACS bask in the spotlight. As the director of the NCI in the 1960s put it, "a secret of really effective working relationships between the Society and the NCI is to let them take the lion's share of the credit and don't get uptight about it. Because they reciprocate by pushing for a big budget for the NCI. Okay, let them get the headlines, what the hell." The formula worked. In the postwar years, the budgets of both the NCI and the ACS expanded exponentially.[12] Scientists would get their gratification from their research, leaving the fundraisers to enjoy a more public image as the symbolic "white knights" leading combat against the disease.

Canada carves the cancer charity pie somewhat differently. The Canadian government has no counterpart to the well-funded NCI (the largest in a cluster of disease-targeted health institutes). The federally-funded Medical Research Council disburses some of its limited tax monies to cancer researchers, but the main funding body for cancer research is the National Cancer Institute of Canada (NCIC). Historically the NCIC has derived its funds entirely from the Canadian Cancer Society (CCS) which, like the ACS, depends on donations. The CCS splits its annual take between research (40 to 50 percent) and services, education and administration.

In both the Canadian and American systems, the owners of the turf have agreed that cancer monies are not split further by body parts. Until very recently, donors to the Canadian Cancer Society, for example, could not earmark their donations to a specific cancer site such as breast cancer or leukemia. In the U.S. as well, cancer reseachers scorn the concept of earmarking funds (although earmarking for cancer in general is a well-accepted practice).

While these agencies depend on public participation for door-to-door canvassers and donors, the public has had little to say about how the funds are disbursed. In a few short years, however, breast cancer advocacy has radically transformed cancer fundraising. In many communities, women with breast cancer have formed small grass-roots self-help groups which raise funds to finance their own activites. Often the incentive for forming these groups is the women's dissatisfaction with Cancer Society services. The survivor-run groups absorb both funds and goodwill that were previously the exclusive province of the established charities. Members take considerable pride in their organizations and the self-help projects they mount.

American activists have had an impact on research funding. Working through the political avenues that influence the NCI, in 1992 the newly formed National Breast Cancer Coalition (NBCC) secured a $42-million allocation for breast cancer research. Activists demanded funds targeted for breast cancer research and a say in how this money is spent. "We want to be part of the designs of those trials," said Sharon Greene, of the Coalition.

While fundraising administrators have long counted on donations and bequests from cancer patients and their families, the NBCC lobby was different. The activists designed and mounted the campaign themselves. Activists like Green were undeterred by the resistance to their demands for policy input. "[NCI administrators] do not want micro-management," she acknowledged. "They do not want anyone telling them how to spend their dollars." The women felt justified in their demands because the lobby belonged to them; and they clearly relished the spotlight that went with their achievement. "I am waiting for the NCI to give us trouble. I can't wait to remind [NCI head] Sam Broder that he got $42 million because we were out stomping the steps," Green told the Parliamentary committee in Ottawa, which invited her to describe the American experience.[13]

When advocacy fundraising began to have an impact, the traditional beneficiaries expressed open concern. In late 1992, advocacy pressure popped $214 million in earmarked breast cancer funds from the American defense budget. Rather than welcoming the new money, researchers responded with anxiety. The increase in funds was "very politically motivated," complained a breast cancer researcher at the Mayo Clinic in Rochester, Minnesota. "To say, 'Here's another $200 million. Please go out and find an idea.' I mean, give me a break." Another prominent cancer researcher explained that science makes leaps in unexpected directions. "It is important for us to follow the clues wherever they are and to realize that the answer may not be in breast cancer directed funds," he said.[14] Researchers were also concerned, said an article in *Science*, that "popularity rather than quality could become important in determining what gets funded, and that these targetted funds could siphon dollars from other basic research."[15]

In Canada, the Breast Cancer Initiative, a government allocation of $20 million over five years earmarked for breast cancer research, sparked similar angst in scientific circles about targeted funds. The power of lobbying was a "worrisome trend," said the president of the Canadian Cancer Society. "The group with the greatest advocacy will get the most money."[16] In fact, politics are hardly new to research fundraising. The NCI was born of assiduous lobbying by the cancer research community. The difference in this case was that breast cancer activists, not researchers, socialites and businessmen, were the ones who felt engaged.

As activists raised the public profile of breast cancer, specialized breast cancer funds began to proliferate. In Canada, one new fund was the Breast Cancer International Centre, started by Avon cosmetics in 1993. The company quickly came up against criticism from activists for not taking survivors' interests into account. The campaign, designed by a group of professional fundraisers, was to raise $10 million a year for five years. They planned to combine drug company donations with public support through sales of a $2 flame-shaped gold pin distributed by Avon's door-to-door cosmetic reps. Half the money from pin sales would go to an international research fund for breast cancer. In a similar campaign in Britain, Avon sold $2 million in crocus-shaped pins for breast cancer research. The Canadian company promoted the pins in magazine ads as "bringing hope to 1.4 million Canadian women." Members of a breast cancer group in Burlington, Ontario called Avon to account, saying, "It is as if they are jumping on the breast cancer bandwagon, but not for our benefit." Company officials, which had expected the campaign to meet public approval, expressed surprise that women with breast cancer saw the fund as opportunistic. No one had told them that fundraisers now shared their traditional turf with activists.[17]

Fundraisers may be the first group of owners to seek a turf-sharing agreement with advocates. Charities operate with high visibility and depend on public goodwill. An overture to advocates by a branch of the Canadian Cancer Society may be prophetic. In late 1993, Canadian breast cancer activists began to organize a grass-roots network of support and advocacy groups. Shortly afterwards, the B.C. and Yukon branch of the CCS invited a member of the network's planning group to attend discussions about sharing the network. "The Canadian Cancer Society needs to find a place for a group of women who are pro-active and politically aware of the course of breast cancer in Canada," a CCS volunteer wrote in a letter about the discussions. "These women will organize with us or without us. We feel an obligation to encourage them to organize under one umbrella ... The CCS, B.C. and Yukon division, needs to be a part of this changing aspect of cancer patient support and activism. If not, we lose credibility and our 'paying customer.'"[18]

Whether the grass-roots groups can best fulfill their mandates independently or in collaboration with established charities is a point of active debate within the movement. In the U.S., the National Breast Cancer Coalition includes traditional fundraising groups, such as the ACS, along with grass-roots groups. Fundraising, however, links charities to donors at one end and to spending programs at the other. Some activists, such as Judy Brady of San Francisco, want to to redraw the fundraising turf to create an anti-cancer lobby that will fight environmental pollution. Brady, while she acknowledges that she welcomed a Reach to Recovery visit, nonetheless urges groups within the women's cancer movement to openly reject a union with the cancer establishment. Institutions such as the ACS and NCI, she argues, have too many ties to the corporate world to get tough with nuclear and chemical polluters. "Unless the ACS takes an approach to fighting cancer which is radically different from their present activities, we will have to work without them in any struggle to rid our society of the poisons which are killing us," she says.[19]

The Support and Information Turf

Cancer Societies have also owned breast cancer support and information services. These activities have long emphasized the importance of early detection and prompt medical care. Appeals for funds are effective because the public backs these goals. Newer cancer charities, some of them specific to breast cancer, also provide services and educational programs. Hospitals may mount their own support programs, independent of outside fundraising groups.

Services include visitor programs like Reach to Recovery, instruction in breast self-exam, support groups and the ubiquitous information brochures. Others are wig banks, home visits, and accommodation for out-of-towners who come into a large centre for treatments. By and large these programs have evolved without significant involvement by patients. "Consumer participation in cancer medicine is a rare phenomenon and, where it exists at all, is often at a trivial level, such as having a suggestion box in a patient waiting room," says an article co-authored by Ross Gray, a psychologist at a Toronto cancer treatment centre. Gray noted that (in 1990) the Canadian Cancer Society had no mechanism for ensuring adequate consumer representation on its National Board and no formal mechanism to ensure survivor representation on its national Patient Services Committee.[20]

The educational messages of the cancer charities typically reflect the views of physicians rather than patients. Rose Kushner made numerous attempts to change this bias in the policies of the American Cancer Society. In 1974, for example, Kushner urged the ACS to review breast cancer surgery practices in the U.S., citing the varied approaches to treating breast cancer in Europe and Japan. She also challenged the Society's definition of informed consent: "the patient and selected members of the family should be thoroughly advised by the physician about the proposed surgery and its rationale." The ACS stubbornly defended both the "proven methods" that it promoted through its educational campaigns — the Halsted radical and extended mastectomies — and the physician's prerogative to dictate the treatment. The ACS, Kushner concluded, was "a conservative organization that moves with the speed of a senile snail."[21]

Established services don't come close to meeting the enormous emotional and information needs of women with breast cancer. Many newly diagnosed women are taken aback to discover that their community has no support group and that information they seek is difficult to find. Frustration spurs women to action if services aggravate rather than alleviate the patients' problems. Jackie Winnow, who was diagnosed with breast cancer in 1985, described a seven-week ACS support group she attended as "very controlled." At one point, she recalled, "somebody had a lot of complaints about a doctor and I wanted to know who that doctor was. The social worker said, 'You can't ask that question because it's not an objective response.' I was horrified." The incident was one catalyst that prompted Winnow to start the Women's Cancer Resource Center in San Francisco.

Activists such as Winnow (who died in in 1991), thrive on the involvement that their projects demand. "We started growing more and more," she enthused. "Now we have our own space. It's a storefront and it's wonderful. It's all wheelchair accessible. We have environmentally safe carpetting inside. We just got a $6,000 grant for a library."[22]

As with the other public turfs, the activist claim to ownership in breast cancer services can destabilize the established community. Turf-sharing threatens the established owners most when the goal of the self-help group is to reduce women's dependence on the medical community. The traditional groups reinforce the power of the medical community. Consumer-driven groups shift the balance of power and the satisfaction of involvement to the woman.

One solution is to work out amicable turf-sharing agreements. The group Y-Me was started in 1979 in Chicago by two women with breast cancer whose support and information needs were not being met. By 1992, Y-Me was the largest consumer-based support program for breast cancer in the United States. Funded entirely by donations, the group's services include a 1-800 information hot line, a telephone counselling service and tailor-made packages of printed material.

"If the American Cancer Society had been meeting that need," said Y-Me's executive director Sharon Green, "we wouldn't have had to exist." Describing the ACS as a huge and regionally variable bureaucracy ("billions of dollars, and chapters in every state"), Green stressed, "We work cooperatively with them, but we find that we move a lot quicker when things need to be done because we have a much smaller bureaucracy. We're breast cancer specific, which makes us different too." The ACS supplies Y-Me with its brochures to include in mailings, while Y-Me encourages women to ask for a Reach to Recovery visitor. Part of the secret of the collaboration is that the services of the two agencies are not identical. "I don't consider our relationship with the American Cancer Society as being antagonistic because their program doesn't do the hot line counselling and the pre-surgical counselling that we do," Green explained.[23]

Owners of the support turf may respond to survivor-run support services by trying to absorb them. We should be cautious of agreeing to such takeovers in the area of support, warns the Honourable Monique Bégin, for many years Canada's Minister of Health. "Women's self-help groups are very threatening to the traditional medical health care system since they question both the sacred status of experts and the authoritarianism of health professionals of all kinds," she writes. "Instead, the egalitarian relationships of self-help groups favour a greater sense of self, more autonomy, and better self-expression of lay women whose knowledge is rooted in their life experience." Government bureaucracies try to absorb these initiatives into their ways of doing things and, in doing so, may kill what is so special about them, Bégin notes. "While this may be the price of success," she says, "it must be opposed."[24]

The Private Turf

In the established order, the private region of breast cancer — the personal anguish — has been our property alone. It wasn't always so. One can imagine that before cancer became the exclusive domain of medical specialists, women with breast cancer may have faced death with the support of their close women friends. In families or communities where breast cancer struck often, caring for someone with breast cancer must have been part of the healing lore passed on from one woman to another, from one generation to the next. We have lost that knowledge.

Glimmers of the intimacy that comes from shared understanding lie in the scattered diaries and letters of women with breast cancer. Fanny Burney wrote letters to her sister Esther, over a period of four months, describing in minute detail her experience of a mastectomy without anaesthetic. She hoped to keep the news from her father, so that he wouldn't worry, but she explained to Esther, "to you I will write the whole history, certain that, from the moment you know any evil has befallen me your kind kind heart will be constantly anxious to learn its extent, & its circumstances, as well as its termination." At the end of the document, she gave Esther explicit directions to show it to others: "I entreat you to let all my dear Brethren male & female take a perusal — and that you will lend it also to my tender & beloved Mrs Angerstein."[25]

Alice James, sister of the famous writers Henry and William James, was cared for by her companion Katherine Loring and dictated sentences of her diary to Katherine up to her last days.[26] James learned she had advanced breast cancer when she was 42.[27] When she was told she would soon die, she was jubilant. From the age of 19, she had been bedridden with debilitating symptoms that had no clear origin. She revealed in her diary, "Ever since I have been ill, I have longed and longed for some palpable disease, no matter how conventionally dreadful a label it might have, but I was always driven back to stagger alone, under the monstrous mass of subjective sensations, which that sympathetic being 'the medicine man' has had no aspiration than to assure me I was personally responsible for." The uncompromising verdict (the cancer had already spread to her liver when it was discovered) lifted her "out of the formless vague," she said, and set her "within the very heart of the sustaining concrete." James hated the condescension of doctors and wrote, "I suppose one has a greater sense of intellectual degradation after an interview with a doctor than from any human experience."

Rachel Carson learned she had breast cancer in 1960. Available accounts say she felt obliged to keep her diagnosis secret because she was mid-way through writing *Silent Spring*, her indictment of the chemical industry in which she linked uncontrolled pesticide use to rising cancer rates. Carson feared that if the public knew she had cancer, her analysis would be dismissed as biased. Indeed, after her death, critics did try to discredit her book on the grounds that having cancer disqualified her from assessing the situation "objectively."[28] Thus, she felt obliged by the norms of science to separate her private persona from her analysis and public persona. We do know that Carson confided the full range of her thoughts and feelings to her most intimate friend, Dorothy Freeman, who was with her as she was dying. During their last summer in Maine together, in 1963, Rachel spoke to Dorothy about death, "using the metaphor of Monarch butterflies whose migration they had watched together: 'brightly fluttering bits of life ... [on] the closing journey of their lives.'"[29]

Just as the wall between public and private arenas has kept women with breast cancer from participating in the public spheres, the same principle of separation keeps us isolated in our grief. Wigs, breast prostheses, make-up and optimistism-at-all-costs are the outward trappings of fear and pain. Even within the perimeters of our assigned territory, we are not true participants as long as our grief remains wholly private. Paradoxically, the taboos against exposing the lived experience of breast cancer disengage us from our feelings. Can a woman truly confront her mortality when her lipstick is just right?

Audre Lorde wrote forcibly about the politics of silence. What is important to me Lorde says, "must be spoken, made verbal and shared."[30] In the harsh light of self-examination following her first breast biopsy, Lorde saw what she regretted most in her life: the occasions when she silenced, out of fear, thoughts she wanted to speak. Her understanding that the ultimate silence — death — might not be far off pushed her to another realization: that silence would not protect her from dying. While silence isolated her, speaking her beliefs had invariably brought her into contact with other women with the same fears where a collective examining of the issues strengthened her.

Through a process of rebuilding lost networks, women can recoup the power that comes from a firsthand understanding of the pain of breast cancer. By passing on our experiences to other women, we can remove the filters that keep us from seeing our choices clearly. Women have begun to recreate the collective knowledge of what breast cancer means. In 1988, when Treya Wilber was dying of the cancer that had metastasized to her brain, liver and lungs, she summoned her friend Vicky Wells into her room. Despite the excruciating pain caused by the swelling in her brain, Treya had chosen not to take any painkillers or tranquilizers so that she could witness the progress of her disease with complete clarity. For an hour or two, she described to Vicky "in the most agonizing terms ... exactly what what going on with her — the precise sensations, the actual feel, of having a brain tumour slowly destroy all normal functions, detail by gruesome detail." Two years earlier, Treya and Vicky had formed the Cancer Support Community in San Francisco. Before she died, Treya wanted to relay to Vicky what she knew from her own ordeal, so that Vicky could help others at the Community who were going through something similar.

Women are now making the private grief of breast cancer a public issue. Just as we must stake a claim in the public areas of breast cancer from which we were excluded, we must also insist that the public share its load of the suffering that has been private. The wall needs to be dismantled from both sides.

The public, which has been soaking up happy stories about breast cancer survivors for years, responded with ambivalence when New York artist Matushka bared her mastectomy scar on the cover of *New York Times Magazine*.[31] The photograph prompted a barrage of mail, with two-thirds of the replies favourable: "The most significant image of the century," said one. "Finally, both sexes know. Now everybody is party to the cure." Another wrote, "I gasped when I saw it, even though this is the same image I've been facing in the mirror every morning for almost seven years." A woman who offered, "Many thanks for your very bold presentation of a terrifying subject that must be faced by all women" added, "By the time I got to our copy ... my husband had torn off the cover of the magazine section to 'protect' me." The hostile reactions included, "voyeurism at its finest," and "Please resist the temptation to shock us in this way. Just assume that we can make rational judgments when we aren't burdened with overly emotional presentations." More significant than the details of the reactions however was the volume of letters received — four times the usual number for a major article. No one was indifferent.

Women who come out of the closet may be pleasantly surprised at the willingness of others to share their emotional involvement with the disease. Deena Apel, a Montreal high school teacher, did not tell her students when she was diagnosed with breast cancer in 1988. "I thought it might freak them out," she says. "I thought they might spend too much time considering my anatomy." After joining an activist group four years later, she spoke at a public rally that was televised. "My students saw me. They questioned me. It was pretty wonderful," she says. "They have mothers, aunts and grandmothers who have the disease. It helps to share and I certainly have not lost any credibility."[32]

One consequence of dividing the breast cancer property into private and public parts was that those who took on public pursuits in the name of breast cancer were spared the emotional messiness. No longer. Women with breast cancer who enter these designated public spheres bring their emotions with them. Researchers, physicians and administrators, it turns out, often do not want their work complicated with our feelings.

Psychologist Ross Gray, an advocate of patients' participation on policy planning committees, surveyed health care professionals' attitudes to having people with cancer sitting with them around the board room table. Professionals in the cancer community, he found, resist having people with cancer on their committees because they raise subjective, emotional issues that medical professionals and administrators would rather not discuss. No wonder the medical system deals poorly with our emotional trauma. Removing the artificial barrier between public and private spheres can only improve this glaring weakness in the system.

Patient No More

After I read Nils Christie's analysis in the early 1980s, I immersed myself in sexual assault literature, including case histories of both criminal trials and civil suits. A central test of Christie's thesis was whether women who had been assaulted regarded the process of testifying as an opportunity or a burden. Popular wisdom says that the courtroom experience is an excruciating ordeal that most women would prefer to be spared. Was it possible that sexually assaulted women might actually want to confront their aggressors?

I found ample evidence in my review of cases that many do. They regard the opportunity to testify as therapeutic. A young Ontario girl named Karen, raped by a neighbour when she was 12, described her feelings after the trial this way.

"I wanted people to know what happened," she said. "I wanted to say in court that he did it. [The criminal procedure] made me feel the whole thing had nothing to do with me. It wasn't the Queen who got raped. It was me. But it was totally out of my hands."[33]

The state had stolen her conflict.

Christie calls for major changes in the legal systems of western democracies so that the victim of a crime can regain the valuable "stolen property," the opportunity to engage the aggressor in a conflict. He advocates a system of victim-centred justice that would combine elements from the criminal and civil procedures, with the emphasis on the civil side. As models, he points to the system of dispute resolution in some African villages, where offender and victim meet face-to-face, surrounded by neighbours, and actively work out a settlement.[34]

The formative experience in Nils Christie's thinking was a study he undertook as a student in which he interviewed the former guards of a prison camp set up in the north of Norway during World War II. Some of the guards had maltreated or killed their charges, who were Yugoslavian partisans, others had not. Christie wanted to understand what distinguished the two groups. After interviewing 50 of the abusive guards and another set who had acted responsibly, he found that the non-killers had often been shown photographs, by the prisoner, of the prisoner's family. The killers had never seen pictures. Those who had seen family photos were inclined to think of the prisoners as people rather like themselves, who had arrived in a difficult situation. They were able to connect the prisoners' experience to their own existence. Those who had not seen family photos described the prisoners as animals — dirty, lice-ridden — a different breed from themselves. The growth and modernization of the prison system, especially in the U.S., alarms Christie. Prisons are an industry that creates jobs in many sectors, to provide everything from the prisons themselves to specialized telephones, weapons, food and medical services. A fantastic electronic industry has evolved, permitting the prison administrators to tag prisoners with wristbands so their numbers can be scanned electronically. The guards never have to talk to their charges. Christie believes that, through such mechanization, we are creating concentration camp conditions in modern prisons. These "state-of-the-art" institutions separate staff from inmates and objectify the inmates. They become commodities.[35]

In the past 40 years, breast cancer treatment has also become increasingly mechanized and depersonalized. Each new diagnostic test and treatment modality creates a new industry. Every new specialty fragments the patient's body and experience further, parcelling her into bits owned by various specialties. Through their "expertise" and professional language, specialists create new and thicker walls between themselves and the diagnosed woman. With new computer programs, patients can put their questions about breast cancer to machines in the waiting room. The rationale is efficiency. The "interactive learning experience," which saves both doctor and patient time, also reduces their opportunity to make human contact.

New tests distance the practitioner from the patient and objectify her. She is transformed from a person with dreams, friends, and physical symptoms to a series of numbers that denote test results. Many tests are ordered because they protect the physician from law suits, not because they add anything to diagnosis. At a public lecture, breast surgeon Susan Love shows a schematic slide of a woman, her breast flattened between two plates of a mammogram machine and the audience of women laughs appreciatively. "Mammography was undoubtedly invented by a man," quips Love. "I keep thinking there should be something we can invent for them." During radiation, patients are shut into double-doored rooms, while an unseen technician carries out the treatment from a console. Some procedures are humiliating in the extreme. In a test for spinal metastasis, the patient has a fluid injected into the spinal column. Dressed only in a hospital gown and leather boots to hold her in place, she is then rotated upside down so that gravity can distribute the liquid. "You are alone in the room," recalls Carole Jones. "You think you are going to fall on your head. It's painful; you go into spasms. But what really got me was the leather boots. Who thinks these things up?" The anxiously awaited genetic susceptibility tests, once available, will provide information arguably more useful to researchers, employers and insurance companies than to the woman herself. The woman's genetic code will become a commodity with a market value; if a gene lends itself to a blood test, control of the information will be virtually impossible.

Women with breast cancer have begun to renegotiate the terms of breast cancer ownership. As we shut the door on the old model we need to consider what a patient-centred system will look like. Many questions revolve around the relationships we will have with health professionals.

Discussing her re-visioned system of health care for women, Monique Bégin cautions, "while physicians and medical experts are natural targets for women's anger, the exaggerated political power such professionals enjoy in our society is conferred by us. We empower them. Our blind faith in science and technology is the cornerstone of our value system. This faith represents our vision of progress in this second half of the 20th century."

Bégin stresses the importance of questioning such fundamental beliefs, "and, consequently, the challenge of questioning the ideology which has legitimized the immense power invested in physicians and specialists and 'experts.' Our actions will be all the more revolutionary and will be all the more significant if they are solidly rooted in a thorough consideration of the relevant underlying values," she says. The process of examining our own personal beliefs is a demanding experience. "To what extent are we familiar with the limitations of science? What do we know of its economics, its priorities, its internal logic? To what extent have we erased from our consciences the meaning of suffering, aging and dying — that is, the meaning of vulnerability?"[36]

As women negotiate an active part in the struggle against breast cancer, the liveliest disputes will be over fundamental values. Already our participation shows up ideological splits. The most profound rifts reflect masculine and feminine orientations to the world. After a diagnosis of breast cancer women are thrust, as dependants, into an intensely masculine milieu: Western medicine. The field of medicine became professionalized in the latter part of the 19th century. This was a time, explains medical historian Dr. Ann Dally, when paternalistic attitudes were especially strong. The male bias was not subtle; medical schools kept women out. (This was rationalized, of course, as for our own good: "More especially is medicine disgusting to women, accustomed to softness and the downy side of life," opined a leading American gynaecologist in 1871.[37]) While striving to exclude women, says Dally, the medical profession also excluded many traditional female traits: "caring, succouring, watching, waiting. Increasingly the emphasis was on discovery and control, power and acquisition."[38]

These masculine values define oncology. Characteristics of the field are specialization, hierarchical power structures, heroic intervention, rational and scientific thinking, and high-tech methods of treatment and diagnosis. The popular war metaphor used to describe the fight against cancer creates a military climate that further valorizes macho behaviour. From diagnosis to death, oncology veers towards the highest cost and the riskiest heroics. Even when the cancer strikes a female organ, male ownership of the struggle seems almost mandatory.

As more women with breast cancer find their voices, the clash between the masculine ideology of the owners and the feminist values of the owned is increasingly obvious. One example is the activist opposition to hormone manipulation experiments. Another is the pressure for preventive research into environmental toxins. A third is the interest in "soft" alternative treatments that enhance the woman's sense of well-being and control. Women with breast cancer are bargaining for non-interventionist, preventive and low-tech solutions.

We are saying: it's our conflict. We want it back.

Notes

1. Nils Christie, "Conflicts as Property," *The British Journal of Criminology*, (Jan. 1977), 17: 1-15.

2. Taylor, pp. 229-239.

3. Mary-Jo Delvecchio Good et al., "American Oncology and the Discourse on Hope," *Culture, Medicine and Psychiatry*, (1990), 14:59-79, pp. 73-74.

4. Patricia Kaufert, "Women and the Debate over Mammography: An Economic, Political and Moral History," unpublished paper, (1994), p. 24.

5. Thomas Ginsberg, "Fighting Hard and Learning to Look Inside," *Globe and Mail*, (Nov. 12, 1993).

6. David Horrobin, Parliamentary Testimony, (Feb. 11, 1992), [from transcript], pp. 9:4-9:5.

7. Horrobin, p. 9:6.

8. *Breast Cancer: Unanswered Questions*, p. 25.

9. Gina Kolata, "Weighing Spending on Breast Cancer," *New York Times*, (Dec. 1993).

10. Deborah Collyar, "From a Night at the Opera to a Lasting Partnership," *Breast Cancer Action Newsletter*, (Aug. 1993), pp. 2-4.

11. Patterson, p. 179.

12. Patterson, p. 171.

13. Sharon Green, Parliamentary Testimony, Ottawa, (Feb. 18, 1992), [from transcript], pp. 10:21.

14. Kolata, Dec. 1993.

15. Eliot Marshall, "The Politics of Breast Cancer," *Science*, (Jan. 29, 1993), p. 616.

16. Paul Taylor, "Breast Cancer Research Gets $20 Million," *Globe and Mail*, (Dec. 16, 1992), p. A9.

17. Vivien Smith, "Breast-Cancer Politics Tangles Avon Campaign," *Globe and Mail*, (Nov. 13, 1993), p. A1.

18. Personal communication from Jan Morrow, (May 1994).

19. Brady, pp. 31-32.

20. R.E. Gray, B.D. Doan, and K. Church, "Empowerment Issues in Cancer," *Health Values*, (1991), 15 (4):22-28.

21. Kushner, pp. 225 and 222.

22. Sandy Polishuk, "Jackie Winnow and the Women's Resource Centre," *Bridges*, (Fall 1991), pp. 72-77.

23. Green, pp. 10:4-10:10.

24. Monique Bégin, "Redesigning Health Care for Women," (Ottawa: Canadian Research Institute for the Advancement of Women conference proceedings, 1989), pp. 34-35.

25. Hemlow, p. 598.

26. Jean Strouse, *Alice James, A Biography*, (Boston: Houghton-Mifflin, 1980), p. 301.

27. Strouse, p. 301.

28. Sandra Steingraber, "'If I Live to be 90, Still Wanting to Say Something': My Search for Rachel Carson," in *Confronting Cancer, Constructing Change*, edited by Midge Stocker, (Chicago: Third Side, 1993), p. 197.

29. Quoted in Patricia Hynes, *The Recurring Silent Spring*, (N.Y.: Pergamon, 1989), p. 30. At the request of Dorothy Freeman, Carson's letters to Freeman will not be available for many years.

30. Lorde, p. 19.

31. Susan Ferraro, "The Anguished Politics of Breast Cancer," *New York Times Magazine*, (Aug. 15, 1993), pp. 24-27, 58-62; and "Letters to the Editor," *New York Times Magazine*, (Sept. 5, 1993), p. 6.

32. Deena Apel, "Address to the Women's Federation of the Combined Jewish Appeal," (Montreal, Mar. 2, 1994).

33. Dianne Kinnon, "Report on Sexual Assault in Canada," (Ottawa: Canadian Advisory Council on the Status of Women, 1981), p. iv.

34. Christie, pp. 1-15.

35. Transcript of an interview with Nils Christie by David Cayley, for "Crime Control as Industry," *Ideas*, CBC Radio, (Toronto: Mar. 10, 1993), pp. 2-5.

36. Bégin, pp. 27-28.

37. Dr. Augustus Gardner, cited in B. Ehrenreich and D. English, *For Her Own Good*, (N.Y.: Anchor/Doubleday, 1979), p. 64.

38. Dr. Ann G. Dally, *Women Under the Knife*, (London: Hutchinson Radius, 1991), p. 204.

Act One
Groups

Never doubt that a small group of thoughtful, committed citizens can
change the world; indeed, it's the only thing that ever does.

— Margaret Mead

Movement

AIDS activists, breast cancer optimists — the disturbing contrast
stayed with me, but settled into the back of my mind. Since coming
out in the newspaper, I'd been relatively quiet. A few women wrote
to me after the article was published. "You sound like an activist,"
said one. "Call me if you decide to start a group." Her name was
Carolyn and we chatted briefly. The idea was tempting, but I was
feeling my limits. After chemotherapy and radiation, a series of
baffling symptoms kept me running to the half dozen doctors
whose phone numbers now dotted my address book. I expected
to relapse at any moment.

Not that I had stopped talking about cancer — I produced a
radio documentary on cancer and the mind-body debate that won
some prizes. After it aired, I was at a crucial juncture.

"You've 'done' cancer. Now you can move on," the man I'd
been seeing for the past year said, hopefully.

"The more you think about it, the worse it gets," my cousin in
Alsace assured me over the crackling phone line. I didn't believe
this, but I could see that life might be easier if I turned my obsessive
nature to something less visceral — Chinese calligraphy, say.

In March 1991, a riveting documentary revived the excitement

I had felt two years earlier, when AIDS activists took Montreal by storm. The radio program was about a group of women in San Francisco who had done what I had only dreamed of doing. They had started an activist breast cancer group. In the report, live from one of their meetings, the airwaves bristled with emotion. These women were angry.[1]

I jotted down the name of the group's president: Elenore Pred.

Pred was a veteran of 1960s civil rights and anti-war demonstrations. She was diagnosed with breast cancer in 1981. In 1988, the cancer spread to her neck. She joined a support group with seven other women. The women began to die: one, two, three, four, five.[2]

Elenore Pred decided to act.

"I called together a small group at my house," she told me when I contacted her. "Twelve women and men from support groups who were angry about what wasn't happening. I laid out the statistics and I said, 'We've got to do something about this.'"

"You have men in the group?" I asked. Sexual politics overlaid on cancer politics could get complicated.

"I have no problem with men who get involved, but our focus is on breast cancer — because there is no prevention and because the numbers are increasing. Other groups include all cancers.

"I contacted a woman in Congress," she continued. "We started a study group and a newsletter. I went to an AIDS group, and one of the men showed us how to do research using the computer."

She explained the group's three purposes: education, political advocacy, and direct support of women with cancer. "That last one is tricky. Doing support takes away energy. You really can't be effective as both a support and an advocacy group. Fortunately, we have a good support organization here in the Cancer Support Community."

I knew about the centre founded by Vicky Wells and the late Treya Wilber.

"We work closely with Vicky," Pred said. "They don't want us to infringe on their financial base and I respect that. The Cancer Support Community gave us meeting space.

"The definition of political action is another tricky one," Pred continued. "We're applying for tax status as a charitable organization. We call ourselves a patient advocacy group, not a political advocacy group."

"But aren't your goals political?"

"Well, in a way. For example, I just came back from a trip to Washington. But it's the difference between asking representatives to support legislation — that's political advocacy — and trying to influence legislation. It's a fine line."

In a matter of months, after decades of repression, a wave of breast cancer activism had swept across America. "We now have a coalition of four or five groups in California. On Mother's Day we had a march in Sacramento with 500 to 1000 people — a lot for us. Burlington, Boston, and Richmond, Virginia all had smaller marches."

My ears pricked up when Pred mentioned Burlington, in Vermont. It's just a two-hour drive from Montreal.

"That's Ginny Soffa," said Pred. "You'll like her." She gave me Ginny's phone number.

She also gave me the names of a few Canadian women who had contacted her, including one in Montreal. I added Margaret Waller's name to the short list of women with breast cancer I knew in the city.

A few months later, in a suburban living room in Burlington, I'm sitting in a circle with members of Vermont's Breast Cancer Action Group.

Plates of raw vegetables circulate.

"Macrobiotic," says the hostess.

Breast cancer food. Chips are coming around in the other direction. Comfort food. We need that kind too. They're black or deep purple, the kind you buy in the health food store.

People introduce themselves, mostly for my benefit, although for a few, this is their first monthly meeting since the group's founding six months earlier. Most are women with breast cancer, one is a journalist who writes about health issues, another is the daughter of a woman with breast cancer. Ginny Soffa, a vivacious, dark-haired woman of about 40, has just returned from a meeting of the National Breast Cancer Coalition (NBCC) and has a pile of newsletters from other Coalition members.

"We need someone to go through all this stuff and summarize it," she says, her voice charged with excitement. "We're up to 116 groups."

A murmur of satisfaction goes through the room.

The Coalition is diverse. Membership includes women's health groups, cancer agencies, health care providers, corporations and religious organizations, as well as the segment that interests me the most — the grass-roots breast cancer groups. NBCC's goals are to raise awareness of breast cancer in the general public and to push for legislation allocating money earmarked for breast cancer research to the National Cancer Institute (NCI). A bill approving some $40 million in new research funds has been moved partway through the lengthy political process. But the coalition anticipates a Presidential veto, because the same bill has a controversial section authorizing research with fetal tissue.

NBCC's board has hatched a plan to overturn the veto, in the form of a letter-writing campaign. A Grass-Roots Task Force, complete with state captains, has been assigned to deliver 175,000 letters to members of Congress and President Bush in October — Breast Cancer Awareness Month. The number is not arbitrary: it corresponds to the projected number of women who will be diagnosed with breast cancer in the U.S. in 1991. State quotas match state diagnoses. To give the numbers emotional punch, letter writers will enclose a photo of a woman who has breast cancer or who has died of the disease.

"It's an in-your-face campaign," says Ginny. She passes around the letter she has written and her photograph, taken when she was eight. "Every day, when they open their mail," she explains, "they'll see our faces, or the faces of our families, and realize their re-election is on the line."

The sheer organization of it all takes my breath away. I wonder, however, about raising research money as the central focus. Women have gained little, that I can see, by the money spent on chemotherapy, radiation and hormonal research. Unless we convey to the public how little past spending has advanced our welfare, and secure a very large say for women in how the money is spent in the future, I worry that more research money will just bolster our status as glorified lab rats. I'm here to learn, however, not to criticize. The Coalition has successfully mobilized an entire nation. I am just one person — with a list of three Montreal women who have expressed tentative interest in forming an activist group.

The three women are Margaret Waller, whose name Elenore Pred passed on to me, Carolyn Badger, who wrote to me after she read my article, and Kathy Glass. I met Kathy through her family doctor, whose wife, Bonnie Klein, is a friend and feminist filmmaker. In mid-September, the four of us come face to face for the first time at a meeting in my apartment.

I suggest that each person explain what brought her to the meeting. Margaret begins.

"I'd rather not be here," she says, carefully. "I really had to struggle to get myself to come. I believe an activist group is the right thing to do. But to be perfectly honest, on a beautiful night like this I'd rather be out riding my bicycle than in here talking about breast cancer."

This is going to be tougher than I thought. I talk about my envy of the AIDS activists. "They are so knowledgeable about the disease. I want that kind of control, that involvement. I can't stand being passive."

Kathy feels the weight of a possible family history. "My mother had breast cancer," she says. "When I was diagnosed, the first thing my teenaged daughter said was, 'Grandma had it, now you've got it — that means I'm going to get it.' I feel helpless. There seems to be absolutely nothing I can tell her that's based on fact."

Carolyn's mother died of breast cancer, too. One of her aunts has the disease and she herself has had a recurrence. With two daughters, she shares Kathy's frustration. A family therapist by trade, she also finds the medical profession's focus on the bio-medical model too narrow. She believes stress played a role in her own cancer appearing when it did. Ultimately, though, she's here because she's an activist. "The political route attracts me. It's the only way to get change."

At the end of the evening, even Margaret wants to continue meeting, although she cautions us that her ambivalence will probably persist. Elenore Pred's group ignited dramatically. By the end of the first evening, they had picked a name, elected officers and taken up a collection. Ours seems destined to evolve slowly. We need to establish mutual trust and flesh out our goals. Given the weight of everyone's obligations, I can't see when we will have time to launch an organization, but everyone is game to try. We decide to meet monthly. A few other women come to occasional meetings, but as our goals gel, a working group of four is comfortable.

By February, we have mapped out our mission statement. Our overriding purpose is to provide a voice for the silent constituency — women with breast cancer. Our goals are to educate — ourselves, other women with breast cancer, and the public — about breast cancer issues; to engage in political action where change is needed; and to build a community of activists in Montreal with links to the movement elsewhere. Educate. Advocate. Network. Everyone is pleased. With the blessing of Breast Cancer Action in San Francisco, we choose our name: Breast Cancer Action Montreal (BCAM).

A newsletter is a natural centrepoint for our activities. We share a bent towards writing and research and I'm eager to put my editor's background to work. We will also sponsor educational forums, prepare positon papers and briefs, and get our messsage out to the media with interviews, articles and letters to the editor. To launch the group, we need an event that will set the tone. A speaker is a way to draw the public, but who to invite?

"Virginia Soffa," says Carolyn, immediately.

Perfect. The American movement is a phenomenon that's making headlines and Ginny is on the Coalition's founding board. She has a lively wit, likes speaking and she lives within driving distance — no small consideration, since our group's kitty, made up of a $20 bill from each of us, is dwindling.

"I'd love to do it!" says Ginny, over the phone.

"We're on," I tell the group.

As we plan details of the event, the group springs to life. We're tired of just talking and reading. Selecting the time and place, phrasing the press release and the poster, planning a publicity strategy — everyone kicks in with contacts and skills they hadn't mentioned in our more philosophical discussions. Montreal's English daily, *The Gazette*, runs a feature article with a large colour photograph of Carolyn, Margaret and me: "We want to give women a voice," says the headline. BCAM's launch is shaping up as a happening.

Meeting

Montreal's Unitarian Church, an organization known for its support of progressive causes, agrees to let us use their meeting hall. At 6:30 PM we arrive with Ginny, wondering uncertainly if the 40 or so chairs set out by the caretaker is the right number. Soon we are setting out more chairs. People, mostly women in their middle years, are streaming into the hall. Their faces have a purposeful set, an intensity that is almost frightening. We have suggested a $2 donation. Some women thrust $20 or $50 bills into the jar. I hand out copies of our first newsletter.

Ginny's talk, "Making Breast Cancer a Public Health Priority" is a lively account of the American strategy and its success. She's an engaging speaker and has learned the art of media sound-bites. ("We keep better statistics on baseball than we do on breast cancer"; "Five American women are dying every hour. If a mass murderer were killing five women an hour, more would be done.") She alludes to the tensions between activist groups and established organizations like the American Cancer Society. "Organizations in the so-called cancer business wanted to take us by the hand and get us to be more sedate. We're saying we're tired of waiting for answers." When the applause dies down, she asks for questions.

A woman with a youthful face crowned by soft grey curls gives a long speech about the Gerson diet. We should all be on it, vegetables prevent cancer. She has a whole satchel of books and she begins holding up them up, urging us to read each one.

"I'd like to hear from this person over here," says Ginny, adroitly, pointing to another raised hand.

"Do you really expect to make a difference lobbying the government?"

"Politicians respond to public pressure," says Ginny. "Our letter campaign shows that grass-roots action can have an impact."

"Mammography is imprecise. Are you doing anything about that in the States?"

"Mammography standards are still a problem," she says. "Only 13 states have laws to assure quality. But since our letter campaign, two senators have introduced legislation for national standards."

"I want to thank you. If you hadn't done this, in a couple of months, when I had my strength back, I probably would have done it," says a woman with a trace of an English accent.

The size of the crowd is gratifying, but I'm beginning to understand what a mixed group this is. In our months of discussions, our foursome evolved a rapport based on an essential like-mindedness. We will have to decide how far we are going to stretch to reach out to the diverse expectations of this crowd, whose urgency is palpable.

"What are you going to *do?*" one woman demands.

"We will be a voice for women with breast cancer," I say, feeling inadequate. The room is filled with fear of this disease. I sense the jagged edges of hopes, dashed before, now wary of anything that smacks of a promise. "We're gratified that so many of you came here. But this is just a beginning. We can't do everything tonight. "

We schedule a meeting for a month away. After we close, many people stay behind. Women who know each other from support groups greet one another and give updates on their lives. The woman with the British accent approaches me holding a crumpled newspaper clipping. It's my article of two years ago. "I want to thank you for this," she says. A group of four native women have driven in from a nearby reserve. Six women in their community have been diagnosed with breast cancer in the last year, they tell us. Reporters mill about, fishing for quotes for the next newscast. "Group ready for radical tactics," announces *The Gazette* the next morning. "It's hard to think of a better health cause, or a more neglected one," says the lead editorial. The media are with us.

Journalists

Over the months, BCAM continues to garner generous media coverage. Many journalists, though, have one or two standard angles they want to promote. One gambit is to contrast research funding for AIDS and breast cancer, the assumption being that AIDS gets more than its fair share.

I refuse to get sucked into a breast cancer vs AIDS contest. Besides, despite assiduous digging, I haven't been able to find out how much money is spent on breast cancer research. The murkiness about research spending bothers me a lot more than the possibility that we are being short-changed. At least some breast cancer research, I'm convinced, will make our lot worse, not better. But I soon learn that this kind of opinion isn't what journalists want for their sound bites.

A variant is that breast cancer research is ignored, and that this presumed imbalance proves women's diseases aren't taken seriously. "As a breast cancer lobby group, I guess you want more funding for research," the researcher will begin confidently, in the pre-interview.

"That's not actually our position," I begin. "We're saying women should have a say in how the research money is spent. We'd like to see more money go towards determining the causes of breast cancer."

At this, the pre-interview often grinds to a halt. The idea that "non-experts" — mere women with breast cancer — might have anything worthwhile to say about research is too risky to tangle with.

Once our group becomes known, women call us. As I talk to women with breast cancer, as well as to journalists, the confusion over basic issues becomes more and more obvious. An example is the question of screening mammography. In the spring of 1992, the Quebec government began to talk about restricting funding to mammography in women under 50. A feminist group immediately circulated a petition in protest. Both the feminist group and the media looked to us for support. Our executive faced a dilemma. Many of our new members eagerly signed the petition. In explaining their reasons for doing so, some of the women clearly did not grasp the difference between diagnostic mammography (for which there was never any threat of a funding cut) and screening mammography.

Our executive members are cool to the protest. Margaret has written a cogent analysis of the mammography issue in our first newsletter, noting the technology's drawbacks. Alas, the analysis is again too complex for public consumption, especially because radiologists are fueling the protest against cuts. The media cannot understand why our self-proclaimed activist group has not hit the streets to protest this supposed insult to women's health.

The launch of the Tamoxifen Prevention Trial, one week after our group's first meeting, provides an opening for us to voice a patient-centred point of view. One of the local TV news shows asks me to appear. The format will be a media standard, two people with contrasting views pitted against one another. Oncologist Richard Margolese, one of the study's principle investigators, will promote the trial and I will voice our group's concerns about it.

I'm intimidated by the prospect of appearing opposite Margolese, a breast cancer specialist who is revered locally and respected internationally. I wrestle with my anxiety. Why should the idea of publicly stating my beliefs be so frightening? We have worked hard to build an organization that voices women's concerns. Now, a year since my conversation with Elenore Pred, the dream is a reality, yet I am afraid. The words that come to me are

Audre Lorde's: ... *the transformation of silence into language and action is an act of self-revelation and that always seems fraught with danger.*

At the appointed time, I arrive by taxi at the studio. The researcher, a young woman, meets me at the door and as we walk downstairs, she asks me what points I will be making.

"Fine, that's perfect," she says, nodding encouragement.

My goal is to express three major concerns clearly and succinctly, and to sound confident. In minutes the interview is over. It goes well.

As the activist movement gathers force, pockets of journalists are digging beneath the surface of the breast cancer issue. Some, like Susan Ince, whose thoughtful pieces appear regularly in *Vogue*, are women whose mothers had the disease. Many other journalists, though, don't want to hear us to talk about issues. They want personal cancer stories, the more emotional the better. They also want me to say I'm fine — cured — living proof that the harrowing treatments are worth enduring after all.

"I do feel well, but the cancer could come back at any time," I explain. "Women with breast cancer live with uncertainty for the rest of their lives."

"But if you're OK after five years, you're cured."

"No, breast cancer can return 10 years later, or 15 or 20."

"We don't want wrong information going out over the air," one phone-in host tells me sharply. She has invited me to be a guest on the same show as an oncologist. "When I want a medical opinion, I'll ask him, when I want a personal anecdote I'll ask you," she says.

Our group makes many people uneasy. "You're setting yourselves up as experts," an angry nurse tells one of our members. "You're coming out against the medical profession."

"Wait a minute," counters Bev. "We're not against anybody. We are for women with cancer having a voice in the system. We are for informed choice. We are for public discussion of issues."

The accusation that we are doctor-bashing dogs us. Many of our group members, including me, approach our regular appointments at the hospital with trepidation. We assiduously avoid personal attacks on individual physicians. Our role is to raise questions about the system, about issues, not about individuals.

Sometimes we get unexpected encouragement for our work. "What you're doing is great," a woman who works at one of the hospitals tells Carolyn. "A lot of us in the system question the tamoxifen trial. We discuss it among ourselves, but we can't voice our concerns in public when the hospitals are recruiting."

Deaths

One stress of activism is the constant reminder that breast cancer kills. The force of this reality hits me a month after our first public meeting, when a woman calls to say she wants to join BCAM. "Forgive me if I lose the train of things," she says at the beginning of the conversation. "I'm on morphine." She gives her address as the palliative care unit of the Royal Victoria Hospital.

Our conversation moves me deeply. This woman is heavily drugged, in the final stage of life, yet she is reaching out to join a new organization. "I can't come to meetings," she says, sounding weary though coherent. "But I want to do something." I ask if I can visit her at the hospital.

Her name is Joanna Manross. When I arrive, the nurse directs me to the patio, off the second floor. Out in the May sun, I see a woman stretched face-down in a hospital bed, talking to a stylishly dressed friend who is seated in a wooden lawn chair. "Sharon?" she says. She introduces me to her friend.

Joanna is about my age. Her pretty face is elongated, with the beginnings of a summer tan and she has light brown hair with a few wisps of gray. She's propped up on her elbows, which are each covered with a huge blister. She seems oblivious to the sores. Her right hand is encased in a glove and the forearm is bandaged to the elbow. Under the sheets, her slight body stretches out behind her and seems to trail off into nothing.

She tells me her story. She was diagnosed only two years ago. She worked in advertising, as a copywriter at *Reader's Digest*. She knew nothing about breast cancer. She had always enjoyed good health. A mammogram showed some tiny calcifications, which the doctor said were nothing to worry about. She read everything she could find about breast cancer. At a checkup six months later, the doctor recommended that they operate. They had hoped to do just a lumpectomy, but when she woke up her breast was gone. The surgery had revealed a large central lump in her breast, nine centimetres, and it was giving off smaller calcifications. Eleven of the 15 lymph nodes they removed were positive. "I knew then the prognosis wasn't good."

She had decided, after reading, that if she was Stage I or II she would opt for diet and supplements. "But when they told me I was late Stage III, I figured I'd better go for the big guns, conventional chemotherapy." Two weeks after the operation, she found big sores growing at the site of the operation.

"I'd read that if the cancer recurs within the first six months, it's a bad sign. So when I had a recurrence after just two weeks ..." Her first treatment after surgery was CAF, the same chemotherapy regimen I had. She began to feel pain in her bones. She hoped it was just muscle fatigue but it persisted and she knew the grim truth before the test results came back. She had a stem cell transplant. "That gave me about six good months," she says. Eventually the pain returned and she was admitted to palliative care. The treatment for pain relief requires attention every four hours.

With the morphine, Joanna feels drowsy all the time but the following week, she says, they are going to insert a catheter that will feed the morphine directly into her spine. They hope she'll feel less sleepy.

We speak a few more times by phone. In early July the notice of her death appears in the paper and I attend the memorial service. In a eulogy, one of her friends reads excerpts of a letter from Joanna, written in her final days.

"I feel as if I have now embarked on a last ski marathon. I first realized the joys of that experience when I spent a year in Sweden. You never know what lies down the next slope — around the next bend. You know there will be dangerous and difficult holes — but sometimes, unexpectedly, you find a beautiful sunny place around a corner. That's like a time with special friends — chatter and the ring of laughter. And then come the hard climbs again. But it's still exhilarating and wonderous. That's how I feel about life now. It's still an adventure — I want to know what will happen next.

"But always, of course, I know there is the finishing line. It's getting nearer now. But I think I'll be able to cope when I get there. I think I'll have decided what it's all about by then."

Joanna is our first member to die. I write a piece in her honour in the newsletter. If our group is to survive, I feel we have to confront the deaths, learn how to cope with them.

One evening, after a radio interview, the show's producer stops me to say how much he likes our newsletter.

"You've read it?" I'm surprised. We only have about 100 subscribers and he's a young man — about 30. I'm sure his name isn't on the list.

"I read every issue." He sees my puzzlement, and explains, "My mother has breast cancer. I also belong to ACT-UP," he continues. "I'm encouraging her to come out."

"Most women aren't there yet," I sigh. "That's one reason our group has been fairly low key." I often feel the media are disappointed we haven't staged lie-ins and marches, or stormed medical meetings — the kind of theatrical tactics for which AIDS activists are known. "But women have been socialized not to express anger. And breast cancer has been in the closet for eons. We can't afford to scare away women like your mother. We have to start at square one, encouraging women to start talking openly."

"In the AIDS movement we're having to rethink some of our early views," he offers. "We used to say, 'turn your grief into anger.' Now we're realizing that doesn't work. You can't substitute one emotion for another. You have to acknowledge the grief, and learn to deal with it."

"How do you do that?" Since Joanna Manross' death, this has been on my mind.

"We're still working on that one," he says. "A lot of people just don't talk about the deaths. Or they talk about them in an unnatural way, without acknowledging the pain. You see these forced smiles. Someone will say, 'Have you heard the news?' And the news will be that someone else has the AIDS syndrome. But they smile when they say it."

Smile, you've got breast cancer.

I find other thoughtful insights in an article by Linda Reyes, a founder with Elenore Pred of Breast Cancer Action in San Francisco. Pred died in October 1991, five months after our first conversation. "Death from this disease is part of the reality we have to face," says Reyes. "I've been through a lot of deaths in two different support groups to which I've belonged ... .the most difficult for me were the young deaths. Ava, 32, a pediatrician with so much to give — I still grieve for Ava. Yet I have never wanted to leave [the group] because people died, though I've seen other group members decide to leave because they couldn't handle it.

"Like too many doctors who counsel their patients not to join support groups, those people thought of death as only negative, and they seemed to feel that if they walked away from that negativity they would be walking toward health. These people made the mistake of seeing everybody else's death as their own. I never did that," says Reyes. "In fact, I find that sort of identification a bit offensive. A person's birth and life are his or her own, so is his or her death — you cannot take it from them."[3]

The deadliness of breast cancer pushes women to form groups and speak out about the disease. Ironically, the pain of these deaths, witnessed firsthand, can also draw us back, towards silence and isolation. Learning to understand death, in both its private and communal significance will be a continual process. By acknowledging the loss of one member, and by speaking publicly about breast cancer as a major killer of women, our group has taken its first tentative steps in breaking the silence about breast cancer's deadly legacy.

This knitting together of acute pain and happiness is precisely what satisfies me most deeply about the formation of our group. Becoming part of a collective entity brings comfort. No longer isolated, we all gain strength. By assuming a public profile, however, we also face uncharted risks. Joanna Manross captured this duality when she wrote of participating in life's great adventure. Without the unseen "dangerous and difficult holes" the process would not be "exhilarating and wonderous." Now that our group is well and truly launched, I share Joanna's thirst to know what will happen next.

Notes

1. Trish Smith on *As It Happens*, CBC radio, (Mar. 13, 1991).

2. Erica Goode, "Fighting for their Lives," *U.S. News and World Report*, (Aug. 26/Sept. 2, 1991), pp. 68-70.

3. Linda Reyes, "From the Trenches," in Brady, pp. 245-254.

Act Two
Testifying

But my daughter, when I told her of our topic and my difficulty with it, said, "Tell them about how you're never really a whole person if you remain silent, because there's always that one little piece inside of you that wants to be spoken out, and if you keep ignoring it, it gets madder and madder, and hotter and hotter, and if you don't speak it out, one day it will just up and punch you in the mouth."

— Audre Lorde, *The Cancer Journals*

Everything You Ever Wanted to Know ...

In the Fall of 1991, when our group in Montreal was still in the throes of planning meetings, I spent a morning talking with a Toronto psychologist named Ross Gray. Gray works at the Sunnybrook Health Science Centre, a major cancer treatment facility, and has written about the need for patient participation in the cancer field. In several articles he talks about empowering people with cancer by involving them in policy decisions. "The record to date is decidedly grim," one paper concludes.[1] Gray proved to be as sympathetic in person as in print. As we chatted, he mentioned that a committee in Ottawa had just begun hearing testimony about breast cancer. I was astonished.

"I haven't heard anything about that."

"I hadn't either, until last week," he said. Another woman with breast cancer whom he knew, Pat Kelly, was testifying that week before the committee. Kelly had co-founded a support group in Burlington, Ontario.

"How does anyone find out what's going on?" I asked.

"With great difficulty," he replied, with a smile. "I keep my ear to the ground all the time, but I always consider myself very lucky if I hear anything."

The House of Commons subcommittee had representatives from each of the national political parties. The members, all women, included Barbara Greene and Edna Anderson of the then-ruling Conservatives, Mary Clancy of the Liberal Party, Dawn Black of the New Democratic Party (NDP) and Pierrette Venn from the Bloc Québécois. Their mandate was to study issues related to the status of women, health and welfare, social affairs and seniors.

The women decided to look at everything and anything related to breast cancer. The hearings began in October 1991 and ran through to the following May. Witnesses ran the gamut, from scientists and practitioners, to health policy makers, fundraisers, and, significantly, women with breast cancer. The text of each presentation, with questioning from the committee members, was published as the hearings went on. The committee's findings and recommendations were summarized in a report in June 1992.

The entire procedure generated the most extraordinary volume of information ever gathered in Canada about breast cancer. The testimonials were not dry scientific accounts. In their questions, committee members probed beyond facts to issues that are essentially political: who controls the money and information, who decides on the direction of research, and what kind of accountability to the public is built into the system.

For the first time in the country's history, breast cancer was on the political agenda. Silence about the disease had ended, at the top, as well as at the grass roots.

Witness

One call to Ottawa and I was invited to appear before the committee. Although I grew up in the nation's capital and came from a politically engaged family, I had never testified before a Parliamentary committee, or even attended such hearings. The staff, however, were friendly and helpful. Committee clerk Christine Fisher rushed me the testimony of previous witnesses, still in galley form. Researcher Sandra Harder helped me focus my presentation. My invitation to appear before the committee had apparently been issued largely on the strength of my radio documentary on the mind-body question. I wanted to use my allotted 20 minutes to talk about research politics, however, including the Tamoxifen Prevention Trial, the absence of long-term follow-up on treatment morbidity and breast cancer researchers' sluggish interest in environmental toxins.

"Fine," said Harder. "No one else has raised those questions yet, and if witnesses don't raise them, they won't go into the final report."

I read with interest the testimony of witnesses who had gone before me. They included several epidemiologists, the heads of major health funding agencies, oncologist Richard Margolese — and two women with breast cancer, Pat Kelly and Sylvia Morrison. The two women, I noticed with pleasure, had made powerful presentations.

The list of things I wanted to say seemed endless, and I spent several days trying to pummel my presentation into a 20-minute package. The shape of my testimony was strongly influenced by a meeting of the National Coalition of Cancer Survivorship (NCCS) I had just attended in Denver, Colorado. I joined the coalition because I felt the need for some contact with an organized group of people with cancer and Canada had no such organization. As a lobby group for the interests of cancer survivors, the NCCS had a newsletter and some useful publications to aid in decision-making. They also held an annual assembly featuring excellent speakers, panel discussions and workshops.

At the Denver meeting, my first, several sessions were eye-openers. In a passionate presentation, Patricia Schroeder, a Congressional representative from Denver for 20 years and a long-time advocate for women's health issues, spoke of a legacy of publicly funded health research that used men as the model. When she asked for an explanation, she was told, "Studying women is too complex. They have so many different metabolic states: pregnancy, menstrual cycles, menopause ..."

Three women who had been treated for Hodgkin's disease two decades earlier gave a panel on the long-term effects of cancer treatments. Too often, doctors took the attitude, "You're cured, what more do you want," leaving patients to sort out the symptoms for themselves. Of even less interest to medical specialists and researchers were social, psychological and economic effects of a cancer diagnosis — family breakdown, employment discrimination, social isolation, fear of recurrence, to name just a few.

If I had had any doubt, these presentations convinced me that research priorities are a political issue; if people with cancer don't get involved in setting the agenda, others will set it for us. Ditto questions of national health policy that dictate who will have access to treatments and insurance. The NCCS also impressed on me the value of group action.

I was still punching away at my presentation when I arrived at my sister Sylvia's, in Ottawa, where I was going to spend the night. Sylvia had just had her second child and was on leave from her job as a lawyer in the federal bureaucracy.

"Just put it away and relax," she told me.

"I can't. I'm not ready."

We argued back and forth. I wanted a tight text I could read. Sylvia urged me to speak extemporaneously from notes. The next morning, we were still discussing what to do about my semi-written testimony as we dropped my niece Jessie at her daycare on the other side of the river and headed back to the West Block of the Parliament Buildings. The infant Nicky, bundled in a blanket, would come to the hearings.

Sandra Harder, the researcher, picked us out from the small gathering in the hallway and introduced herself. She brought me into the room and introduced me to another woman, about my age.

"This is Carole Jones, a friend of mine," she said.

"Are you testifying too?" I asked.

"No, I'm just here to listen. I do have breast cancer though. I'm glad you're doing this. It's so important that they hear survivors' point of view."

A rectangle of long tables equipped with microphones occupied most of the room. The end of the room where we were standing had about 20 chairs, hooked up with translation devices, for the audience. A sprinking of people — no more than 10, including Carole, Sylvia and Nicky — had taken seats.

A little after 9:30, the members took their places and introduced themselves: Sandra sat at the far end, next to Edna Anderson who was chairing the meeting for an absent Barbara Greene. Dawn Black and Mary Clancy sat along one side of the rectangle. A cancer researcher named Dr. Louis Ciminovitch, who was speaking before me, took a place on the third side of the rectangle, facing the chair.

When my turn came, I put my notes aside.

I managed to cover most of the ground I had mapped out for myself: the need for a research audit, the need to consult patients about clinical trials, the lack of long-term follow-up on side effects, my concerns about the Tamoxifen Prevention Trial, the volume of chemotherapy research, the relative absence of research on industrial causes. My conclusion, the need for a network of groups that would provide a voice for women with breast cancer, came out in the question period, when Mary Clancy asked me to name the one thing I would ask for if I could "wave a wand."

"I would build a commmunity of women breast cancer survivors who would have a strong voice and who would speak to whatever issues they felt needed to be addressed, so that our side is heard ..." I replied.

Suddenly I was caught off guard by a question from someone who seemed to appear from nowhere.

"Ms. Batt, I apologize for being late ..."

The newcomer was Mme Gabrielle Bertrand, a Member of Parliament from the region south of Montreal. After some welcoming remarks, she said, "I see that your group has decided to take political action. I would like to know what that implies?"

"I am talking about a range of activites, which would include advocacy," I responded. "It would include eduating the public, educating other women, trying to improve the quality of information available, providing a network that could mobilize if there were some particular issue we felt was important ..."

"I've never heard any complaints from women around me who have gone through this trauma. It seems to me the doctors are enlightened and they work competently ... The Canadian Cancer Society does a lot of good work ..."

"I was not aware of any problems until I had cancer," I said.

I felt unnerved by the intervention, which I sensed carried an undertone of disapproval. Our exchange continued back and forth, and eventually ended with Mme Bertrand striking an optimistic note.

"I think that the work that needs to be done with women in general is to raise their awareness and to tell them not to be afraid to talk about it and to see their doctor as soon as possible when they have some concern. That's what the positive outcome can be. If it is caught in time, there is a great deal of hope for recovery."

Soon it was over, and I returned to my seat. Carole Jones smiled and nodded her encouragement. A woman sitting next to Sylvia, a Toronto researcher named Kathleen Pritchard, took the stand.

Parallels

In Washington, the the U.S. government was also hearing testimony about breast cancer. The occasion was the 20th anniversary of the War on Cancer, a Nixon initiative designed to wipe out cancer. In December 1991, a subcommittee of the House of Representatives took stock of the investment's impact on breast cancer.

Surgeon and activist Dr. Susan Love testified, so did Devra Lee Davis, and the director of the National Institutes of Health, Dr. Bernadine Healy. Like the researchers in Canada, they told a story of past failure and future hope.

"Every four minutes a woman is diagnosed with breast cancer and every 12 minutes a woman dies of breast cancer," said Susan Love, speaking as both a surgeon and as chairperson of the Research Task Force of the National Breast Cancer Coalition. "Yet there has been no substantial change in the mortality of breast cancer since the 1930s."

"Breast cancer today afflicts one out of nine American women," began Devra Lee Davis, "robbing them of an average of 19 years of life."

Bernadine Healy described a young mother whom she encountered on Capitol Hill shortly after her appointment as director of the NIH. "She had advanced breast cancer. Despite the ravages of the disease on her small frame, she was here on the Hill pleading with legislators to listen and to help. As I bid her farewell, she took my arm and said, 'Dr. Healy, hurry.'"

American women with breast cancer were heard in Washington, too. In October 1991, Ginny Soffa gave her views on the Women's Health Initiative, a large and newly approved project to look at leading diseases in postmenopausal women. The trial would assess the effects of dietary change, supplements and hormone replacement therapy on breast cancer, heart disease, osteoporosis and stroke. Ginny voiced the concerns of her Vermont organization. The study population (women aged 45 to 79) was too old to use in a prevention study, she said. Moreover, she continued, "I get the impression that the National Institutes of Health cannot study prevention without it translating into a drug treatment."

Meanwhile, the hearings in Ottawa continued and I began to attend them whenever I could. The researcher had done a thorough job of digging out diverse points of view and the unexpected revelations of witnesses held me in thrall.

"Now in terms of physical examination of the breasts," said Anthony Miller, Director of the National Breast Screening Study (NBSS), "I think our study has demonstrated that it is rarely performed well by physicians. The reason is that the physicians just do not take the time. They do not actually know what they are looking for."[2]

Sharon Green, of the American breast cancer information group Y-Me, described the impact the grass-roots lobby had on researchers at hearings in Washington. "The researchers saw that they have to be nice to these women because they could get the money ... we respected the researchers because they're going to listen to what we think we need. We want to be part of the designs of those trials."[3]

Physiotherapist Cynthia Webster said that, contrary to what was expected when conservative surgery was introduced, a lumpectomy does not greatly reduce the risk of lymphedema — the painful swelling of a woman's arm after breast surgery. "It has become evident in my practice that the number of lymph nodes is very significant. If they've excised 20 or more nodes, you have 100 percent guarantee you will have lymphedema in your lifetime. Fifty percent is usually around eight to 10 nodes." Furthermore, she added, "if a woman, before her breast surgery, has swollen hands when she flies on an airplane or gets them in the summer or has them when she's hiking, I can guarantee you she has a high risk of getting lymphedema."[4]

Sometimes, one witness would vehemently contradict the testimony of another. To me, these exchanges signalled sensitive areas. I wondered what the committee would make of them.

"Oh, the contradictions are part of the hearings process," explained Sandra Harder. "It's up to the committee to try to sort out them out by questioning different witnesses."

To do this, the committee heard from a number of people whose views were known to be off-centre. These included David Horrobin and Rudy Falk, two researchers with unorthodox approaches to cancer treatment. Pierre Blais, a one-time government employee who was dismissed in a dispute over the Même breast implant, had an entire evening session to himself.

Throughout the eight months of hearings, women with breast cancer continued to come forward, and the Parliamentary subcommitee even travelled to Washington to find out first-hand how the American approach to breast cancer compared to Canada's. The biggest black marks on the American record were the estimated 85 million citizens who either lacked basic health coverage altogether, or were uninsured, whereas in Canada health care is understood as a basic right. Sandra Harder observed that, "in the United States it tends to be approached as a consumer good or a product which is subject to the vagaries of the marketplace."[5] On the plus side, the visiting delegation found that the NCI could provide data on site-specific cancer research, data which the NCI in Canada was unable to provide. As well, the Office of Research on Women's Health, set up in 1990, was a positive response to past neglect of women's health issues.

Call to Action

Over the months the hearings took place, Carole Jones and I were regulars in the audience. We often had lunch together before I drove back to Montreal. She was one of the 20 to 30 percent of women with a tumour that is diagnosed as early — node-negative, small and apparently not aggressive — and who learns she has metastasis despite all the recommended treatments. During the hearings she was undergoing chemotherapy and was often tired. On her doctor's advice, she reluctantly took a disability leave from her job as conference organizer at Carleton University. She had an earthy humour and always spoke her mind. I enjoyed comparing notes with her after a morning of listening to testimony.

"Do you *believe* what that bozo said," she would mutter, as we worked our way along the cafeteria line, pushing our trays. "Honestly!"

Like me, she felt the hearings offered hope for significant change. The sparse attendance, and particularly the absence of reporters, dismayed both of us. On most days, the audience section of the hearing room was nearly empty. With virtually no media coverage, the public was oblivious to what was going on. We began to hatch a plan for a letter-writing awareness campaign, like the "Do the Write Thing" campaign the American women had orchestrated so effectively.

Two other women were soon part of our planning team — Pat Kelly of Burlington and Jill Jackson, a friend of Carole's in Ottawa who also had breast cancer. Our group drew up a letter and a brochure and worked out a plan for distributing 5,000 copies. At Carole's birthday party, friends gave cheques for postage and printing instead of gifts. She corralled her friends to stuff envelopes. The mailing went out across Canada requesting recipients to back a national policy to combat breast cancer. Each person was to send the form letter to their Member of Parliament asking him or her vote to implement the Committee's recommendations, due to be tabled in the House of Commons in June. We encouraged them to enclose a photo of a woman with breast cancer and send a copy of letter and photo to our box number.

Along with the thousands of replies were disheartening letters from women who couldn't find the services they needed. "This one just lost her mother, and she's writing to say how she feels," Carole testified before the Parliamentary Committee. "This young girl is 22 and has just found out she has breast cancer. She wants to know where she can find a support group."[6]

Carole, ever resourceful, again seconded her friends to reply to the letters. Meanwhile Jill, after months of research on experimental treatments, entered the hospital in Sudbury for high-dose chemotherapy and a bone marrow transplant.

Unanswered Questions

The subcommittee's report came out in June, 1992. *Breast Cancer: Unanswered Questions* was an impressive document. It had the same sweeping scope as the hearings, but its author, Sandra Harder, had distilled the reams of testimony to 50 pages of vigorous prose, with 49 recommendations. Together they painted a clear, if dismal, picture of breast cancer in Canada.

Throughout, the report acknowledged the contribution of women with breast cancer, giving activists credibility at the national policy level. "As a subcommittee we are supportive of the actions of the survivor groups from whom we have heard," the report read.

"We predict that the formation of similar groups across Canada will make important contributions to the direction of breast cancer research and treatment, to the quality of life for breast cancer patients, and to the level of public knowledge of this disease."

To aid in this process, the report recommended a national conference of breast cancer patients, survivors, their partners, friends and families, planned and coordinated by survivors of breast cancer. The goal would be to assist in developing a national network of survivor groups. *Unanswered Questions* also recommended lay participation in the research process and consultation by cancer research agencies with breast cancer survivor groups.

According to Canadian government regulations, the ruling party must respond to a report by an all-party committee within 150 days. In the same period, affected institutions, as well as individual citizens, can comment on the report. This public reaction gives the government a sense of what policy changes might fly politically, or whether they need to act at all.

While Canada's official process moved stepwise along its even path, Washington's response to the U.S. breast cancer lobby matched the movement itself for shock value and sheer drama. The high point occurred during the Presidential election campaign in October 1992. Senator Tom Harkin, a champion of the breast cancer cause (he lost two sisters to the disease), tried to have $300 million for breast cancer research transferred from the defense budget to the National Cancer Institute. Harkin's strategy was blocked by a budget agreement that forbids transferring funds from military to domestic programs. But Harkin hit on a way around the rules: use the defense budget to fund breast cancer directly. The House of Representatives agreed to support the plan, but the White House budget chief cried foul — the move would break the spirit of the budget rule. Harkin and his allies objected. The Defense budget has allocations for prostate cancer and AIDS research, they argued, why not breast cancer?

"I think Bush was so afraid of looking sexist during the campaign," said Virginia Soffa, "he let it through. Now," Soffa added, "we have $210 million earmarked for breast cancer research in the Defense department which is looking for non-military ways of using its technology." The money would be administered by the

Army, an odd alliance for breast cancer activists. The miraculous thing about the huge allocation, Soffa said, was that it came about through a combination of unforseeable circumstances: the end of the cold war, a lame-duck president, Senate support for the advocates' cause, and timely work by the activists themselves.

In Canada, the appointed day came and went: no government policy on breast cancer. BCAM had submitted a response to the report. So had other grass-roots groups and the major cancer agencies. In early December, things began to budge. The government would unveil the policy on December 15, with press conferences in three cities: Toronto, Montreal, and Calgary. Members of BCAM were invited to attend the Montreal announcement at the Sheraton Hotel. I called as many people as I thought would be free at 10 AM on a Tuesday.

The crux of the announcement was that the government would launch a $25 million initiative, over five years, for breast cancer research and education. The bulk of the money, $20 million, would go to a Breast Cancer Research Challenge Fund, which would invite matching contributions for business and industry, non-governmental organizations and citizens. The money would be administered by the NCIC, and directed by a Management Committee with approximately 10 members. The Management Committee would include women with breast cancer as well as scientists, policy makers and health professionals. The other $5 million would be streamed into breast-care information projects in five cancer centres across the country ($2.7 million) and into support for various provincial programs for screening, to improve the standard of care, and to educate health professionals ($2.3 milliion). No money was allocated for women with breast cancer or the groups to which they belonged.

Although the government identified breast cancer as an area of policy concern, the details of the response implied a course of more of the same, with minimal input from women with breast cancer. The NCIC would have a tad more money, and it would be targeted for breast cancer. Yet *Unanswered Questions* had criticized NCIC for its closed-shop atmosphere, its inability to track its own spending, and its lack of public accountability. The new Management Committee, with its unspecified number of breast cancer survivors, was the only concrete attempt in the initiative to draw women with breast cancer into decision-making.

In short, the published government response did not convey the same enthusiasm for survivor and activist participation that came through in the Parliamentary report. Significantly, the government did not endorse the concept of a survivor-organized national conference as the launching platform for a national network of survivor groups. Instead, the report said, the health department would encourage representatives from patient groups to participate at a national workshop on breast cancer. The government would convene this workshop and the Cancer Society, the Medical Research Council and the NCIC would all have a hand in organizing it. By my reading, this meant a few women with breast cancer would be guests at a meeting designed by and for professionals.

Despite my disappointment in the tone of the government response, the announcement did put an official stamp on breast cancer as a problem meriting policy attention. Like our American counterparts, Canadian women with breast cancer had entered the public debate that would shape future decisions. Also significant for me and for members of BCAM was the discovery that women with breast cancer in other communities had formed groups and were speaking out too. Perhaps we were still on the sidelines of the major institutions, but our individual voices were now a chorus that no one could ignore.

Notes

1. Ross E. Gray and Brian D. Doan, "Empowerment and Persons with Cancer: Politics in Cancer Medicine," *Journal of Palliative Care*, (1990), 6:2, pp. 33-45.

2. Anthony Miller, *House of Commons Proceedings*, (Nov. 20, 1991), 5:12.

3. Green, (Feb. 18, 1992), 10:21.

4. Cynthia E. Webster, *House of Commons Proceedings*, (Mar. 30, 1992), 14:4.

5. Sandra Harder, *House of Commons Proceedings*, (Apr. 27, 1992), 15A:9.

6. Carole Jones, *House of Commons Proceedings*, (Apr. 27, 1992), 15:20-24.

Act Three
Seismic Shift

Many of the scientists at [the Fifth International Conferenence in]
Montreal spoke of avoiding future conferences. Some even considered
leaving AIDS work altogether. One prominent AIDS clinician, a cancer
specialist by training, shook his head after a particularly unpleasant
session. "I kind of enjoy treating women with breast cancer. Maybe that's
what I should be doing. It would be a hell of a lot easier than this."

— Robert M. Wachter, Program Director for the Sixth
International Conference on AIDS, in *The Fragile Coalition*[1]

An Invitation

In March 1993, I receive a phone call from a woman at Health
Canada, in Ottawa. "We're having a national breast cancer conference in November and we'd like you to chair one of the
planning committees," she says. "Are you interested?"

I'm not sure. The government's failure to endorse a conference organized by and for women with breast cancer, has left
me cool to the whole federal initiative. This meeting is apparently
the one described in the government report as a "national consensus workshop," which would be organized by the government and
various established cancer institutions. The goals, stated in
bureaucratese, had not implied to me a prominent role for women
with breast cancer.

In fact, by this time, the government report is a dim memory.
BCAM, by contrast, is ticking merrily along. Our group is sponsoring

a panel discussion on breast cancer prevention that is shaping up as a major happening. With the planning of our very own event in the home stretch, I can't work up much enthusiasm for a government-run conference.

"What would this committee do?" I ask the woman from Health Canada.

"It would be one of four planning committees for the conference." She sounds excited. "Your committee would plan the part of the program dealing with breast cancer support groups. We will ask Pat Kelly to be the vice-chair. The other committees are on prevention and screening, treatment, and research."

"I'd rather be on the research committee," I tell her, "or prevention." I want a say in the important policy areas, not a marginalized role on a committee confined to support groups.

"The other committees already have chairs," she says, sounding uncomfortable.

"I'm not saying I want to be the chair. I'd be happy to be a member."

"But the chairs get to choose their own committee members. That's how it works. I could suggest your name, but I couldn't guarantee you would get on one of those committees." She sounds frustrated, as if I'm not getting the point. "If you were chairing the Support Group Committee, then *you* could suggest people to be on the other committees."

This doesn't seem like much of a carrot. I try another tack.

"How much time will it take?"

"Well, probably quite a lot."

"Is there any compensation?"

"No. None of the chairs will be paid. We couldn't afford that — the conference is already costing a lot. Of course, we would reimburse your expenses when you had to go to a meeting."

I explode. "Then you're not serious about having women with breast cancer involved. Researchers, academics, doctors — meetings like this are part of their job. It's a career opportunity. You all make your livings off our misfortune. We will never have a say in the process if we have to work on the same basis as people who have fat salaries and secretaries!"

A long silence. "I understand what you're saying. I'll have to get back to you."

Weeks later she phones back with an offer. A per diem when I go to meetings. A per diem for days worked. Plus expenses. Someone is working on a contract. Apparently she has fought hard to get this through the system. Pat Kelly will get the same offer.

It's already April and the planning group, including the other chairs, is having a meeting in Toronto. If I want to, I can come and meet the members. Attending a meeting, I conclude, is the best way to decide whether I want to get involved.

Close Encounters

The members are Lise Mathieu, Dr. Sylvie Stachenko, and May Smith, all from the preventive health division of Health Canada; the chairs of the other three subcommittees; Dr. Roy Clark, chief radiologist from the Princess Margaret Hospital in Toronto; and representatives from each of the groups that are sharing the funding load with the government. Elizabeth Kaegi represents both the Cancer Society and the National Cancer Institute of Canada (NCIC), and Carole Grafstein represents the Canadian Breast Cancer Foundation (CBCF). Two companies that will provide administrative support each have representatives. Pat Kelly, driving in from Burlington, hasn't yet arrived.

Dr. Sylvie Stachenko, who is chairing the meeting, is about my own age. With her tiny frame and unpretentious manner, I find her the least intimidating person in the room. She begins with an introduction about the purpose of the conference.

"The Breast Cancer Forum will bring all the different sectors together," she begins. It's time, she says, that all these different players — researchers, practitioners, policy planners, the funding agencies, people involved in the screening programs — became partners instead of working independently. "But what will make this conference really different," Dr. Stachenko continues, "is the participation of women." As she heads into her conclusion, she is verging on passion. My interest begins to pick up.

The concept of the Forum is to bring the diverse interest groups together for three days to discuss issues and define priorities. Out of it will come a national policy document proposing action on all fronts: treatment, research, prevention, screening, and a network of survivor groups. The planning group envisions a highly participatory process, very different from most conferences where delegates sit and listen to appointed speakers. About half the space on the program is devoted to typical conference presentations, but the rest of the time is designed to engage the entire assembly in active discussion of issues. This process is the essence of the Forum.

As background to these discussions, each subcommittee will develop a six-page postion paper on the issues in its broad area of responsibility: the research subcommittee will map out directions for research, the treatment subcommittee will propose directions for treatment, and so on. Developing these papers is a process in itself, involving concentric circles of participants. The sub-committee chairs and vice-chairs are at the core, surrounded by the members of their committees. Next the subcommittee assembles another circle, a working group of 30 to 45 members who will assist by helping to research the position paper or by critiquing drafts of it. The delegates are yet another circle of participants. They will receive all four position papers in their binders at registration and, on Day One, listen to representatives from each committee present a one-hour oral plenary highlighting the issues. A good part of the next two days will be spent discussing the issues at round-table discussions, all duly recorded by rapporteurs. The discussions will be distilled into a document that will be launched to the general public — the outermost circle.

Some rules have been established. Funding for the conference will come from the government and the cancer funding agencies, not from industry. Money from pharmaceutical companies, in particular, is off-limits. The venue for the meeting will be Montreal's convention centre, the Palais des Congrès — the very site of the Fifth International AIDS Conference.

When Sylvie Stachenko finishes, other people begin to describe what they have done so far. The meeting lasts the entire day. By the end of it, I'm still not much wiser about what is supposed to happen at the Forum, but I am convinced the women from Health Canada are sincere about wanting the participation of women. Throughout the discussions, they listen attentively to what Pat and I have to say. When the question of delegates at the conference comes up and we propose that one-quarter of the 600 places be assigned to women with cancer, they don't flinch.

By the end of the day, I'm veering towards signing on. One question, though, is how we will form our committee, let alone find our 150 delegates. The other committees have the university and

cancer treatment infrastructure from which to draw representatives. We have a constituency that is largely invisible and
silent.

Once again, the women from Health Canada are eager to
support us. "I can see that each of the subcommittees is going to
encounter very different problems preparing for the Forum," one
of them says. "Health Canada will provide assistance wherever we
can to help the subcommittees do their work."

SAN Subcommittee

The first job for Pat and me is to form a subcommittee, which soon
acquires the acronym SAN, for "Support, Advocacy and Networking." Our concept is a group of women who will speak their
concerns directly, not through the bureacracy of the Cancer
Society. The committee needs to reflect the country's geographical and cultural diversity, the Health Canada people remind us.
Pat and I divide the country in two — east and west. By mid-June
we have a subcommittee, comprised mainly of women with breast
cancer: Hilary from Saskatchewan, Maureen and Marion from
Nova Scotia; Ninon Bourque of Ottawa, and Rosemary Gadler of
Montreal; in Winnipeg, Sonia Hernandez; Frances Hanna, a
Métis woman from Peace River, Alberta; Jan Morrow in Kelowna
B.C. Neil Docherty, from Toronto, will provide a spouse's perspective. Neil's wife Nina belonged to Pat's support group and died of
breast cancer in April. We invite Ross Gray to be our member from
the institutional milieu. Three other members are resource
people from Health Canada and the consulting group hired to
work on the Forum planning. Health Canada has given our
committee an budget so we can meet three times before the
Forum, with conference calls in between. Pat and I have our own
budgets for travel, phone calls and faxes. We strike our working
group and begin to spread the word to potential delegates, from
Newfoundland to the far reaches of the Arctic.

Women with breast cancer need to tell their stories and the SAN
subcommittee is no exception. At our first face-to-face meeting in
Toronto, the first half of the day is taken up with a go-round-the-
table at which everyone talks of her cancer experience and the
issues it raised. Delayed diagnoses, negative surgeons, biases and

voids in information, poor follow-up for complications like lymphedema, support groups that don't, spiritual quests — the recurring themes are the ones that come up whenever women with breast cancer speak frankly. Different as we are, and still strangers, our group feels a strong kinship. The task is to seize these strands of frustration and weave them into a paper that speaks for everyone.

We decide to form five working groups. Three of the groups will develop a patients' perspective on the themes being addressed by the other subcommittees. Many of the problems we've identified suggest weaknesses in one or more of these areas. Ninon agrees to head the Prevention and Screening group, I take Research, and Jan will chair Treatment and Care. Pat will chair a Survivor Network group and Rosemary will head a group on psycho-social issues. The others join one or more groups, according to their interests. Each chair is to add members to her working group and come up with a draft of a working paper by the end of the summer. As we begin talking about additional projects — a questionnaire, a photo exhibit — I sense that people are starting to feel overwhelmed. Still, there's an excitement in the room. We are part of something important. I leave the meeting bouyed with optimism.

Later I speak to Neil Docherty, who was unable to attend the first meeting. Neil is a TV journalist with an investigative program called *The Fifth Estate*. His wife Nina was 39 when she died of breast cancer in April, leaving him with two sons, three and seven. Neil's courtly manner turns fierce when he talks about breast cancer. "We've got to wrest power away from the research community!" he declares, during one conference call. He joins my research working group.

At the June meeting of the organizing committee, the chairs review their work. When I describe the SAN subcommittee's working groups, the response is swift.

"I'm concerned about this shadow cabinet, you've set up," says Mark Levine, an oncologist who heads a major cancer centre in Hamilton. "My subcommittee is looking at treatment and care. We have a patient representative, a woman from your own organization, recommended by you, to make provide the patient's perspective. Now you've set up a working group to prepare a paper on treatment and care. The spirit of the Forum is supposed to be partnership, not confrontation."

"How is this confrontation?" I'm completely unprepared for this. "These working groups are a way for our committee members to study the issues in each main area, so they that they can take part in the Forum discussions. The Forum is supposed to be participatory — but women with breast cancer aren't used to attending conferences, to sitting on policy committees. We've never been invited before. We want to ask informed questions, to discuss policy, not simply give patients' experiences, or listen passively. Our members need to do some advance work if they are going to be up to speed on policy issues."

"I share Mark's concerns," Ron Buick joins in. Buick chairs the research subcommittee. "You're developing an alternative platform. What do you intend to do with it? While members of my committee are presenting their ideas, will you be off in another room holding a counter-session?"

"Of course not." I say. "Members of our group who have concerns about research will be *at* your session, asking questions and voicing their opinions."

I'm starting to understand the subtext for this anxiety: AIDS activism. For me, the show of patient power at the AIDS conference in Montreal was a beacon to guide us out of the funk of patient passivity. I can sense that for Buick, Levine, and health professionals in general, even an oblique allusion to AIDS activists is a toreador's taunting red cape.

I never for a minute imagined women with breast cancer mimicking the more theatrical tactics of AIDS activists. Even the AIDS protestors toned down their demonstrations after the meeting in Montreal. At the closing ceremonies of that conference, Randy Shilts, chief chronicler of the AIDS struggle (now dead of AIDS-related causes), was disturbed enough to scold the activists in his speech at the closing ceremonies. "Expressing your anger can give you a warm, fuzzy feeling inside," he said, "but this conference is not supposed to be a therapy session ... it is not enough to be angry, if that anger is not paired with intelligence about its best tactical timing and its best strategic targets."[2]

Our age, and our socialization as women, will also shape the breast cancer activist movement. As a group, we are at least a generation older than ACT-UP's membership. Women — activists included — rarely translate outrage into boisterous demonstrations. I am more worried that women with cancer who come to the conference will simply listen, talk among themselves and go home, as frustrated as ever about the gap between the issues as we perceive them and as researchers and practitioners define them. Few women, I know, will come to the conference feeling as prepped on the issues as Pat and I. Even Hilary, one of the more politically experienced of our committee members, likens our preparations to "cramming to get a Ph.D. in six months."

Pierre Beaudry, who is from the consulting group hired to work on the conference, attends the meetings of all the subcommittees, including ours. Over the months, his enthusiasm for the SAN group has swelled to the point where he is ready to start a fan club on our behalf.

"I can assure you," he now tells Levine and Buick, with Gallic passion, "that the women on this subcommittee have no intent to disrupt the proceedings. They, as much as any of you, are ready to work in partnership with the other committees!"

Someone proposes a compromise — that the subcommittees circulate drafts of their working documents to one another, well in advance of the meeting. That way, committee members will be able to flag contentious issues in advance. At the conference itself, no one will be caught off guard by unanticipated opposition to their proposals.

All agree. Open communication is the byword.

Throughout the summer and early fall, the SAN subcommittee and its working groups beaver away on our papers, on the questionnaire, and on two breast cancer awareness projects — a photo exhibit and a balloon release. In just a few months, the SAN subcommittee covers an astonishing amount of ground. As we hurtle towards the Forum dates, the pace of meetings and conference calls becomes hectic. Excitement mounts; so does the tension.

Then, in September, our committee learns that the government's Breast Cancer Initiative, the new name for the $20 million research fund, has set October 15 as the closing date of its first Request for Proposals (RFPs) — one month before the Forum. At our September meeting, members assail the Fund on two counts. First, the mid-October closing date means the proposals funded in the first year will not reflect discussions at the Forum. Second, the Management Committee has declined to publicly identify the women with breast cancer in its membership.

"We can't let them co-opt the Fund," declares Neil.

"We want a representative on that Fund, and we shouldn't be silent," Valerie concurs. And so on, around the table. The SAN subcommittee votes unanimously that Neil, Pat and I write to the Assistant Deputy Minister of Health asking for an appointment to discuss the matter. Our first act of advocacy.

"Will our group keep meeting after the Forum?" asks Marion as we leave the seminar room. "I'm really getting into this!"

The letter to Ottawa gets an immediate response: I'm invited to meet with Kay Stanley, the Assistant Deputy Minister. The mood at the Assistant Deputy Minister's office is cordial. Two staff members explain the background to the decisions and listen as I reiterate the subcommittee's objections. Stanley then proposes a number of ways out of the impasse. She assures me the government takes the Forum very seriously. A special call for proposals can be issued after the Forum, she says, to generate applications in any areas that are wanting. She believes in the value of consumer representation, she emphasizes, and in the transparency of process within public bodies. Unfortunately, Committee members have been appointed for two years and unless someone resigns no openings will be available before then. In the interim, she suggests that our subcommittee find a suitable person among the current members to act as a consumer rep. She also proposes that the Fund issue regular bulletins, in the form of a letter or newsletter, to keep the public informed about its work.

Not exactly a victory, but the SAN group has shown some muscle. With the Forum just a month off, Pat and I are preparing the subcommittee's Plenary presentation for the first day. Advocacy participation on research committees will be part of my text.

The Forum

The National Forum on Breast Cancer is a three-day event, Sunday through Tuesday. To ensure a good turnout from women with cancer, several of the sponsoring agencies have committed themselves to subsidizing the costs for applicants with cancer from out of town. The local Cancer Society provides free accommodation in its lodge; the Canadian Breast Cancer Foundation seeks corporate backers and bargains with hotels and airlines for bonus rooms and seats; Health Canada pays the travel and accommodation costs of all members in our working group and finds pockets of money to assist other women in need. Conference fees aren't a problem — there are none. Officially, registration closed on September 30, but as word of the Forum spreads, we are all inundated with calls from people who want us to "get them in." Rules are stretched for those from an underrepresented sector or region of the country. The word from the Secretariat is that close to 150 lay delegates will indeed be at the Forum.

Pat and I have each spent the past week writing our respective portions of the SAN group's plenary presentation, which we will deliver Sunday afternoon. A rush of anticipation has us both in high spirits. We work together to smooth out kinks in our two texts.

Early Saturday morning, I head down to the Palais des Congrès, a vast high-tech convention hall straddling a freeway that cuts the city in two. Most delegates are housed in a variety of hotels within a two block radius and by noon they begin to drift in to register. Some are setting up booths in the foyer. The press office is abuzz with activity. Drawing from their professional expertise, Neil and Ninon have devised a press strategy for the SAN group. The goal is to maximize the exposure of our subcommittee and of survivor issues. Pat and I will be the subcommittee's official voices for the English media; Ninon will explain our goals to the French media. We encourage the rest of our members to comment on the proceedings at every opportunity, to tell reporters their personal stories and to highlight issues from their region of the country. From his vantage point as a TV journalist, Neil reminds everyone of the intrinsic power of cancer stories, told by someone living with the disease. On Sunday at noon, with his two sons and another family, he himself will participate in a balloon release event in honour of the fourteen women a day who die of breast cancer in Canada.

BCAM has planned a pre-conference rally on Saturday, outdoors, under the guidance of Joy Laverdure. It features an introductory speech by two of our members, a minute of silence, and a ceremony at which all present pin black and pink ribbons on a large BCAM banner, in honour of women who have died. The finale is a performance by the Raging Grannies, a group of activists who costume themselves in outrageously dowdy hats and dresses and sing satirical songs. At two PM, with November drizzle falling on a near-empty square, Joy valiantly gets the proceedings underway. Suddenly, dozens of colourful umbrellas dot the square and reporters with mikes and TV cameras begin weaving through the crowd. The umbrellas, the banner, the tears and the Grannies are made for TV. That night, and on television broadcasts for the next three days, the rally provides opening visuals for much of the Forum coverage.

The entire first day of the Forum is a plenary in the vast main hall where two giant screens flank the speakers' platform. At the opening ceremonies, a politician from Quebec City puts everyone in a testy mood with an interminable speech about the province's yet-to-be-launched mammography screening program. It takes Carole Jones to re-engage the crowd with her poignant testimony. "I can't honestly say the good days outnumber the bad any more," she says, adding that her decision to work with other women who have breast cancer means losing friends. She asks for a moment of silence and I think of Jill. It's almost two years since Carole introduced us at the hearings. Jill died one year ago, at 34. Her mother is in the audience.

Before the subcommittees give their plenary presentations, another woman with breast cancer speaks — children's entertainer Sharon Hampson of the group Sharon, Lois & Bram. This is a Canadian breakthrough of sorts. While high-profile American women with breast cancer have been coming out of the closet since the 70s, beginning with Betty Ford and Shirley Temple Black, well-known Canadian women have been largely silent about having cancer. The Organizing Committee spent a good part of one summer morning trying to come up with the name of a survivor with a public profile to speak on opening day. Finally, a Health Canada official joked that it was a lost cause, "unless the oncologists in the room can persuade one of their famous patients to come out." By the next meeting, Sharon Hampson had agreed to make her diagnosis public. "I've never kept it a secret from friends," she tells me. "But I haven't spoken about it to an audience." In her 20 minute slot, she talks candidly about the discomfort of intense hot flashes brought on by tamoxifen, the uncertainty cancer has brought to her own life, and her anxiety for her daughter.

At the lunch break, our subcommittee holds a press conference. The highlight is Catch the Wind, which evolved from an idea of Neil's son, Bruce. After Nina died in April, Neil's two boys, Bruce and Liam, wanted to do something special on Mother's Day.

They wrote a message and sent it aloft in a helium balloon to their mother, who had asked them to think of her in the clear blue sky. The ceremony was a healing moment for the boys, and Neil as well. Now, to commemorate the 14 women who die each day in Canada of breast cancer, Bruce, Liam and three children from another family, gather in the outdoor square with 14 balloons. Neil speaks poignantly about breast cancer's toll on families, while the boys let slip the first round of balloons. Soon images from the ceremony join the swelling collection of Forum iconography.

Our plenary is the subcommittee's main chance to influence the formal proceedings. Pat and I have one hour to present. We will begin with a 10-minute clip from a video based on interviews of women with breast cancer. Wrenching testimonials from three women, including Carole Jones, will be projected on two huge screens flanking the platform. Next, I will introduce the subcommittee members, who will come up on stage as I call their names. Then I'll speak briefly about my evolution from patient to advocate; over to Pat, who will do the same. Back to me, for the main portion of my presentation, in which I will highlight issues in prevention, screening and research from the patient's standpoint, underlining that we want advocacy representation on decision-making bodies. Finally, Pat will talk about issues in treatment, care and support, bolstering her points with quotes from the cross-Canada survey, and closing with the vision of a national network of breast cancer groups.

After the dry run, committee members give both Pat and me the same advice: "More passion! Otherwise it's great." Now for the real thing. A haze of harsh lighting separates me from the audience but my nervousness dissolves. In the thick of my address, I hear a surge of applause. Another burst of applause, and another. Later I find out that the rousing response was led by a BCAM claque whose members sustained some withering looks from those around them. When we finish, Pat and I meet in centre stage and hold our hands aloft to a standing ovation.

Other women at the conference are also having an impact. Posters are arranged around the periphery of the reception room and a beaming Darlene Betteley shows me hers. "Prosthesis or Not? A Personal Choice! Personal Conflict with the Canadian Cancer Society" has a five-point summary of Darlene's saga, illustrated by a photo of Darlene, a copy of a Reach to Recovery volunteers' handbook with the offending dress requirement highlighted, some newspaper clippings, and the quasi-apologetic letter sent to her from the Cancer Society. The poster has already sparked discussion among startled Reach to Recovery volunteers, who had not heard of Darlene's resignation before. Later in the conference, Darlene spends 15 minutes chatting about her case with the embarrassed but genial President of the Canadian Cancer Society.

The press are at out in force and Neil's prediction about the power of survivor's stories proves accurate. Never has the disease had so much coverage in the Canadian media, never have reporters given women's opinions so much credence. Yet the mood is very different from the AIDS meeting. "We don't want to bash the medical profession," says Ninon with her engaging smile, "but we do say they have to start listening to us."

The most potent yeast at the conference, though, proves to be the round-table discussions, which are off-limits to the media. I had been skeptical about how these would work — whether women with cancer would speak up, whether professionals would listen to us. The amount of time blocked out for the discussions is formidable. On Day 2, 90 minutes in the morning and two hours in the evening; on Day 3, another 90 minutes. Delegates choose a discussion topic at registration — prevention, screening, research, communication, etc. — and are then assigned to a round table with about ten other people. The compositon at each table remains intact for the three sessions, and progresses through three tiers of debate: first, defining the issues, then setting priorities, and finally developing action strategies. A leader guides the discussion at each table and a rapporteur takes notes, which are typed and distributed in time for the next discussion.

Two BCAM members, Joy Laverdure and Bev Campbell, choose a table on communication and find themselves the only lay participants in a nest of physicians. "Surprise" and "happiness" are the words Bev uses to express her reactions as the talk gets underway. "They spoke to me like I had lost my breast but not my brain," she says later. In another room, Darlene Betteley joins a discussion on the causes of breast cancer in a group at which women with breast cancer predominate. In their midst is the director of molecular oncology at a large cancer institute. "He said, 'You women have so much wisdom,'" Darlene recalls later.

"He had tears in his eyes. He told us he wished his wife could be there to join the conversation." Beth Savan, a biological scientist whose book *Science Under Siege* critiques mainstays of the research process such as peer review, is astonished at the extent of common ground among discussants at her table on research. Participants include Judy Erola, of the Pharmaceutical Association of Canada, and Lewis Slotin, head of the Medical Research Council of Canada.

At another research table, Neil assails a group of researchers, physicians and hospital administrators about the endless chemotherapy studies, and the persistent use of chemotherapy for metastatic disease. The discussion moderator is NCIC director David Beatty. "He agreed with me," says Neil, eyebrows raised. "In fact, they all agreed with me." Neil then siezes the moment to press a stickier point — advocacy representation on research committees. "Of course they all yattered on about peer review. So I just kept telling them we weren't going to go away, and they might as well start listening to us."

That evening, Beatty invites Neil to join him and Ron Buick for a beer.

"A boys' night out!" I laugh, when he tells me this.

He grins. "But I think I got through to them."

I remember the Honourable Pat Schroeder's advice to the NCCS audience on lobbying for the Women's Health Equity Act. "When Gilda Radner's husband came to the Hill to lobby, he got in to see everyone," she said. "Men listen to men, so it's good to have men join the lobbying."

The international speakers are on the program largely as lures to attract leading professionals to the conference. While some women with breast cancer opt out of these sessions in favour of more intimate hallway exchanges, many others listen attentively. On Monday morning, Richard Peto of Oxford presents the combined results of randomized clinical trials on all the standard breast cancer treatments. Up on the big screen to the left of the podium, slide after slide illustrates the nil effect of various standard treatments on the death rate. "Radiation has a net effect of zero on survival" Peto announces, matter-of-factly, as women who have gone obediently for radiation treatments gasp their disbelief.

Peto launches an appeal for his concept of an ideal research program: large randomized clinical trials that look exclusively at treatment effects on length of life. "Quality of life matters, but should not be assessed in the same study as quantity of life," he argues. "If consent procedures are made more complicated, we slow things down. Activists should collaborate with researchers on how to make trials simpler and more effective." Big. Fast. Simple.

I go to the mike. "You say any gains from radiation are cancelled out by the earlier deaths from side effects. What implications does that have for clinical practice?"

Peto, whose intense, craggy face is thrown mega-sized on the right-hand screen, runs his hand dramatically through his mane of wavy hair.

"You cannot treat breast cancer without hitting the heart!"

He goes on to nuance his reply with some codicils about improvements to radiation equipment and the possible differences between post-lumpectomy and post-mastectomy radiation. Evidently the big, fast, simple randomized trial that would answer my question more precisely has yet to be done.

Therapist Wendy Schain, the next featured guest speaker, is quick on her feet and not shy about challenging linear logic.

"I'm reminded, listening to Richard Peto, that men are from Mars, women are from Venus," she says. "Having us together on the same stage might have been someone's idea of science and sentiment." After a pause, she repeats: "You cannot treat breast cancer without hitting the heart."

Coming from her, the statement takes on an entirely different meaning. Schain, who has breast cancer herself, brings quality-of-life issues to the forefront. Cancer treatments wound us emotionally. Trials that ignore quality-of-life issues that are important to women will be skewed, she points out, because women might not participate properly. "If treatments are too noxious, people will drop out." All clinical trials should involve researchers from the social sciences, as well as the biological sciences, she says, to applause. She credits activism with giving women more say in the treatment process.

In the early hours of Tuesday morning, an earthquake shakes Montreal. In the activist camp, the event takes on mythic significance. *The earth moved. Did you feel it? A paradigm shift!*

Tuesday is the last day, and the program moves to a close: the last round of the discussions — action proposals; panel discussions on media coverage and privacy; the wrap-up plenary given by the chairs. I spend much of the afternoon sequestered in the SAN subcommittee room, preparing a final statement. I want to sound optimistic without being Pollyannaish. In the end I highlight the round tables as a model for collaboration, the openness of the scientific community to change, the need to broaden the focus of research, and the importance of keeping women with breast cancer involved in policy discussions. Pat urges caregivers to support a woman's choice of treatment. She summarizes the discussions about a national support network, which participants agreed should be survivor-driven, community based and fully accountable.

I feel exhausted but satisfied. It's been seven months since I was first approached about heading the subcommittee. My hope was that women with breast cancer would come to the conference in numbers, that they would participate, that we would find our voice. I can't believe that we will ever step back to the days of silence and shame.

As I chat with departing delegates in the Foyer, the picture clouds. For some women, the round-table discussions were a waste of time, if not a disaster. "The usual problem," says one woman curtly, "the men did all the talking." One of the Native women is still stunned that the entire program was developed with no attention to the spiritual, "no mention of the Creator." When I ask a journalist in her 30s what she thought of the Forum she replies, her voice dead, " I don't think they should have sent women to cover this." For many women, especially those undergoing treatment, the program was simply too long, too intense, too tiring.

A Question of Conflicts

When I try to reconcile the press' glowing reports in the days that follow the Forum with the distress felt by many women who participated, the most satisfying explanation I can come up with is Nils Christie's concept of conflicts as precious resources. Those of us with cancer face a conflict that has precious value. The medical system, casting us in the role of patient, disengages us from our conflict with the disease.

I hope some of the trauma women expressed after the Forum comes from struggling more actively than before with breast cancer as a conflict. If we acknowledge our place at the centre of this drama, we will feel turmoil. We will have to confront the truth about unchanging death rates and the inadequacy of current treatments. But we will gain the reward of being engaged. I don't believe struggles with professionals need to be acrimonious. But they will take the courage to act, and to speak out. At the Forum, for example, the aboriginal delegates made their vision — of cancer as a spiritual encounter — a reality. They retired to a secluded room one evening and held a sweetgrass ceremony. They also persuaded the Health Canada organizers to make room for Rita McComber of the Kahnawake reserve to say a prayer at the closing ceremonies. Small triumphs, perhaps, but real steps to reclaiming breast cancer as theirs.

In the wake of the Forum, Hilary Craig and her group of delegates from Saskatchewan best illustrate for me the momentum towards change. Upon their return home they called local reporters, who were eager to interview them. For a week, they ruled the airwaves in Saskatchewan. Community interest was so high they called a public meeting to talk about the Forum with people who had been unable to attend. A crowd of 100 turned up. Each woman who had gone to Montreal told her version of events at the Palais and answered questions. In the months that followed, the women started their own organization, Breast Cancer Action Saskatchewan, which issued pink tee-shirts to commemorate November 14 to 16. The tee-shirts read: *The earth moved ... the paradigm shifted ... and the dinosaurs dropped.*

As activists, we have moved one more step away from the prison of silence. From forming groups where we can talk among ourselves, we have progressed to putting our views on the public record, and still further to active engagement in policy debates. As the 1993 calendar closes, I envision another year of gradual gains. The reality is something else entirely.

Notes

1. Robert M. Wachter, *The Fragile Coalition: Scientists, Activists and AIDS*, (N.Y.: St. Martin's, 1991), p. 14.

2. Wachter, p. 14.

Act Four
Real Choices

Which is easiest to do,
Un-dish-cover the fish, or dishcover the riddle?

— Lewis Carroll, *Through the Looking Glass*

Something Fishy

March 13 was a Sunday. My phone began ringing around seven
AM. First friends, then reporters.

"Turn on your radio."

"Get the paper"

"Ms. Batt? Of BCAM? What do you have to say about this story?"

The headline, splashed across the front page, read: "City M.D.
tied to research fraud: U.S. probe casts shadow on key breast
cancer studies."[1] The dateline was Pittsburgh and the journalist,
John Crewdson, was a *Chicago Tribune* reporter working out of
Washington.

I read the story, my mouth open in astonishment. Dr. Roger
Poisson, a breast cancer surgeon and researcher at St. Luc hospital
— an easy mile from my apartment — had submitted false data to
a series of major research trials over a period of almost 13 years.
Not just any trials, but the large clinical trials that have set the
standard for breast cancer treatments around the world: B-06,
published in 1985 which ushered in the lumpectomy era; B-13,
published in 1989, which underpins the practice of giving
chemotherapy to women with Stage I disease; B-14, which showed
that tamoxifen benefits women with estrogen-positive tumours;

B-16, which showed that tamoxifen plus chemotherapy gave longer disease-free suvival for women over 50.

In some of the trials, Poisson had contributed large numbers of patients — up to 16 percent of the total volunteers in a single study. From 1977 to 1990, he had entered 1,511 women into 14 different breast cancer research trials. He had altered the files of at least 99 patients so that the women would be eligible. The discrepancies were deliberate falsifications, not clerical errors. For some patients, Dr. Poisson and his staff kept double records, one set labelled "true," the other "false." The false files went to the NSABP headquarters at the University of Pittsburgh, home of Bernard Fisher's huge breast cancer research empire.

Implicit in the story were shocking breaches of trust, beginning with Poisson's patients but casting a vast net that ensnared thousands of others: researchers who didn't cheat, other women who volunteered for trials in good faith, women with breast cancer who made treatment decisions based on the study outcomes, physicians, journal editors, and the American public, whose tax dollars underwrote the massive research program over several decades.

Poisson's patients were those most immediately betrayed. While some of the tampering would not affect the patient's treatment decision or her well-being — a fudged date of diagnosis, for example — other cases made me shiver. One woman was treated for a less-advanced condition than she actually had; another had a history of congestive heart failure and was entered in a trial testing the potent drug Adriamycin; a third had cancer diagnosed in both breasts but was classified as having only one breast affected and so had radiation to only one side of her body. In another case, the Poisson team continued to submit data to the NSABP for two years after the patient had died. They enrolled women before they had signed consent forms. They entered in trials two patients who had explicitly refused consent.

A second jarring aspect of the story was that various parties had known about the falsifications for years. The NSABP was first alerted to the trouble in mid-1990, when Fisher's staff came upon two different files for the same patient. Except for the dates of the woman's surgery, the records were identical. The staff examined other files from St. Luc and found more discrepancies. The NSABP waited for the results of the next scheduled audit, in September

1990, and they found more alterations. They waited five months to report the problem to the National Cancer Institute (NCI). Over the next three years, the health department's Office of Research Integrity (ORI) confirmed the fraud in a detailed investigation and prepared a report. But the editors of the *New England Journal of Medicine*, which published some of Fisher's key articles, had not heard of the fraud until Crewdson called them a week before breaking the story. Nor had Poisson's 99 patients been advised that their files were altered. The ORI and the NCI had been urging Fisher for more than a year to publish a corrected analyses of those studies in which the outcome might be affected, said Crewdson. But the NSABP intended to make nothing public until at least June — after the other members of the research group had been told about the problems at St. Luc.

"I am appalled," I told the first reporter who called. "It's an incredible story. The ramifications are too big to even grasp."

Poisson's name was only vaguely familiar to me. Like other sectors of Montreal, the medical community divides roughly down the centre of the city — English to the west, French to the east. Most of BCAM's members were west-siders, treated in the cluster of teaching hospitals associated with McGill University: the Royal Vic, the Montreal General, the Jewish General and St. Mary's. St. Luc is one of the parallel cluster of hospitals, linked to the *Université de Montréal* medical school. Our group was just beginning to extend its membership into the French milieu, so our grapevine about various physicians had significant east-side gaps.

Carolyn, however, remembered Poisson clearly.

"He was at the Forum," she told me after she read the story. "In fact, I got him on a committee."

Poisson, she explained, heard about the Forum and called the BCAM number to get more information. Caroline chatted with him for some time. "He seemed pleasant and genuine," she recalls.

His interest in the Forum impressed her as well. "I liked the fact that he was willing to make contact with an activist group," she adds. "A lot of doctors would never call us for information."

Although Carolyn, too, was aghast at the fraud, we both saw his wrongdoing as the symptom of a larger malaise. The case exposed faultlines in the medical research structures; the reward system in the research milieu; the code of secrecy that prevails in professional circles; the conflict of interest inherent in the physician-researcher role; patients' vulnerability to abuse of their files and of informed consent requirements. Poisson's defense — that he believed women he entered into studies would get better treatment — fed suspicions among members of our group that the system had two standards of care.

This was not the first time I'd heard that patients who are on protocol get a higher standard of care than those who are not in studies. Physicians who participate in research have a budget from the research group to hire administrative staff, to carry out regular follow-up tests, and so on. Over a 15-year period, St. Luc netted more than $1 million in NCI funds as a result of Poisson's enthusiastic participation as a trialist. Such an infusion of funds into a hospital budget might well be an incentive to favour patients who agree to enter studies.

As a patient who was in a study myself, I was certainly aware that my progress was being followed closely. I did not always experience this as a plus. During the eight months of my treatment, so many people were poking me and irradiating me and giving me conflicting information, I felt alienated from my body and from the treatment "team." One low point was an impromptu photo session with a young, male radiation technician, when I was stripped to the waist and positoned for a radiation. The technician, who explained that the photo was needed at the study headquarters in the U.S., seemed both embarrassed and unfamiliar with the camera. Other members of BCAM felt that their physicians did not spend much time with them or take sufficient interest in their case because they were not study subjects.

In her book *Alternatives*, Rose Kushner explained in detail the controversy over randomized clinical trials, adding that "we women are its victims." Fisher and his colleagues at the NSABP firmly believed in prospective clinical trials, in which large numbers of patients are assigned at random to different treatment groups and followed over a period of years. Critics of large-scale clinical trials argued that the controlled randomized clinical trial makes sense in theory, but randomizaton is an unattainable ideal.

Kushner was ambivalent about the debate. As an avid proponent of women's choice, she went to Dr. Thomas Dao precisely because she had decided against having a Halsted radical.

Dao was one of the few breast specialists in the United States in 1974 who was bucking the current norm and doing modified radicals. "To me," she said, "the requirement for randomization is difficult to understand, because ... as soon as a woman makes up her mind to see a doctor, she is already 'self-selected.'" Despite her reservations about clinical trials, she was frustrated by the impasse in treatment progress because neither women nor their physicians wanted to participate in trials. She worried that "the year 2000 will have come and gone and we will still not know whether breasts must be amputated to treat breast cancer."[2]

Dr. Poisson, according to his own defense in letters to the NSABP and the ORI, was an exuberant trialist, who chose not to be bound by the formalities of consent forms and trial eligibility restrictions, if it would mean a "nice case" would be "denied the right to enter a good protocol just on account of trivial details."[3]

"I'm not ashamed of having done my best to enter as many patients as possible in the various protocols," he wrote in a letter to Fisher. "However, obviously I'm paying attention too much to the great lines, the spirit, the philosophy and the reason behind the protocols and not enough to the forms or the details of the fine print. I see the forest and not enough of the trees."[4] He concluded gallantly by saying that his wife and co-investigator, surgeon Sandra Legault, "has nothing to do with the whole affair."

In their report, dated August 1991 and labelled "confidential/sensitive," the ORI investigators concluded that the changes to the files did represent falsifications. The nature of the tampering, from both a research and a medical standpoint, ranged from trivial to serious.[5] The pattern of falsification, they said, reflected a "utilitarian ethic which gave precedence to a high accrual rate over compliance with rules that the investigator thought ... would not affect the outcome of the trials." The ORI experts noted that a certain "sloppiness" had been considered acceptable in the early days of oncology clinical investigation, so that Poisson's disregard for eligibility criteria had historical roots; however, the field had long since matured and such carelessness is no longer considered tolerable. They felt Poisson had shown disrespect for the truth and deluded himself in thinking he was complying with the "spirit" of the protocol. Since they could not be certain whether they had found only the most clumsy changes, the ORI experts questioned whether any data from St. Luc could be considered reliable.

The ORI barred Poisson from further participation in U.S.-funded studies for eight years — at which time he would be 70 years old. The investigators cleared the junior staff from responsibility; similarly their findings did not implicate the hospital's other physicians, whose photocopied signatures had sometimes been added to the false documents without their knowledge or consent.

In his response to the report, Poisson suggested that on the clinician-researcher continuum, his orientation was towards the clinical pole. "I aways tried to do the best for my patients," he wrote, "and I strongly felt that for a patient to be in any official protocol, regardless of the arm, was better than to be treated off protocol ... I am not a Ph.D. in research. On the other hand, few would contest that I am a good surgeon and that I was devoted to the NSABP."[6]

As the story unfolded, reactions split along two lines. Many in the research community insisted the system had worked. The falsifications had been found and investigated. "One of the strengths of a multi-centre study is that the chance of a wrong conclusion because of one sloppy centre is much diminished," said Montreal oncologist Michael Pollack, in response to Crewdson's article.[7] Later the same week, senior investigators from six Montreal hospitals wrote a collective letter to local newspapers saying, "the system worked as it was intended to from the beginning. The integrity of the process and the efforts of men and women who contribute to the results as participants and investigators is strengthened by this process."[8]

Newspaper editorials generally took a less sanguine view. "Betrayal of trust" said one. "Grievous damage" and "scary attitude" wrote two columnists. Medical ethicists were another group of critics. "Dr. Roger Poisson ... may well go down in history as being guilty of one of the most serious breaches of the ethics of human experimentation," wrote Arthur Caplan of the University of Minnesota Medical School.

Judith Swazey was another critical voice in the scientific community.[9] Swazey heads the Acadia Institute in Bar Harbour Maine, and is a long-time student of professional ethics. "He destroyed trust," she said of Poisson in a radio interview. "In cases where he didn't get proper consent, he used people as guinea pigs."

Swazey has studied scientific misconduct for 20 years, and her studies included a national survey of faculty and doctoral students in various fields of science. She rejected the view of the Poisson incident as an isolated case: "… misconduct problems are certainly not epidemic in science but they are more common than many people would like to believe."

The failure to disclose the facts of the Poisson affair to the public was also familiar to Swazey. "It's a pattern we've seen over and over," she said. "Knowledge that something is wrong is kept in-house." Insiders, she explained, are very reluctant to make that knowledge public outside of their professional group. "They view it as an act of disloyalty to their colleague. They think if they ignore it it will simply go away and not be discovered."

Swayze blamed the scientific system. "There is pressure to enrol patients, there are high political stakes." We should ask, she said, if we are putting too much pressure on researchers, and why it took so long to get the story out in the open. Deception in research will never go away, because scientists are human. "What bothers me is the way institutions react. I certainly think we can do a much better job of how we respond to allegations of misconduct, [of] how openly and well they are dealt with."

A Debacle

Late in the week, a patient of Poisson's called to ask if our group planned to "do something."

"What do you suggest?"

All week I had answered calls from patients who phoned BCAM, from St. Luc or elsewhere. I listened to their stories, shared their indignation, and gave them any information I thought might be helpful. Reporters were hungry to get patients' views on the affair so if someone indicated she wanted to speak to press, I played liaison. Only one of BCAM's active members, Denise, had been treated at St. Luc, and she was Legault's patient, not Poisson's. We had not considered doing anything specifically on behalf of Poisson's patients.

"I feel isolated," said the woman. "The whole thing is eating at me. I'd like to meet with other patients, away from the hospital, and just talk about everything. Maybe together we can come up with a plan. I can't do it by myself, but your group could sponsor a meeting."

If BCAM could provide a service to patients from the hospital by providing a meeting spot and some moral support, why not? I thought. Joy liked the idea and agreed to coordinate it. She booked the church hall for the following Wednesday and assembled a committee: Denise and two patients from St. Luc who had phoned us. Almost a week had gone by since the news broke. We felt we should act quickly. Out went a press release.

Denise returned from work on Tuesday to find 25 messages awaiting her. Maybe we would have a bigger turnout than we thought. Some patients assumed the meeting was being called by the hospital. They asked if they needed to bring their files. Others stressed that they didn't want to see Poisson's reputation tarnished. He was a good doctor. Callers' interest was intense; so was their anxiety.

The next day, the day of the meeting, Dr. Legault called me. What did we plan to do? she asked. She was concerned that we wouldn't listen to patients who supported her husband. The press was only printing negative letters, she charged. I told her she should call the papers if she didn't like their coverage. We did not intend to censor anyone's opinions — the meeting would be an open discussion.

A wild thought flew through my mind: she and Poisson might actually attend.

"The meeting is for patients," I reminded her. "It wouldn't be appropriate for you or your husband to be there."

"My husband isn't well enough ..." she began. I'd heard on the news that Poisson was hospitalized for "a strong allergic reaction." He had just been released. "You don't think I should come ... ?" She sounded slightly hurt.

"Of course not. Patients would be intimidated."

The next call was a TV news reporter.

"What time does the meeting start?" he asked. "Reporters aren't allowed in," I told him.

I was beginning to feel nervous about the whole thing.

That evening, I arrived at 7:15. Joy's team was well organized. Two people would take names and phone numbers as people come in and hand out brochures about our group. Two others would monitor the door, letting patients in and keeping reporters out. Ginnette, Rose Mary, Ruth, Gabriella, Ruby, Zelda and Rose were all there to lend a hand. Denise would chair the meeting. About 50 chairs were arranged in concentric circles. There were two flip charts, a table with tea, coffee and cookies.

People had already begun to arrive. In droves. They were coming in too fast for the door monitors to get all the names. We started putting out more chairs. The mood — urgent, anxious — reminded me of our first meeting. By 7:30, the room was packed, with 80 or 100 people. Denise looked rattled.

"Dr. Legault is here," she said, gestering towards the window.

"Which one is she?"

Small, blond, 40ish, pretty, someone else whispered.

I picked my way through the throng. Four people who seemed to be together were sitting in the back row. I lean over the blond woman.

"Dr. Legault? ... I asked you not to come."

"I thought it best that I be here. I heard there would be reporters."

As we spoke, the TV journalist and his crew were banging at the door, explaining the sacred ritual of the set-up shot, trying to push through each time Lorraine cracked it open for the patients still arriving.

"We're not letting them in."

"Well, good. I agree with that." Legault hesitated. "What's wrong with me staying?" That same wounded tone. I was standing over her and she seemed very tiny. She had a cane.

"We want patients to talk freely. Your presence will be intimidating."

"Well, all right ..."

She made her way to the door and I went back to my seat, behind Denise.

Denise began her introduction. She described herself — a patient at St. Luc, distraught by these revelations; and she described BCAM — a voice for women with breast cancer, an educational group that encouraged patients to be informed and in control of their situation. She suggested some different avenues we might take and said she wanted to hear from the group.

A woman to our right stood and said she had had a lumpectomy. Was that an effective treatment, she asked the crowd.

Over to the left, someone else stood and testified that she too had had a lumpectomy. Now she was fine. A lumpectomy is less traumatic, she said.

The woman sitting next to Legault stood and said that our group was not competent to give people the medical advice they wanted. "And a doctor who could have responded to your questions was asked to leave!" she cried, indignantly, referring to Legault.

The next woman who got up began a long story involving a very aggressive tumour, delays, many doctors, aggressive chemotherapy and radiation. I was trying to grasp her point when someone tugged my sleeve.

"You've got to so something," she said urgently. It was one of the women I had asked to attend as a resource. "I've been to a lot of public meetings — I would say you have a very well organized faction that is here to disrupt the proceedings — including someone who works at the hospital."

Crowd control was not my forte. I felt overwhelmed by the size of the crowd, and the emotions. "What should I do? "

"I don't know, but you've got to think of something."

Several people began talking at once. One wanted to know if she was one of the 100 patients whose records were falsified.

If you take out the 100 patients, it doesn't make any difference, someone retorted. "The results are the same." The emotional temperature of the room moved upwards.

Ginette, a young nurse who belongs to our group, rose to explain that the results of the studies were being reanalyzed. When the new analysis was published we would know the answers to some of our questions. Right now, we couldn't know if the falsifications had changed the results.

A woman stated that she was not a patient of Dr. Poisson's, but that it was very serious to falsify data. Poisson had broken the confidence of patients.

Another woman retorted that she had confidence in Dr. Poisson.

Again the tone was veering towards something nasty, confrontational. Deena stood up. "We have to understand what this means," she said. "We all need to have confidence in our doctors, in research results." She tried to shift the discussion to the ethical questions of openness and trust, away from testimonials.

Now Rose stood up. "We all hope we had the right treatment. The problem is, our treatment is based on research. What we want for ourselves, and for our daughters, is accurate research, accurate information on which to base our decisions. We're not here to decide whether Dr. Poisson is a good doctor or not. We're here to talk about the consequences of falsifying research."

"Doctors are human. They all make mistakes," responded a man.

It was 8:50 PM. All around, faces showed the strain of agitation and fatigue. We heard a clatter at the door, and a stream of reporters burst into the hall, cameras aloft, microphones thrust out. Some participants left. Members of our group stayed behind to be interviewed; so did 30 or so patients.

Under the glare of TV lights and cameras flashing, journalists scuttled about, buttonholing everyone who was willing to describe what had gone on. Many had already interviewed Dr. Legault, who had held court on the sidewalk throughout the meeting. The melee in the hall rivalled the chaos of the meeting. The reporters were in clover. A TV journalist from *Radio Canada* cornered me. One of his crew beamed a light in my face, the other aimed the camera. "People were upset that you couldn't answer their questions," he charged.

His goading worked. "The point of the meeting wasn't to discuss medical questions," I cried. "We make no pretense of having medical expertise. The point was to discuss our concerns, as patients, about the falsification of research data and patient's records. Unfortunately, Doctor Legault decided to come to the meeting, with a group of Dr. Poisson's supporters. We were not able to have an open discussion."

A few hours later, a report on the meeting played on the late-night news. I appeared briefly, distress clearly written on my face. The meeting had one good outcome, the report concluded — it gave patients the chance to exchange phone numbers. The next morning a radio account awakened me: a clip of an outburst from Deena, outraged at Dr. Legault's presence at the meeting, juxtaposed with Dr. Legault, chastising our group. In the French tabloid, *Le Journal de Montréal,* the meeting was a *soirée houleuse* (tumultuous evening). The report was sympathetic to Poisson supporters and to Dr. Legault, who was described as having been "bluntly shown the door." A *La Presse* story, more sympathetic to our group, headlined a meeting that "degenerated into squabbling" (*se déroule dans la bisbille*).[10]

At BCAM's post-mortem get-together, we all agreed on one thing: the event was a disaster. The last thing we had wanted was to send patients home more upset than when they had arrived. We had not been prepared for the size of the gathering, much less for the presence of an organized lobby group or an acrimonious debate. Overnight, our hard-won reputation as an articulate, coherent voice had acquired an ugly counterpoint — we were seen as raucus and divided.

But the meeting had highlighted a genuine difference in the way women with breast cancer respond to activism. Many cancer patients have profound feelings of loyalty to their physician. They shrink from any action that could be interpreted as lack of gratitude. They frame the problems they encounter as being beyond control — they are "part of life" or "human error" rather than the result of a system with terms that can be negotiated. Even women who identify with an activist philosophy may feel too vulnerable in the months after their diagnosis to speak out and run the risk of antagonizing their treatment team.

In the past, BCAM had dealt with these realities by directing our critique at systemic issues, not at individuals. The Poisson Affair forcibly brought home to us that the system is made up of individuals. A crisis that involves real choices puts the lives and reputations of real people on the line. Not only was Poisson's professional reputation in ruins, his patients faced agonizing decisions about whether to disrupt the continuity of their medical care by changing doctors or hospitals.

Meanwhile, the NCI announced its intention to sue St. Luc to recoup the $1 million-plus the hospital had received from the NSABP over the years. Patients had good reason to worry about what would happen to them and their files if such a suit proceeded. The hospital announced that it did not have the money and intended to fight any suit. In hindsight, we marvelled at our own naiveté. ("We thought we could just serve tea and cookies and have a friendly little discussion," someone laughed ruefully.)

What started as the Poisson Affair, however, was no tea party. As the weeks went by, more shocks followed in quick succession. Bernard Fisher resigned as head of the NSABP. Recruitment for all NSABP trials was put on hold. The ORI widened its investigatory net to other hospitals, including the one where I had been treated and entered in a clinical trial. In Washington, a series of hearings probed the upper reaches of the National Cancer Institute.

The most significant commotion was no longer in Montreal. As events in Washington, Bethesda and Pittsburgh gathered momentum, the events at St. Luc were at the tail of a floundering whale.

Shake-up

Bernard Fisher resigned from his post as head of the NSABP at the end of March, at the request of officials at the National Cancer Institute. Over a 40-year period, the NCI had poured over $119 million into Fisher's centre at Pittsburgh, allowing him to mount some 31 comparative studies of treatments in cancer of the breast and bowel. Ostensibly, at least, the last straw for the NCI was Fisher's failure to tell the agency about questionable data at St. Mary's hospital, which Fisher had known about since September 1993.

My hospital. Could the drama become any more surreal, I wondered, as I skimmed the newspaper accounts. "Investigators swooped down on St. Mary's in mid-afternoon on Monday," said one. The six-person team, made up of investigators from the NSABP, the NCI and the ORI, told hospital staff late Sunday they would arrive the next day. The cue for the high-level audit, they said, was a changed date on a single file, uncovered in a routine check the previous fall.[11]

Two weeks later, the auditing team left, having combed through two-thirds of the hospitals 285 research files. They found a total of five irregularities, involving three patients, all of them in the Tamoxifen Prevention Trial. The investigatory team wasn't sure if the changes, altered dates of laboratory tests, were fabrications. They left without completing the audit, after issuing a statement to say they would return at the end of the month and complete their report promptly.

South of the border, meanwhile, Congressional hearings into the NCI's part in the whole affair got underway, chaired by Congressman John Dingell of Michigan. When the congressional hearings began April 13, the affair took on Watergate overtones. American politicians moved to the fore in the news stories and I lost the flow of what was happening. From the beginning, many of the principles, such as Poisson and Fisher, issued statements only through their lawyers. Most of the manoeuvring seemed less about women with breast cancer than about powerful people and institutions playing with a volatile situation to advance or protect their interests.

When NCI director Sam Broder was asked to explain why the NCI had not disclosed the Poisson fraud to the public, Broder said Fisher's "formidable intellect" and "formidable renown" had intimidated his officials. The NCI also complained that the NSABP was slow to verify the cause of the deaths of women diagnosed with endometrial cancer while taking tamoxifen. Zeneca, the company that manufactures tamoxifen, tabled a memo detailing conversations in which the company grappled with the increasing number of patients on tamoxifen who were developing endometrial cancer. According to the memo, Fisher worried about potential negative media coverage if the company changed its consent forms for the European prevention trial.

The NSABP's defenders had used the "bad apple" analogy to contain the initial public outrage at Poisson's fraud. Now the NCI was using the same strategy: dump Fisher and turn the breast cancer research empire over to new management. After firing Fisher and his chief statistician, Carol Redmond, the NCI invited bids from other researcher groups willing to take over the NSABP program. Breast cancer research was up for auction.

Fissures

St. Mary's is a small community hospital, tucked away on a one-way street on the edge of a residential neighbourhood. On May 18, the oncology ward is crowded. Everyone is griping because the doctor was an hour late for the clinic and now our appointments are bumped forward. Business as usual — at least on the surface.

What's changed since I was here last December is that Bernard Fisher's international breast cancer empire is on the verge of toppling, ostensibly because of a discrepancy in one file at this very hospital. Since my files are part of the hospital's collection[12] I feel the investigation concerns me too.

"How does it feel to be investigated?" I ask my oncologist. He has declared me roadworthy for another six months, barring an unforeseen calamity.

"Terrible. Like a witch hunt. Why St. Mary's and why now? The NCI knew months ago that one of the files here had a discrepancy. Why didn't they investigate then?"

"Are they finished?" I haven't read anything in the papers about

St. Mary's since the investigating team left town, leaving the audit hanging in mid-air.

"No."

"But don't you agree that the public should have been told about St. Luc ages ago?"

"You tell me. When the NCI found out about it, they ordered the NSABP not to say anything."

Now that the white heat of judgement has turned from Poisson and St. Luc to the two big American agencies, I've begun to wonder if the public will ever be able to sort truth from self-serving posturing. I'm awed by the myriad of investigatory bodies that kick in when a scandal erupts in the U.S., but the tons of paper that are generated can obscure as much as they reveal.

"I believe the NSABP is a good group," says my doctor, with conviction. "It's well run. Far better run than a lot of the others. And treatment changes in the last 20 years have made a difference. Not dramatic, but early detection is making a difference. So is chemotherapy."

"What about my file — was I in an NSABP trial?"

"No, you were in a CLGB study — the Cancer and Leukemia Group B. The ORI and NCI auditors checked those files as well — including yours. It's right here," he says, gesturing wearily to a stack of files a few inches thick. "No mistakes."

This seems like a good time to clear up the mystery of my treatment plan, which has baffled me for five-and-a-half years. Once the treatments were over, I hadn't particularly wanted to revisit the decision I made in that time of crisis, but the experience with the tumour board had undermined my confidence in the whole process.

"I never understood why was I given CAF when the tumour board recommended CMF and tamoxifen."

"Well I don't remember your specific case," my doctor says, "but I can guess what happened. It's the policy at this hospital to offer every patient who is eligible the chance to go into a trial. Usually these are NSABP trials — that was our first choice. But you were Stage II and the most recent NSABP trials were geared to earlier stage patients. Since you weren't eligible for an NSABP trial, the tumour board would have recommended that you have the standard treatment — CMF. Probably I found out later you were eligible for this CLGB trial. We didn't put many patients into that study — you were one of just a few. But it's an important study," he says, brightening just a shade.

I've waited five years to understand how the crucial decision about my treatment was made. Now, the mystery is resolved by the regulatory fine print of research administration: trial eligibility criteria. As the endpoint of my lengthy quest, it seems wanting.

"Well, you should have told me what was going on," I say. "I was totally confused."

Even as I speak, I know that a discussion of trial eligibility rules would have been even more tedious to me in the weeks after my diagnosis than it is now. My mind was attuned to the immediate crisis in my own life.

Now, my real interest is in the big picture and how to change it. The Poisson Affair exposes longstanding fissures in the cancer infrastructure. They include: the focus on treatment and the "big research" model for answering questions; the mysterious world of breast cancer researchers, insulated from women with the disease; the paternalistic attitudes and the hierarchies; the quantity- over quality-of- life mindset; the emphasis on control; the science-business-government triumverate; the role of the emerging activist movement in the whole. The Poisson crisis could be a constructive hiatus that allows everyone to take stock and rebuild the structure. More likely, the result will be a patch-job, and more of the same.

Women with breast cancer need to evaluate the legacy of the Fisher years using our own interests as the yardstick. The accuracy of studies carried out under the auspices of the NSABP is only the most obvious area of concern to us.

Since the NSABP program underpins much of what western medicine defines as standard treatment for breast cancer, we need to assess what these studies tell us about the usefulness of various breast cancer treatments. At a meeting of clinical oncologists in Dallas on May 18, Fisher reviewed the results of 22 published studies, with and without Roger Poisson's data, and declared the results "monotonously similar." Fisher's reanalyses are unlikely to be the last word since audits of other centres continue to turn up new cases of fraudulent data. Eventually, however, a penultimate review of the NSABP program of breast cancer studies will likely appear, with all certifiably fraudulent data removed. Regardless of the results, this type of narrow recalculation is not enough.

Defined as the Gold Standard in breast cancer research, the results of NSABP studies have consistently overshadowed the results of smaller studios carried out elsewhere to answer essentially the same questions. A salutary effect of the data-fraud escapade would be to remind all concerned that a Gold Standard is an unattainable ideal that depends upon an oversimplification of reality. The very weight of its "formidable reputation" removes it from scrutiny. A statement by NCI director Sam Broder, in mid-June, that he wanted to return the research project "to its previous glory"[13] suggests that this will not be a moral drawn by establishment leaders.

Fomenting a crisis over the tarnished results of the Fisher oeuvre does not aid women trying to make a decision in a time of extreme duress either. The sad truth is that breast cancer research has not shown dramatic treatment benefits. This is why re-analyzing Fisher's studies is unlikely to reveal that mastectomies, for example, are vastly superior to lumpectomies.

As befits a Gold Standard, results of Fisher's studies have tended to be translated too dogmatically into standard practice. The routine use of radiation after a lumpectomy and the hyping of tamoxifen illustrate the transformation of potentially valuable insights to the status of Great Truths. Research results should not overwhelm personal and practical considerations that are equally important to the woman's treatment decision.

The NSABP research empire embodied certain values about how breast cancer research should best be done. The stress on size, on quantitative measurement, on tests of interventions, and on randomized prospective studies all reveal a bias towards the male values of heroic intervention and control. The rush to control the NSABP crisis with firings and by implementing more thorough audits similarly reflects a macho-authoritarian vision of problem-solving. Now is the time to propose an approach to breast cancer research that is informed by a more balanced set of values.

BCAM's prevention panel in April is our group's first chance to reposition itself since the meeting for St. Luc patients. From the beginning, we have defined prevention as one of the most important questions about breast cancer. All three of our panelists are prominent advocates for change: Devra Lee Davis, John Bailar, and Judy Brady.

Although the panelists all build their arguments around what I think of as the feminine value pole, they differ significantly in what they think causes breast cancer and how it can be prevented. Even with the scope of discussion narrowed to the point where everyone agrees on the general aims, I realize the decisions we must make are not obvious.

Real Choices

The cancer establishment is at a crucial juncture. So is the breast cancer activist movement. At last we confront real choices.

One set of choices will define the movement's stance towards doctors and researchers. Knocking the professionals can be a too-easy outlet for our frustration. As Robert Wachter points out in his analysis of the AIDS movement, many physicians and health researchers are liberal democrats, basically sympathetic to activist goals. Much activist anger is justified, but lashing out blindly alienates even the most tolerant. We have gained a measure of participation and we need to consider how to use those gains to our advantange, not squander them. Wachter argues that the AIDS struggle will be won by a fragile coalition between activists, scientists and policymakers. My experience with the National Forum on Breast Cancer suggests that a similar alliance in breast cancer is possible.

Furthermore, failure to forge professional alliances could be disastrous. Margaret Waller, one of BCAM's founders, points to the ruins of mental health reform as a worst-case scenario. In the 1960s, patients' rights activists rebelled (with good reason) against a system in which those in severe mental distress were institution-alized and drugged. Mental health activists failed, however, to build alliances among sympathetic professionals or to create an alternative structure. Patients' malaise gave governments an excuse to cut funding. When hospitals emptied their psychiatric wards into the streets, the former inmates were left to fend for themselves. Our goal is not to become street people. Many of us need medical care. We want a humane system that provides for those needs and we deserve no less.

The targets of our wrath, and our efforts for change, should be the inhumane values entrenched in the system. Stock tactics for exploiting us include the opportunistic manipulation of our vulnerability, especially of our deepest emotions: fear and hope. Our best weapon against these systemic poisons is our own voices. As we speak out, we will find that many professionals share our eagerness to reject the values of oppression.

Another set of choices are the priorities we push for in cancer policy. An approach that promotes primary prevention is long overdue. Modern industrialized countries — with the intriguing exception of Japan — have the highest breast cancer rates in the world. We need to confront this reality and its many ramifications. After a century of effort, high-tech medicine has not brought the incidence of cancer down or significantly changed the death rate.

We need to face the limits of medical technology. We know from the examples of heart disease and lung cancer that science can also be harnassed in the interest of low-tech, preventive approaches. But the discoveries are only useful if we adopt strong social and political measures to implement what we learn. We don't need more studies to prove that radiation and toxic chemicals are bad for our health. The existence of polluting industries in our countries is not secret. We know that the biotech, pharmaceutical and nuclear industries are powerful lobby groups. Those of us with cancer are in a unique position to challenge the overblown claims of these commercial interests.

A third set of choices has to do with the shape our own movement takes. Five years ago, in the first flush of coming out, I made the flattering assumption that a cancer activist movement would be self-purifying. Those of us who are fighting for our lives, I thought then, would have no time for self-deception and ego-trips. We would transform the awareness of our mortality into moral courage.

After several years as an activist, I no longer believe this malarkey. Women with breast cancer are subject to human foibles; the movement we are still building is susceptible to internal stresses and harbours its share of pettiness and power struggles. We are individuals with differing world views. We can harness this richness or splinter into bickering factions. As activists, we must insist on openness and accountability from the leaders and organizations that act in our name — in short, we must demand of ourselves the same standard of behaviour we want from others.

Notes

1. John Crewdson, "City M.D. Tied to Research Fraud," *The Gazette*, (Mar. 13, 1994), p. A1.

2. Kushner, pp. 228-233.

3. Lyle Bivens, "St. Luc Hospital NSABP Project Report," and related documents, [Rockville, Md: Office of Research Integrity], (Feb. 10, 1993), p. 4.

4. Bivens, p. 5.

5. Bivens, p. 28.

6. Bivens, pp. 84-85.

7. Carolyn Adolph, "Patients Angered by Cancer Work," *The Gazette*, (Mar. 14, 1994), p. A1.

8. R. Margolese, H. Shibata, A. Robidoux, M. Thirvell, J. Keyserlingk, D. Stern, "Results of Flawed Cancer Study Still OK," *The Gazette*, (Mar. 17, 1994), p. B2.

9. Judith Swazey, interviewed on *As it Happens*, CBC Radio, (Mar. 15, 1994), and *Quirks and Quarks*, CBC Radio, (Mar. 19, 1994); see also Judith P. Swazey et al, "Ethical Problems in Academic Research," *American Scientist*, (Nov./Dec. 1993), pp. 542-553.

10. Claire Harting, "Soirée houleuse des patientes du Dr. Roger Poisson: Des femmes à la défense du médicin," *Le Journal de Montréal*, (Mar. 24, 1994), p. 5; and André Noel, "Une assemblée de patientes du docteur Roger Poisson se déroule dans la bisbille," *La Presse*, (Mar. 24, 1994), p. A2.

11. Carolyn Adolph, "Cancer Work at St. Mary's Investigated," *The Gazette*, (Mar. 30, 1994), p. A1.

12. In Canada, a patient's file belongs to the doctor who holds it, although the patient has a right to examine and copy it. See *DES Action Canada Newsletter*, (Fall 1993).

13. "Chief of Cancer Study Apologizes on Leaving," *New York Times*, (June 14, 1994).

FIVE

Brugge

*Come to the Lancet conference, where the aim
is to challenge dogma and redirect research
efforts along more fruitful lines.*
— *Lancet*, Feb. 6, 1993

Brugge
April 1994

*In the 19th century it was British travellers ... who rediscovered
Brugge and spread its fame as a perfectly preserved medieval town.
A novel by Georges Rodenbach, Bruges the Dead, brought more visitors
but created an image that has been difficult to throw off.*

— Fodor's travel guide to Belgium, on Brugge

"The Challenge of Breast Cancer" is billed as a conference with
a difference. "This is not a meeting for the fainthearted," declares
the brochure. The call for papers appeals to "self-styled
revolutionaries" while supporters of the status quo are warned to
be there, "if only to defend their research budgets." The place for
this historic duel between scientific iconoclasts and the old guard
is the picturesque medieval town of Brugge, in Belgium.

Britain's premier medical journal, the *Lancet*, had thrown
down the gauntlet in an unusual editorial in February, 1993. With
considerable fanfare, a year earlier, the *Lancet* had published
world overviews of clinical trials to test the effects of tamoxifen
and cytotoxic drugs as adjuvant breast cancer treatments. Back
then, the articles were hailed as evidence that the use of systemic
drug treatments — especially tamoxifen — helped prevent the
spread of early breast cancer. Now, with the clatter of scales falling
from learned eyes, the *Lancet*'s editors thank *Vogue* magazine for
drawing attention to "the ineluctable truth": women still die of
breast cancer. This, says the editorial, despite "the media hype, the

triumphalism of the profession in published research, and the almost weekly miracle breakthroughs trumpeted by the cancer charities ..."

I haven't been to Europe since my cycling trip of 1988 when I discovered the lump in my breast. Superstition has held me back. For me, walled villages with winding cobbled alleyways evoke the spectre of breast cancer. *Move towards fear*, the saying goes. I book my flight for Brugge.

An incentive beyond the promised scientific iconoclasm is that two American activists, Kay Dickersin and Susan Love, have landed a slot on the program. Along with Hazel Thornton, a British woman with breast cancer who writes patient's viewpoint pieces for the *Lancet*, they will talk, on Day Two, about the patients' role in research. The American women have also called on activists from other countries to attend an informal pre-conference meeting, to form the beginnings of an international consumer-driven advocacy network. While this movement is well underway in the U.S. and Canada, I am not aware of activist groups on other continents.

"We've found one in Ireland," says Kay, hopefully, when I call her to say I am coming. "We've put feelers out all over, but you're right, it is still a North American thing. Do you know of anyone in Australia ... ?"

At the appointed time I arrive in the lobby of the Holiday Inn, in central Brugge, to find Kay chatting with Stephanie Clark, a *Lancet* editor and one of the conference organizers. The only other person in sight is a bulky man leaning against the check-in desk. He looks more like a journalist than a medical researcher.

"He's from ABC-TV," confirms Kay.

Press passes have been judiciously allocated. I had tried myself to obtain one, in the hope of circumventing the hefty conference fee, but Clark tells me that with a few exceptions the press will be charged the same fee as everyone else. In keeping with the meeting's ground-breaking ambitions, the journal has opted not to seek pharmaceutical company support — unusual for an international cancer conference. To keep costs down, even the speakers have to pay their own plane fares. Nor has the *Lancet* seen its way to granting women with cancer a special rate. With a $700 fee, on top of accommodation and plane fare, even if there are breast cancer activists in far-flung corners of the globe, I can't see many pilgriming to Brugge.

"These are the women who replied," says Kay, handing a sheaf of papers to a woman who has just joined us. She is Barbara Balaban, a social worker who runs a breast cancer hotline at Adelphi University in Long Island. "It's hard to tell who is actually coming."

Barbara rifles through the papers. One form is from Israel, two from Peru, another from Australia. Barbara concludes that they wanted to attend but couldn't afford the trip. I had hoped Belgium, at least, would supply a contingent. Belgian women rank high in breast cancer incidence, so even tiny Brugge would have a quota of women affected. But there were none to be seen.

And so we are five: Susan Love, Kay Dickersin and Barbara Balaban from the U.S., Hazel Thornton from Britian and me. We create a meeting space in the hospitality area, between the hotel registration desk and the tables set up for conference registration. A woman journalist from ABC sits on the periphery of the group taking notes. Love, crosslegged on the floor, in jeans and a sweater, resembles a college student taking a break from her studies more than a celebrated surgeon-author-researcher-activist.

Hazel tells us she became a consumer advocate after being asked to join a study on ductal carcinoma in situ (DCIS). The DCIS trial had a radiotherapy treatment arm, one with five years of tamoxifen, one with tamoxifen and radiotherapy and a control (no treatment) group. During the two weeks in which she had to make her decision, she discovered papers which showed no benefit for radiotherapy, but potential after effects, although the trialists claimed to have no idea which treatment was best. To decide about hormones, she had to obtain information from her dossier. She was so appalled by the prospect of being randomly assigned to one of the four treatment groups that she wrote an article, "Breast Cancer Trials: A Patient's Viewpoint." In her article, she concluded that it was unethical to expect the woman to do her own research, and that trial candidates were deprived of support from their physicians during the most critical two weeks, because trialists did not want to influence the woman's decision. She declined to enter the trial. The *Lancet* ran her article alongside its world overview on breast cancer treatment.[1] Hazel has since penned a dozen articles and letters on the ethics of randomized trials. Despite her passion for the cause, Hazel is a self-declared loner. She hasn't tried to rally other British women to action and steadfastedly resists Kay's cajoling efforts to push her in that direction.

Susan Love recaps the American womens' accomplishments of the past few years — the burgeoning of activist groups since 1991, the letter campaign, the money appropriated from the Army budget for research, the new, political commitment to breast cancer, helped by the movement's support in high places. "Clinton's mother died of breast cancer in January," she points out. The wife of a prominent NCI official also has breast cancer. Love agrees with Hazel: women with breast cancer must be part of the research planning. "Of course the scientists would like us to be the women's auxiliary, and just raise money," she says cheerfully. In her activist hat, Love jettisons her scientist identity, talking of breast cancer researchers as The Others. "I don't have breast cancer — yet," she says, grinning up at Kay who is sitting on a couch. "But I think maybe it's contagious." She helped get the movement rolling, she explains, now she wants women with breast cancer to lead it.

Kay Dickersin started a survivor-run support group for women with breast cancer after her diagnosis because her city, Baltimore, Maryland had none. When the National Breast Cancer Coalition (NBCC) was formed, she turned from support to advocacy work. Two of her three sisters have been diagnosed with breast cancer since then, and they are part of the breast cancer gene study headed by Mary-Claire King in Los Angeles. A scientist herself, Kay has a doctorate in epidemiology. As an activist, she is most interested in the participation of lay women in research.

"We need more people in the movement," she sighs. Her volunteer work with the National Coalition is squeezing time from her family life and her teaching job at the University of Maryland. "There's so much to do. We're going to burn out." She notes that activists who don't have breast cancer, like Love and Barbara Balaban, are vital.

Barbara set up the breast cancer hot line at Adelphi, on Long Island. "Are you involved in the pesticide research project?" I ask.

"Is she involved!" laughs Susan Love. "She started it!"

Barbara explains how the project grew out of the Island's high rate of breast cancer and the refusal of politicans and scientists to look at the possible role of environmental contaminants. She organized the November 1993 workshop on environmental causes of breast cancer, co-chaired by Love and Devra Lee Davis, which generated funding for research into toxins and breast cancer.

The others turn to me. "What's happening in Canada?"

I explain how the Parliamentary inquiry that eventually resulted in the National Forum on Breast Cancer raised public awareness of the issues and helped stimulate the nascent grass-roots movement. Like the American cancer researchers, those in Canada would like advocates to lobby for funds and hand them the money with no strings attached, I say. But with support from federal policy makers, we worked on an equal footing with researchers at the Forum. Now, I explain, we have a say in helping to set research priorities — but not study and trial design.

"The peer review system won't change without a political battle," I add.

"Of course not," says Love. "But by raising the money, we can negotiate for a say."

"Bernard Fisher is opposed to consumer participation in research," Kay interjects. "He said that at the 1993 meeting of the American Society for Clinical Oncologists — and got an ovation."

The talk turns to Fisher's ousting and the NSABP. Love gives her summation of the situation, then flashes her grin at the journalist. "Not for quotation," she says.

I want to know more about events in England, especially two activist groups I've read about. One, called Radiation Action Group Exposure (RAGE), was organized by women with breast cancer who suffered radiation damage from their radiotherapy.

"That would be Lady Audrey Ironside and Jan Millington," says Hazel.

"Are they here?"

"Oh, no. The women in RAGE are very ill."

I'm shocked to hear this, though it seems obvious on reflection that they would not take legal action over radiation injury unless they were faring badly. Later I learn that a lawyer involved in the womens' injury claims is here at the Brugge meeting.

"What about the group from the Bristol Cancer Centre?" I wonder.

Hazel brightens. "Heather Goodare! She's right over there, in the blue cape."

An animated woman with a bob of white hair is part of a small gathering near the registration desk.

Our group is breaking up, with no real plan except to find women in more countries and to keep in touch. Susan Love, explaining that she wants to work out the kinks from the long plane trip, jogs off towards the nearest exit. Someone suggests a newsletter as a practical means for communication. Kay looks hopefully at me. Another newsletter is too exhausting to contemplate right now. "Let's get Hazel to introduce us to Heather Goodare," I suggest, steering Kay towards the knot of new arrivals.

They are all from England: Heather, Hazel's husband and a short, gray-haired woman named Ann Johnson. I wonder if she has breast cancer too. "Ann's an oncologist," says Hazel.

She doesn't look like an oncologist, I think to myself, but before I can pinpoint how she is different from the generic oncologist in my mind's eye, I catch Heather saying something about tamoxifen.

"… so I told them this was a quality of life issue and they should put a warning on their consent forms. Or they could get in BIG trouble."

"Hot flashes?" I ask.

"No, singing voice! I lost my singing voice when I took tamoxifen," declares Heather.

"I've never heard of that one," I say, all ears.

"Of course not, they don't tell you," she says. "But doesn't it make sense? When you take a drug that affects female hormones, it changes the upper registers of your voice. I couldn't sing anymore, and I couldn't yell at my husband either." She laughs.

"I told them at Zeneca that Kathleen Ferrier refused to have hormonal treatments. In those days, that could mean an oophorectomy."

"Who is Kathleen Ferrier?"

She and Ann exchange glances, then look at me.

"You don't know about Kathleen Ferrier? The opera singer?"

"She's too young," says Ann, in my defense.

"Kathleen Ferrier died in 1952," Heather explains. "Of breast cancer. She refused to let them remove her ovaries because she had been told it might ruin her singing voice and she wanted to go to the grave with the voice God gave her. She sang two performances of Orpheus that were glorious. Then she died. She was 42."

In my book this is compelling evidence, but I wonder how it would go down in Zeneca's boardroom. "What did the drug company say?" I ask.

"Well of course they didn't take me very seriously at first. So I wrote a letter to the *Lancet* that was published. I said that because I have breast cancer I could accept permanently losing my singing voice as a trade-off, but I should have been told about it so I could make an informed choice. But imagine if you were a singer who was thinking of going into the prevention trial! You should know that you could lose your voice. Well, after my letter appeared in the *Lancet*, the trialists changed their information forms."

"Bravo," I say, impressed.

Kay has a pre-conference dinner meeting with the other conference speakers. Heather and Ann invite me to join them at a pub opposite their hotel. I accept eagerly. I'm curious about Ann and I want to learn about the Bristol affair.

Heather's Story

The pub is a neighbourhood gathering-place on one of the canals, away from the touristy town centre. Warmed by a delicious house soup, a tankard of Belgian beer and a heaping plate of mussels, I settle in to hear Heather's story.

Heather was in her mid-fifties when she learned she had breast cancer, in 1986. She was married, a former editor, with a 15-year-old son. She collected every book and pamphlet she could find about breast cancer and brought them to the hospital where she read them on the sly ("I had an instinct some of them might be thought somewhat subversive"). Her surgeon was "into lumpectomies" so she emerged from the hospital minus a five-centimetre lump and six lymph nodes (two positive), but with her breast intact.

An old publishing colleague told her about the Bristol Cancer Help Centre. Heather decided to spend a day there to help cope with her depression and emotional turmoil. Her GP encouraged her to go, but her oncologist sniffed, "I don't care if you go to Bristol and stain yourself yellow with carrot juice, my dear." Feeling patronized and snubbed, she stuck to her guns. Her husband found money to pay the costs, and they set out together.

Bristol, by oncology standards, was a daring experiment. Begun in 1979, the centre soon won international aclaim for its gentle, holistic approach to cancer treatment: touch "healing," psychological counselling, art therapy, relaxation exercises, meditation and a low-fat diet of vegetables and protein from soya. These treatments were offered on a user-pay basis to cancer patients, nearly all of whom had undergone conventional medical treatment. About one-third of the patients who went to Bristol had breast cancer.

On their first visit, patients could go for a week-long course, or for a single day. Heather opted for the one-day course. The counselling, in particular, affected her profoundly, and her husband as well.

"What we found at Bristol was very simple, really: people who listened and reminded us that we were in charge of our own lives, that we did have choices."

On her return, her oncologist recommended both tamoxifen and radiation to her breast. The oncologist dismissed her fears of side effects from radiation and assured her tamoxifen had no side effects.

"I wasn't given the full facts, so I had no real choice," she says of both the radiation and tamoxifen. She suffered fibrosis from the radiation, which has become steadily worse, and developed endometrial polyps from the tamoxifen, as well as the damage to her singing voice. She had been a serious amateur singer so she felt the loss of her voice acutely.

Heather returned to the Bristol Cancer Help Centre a total of six times in the first year after her diagnosis. She was so struck by the gap in emotional support for cancer patients, she took a counselling skills course at her local community college so she could help other cancer patients. "That one-year course became a two-year certificate, then a full post-graduate university diploma."

She now has a private practice as a counsellor to a clientele which includes many people with cancer. She also wanted to help health professionals face up to the psychological and emotional implications of the disease — not just on behalf of their patients, but in themselves.

"Health professionals have difficulty just saying the word cancer," she says. "One of the staff at my local clinic even ticked me off for saying it. 'We don't use that word here,' she told me.

"Not all patients need or want professional counselling," says Heather, "but all of them need to be listened to. And if they think that it was the boss, or British Nuclear Fuels, or their divorce, or their Chinese horoscope for that matter, that caused their cancer, what the professionals think about it is largly irrelevant. Their search for meaning may be a very important part of the healing process."

In mid-1986, the staff and patients at Bristol decided they would like to see the benefits of the centre validated scientifically. They invited a team of doctors and scientists to discuss how this could be done. Two studies were proposed, one to evaluate quality of life, the other, disease progress and length of life. Money for the research came from Britain's two major cancer charities, the Cancer Research Campaign and the Imperial Cancer Research Fund. Heather was among the participating patients. She religiously completed the periodic questionnaires that came in the mail asking about her quality of life.

Four years later, a paper on the Bristol Cancer Help Centre appeared in the *Lancet*.[2] The results were a bombshell. The 334 women who attended Bristol were twice as likely to die, and three times more likely to suffer spread of their cancer, than a control group of women who underwent conventional treatment only. The day before publication, the sponsoring charities took the unusual step of calling a news conference to which they invited 100 journalists.

Heather heard the news on television and was outraged. The report said nothing of quality of life, nor had anyone contacted her to inform her in advance of the devastating finding — which made so little sense as to be unbelievable. The researchers speculated that perhaps the Bristol women died earlier because of their stringent diet. The study made headlines worldwide and struck a blow to the concept of complementary healing techniques. Within weeks, however, the researchers admitted the study was fundamentally flawed. A comparison of the control and study groups showed the women from Bristol suffered more advanced disease to begin with than the women who did not attend. The groups were supposed to have been matched for stage of disease but they were not.

Two months after the study was published the lead researcher, Professor Timothy McElwain of the Institute of Cancer Research, committed suicide. The project was abandoned in May 1991, but the study was never fully retracted, nor did anyone take responsibility for the fiasco. Attendance at Bristol plummeted and the Centre — which had hoped the study would provide the basis for expansion — nearly went into receivership.

A group of women, including Heather, formed the Bristol Survey Support Group. They became the first group of patients to challenge a scientific study in which they were the subjects. In April 1992, they put together a large dossier on the study and lodged a formal complaint with the Charity Commission, demanding an inquiry. The Commission complied. When the 19-month inquiry was completed, the report severely reprimanded the charities for poor supervision of the research they funded. The group felt vindicated.[3]

Heather's complaint was familiar to me: "the polarization of orthodox and complementary medicine doesn't serve the interests of patients."

The inquiry got the attention of the cancer establishment. *Lancet* editor Robin Fox beefed up the journal's statistical review procedures and expressed profound remorse. The words "Bristol Cancer Help Centre" would be found tattooed on his heart after he died, he declared. Gordon McVie, the scientific director of the Cancer Research Campaign, concurred with Heather's contention that women in the trial should have been told the results before publication. The researchers had shown "bad manners," he said.

Heather puts it more bluntly: "They used us as guinea pigs."

And despite Fox's remorse, the Lancet still hadn't formally retracted the study, Heather noted. She sent letters to the journal requesting they do so, but three months later, no retraction had appeared. Disappointed, Heather wrote to the *British Medical Journal* (BMJ).

"The competition!" she says with a wicked smile. Heather understands cut and thrust. BMJ editors not only decided to publish her letter, they asked her to expand it.

The Bristol study is like David Spiegel's study (see "Alternatives"), but through-the-looking-glass. And while Spiegel was so cautious about accepting the evidence of his data — that emotional support lengthens the life of women with breast cancer — that he refrained from submitting it for publication for several years, the results of the Bristol study were rushed into print halfway through the agreed-on study period.

"Was there malevolence behind the Bristol scandal, or just incompetence?" I ask Heather.

"Incompetence is all that's been proven," she says.

I want to hear Ann's story, too, but jet lag and the beer are taking their toll, and the sessions start tomorrow at nine AM. We head out along the moonlit canal, back to our respective inns.

The Conference: Day One

Robin Fox opens the meeting with a mild-mannered, editorly account of the Lancet's goal in launching its first-ever conference: mix disciplines — clinicians, scientists — and women who had experienced the disease. By my math, we are only about five acknowledged survivors at a meeting of several hundred; but I'm glad for even a gesture of inclusion. Fox then turns to the conference's scientific chair, Michael Baum, of London's Royal Marsden Hospital.

Baum has a more vigorous presence. "Breast cancer is at a delicate moment," he declares dramatically. "At Brugge we can seize this moment." Adopting the Lancet's tradition of iconclasm, he says, our gathering will beam the guiding light for future breast cancer research. As a tone-setting opener, the committee has selected a paper called "Have we Missed the Forest Because of the Trees?" by a retired surgeon named Jim Devitt. Baum describes Devitt as "an architect of the idea that lymph node metastases express rather than determine the extent of the disease." Now, says Baum, Devitt will be the "demoliton expert" of this same idea.

I've never heard of Devitt so I'm surprised to note that he fashioned his revolutionary concepts in my sleepy home town, Ottawa. He describes four cases of women with breast tumours that appear identical on diagnosis: 1.5 centimetres, one positive lymph node and no distant metastasis. Under the currently accepted system of characterizing breast cancers, the four women have the same prognosis — yet over time, each woman's fate is radically different from the other three.

"Within a year Mrs. A. has extensive liver involvement. She dies. An autopsy shows little else. In two years Mrs. B. has multiple pulmonary shadows. She dies. Mrs C. has skeletal metastases within four years. She is treated with radiotherapy and her disease waxes and wanes for four years. She dies and an autopsy shows tumours in many organs. Mrs. D., after three years, has a recurrence and then has no further disease for the rest of her life."

Why, he asks, do four women with an identical diagnosis have such different outcomes? Why do women with breast cancer have worse death rates than women without, for their entire lives? Why have the age-specific mortality rates remained unchanged for 50 years?

His examples capture the frustrating unpredictability of breast cancer, the near uselessness of the standard prognostic system, and the hopeless inadequacy of current treatments. Devitt proposes that a breast tumour may not be the origin of the metastasis, but the reverse — the local manifestation of a systemic disease. We have, he concludes, lost sight of the forest because of the trees. "Let's look more intensively at the woman, and less at the tumour," he says, illustrating the point with a slide of a lake and forest scene: Maligne Lake, in the Rockies. "Perhaps the name is significant," he adds. (Maligne = "shrewd" and "malicious.")

Devitt's talk is refreshing, partly because of its simple clarity, and partly for its message: *look more at the woman, less at the tumour.* Could the conference be heading towards a holistic approach?

By the coffee break, the clear light has dimmed a bit. Most of the papers in the first session are about molecular properties that may affect tumour growth. "Bombesin (BBS) receptors were identified by covalent crosslinking methods and competitive binding assays," says an American reseacher. "Trophoblasts show maximum staining for both SCF-1 and CSF-1 receptor at the highly proliferating and invading cells of the villous sprouts," says a woman named Scholl, from the Curie Institute in France. What happened to the forest? I wonder.

The presentation most readily comprehensible to lay listeners argues that the conventional staging system for predicting outcome, known as TNM (tumour size, node involvement and presence or absence of metastases), needs to be replaced. The presenter proposes a system that will integrate new prognostic factors.

Heather Goodare goes to the mike.

"Can psychosocial factors go into the revised model?' she asks.

"If they are measurable."

"Very good answer!" interjects Baum, who is proving to be an irrepressible editorializer. He turns to the other side of the room, where someone else has a hand up. "Dr. Mittra, go ahead."

"We should ban the search for YAPIs," says the man. YAPI, he explains, means "Yet Another Prognostic Indicator."

At the coffee break, Nancy Evans, president of the San Francisco group Breast Cancer Action, joins a knot of us. She passes me a book, called *The Immortal Cell.* It's by an American cell biologist, Gerald B. Dermer, who decided, after 20 years of research on cancer cells that the bulk of current research is useless because it's done on cells in a petri dish (in vitro), rather than cells in the body (in vivo). Dermer argues that because cells cultured in petri dishes, called "cell lines," can grow forever — they are immortal — they provide science with an incorrect model of cancer. Nancy thinks it's an important book.

"Cell lines," I say. That's what they were talking about all morning."

She nods.

A gong sounds and people start moving back into the conference hall. The next sessions are about epidemiology and primary prevention. Two highlights are papers about exercise and organochlorines, both based on research in California. The encouraging news comes from a retrospective study that found a strong correlation between the number of weekly hours spent exercising, from menarche into adulthood, and breast cancer. Women who exercised four or more hours per week were less likely to have breast cancer. "Physical activity is modifiable," emphasizes the researcher. She recommends that exercise programs be a high priority for adolescent and healthy women.

Then comes the discouraging news — for those of us seeking clear signs for ways to prevent breast cancer. A new study failed to show a link between pesticide residues or PCB residues and breast cancer. A team of researchers, including Mary Wolff, whose highly publicized study showed a correlation between breast cancer and DDT residues in breast tissue, found no relationship between breast cancer and organochlorine residues in the blood. The study used blood samples that were taken in the 1960s from women in the San Francisco bay area, and frozen. From a total of 57,040 women in each of three ethnic/racial groups (white, black and Asian), the researchers took a random sample of 50 women from each group who were diagnosed with breast cancer six months or more after the blood draw. Each case was matched to a cancer-free control. The analysis comparing the cancer and non-cancer groups showed no difference in blood concentrations for either of the two contaminants, PCBs and the DDT metabolite, DDE.

Two other attention-getters are on "chemoprevention," one using a drug resembling Vitamin D, the other, the infamous (to many feminists) Pike/Spicer pill.

Michael Sporn, from the Laboratory of Chemoprevention at the National Cancer Institute, distinguishes the new, chemo-prevention approach from the old cell-kill approach, which he calls "a terrible albatross around our neck." The benefits of vegetarian diets, he says, might come from chemicals in foods that regulate gene expression without producing toxic effects. I sigh inwardly. Where he is heading with all this is not towards vegetarian diets, but pharmaceutical drugs designed to mimic the anti-cancer effects of vegetarian diets. In particular, his research team is looking at synthesized analogues of Vitamin D, which they call deltanoids.

He gets to the crunch. They need to test the drug on humans and since the idea is to prevent cancer with these agents, not treat it, they want to give the drugs to women who don't have breast cancer, probably in combination with tamoxifen. "We have to overcome the notion that it's unethical to do pharmacological research on symptom-free people," he said. "It's a major fallacy that people are healthy until they have cancer."

Malcolm Pike's paper is titled, "Changes in mammographic densities induced by a hormonal contraceptive designed to reduce breast cancer risk." He begins by reminding us that Japanese women have one-sixth the U.S. rate of breast cancer, then adds, "The Japanese do enormous amounts of physicial activity and eat a diet that is eight percent fat. You would never want to live like a rural Japanese woman. You would have menarchy at age 16 and would never weigh more than 100 lbs."

He goes on to describe the elaborate regimen he and his colleagues have devised to knock out women's hormonal function and replace it with a system that will cause them to menstruate every four months.

The women had a baseline mammogram, and annual mammograms for two years. Radiologists read the mammograms without knowing which group the women were in and the results showed the drug had significantly reduced the mammographic density of breast tissue for those women in the experimental group. Evidently the drug did something to the women's breasts. Pike was pleased. "We need $50 million to do the next stage of research," he pitches.

I'm incensed by Pike's lego concept of women's hormones, not to mention his flippant style. I'm trying to formulate a pithy question that will challenge his arrogance when a man on the other side of the room takes the microphone and directs a question to Pike:

"I've been listening to your story for some time," he says. "It's a fascinating story, but it's only a story. You keep forgetting about pregnancy, about all the other realities of a woman's life ..."

I lean to Nancy Evans, sitting next to me. "Who is he?"

"Graham Colditz. He directs the Nurses Health Study, at Harvard."

"... It suggests to me," Colditz continues, "you have insufficient gynaecological experience to understand the problems with long-term pharmacological intervention."

"I have *no* gynaecological experience!" Pike replies, triumphantly. After a dramatic pause, he adds, "However, one of my collaborators does. Look," he insists, "We are not *forcing* anyone to take this. We just tell them, 'Here is a contraceptive that is better than the Pill because it prevents breast cancer.' And they love it! They don't want to come off it." (This isn't quite true. The program abstract notes that one of the 14 women in the drug group was withdrawn from the study because of "poor compliance.") The big problem, Pike insists, is the cost. "I was forced to take them off the drug because it cost $500 a month. In a few years, I hope to get the cost down to $20 a month." He doesn't say how.

At lunch, I sit with Heather, Ann, a young gynaecologist from Belgium, Gordon McVie of Britain's Cancer Research Campaign, and Robin Fox of the *Lancet*. The NSABP scandal, and Bernard Fisher's firing, dominate the conversation. I had thought the Poisson affair and its fallout might be a remote matter in Europe.

"Not at all, it's very big in Britain," Heather assures me. McVie has just been on a radio program giving a viewpoint on the medical establishment's obligation to inform patients, and on the scandal's possible impact on the tamoxifen prevention trial.

When McVie realizes I am from Montreal, he leans across the table intently. He wants to know all about our meeting for Poisson's patients.

The doctor from Belgium is listening with astonishment to Heather and I — women with breast cancer at a medical meeting! "There's no money for anything like that in Belgium," he says. I tell him I'm disappointed no Belgian women have come to the meeting. He nods dolefully. "There are hardly even any physicians here from Belgium," he points out. "And there's no interest in prevention, even though the rate of breast cancer is very high." Professional consciousness of the breast cancer problem is low despite the country's high incidence, he explains, and the treatment of breast cancer is very fragmented. Surgeons and gynaecologists both treat women for breast cancer but they don't speak to one another, let alone to oncologists.

The final session of the day, titled Secondary Prevention, turns out to be a grab-bag of papers about metastases. Several are cell line studies, and once more we are mired in prognostic indicators and the jargon of cell biologists.

Montreal oncologist Richard Margolese is the first to take the mike in the question period. "Speaking in the iconoclastic spirit of this conference," he says, "I'll be provocative and ask, What good is this research? It's not going to stop the spread that has happened."

"Um, that's not the sort of question you'd want to get from a grants panel," says one of the presenters, taken aback. "You're right, it's not going to be much good for therapy, but then we haven't advanced much beyond the knife in the past 50 years." He pauses. "Well, it might help us understand what is happening and later help us develop a therapy."

"That's no good," says Margolese.

"I know it's no good."

Despite such fencing, the program so far has kept any revolutionary tendencies within bio-medical bounds. Except for Heather's brief intervention, no one has mentioned psychosocial issues at all. I hope the discussion of consumer advocacy in research, slated for the next day, at 8:30, will shake things up a bit. The second, and final, day will also feature Baum laying out his vision for a new direction in breast cancer research, and a debate about the future of toxic chemotherapy in breast cancer treatment.

As I head for the door, I hear someone behind me mutter, "Where are the iconoclasts? Where are the *radiologists?*"

It's the lawyer from England who is involved in the radiation injury claims.

The Conference: Day Two

For the "Patients' Role in Research" panel, "Sue Love" has done a Clark Kent transformation, shedding jeans and sneakers for a skirt and boldly checked jacket. She is now "Dr. Susan Love, M.D., Director of the UCLA Breast Centre." I watch, fascinated, as she walks the tightrope of surgeon/ activist before this mostly medical audience.

She steps immediately from the safety platform onto the wire. "Is breast cancer a political issue?" she asks rhetorically, following through with the medically incorrect response: "Yes."

Her talk elaborates on why breast cancer, more than other diseases, has been politicized. Women are more frightened of breast cancer than of other, equally deadly diseases, she says, and women are angry about the simplistic way medical professionals present breast cancer to them. As she talks, she shifts her weight adroitly from the professional perspective to the activist one, then back to the professional.

Heart disease, diabetes, and alcoholism are definitely more common than breast cancer, she says in her professional persona, gesturing to a slide which shows breast cancer incidence well down on a list of female conditions with deadly potential. But, she points out, shifting back to the lay woman's reality, treatments for breast cancer are uniquely mutilating.

"Breasts define women. If you see someone walking down the street and you're not sure if it's a man or a woman, you look for breasts." And breasts, she continues, are integral to a woman's sexuality and to motherhood, not just in breastfeeding but as a symbol of the nurturing role.

A second source of fear, she says, is the suffering breast cancer causes. "Breast cancer is not a nice, easy death." Third, women feel no sense of personal control over whether they get breast cancer, "unlike heart disease and osteoporosis."

Love moves to the sensitive issue of women's anger at the medical profession. "Women are angry because of medicine's approach to the disease, and to women."

She runs through the litany of misrepresentation, over-simplification and wishful thinking that has fuelled the current movement. When condemning the medical stance, she includes herself among the guilty. "We view the disease as observers," she says, acting out the surgeon, looking down at the woman on the operating table, then the woman on her back, arms spreadeagled. "I [the surgeon] might worry that the surgery isn't perfect, the breasts aren't perfectly symmetrical. The woman may be happy even to still have a breast.

"Early detection is not prevention," she says. "We've mis-represented early detection by implying that all breast cancers start as a grain of sand, grow to a pea, then a grape, then a lemon then a grapefruit. That's an oversimplification. If you have a cancer that you can't detect until it's five centimetres, is that early detection? If you have a tumour that is detected when it's one gram, but the woman has five positive lymph nodes, is that early detection? We've got to stop presenting mammography screening as the answer."

On breast self-exam: "There has never been a study to show it reduces death. We use it to put the blame on women. Think of all the money we've spent on whether to do BSE up and down or in circles …"

Then, surgery: "Women who were given a mastectomy and were told 'We got it all,' who then come back with a local recur-rence or metastases, are angry."

Lymphedema: "We never talked about it. The attitude was, 'You're lucky to be alive.'"

Prophylactic mastectomies: "There has never been a study to find out if they reduce risk in women; it doesn't reduce any of the risk in rats. Women who have had a prophylactic mastectomy and who then got breast cancer are angry."

Breast reconstruction: "We've promoted it, saying it looks good, but we don't talk about what it's going to feel like. To the feeler, it doesn't feel the same. To the feelee, it doesn't feel at all."

Adjuvant chemo: "We say it reduces risk by one-third. That sounds impressive, but it means, for example, if you have a nine percent chance of recurrence you can reduce it to six percent, if you have negative nodes."

Tamoxifen: "Because the side effects are less than with chemotherapy, we've promoted it as if it were a vitamin. But tamoxifen causes endometrial cancer. Women who were told tamoxifen had no serious side effects are angry."

Chemotherapy: "We seldom tell them anything ..."

Paternalism: "Women are angry about being told 'If you were my wife ... ' My job is not to put myself in the woman's place. My job is to help her understand her situation and her values, so she can make the right decision for her."

The goal of research: "They want prevention. They are worried for their daughters. They don't want more chemo." She shows a chart illustrating the dramatic upswing in funding for breast cancer research in the U.S., from November 1990 and the first discussions of the National Breast Cancer Coalition, to the large award of army funds to breast cancer in late 1992.

But, she underlines, slipping almost imperceptibly back into her activist garb, "There's no free lunch. We are not the women's auxiliary." She lists the goals of the NBCC: support, representation and accountability. "The cure for breast cancer," she concludes, "is political action."

Now it's Kay Dickersin's turn. She too, alludes to her professional status, but her perspective is unambiguously personal. "I'm an epidemiologist, but I'm here as a breast cancer patient. I'm not used to telling my personal story when I'm talking to scientists."

She talks about being diagnosed seven-and-a-half years ago, at age 34 and about having no family history in first degree relatives. "Since then, two of my sisters have been diagnosed."

She elaborates on the NBCC letter-writing campaign, Do the Right Thing and it's impact: $410 million appropriated from the Star Wars budget. "I like that," she says. "Breasts, Not Bombs."

We needed a research plan, she says, and explains the evolution of the new American Secretary of Health and Human Services action plan for breast cancer. She summarizes some of its highlights ("my personal favourites"):

Involve consumers at all levels; establish tissue banks; continue funding from the Department of Defense (it doesn't take money away from other diseases); extend the scope and depth of quality of life and psychosocial research; establish registries of clinical trials; move on from mammography: we don't need yet another study; establish protection for women when genetic research is done; set research priorities: in prevention, emphasize etiology, environmental risks, an understanding of the action of risk factors at the molecular level. In treatment, ensure accessibility to all randomized trials (tell women what's going on and how to join). Identify prognostic markers to aid treatment decisions. Develop "smart bombs" — not dumb bombs like cytotoxic chemo. "Overall, though, we want less attention to new treatments and more money dedicated to learning the causes of breast cancer."

We also need better dissemination of research results, she says. Women want a more effective support system, and attention to their quality of life not just postponement of death.

"Women with breast cancer need to be involved in research funding decisions and the entire research process," she insists. "If a consumer had been involved in the NSABP, the re-analysed data would have been disseminated sooner."

I'm struck by how similar Kay's list is to the one we've arrived at in Canada, by a different route. The Americans have put the activist case in compelling, pragmatic terms. When Hazel Thornton moves to the lectern, her style is very different. She presents in a literary style, studded with quotes from poets and philosophers. But the surface elegance is a deceptive cover for some very hard-hitting views.

Patients, she says, can bring to research "a type of observation that is fresh and uncluttered" — that may even help scientists regain the clear and unprejudiced vision that they need. She cites research which found that medical students lose ethical sensitivity from their first year of med school to their last, and that they have "startlingly poor" powers of observation. She sees the shock of diagnosis as a salutary aid to perception: "the patient is compelled to observe and attempt to understand a world perhaps hitherto unknown to her."

Since research is for the benefit of the patient, she reasons, patients should help define their aims and priorities, and participate in the design and monitoring of studies. Trial accrual would be more rapid if aims of the trial and aims of the patients coincided. She cites the leadership of AIDS patients as research participants, and firmly refutes the contention that rushed approval of the drug AZT demonstrates the pitfalls of patient involvement. Rather, patients learned the need for unhurried, controlled evaluation and trialists learned the importance of taking *both* parties' needs into account. "The main impediment to implementing such a proposal," says Hazel, "is the inequality of the parties."

Turning to breast cancer, she takes aim at current treatments, "an attempt to bludgeon cures"; at trials, with their "evermore complicated protocols"; and at prevention trials, in which "we are pulling healthy women into the consulting rooms, with earlier, smaller and non-invasive cancers ..." The result," she says, is "acute distress and anxiety to vast numbers of women without the disease" not to mention expending enormous resources and worsening the quality of life of the afflicted "for meagre 'survival' gains."

She calls on the profession to work hard to bring patients into the process, even though we may criticize the direction and quality of research. The profession "must learn not to be dismissive and patronizing of the patients' views of research."

Researchers will no longer have to bear all the criticism, she points out, once they begin to share the responsibility of research decisions. She closes with the image of a staircase, on which induction and deduction go up and down. Researchers and patients use the same staircase, she observes, so "please let us contrive to meet on the landing by the invigorating open window of science and talk!"

Applause for the session is fulsome, but I have no illusions that everyone accepts the changes proposed. Sure enough, Baum interjects:

"I have a problem with consumers sitting on our boards. How are they qualified? You, Hazel, are an exception. You have *immersed* yourself in the subject. I worry that patients will bring the busybody values of middle-class women ..."

"That word 'busybody' has got my hackles up," says Kay, coldly.

Baum, thankfully, refrains from responding and someone else takes the mike.

The program now turns to an evaluation of the current treatment paradigm, with its emphasis on early detection, surgery, radiotherapy and adjuvant chemotherapy. Richard Margolese is slated to give a keynote address on seeking a middle ground. Knowing his long association with Fisher and the NSABP, I wonder how critical he will dare to be. He surprises me.

He says we have indeed made progress from the 1960s, when the key treatment issue was to determine the best way of getting out all the axillary nodes. The 1970s were a turning point. Early diagnosis became a goal, the concept of adjuvant chemo was introduced, along with the idea of tumour markers to guide treatment decisions, such as ER positive or negative receptors.

Bernard Fisher embarked on his program of clinical trials to determine the biology of local and systemic control. Up to 1980, says Margolese, the results showed some improvement, "but we haven't moved since then." Where we lost our perspective, he says, is with node-negative treatments. "A lot of energy was dissipated in a not-very-organized program of research."

For the future, say the year 2000, Margolese predicts that biologic therapies will play a big role. He means the genetic therapies based on controlling tumour growth. The chemo approach will not succeed, he predicts. Advances will be unimportant in the overall picture because the body adapts. "We've now exposed cancer cells to about 50 agents. The cell adapts."

A reaction is mounting against science, he says. "We are depicted as Dr. Strangeloves and subjected to adjectival attacks. We are seen as technocrats." His defense of the NSABP program is that, "we have prolonged life, and that's marvellous." He urges a middle ground, where we don't have change for change's sake.

The NSABP theme triggers another of Baum's intejections. "The lesson of the NSABP is less audit, more pragmatism," he says. "The small bully-boys at the NCI decided they would sacrifice Bernard Fisher!"

Many in the audience apparently sympathize. The outburst gets an ovation, but not everyone joins in. As people head down to the dining room for lunch, conversation revolves around a single theme — Bernard Fisher and the NSABP.

At lunch I sit next to Ann and we discuss the injuries sustained by the women who formed RAGE. I am less and less certain that the treatment I had, lumpectomy plus radiation, is preferable to surgery without radiation, even if that means having a mastectomy. Are radiation injuries from radiotherapy to the breast very common, I ask her?

"It depends a lot on the woman's breast," she says. "Fibrosis is a problem for many women. The easiest breast to radiate properly is perfectly symmetrical. But not many woman have that shape. If the woman has pendulous breasts, radiation is less satisfactory. If she's very thin, the chance of internal scatter is greater. In most cases, I think a mastectomy less likely to give trouble later. But of course if the woman says she wants to keep her breast, that's an important factor."

Ann's direct, common sense approach is all the more refreshing because it is so unusual. ("Treat people like individuals — what a radical idea," says Nancy Evans dryly, when I tell her about Ann.) Heather has urged me to see a poster Ann has up today, but I haven't had time. And I don't want to miss any of the final program.

The highlights of the Friday afternoon schedule will suggest in which the direction the conference's organizer's intend to nudge future research. First, Michael Baum's proposal for a new paradigm; then a debate on the pros and cons of continuing chemotherapy treatment and research; and finally, the Young Investigator Award, a sort of "Editor's Choice" of the most promising paper given at the conference.

Baum begins by explaining that a paradigm is a framework of shared assumptions and presuppositions. A paradigm shift is embarrassing because it implies the current paradigm is wrong. One hopes that a shift will have the assent of the relevant community. (Amen, I think, but his definition of "relevant community" is different from mine.)

He identifies three paradigms in the history of breast cancer. First were the ancients, with their idea that cancer arose from an excess of melancholia. The treatments were coffee enemas and diets to get rid of excess of bile. These ideas, he says in an aside, are "re-emerging in the lunatic fringe of alternative therapies."

The shift to a second paradigm came with the invention of the microscope. Cancer was interpreted as a cellular disease that began at the tumour site and spread centrifugally to other parts of the body. The paradigm shifted from the systemic to the local. Surgical treatments such as the Halsted radical mastectomy followed from the hypothesis of centrifugal spread.

The third paradigm was that promoted by the Fisher brothers of Pittsburgh. Bernard, a surgeon, and Edwin, a pathologist, argued for a paradigm in which breast cancer was a systemic disease, not a local one. Adjuvant chemotherapy rather than extensive surgery, would be the treatment method likely to succeed. The outcome of adjuvant treatment gave some support for the contemporary model but clinical trials also revealed inadequacies.

The trials showed the extent of surgery made no difference to outcome. As Baum is explaining this, it occurs to me that researchers and women rejected the Halsted for completely different reasons. Before researchers could condemn the treatment as barbarous, they needed proof that the length of the woman's life was not shortened. But for many women, the pain and mutilation were not worth an extension of life. If the clinical trials of radical breast surgery had shown even a small benefit in length of life, I wonder if doctors would still feel justified in imposing the Halsted.

While the surgical portion of Fisher's research program gave the expected result, says Baum, adjuvant chemotherapy did not change the mortality rate as expected. Breast cancer returns in the distant organs of women who have had systemic therapy, though it may take longer to do so. Liver and skeletal metastases are inexplicably more common than lung metastases. The studies that show that timing of surgery affects outcome suggests that surgery may be an adverse event.

Baum begins to explain his new paradigm: metastases are the result not only of cellular transmission of breast cancer, but also of subcellular transmission — a mechanism Baum calls "in-vivo transfection."

I look blankly at Nancy Evans.

"He's suggesting the cancer can be spread by a virus." She makes a gesture meaning "it seems plausible."

"This may sound far-fetched," Baum continues, "but several remarkable studies support this conceptual revolution." He says his model opens up fertile areas for research. Therapies based on anti-viral drugs might be the next therapeutic advance. As for more aggressive chemotherapy, his assessment is blunt: "it is unlikely to achieve additional benefit."

He concludes with some high-minded statements disclaiming any premature commitment to the paradigm he proposes. "Personal satisfaction is the death of the scientist," he declares. His goal, rather, is "to open minds to the study of history and scientific philosophy."

At least, I think to myself, everyone acknowledges the mediocre effect of current treatments, but Baum's concept of a new paradigm is far from that proposed by activists. Women with cancer are urging a shift from strictly biomedical analyses and treatments to a model that embraces the woman's psychosocial and physical environment, that values prevention rather than treatment. Baum's vision is one of new biological treatments.

In the question period, a man in the audience picks up on Baum's slam at alternative medicine.

"Thirty percent of patients go to alternative healers. Don't you think it's counter-productive to make comments like 'lunatic fringe'?"

Baum is unrepentant.

"The demarcation between alternative and orthodox medicine is intellectual integrity. Do you have the intellectual integrity to challenge your beliefs?" he asks. "… to abandon anecdotal evidence and put it in the historical bin where it belongs?"

The debate on chemotherapy is the last major item on the program. Two American oncologists, Craig Henderson and John Forbes, will argue opposite sides of the statement, "Chemotherapy in the management of breast cancer has a dim future."

I'm hoping for some ferocious verbal sparring to bring the issue to a head before we leave. This doesn't happen — but something else does. In the midst of Henderson's presentation, he describes a study to illustrate one of his points.

"In study #8541," he says, "the women were randomly assigned into three groups. They had four or six months of the chemotherapy regimen cyclophosphamide, doxorubicin and fluorouracil. Four months at a high or low dose, or six months at a moderate dose."

The study has not yet been published, but I know it well: I'm one of the 1,572 women who was in it.

Henderson, of course, is oblivious to my shock, as he clicks the slide carousel forward and the results go up on the screen. Three lines show the probability of disease-free survival over a five-year period for the women in each group. One line descends more steeply than the others. More of those women have had disease recurrences. Nervously, I check the labels. The women who had the lowest dose, for four months, were most likely to have a recurrence. I was in the six-month, medium-dose group.

"There was no difference between the high and the moderate group," says Henderson.

The study suggests limits to chemotherapy at both ends of the dosage scale. Reduced dosages are easier on the patient but effectiveness drops. Increasing the dosage did not improve effectiveness but did increase morbidity (negative side effects). These ran the gamut, from nausea to death, and were clearly most serious, and most frequent, in the high-dose group.

One telling point is that the super-chemo trials are having to close down because of inadequate accrual. Recruitment is difficult because doctors, already convinced that more is better, are advocating bone marrow transplants to women outside of clinical trials.

John Forbes, the chemo advocate, makes his presentation. The moderator calls for a show of hands from those who believe chemotherapy treatments have a dim future.

About two-thirds of the hands go up.

"Those who see a bright future chemotherapy?"

The remaining one-third raise their hands.

"It's a draw," declares the moderator.

Suzie Scholl of the Curie Institute, a woman who presented one of the early papers on growth factors, wins the young investigator award. The future, it seems, is in molecular biology.

Ann's Story

Ann and Heather have invited me to spend Saturday morning cycling around Brugge. As we secure purses and maps into our rear racks, I mention how startled I was to see slides showing the results of the study I was in.

"Imagine how I would have felt if I was in the group with the high recurrence rate."

"Exactly," says Heather. "It's what I've been saying. Patients who volunteer for studies should be the *first* to hear the results. Before the scientific community and certainly before the study appears in the paper. It's the least they could do for us."

She explains the procedure she has in mind.

"As soon as the study is ready for publication, they would send all the patients a letter telling them the research is about to be published. The letter would have a brief statement of the results and what they mean — just a few paragraphs. At the end, they tell you who to call if you want to discuss the results with one of the researchers. How's that?"

"Perfect. Courtesy and accountability. After all, we've donated our bodies to science — and we're still using them."

They laugh.

Because of her research, Ann doesn't believe in randomized trials in breast cancer — that's one of the points she made in her poster. I ask her to start at the beginning.

"I always wanted to be a surgeon," she says. "From the time I was 14. Now I think I made a mistake, I should have been an academic."

She applied to medical school in the early '50s, at a time when women's access to medical training was restricted by quotas. "I made about 15 applications," she recalls. "I told each school it was my first choice. But I was super-confident. I didn't imagine I wouldn't get in somewhere." Sure enough, her true first choice granted her an interview and she was accepted.

After graduation Ann trained in surgery. She married during her first research placement and decided that surgery and home life don't mix. By chance, she was working with radioisotopes, which she found fascinating, so training in the hospital's radiotherapy department seemed a natural progression. By now she had a baby at home and had to work part-time. "I didn't mind, in fact I liked it. But of course I didn't get any promotions in those years."

In the 1970s she began doing research on the effects of cancer therapy with a colleague, Dr. Hugh Thomlinson.

"He was a brilliant man," says Ann. "He had made a name for himself doing basic research in radiobiology. Then he fell out with the Medical Research Council over the neutron trial. He said the design of the trial was no good, that it wouldn't answer the question. Instead of listening to him, they put him off the committee. So he left. He resigned. He couldn't compromise. He gave up radiobiology. It was a disaster for him, and for the field. He was near the top of the tree. And they still haven't sorted out the neutrons."

After he left basic research, Thomlinson came to the clinic where Ann was working. "So that's how we got working together. As it turned out we agreed on a lot of things. He had been working with rats and so he didn't know anything about breast cancer — but I did. He realized he could test his ideas on breast cancer, because the tumours are near the surface. He got me on his grant."

Thomlinson hypothesized that the shrinkage rate of tumours would differ in response to therapy. Rapidly growing, poorly differentiated tumours would shrink rapidly, and well-differentiated, slow growing tumours would shrink slowly.

To test the hypothesis, he and Ann administered therapy to women before they had breast surgery, a treatment that later became known as neoadjuvant therapy. They gave a sequence of single agents, including different cytotoxic drugs, hormones and radiation. Using calliper measurements, they measured how much the tumour shrank in response to each agent.

"Did you give Adriamycin?" I ask.

"We tried it," says Ann, "but I don't use it any more. We found a less toxic drug in the same family, mitozantrone, that had less cardiotoxicity and caused less hair loss. The tumours shrank just as much."

Their rule in giving therapy before surgery was to always use the minimum treatment necessary to shrink the tumour.

"Most of the slow-growing tumours responded to a single drug," says Ann. "For some of the more aggressive tumours, we had to give combination chemotherapy at weekly intervals. Others responded only to radiation. Tamoxifen had varying effects. Sometimes it shrank the tumour, but 17 percent of the tumours actually grew in response to tamoxifen."

Every tumour, they concluded, has a unique rate of shrinkage, and should be treated individually.

"So, that's why clinical trials with random assignment are out?"

"That's right," says Ann. She adds that she doesn't disagree with randomized trials for other purposes. "We've been able to demonstrate which type of chemotherapy drug or hormone treatment is suited to which particular type of tumour. That's our most significant contribution."

As we cycle, Ann notices a sign for the lace museum and we go in. Medieval Brugge was famous for the skill of its lacemakers. The display cases show samples of various intricate patterns made by combining different stitches. I wonder at what age young girls began learning the trade and how many hours a day they worked.

In the gift shop, Heather tells the saleswoman that we are here for the conference on breast cancer. The saleswoman brightens. Breast cancer! Local women still come to the museum for lacemaking classes, and one has created a card for a local breast cancer support group, she tells us, pulling a greeting card from the rack behind her.

The card's photo is a whimsical creation, a lace brassiere hanging from a clothesline, against a black background. A perky bird sits nestled in one of the cups — presumably the unused one. The women of Belgium are not oblivious to breast cancer, after all. The perfect souvenir. We all buy one.

Back on the winding cobbled road, Ann continues her story as we head along the outer wall, towards the main entrance to the town.

I ask her what Dr. Thomlinson is doing now.

"He died in 1989, two years after his retirement," she says. "The Medical Research Council withdrew their support, 18 months before he retired. He had applied for an enlarged program for his last few years but was told to get on with publishing what he had already done, while I wound down the clinic."

Thomlinson regarded the clinic, which was entirely devoted to the treatment of breast cancer, as his most important achievement. His salary was secure until his retirement, but Ann and the other clinic staff would have lost their jobs when his research grant expired in 1985.

"Our wonderful patients did not accept this. They set to and raised enough money to keep us open until Dr. Thomlinson's retirement date in 1987. They raised about £200,000 — almost as much as the grant that was rejected! This meant that we were able to finish the treatment of all the patients on our books." She had to stop seeing patients so that she could devote herself to writing up the research. "My former patients are still my friends," she says. "A group of us meet regularly for a pub lunch."

Professionally, her colleague's death leaves her more isolated than ever. She sees writing up their research as her final professional task. "The marvelous thing," she says, "is that the patients' efforts saved the research from extinction."

We are back at the Adornes, their hotel. Ann and Heather are driving home and must leave by 1:00. I have the afternoon for sightseeing.

With the usual flurry of hugs, photo-taking and promises to write and exchange material, we say goodbye.

As I head out of the courtyard, Ann calls after me, one last thought.

"I think I know what made me different."

"What's that?"

"Two things, really. First, I trained in all the specialties: surgery, chemotherapy and radiation. I could see the whole picture."

"And the second?"

"The other was an accident. Because of my family situation, I didn't move around trying to get promotions, like the others. I couldn't do that and in the end it made me privileged. I stayed in one place, so I got to see the women over the long-term. I got to know them and to see how the treatments affected them years later."

That's a beginning, I think to myself, nodding my agreement. But I also know Ann is being modest — no small part of her difference.

Meandering by myself through the streets of Brugge, lined with spruced-up medieval guild houses, I think about constancy amidst change. It occurs to me that my visit here is an anniversary: it's five years since I came out. In cancer mythology, the five-year anniversary is a benchmark. Before breast cancer activists challenged the dogma, five years was the point when a woman was supposed to be able to rest easy, believing she had "beat the Big C." Looking back upon the recent years in which women with breast cancer have been challenging the status quo, I know they mark a different kind of turning point. We still can't rest easy about the future of breast cancer — but there's no turning back.

Notes

1. Hazel Thornton, "Breast Cancer Trials: A Patient's Viewpoint," *Lancet,* (Jan. 4, 1992), Vol. 339, pp. 44-45.

2. F.S. Bagenal, D.F. Easton, E. Harris, C.E.D. Chilvers, T.J. McElwain, "Survival of Patients with Breast Cancer Attending Bristol Cancer Help Centre," *Lancet,* (Sept. 8, 1990), Vol. 336, pp. 606-610.

3. Richard Smith, "Charity Commission Censures British Cancer Charities," *British Medical Journal,* (Jan. 15, 1994), Vol. 308, pp. 155-156.

Index

Abel, Ulrich, 100-101, 103-104, 105, 106
Activism, 193, 344, 366
  fundraising, 296-299
  professional alliances, 372-373
  research committee representation, 293-295
  see also AIDS activism; National Forum on Breast Cancer (Canada); Personal autonomy
Ader, Robert, 146
Adjuvant therapy. *see* Chemotherapy; Radiotherapy; Tamoxifen
Adriamycin, 18-19, 246
Advertising, 43, 213-214, 218, 243-246, 250
AIDS activism, 27, 286, 324, 344, 372
Alan Guttmacher Institute, 128
Alienation, 287
  see also Depersonalization; Personal autonomy
Alternative treatments, 139-165
  Bristol Cancer Help Centre, 381, 383-384, 385-387
American Cancer Society (ACS)
  advertising, 218, 243-244
  appeal to the wealthy, 217, 219, 234
  connections to pharmaceutical industry, 247
  fundraising and lobbying, 217, 219-220, 244, 295-296
  implicit denial of realities of cancer, 230, 234; Look Good, Feel Better program, 228-230, 232-233; prostheses, 223-226; Reach

to Recovery program, 218, 222-224, 227-228, 230, 231, 232
  interferon research, 248-249
  mammography screening guidelines, 32, 41
  National Breast Cancer Detection Demonstration Project (BCDDP), 38, 39-40
  radiotherapy guidelines, 74
  use of the media, 264-265, 267
  see also American Society for the Control of Cancer (ASCC)
American Society for the Control of Cancer (ASCC), 215-217, 262-263, 264, 295
  Women's Field Army, 216-217, 218, 262
  see also American Cancer Society (ACS)
Angell, Marcia, 105-106
Apel, Deena, 305
Atomic bomb survivors, 80-81, 200
Avon cosmetics, 298

Badger, Carolyn, 315, 316
Bailar III, John C., 38-39, 40, 42-43, 119, 192-193, 197-198, 371
Baines, Cornelia, 32, 36, 44
Balaban, Barbara, 379, 380-381
Batt, Sharon
  alternative treatments, 141, 142, 143-144, 151-152
  Brugge conference, 378
  charitable organizations, 221-222

see also Alternative treatments
Minton, Dr., 274
Misconceptions, 25, 208
  linked to advertising campaigns,
    243-246
  risk of breast cancer related to
    age, 35-36
  see also Early detection
Montreal, 188
  cancer studies, 26; Poisson Affair,
    355-368, 391; St. Mary's Hospi-
    tal, 367-368
  see also Breast Cancer Action
    Montreal (BCAM); National
    Forum on Breast Cancer(Canada)
Morrow, Jan, 342, 343
Moss, Ralph, 246, 247, 248
Mushlin, Alvin, 47

Napoli, Maryann, 42-43, 50, 52-53,
  67
Narod, Steve, 171, 174
National Association of Radiation
  Survivors, 200
National Breast Cancer Awareness
  Month, 245-246
National Breast Cancer Coalition,
  297, 299, 314-315
National Breast Cancer Detection
  Demonstration Project (BCDDP),
  38, 39-40
National Breast Screening Study
  (NBSS), 32, 33, 44, 45-48
  efforts to discredit, 44-45, 242
  prevention studies, 189-190
National Cancer Institute (NCI),
  61, 74, 81, 333
  breast screening workshop
    (February 1993), 31-33, 34-37,
    43, 44-51
  chemotherapy, 93-94; Alert, 90-
    91, 92, 276
  funding, 295-296, 297, 335
  interferon research, 248-249
  lack of research low-fat diets, 190-
    191, 194

  mammography screening
    guidelines, 32, 35, 42, 50-51
  optimistic reports, 266-267
  Poisson Affair, 366, 367, 368;
    knowledge of falsified data, 357,
    368
National Coalition of Cancer Sur-
  vivorship (NCCS), 83, 328-329
National Forum on Breast Cancer
  (Canada), 338-342, 346-353
  Aboriginal ceremonies, 354
  Support, Advocacy and
    Net-working subcommittee,
    342-346, 349, 353
National Surgical Adjuvant Breast
  and Bowel Project (NSABP), 61,
  277
  chemotherapy, 94-95
  falsified data, 355-358, 359-360,
    368; knowledge of, 356-357;
    patient responses to disclosure,
    362-366; results of disclosure,
    366-368, 370-371
  radiotherapy, 76-77
National Women's Health Network,
  194
NBSS. see National Breast Screen-
  ing Study
NCI. see National Cancer Institute
  (NCI)
Nelkin, Dorothy, 177, 181
Nikkel, Karen, 65
Noyes, Diane, 228-229
NSABP. see National Surgical Ad-
  juvant Breast and Bowel Project
  (NSABP)
Nysbrom, Lennarth, 45

Oophorectomies, 100-101, 116,
  179, 180
  hormone induced, 133
Oral contraceptives, 118, 123-126,
  130
  Pike/Spicer pill, 134, 390-391
Ovaries, 100-101, 172
  see also Oophorectomies

related to menstrual cycle, 68-70
techniques: Italian, 78; one-stage, 65-66; related to survival rates; 19th century, 55-57, 58; two-stage, 8, 66; wide excisions, 78
without radiation, 77, 78-79, 87
see also Lumpectomies; Mastectomies
Survival rates, 8
related to chemotherapy, 95-96, 102, 104
related to mammography screening, 46
related to radiotherapy, 76-77, 78
related to support groups, 140-141
related to tamoxifen, 121
related to timing of surgery and menstrual cycle, 68-70
related to type of surgery, 57, 60, 61
Susan G. Komen Breast Cancer Foundation, 219
Swazey, Judith, 360-361
Sweden, 42, 44
Swift, Michael, 178

Tabar, Laszlo, 45
Tamoxifen, 119-121, 245, 404
effect on survival rates, 121
as a preventive treatment, 114, 128-129, 135, 179, 180, 194-197, 198, 320
risk of complications, 122
side effects, 121-122, 382-383, 384; endometrial cancer, 277, 394
Tancredi, Lawrence, 177, 181
Taylor, Kathryn, 8, 11, 18, 94
Thomlinson, Hugh, 403-404, 405
Thornton, Hazel, 79-80, 379
Three-Mile Island disaster, 82-83
Treatment options, 290-292
see also Alternative treatments; Chemotherapy; Personal autonomy; Radiotherapy; Surgery; Tamoxifen
Tri-State Leukemia Survey, 81

Trials. *see* Research trials
Tumours, 116, 117, 120, 387-388, 404
Two-county trials (Sweden), 44

Urban, Nicole, 254

Visualization, 140, 145, 148, 151

Waller, Margaret, 315, 316, 320, 372
Watson, James, 172, 174, 251
Weber, Cynthia, 332
Wells, Vicky, 151, 155, 304
Westin, Jerome, 201-202
Wilber, Ken, 150-151, 152-161
Wilber, Treya (Terry), 150, 152-161, 304
Winnow, Jackie, 300-301
Wolf, Naomi, 235, 236
Wolff, Mary, 202
Women's Cancer Resource Center, 301
Women's Community Cancer Project, 243
Women's Health Initiative, 191, 331-332
World War II, 19, 93

X-rays, 79-80, 81, 82-83, 178-179
see also Mammography; Radiotherapy
Xenoestrogen hypothesis, 131-132, 202, 203, 245

Y-Me, 301-302

Index created by Christine Jacobs.